The Subject in Crisis
in Contemporary
Chinese Literature

The Subject in Crisis in Contemporary Chinese Literature

Rong Cai

 University of Hawai'i Press • Honolulu

Printed in the United States of America
09 08 07 06 05 04   6 5 4 3 2 1

Library of Congress Cataloging-in-Publication Data
Cai, Rong.
   The subject in crisis in contemporary Chinese literature / Rong Cai.
     p. cm.
   Includes bibliographical references and index.
   ISBN 0-8248-2761-9 (alk. paper) —
   ISBN 0-8248-2846-1 (pbk. : alk. paper)
   1. Chinese literature—20th century—History and criticism. I. Title.
   PL2262.C25 2004
   895.1'35209—dc22

                       2004003460

Designed by University of Hawai'i Press Production Department

Printed by The Maple-Vail Book Manufacturing Group

To Bin and Xin,
and the memory of my parents

Contents

Preface

My interest in the human subject's representation in post-Mao literature grew out of my reading during the period this book covers—the twenty years or so following the Cultural Revolution (1966–1976). Many in post-Mao China shared this interest: drastic reimaginings of the subject in literature echoed the society's desire to question, probe, and replace the subjectivity previously informed by the Communist ideals, which had begun to lose credibility as the nation reexamined its history and its priorities. The demythicizing of the revolutionary self and the emergence of a non-Maoist subject aroused complex emotions in contemporary readers as common beliefs were challenged and unorthodox ideas of the self were explored and constructed under new sets of ethical and aesthetic principles. As a reader who enjoyed good stories and saw reflected in them my own subjectivity in the making, I was fascinated by the works that I discuss in this book, as well as numerous other examples of the trends in the busy literary world of the day—literature of the wounded, reflective literature, searching-for-roots literature, avant-garde fiction, new-realist writings, and cultural productions of the 1990s. A student of Chinese literature and society, I came to those texts with an urge to identify, discern, and analyze the post-Mao permutations of the subject, as one act in the ongoing national drama of modernization, against historical, ideological, and literary paradigms that defined the modern self, from the May Fourth era to the post-1989 era. In particular, two parallel discourses of the subject during the 1980s intrigued me. China's most prominent philosophers and literary scholars, such as Li Zehou, Wang Ruoshui, and Liu Zaifu, noisily advocated an autonomous, Enlightenment humanist subject; their theories were brought into practice by writers from the preliberation generation, the rightist generation, and the educated-youth *(zhiqing)* generation. In contrast, there was an equally conspicuous discourse of disenchantment in literary productions: post-Mao literature teems with what I call problematic subjects, beings who suffer either from highly symbolic physical deformities or a paralyzed agency that debunks their apparent normalcy. This contingent of problematic beings repeatedly draws our attention to the deficiency and inadequacy of a subject that cannot always be contained in the Communist past, a history to be transcended in the post-Mao design of modernity.

The intense intellectual and literary inquiries in the 1980s were often taken to be an exhilarating symphony of humanism and Enlightenment subjectivity by its performers: writers, critics, and literary and cultural historians. During the 1990s, however, the preceding decade was characterized as radical, idealistic, elitist, and utopian, and much of the reassessment centered on critiquing its formulations of the idea of the self. But it would seem that there was already dissonance in the multitude of problematic subjects in literary creations. How do we explain the stubborn presence—in literature of the 1980s and 1990s alike—of the crippled agent who fails to recover humanist autonomy, contrary to what was envisioned in the post-Mao theory of the subject? The incongruity between the theoretical celebration of Enlightenment agency and textual realities ultimately points to the anxieties and tensions imbedded in the project of subjectivity that were often ignored in the hope for quick renewal. What are these anxieties and tensions, and what do they reveal about the redeemability of the post-Mao self and the writers' concerns about their ability to establish a new national subject for a postrevolutionary China, a historical task the intellectuals had assigned themselves? These are questions I bring to bear in my look at the problematic subject and its representation in post-Mao literature. My dual focus in this book is the topography and nature of the problematized agent and how its representation punctured post-Mao optimism, foreshadowing the eventual abandonment of the move to rethink subjectivity.

I investigate two incarnations of the subject: not only the literary characters within the texts but also their creators—real subjects in history, Chinese writers whose own agency was being tested and instituted in the post-Mao search for a new subjectivity. This book is not meant to be a comprehensive survey of post-Mao literature or an exhaustive study of the work of any single author. I have selected for detailed analysis literary samples from two periods: the mid-1980s, the highest point of the New Era (1976–1989), and the late 1980s to mid-1990s, when China's accelerated reforms and changing social priorities not only generated new concerns in the imagining of the subject but posed fresh challenges to the intellectuals' own position and prestige in society. The chosen texts are by five well-known and prolific writers in post-Mao China, Han Shaogong (b. 1953), Can Xue (b. 1953), Yu Hua (b. 1960), Mo Yan (b. 1955), and Jia Pingwa (b. 1952), all of whom have been publishing actively for two decades. For the sake of thematic coherence, I have taken only a small portion from each writer's work to demonstrate certain aspects of the subject in crisis. A critical study of the crippled subject offers us a unique perspective to gauge the complexity of China's quest for modernity, allowing us to delve beneath the euphoria of the 1980s and the confusion and frustration of the 1990s to arrive at a fuller understanding of the self's multifaceted experience in the post-Mao era.

I accumulated many debts while I conceived and eventually finished this project, which originated with the doctoral dissertation I completed at Washington University in St. Louis in 1995. Though the final product differs considerably from its earlier incarnation, I remain extremely grateful to the official readers of that dissertation, Robert E. Hegel, the late William Matheson, Robert K. Weninger, Beata Grant, Naomi Lebowitz, and Milica Banjanin, for giving me the freedom to explore the subject and for providing me with timely feedback and astute commentary that propelled me through the process. Years later I am still reaping the benefits. My interest in Chinese literature was cultivated by Robert E. Hegel, Beata Grant, and William Matheson, whose vast knowledge and enthusiasm opened my eyes to the excitement and intricacies of the Chinese world that often escaped the intuitive native reader.

Many people have read earlier versions of parts of the book and offered invaluable suggestions. In particular, I thank David Wang, Mark Selden, Howard Goldblatt, Kim Besio, Woei Lien Chong, Gang Yue, and anonymous readers at the University of Hawai'i Press for raising challenging questions and compelling me to think and to redefine my approach. I owe a special debt to Robert E. Hegel and Yi-tsi Mei Feuerwerker, who read the entire manuscript twice with meticulous care and enormous patience and shared with me their scholarly expertise. Their insightful comments and suggestions have contributed to the coherence of the argument as a whole and have helped me detect both gaps and repetition. I have benefited greatly from their probing questions, which prodded me to reexamine my assumptions, broaden my scope, and reset my parameters. But for their exemplary generosity, encouragement, and unfailing support during various stages of writing, this project would not have reached fruition.

With deep gratitude, I acknowledge the encouragement and continuing support from my home institution, Emory University. A generous funding from Emory College and the Graduate School of Arts and Sciences at Emory University helped defray the production cost of a paperback edition of this book. I would also like to thank the authors and critics I have quoted; their studies on modern Chinese literature and society have been a valuable source of inspiration. I presented certain sections of the book at conferences; I am grateful to the audiences for asking questions and suggesting perspectives. Thanks also go to the editors at the University of Hawai'i Press; their collective wisdom greatly strengthened the final product.

Portions of several chapters appeared in different form in earlier publications. They include: "The Subject in Crisis: Han Shaogong's Cripple(s)," *Journal of Contemporary China* 5 (spring 1994); "In the Madding Crowd: Self and Other in Can Xue's Fiction," *China Information* XI, no. 4 (spring 1997); "The Lonely Traveler Revisited in Yu Hua's Fiction," *Modern Chinese Literature* 10 (1998); "Problematizing the Foreign Other: Mother, Father, and the Bastard in Mo Yan's *Large Breasts and Full Hips*," *Modern China* 29 no. 1 (January 2003). I am thankful to the publishers for granting me permission to reuse this material.

Finally, special thanks go to my family. I thank my parents for their understanding and support of my studies in the United States. Over the years my sisters have been a tremendous help: Min fulfilled my share of filial duties during the difficult period when my parents were seriously ill, and Xia always ungrudgingly took time away from her own research and writing to track down information for me whenever I needed her assistance. I deeply appreciate the moral support Bin and Xin gave me. Their faith in me and good-humored nudging kept me going until this book was done.

1 Introduction

The late 1970s and the 1980s in post-Mao China were an age of ideas and ideals. Thanks to Deng Xiaoping's more liberal cultural policy, Western theories of various persuasions surged in with unprecedented speed and force. Despite their sometimes conflicting and mutually deconstructive theoretical premises, Western concepts of all sorts were eagerly swallowed up, hastily digested, and hurriedly circulated by the intellectually starved Chinese critics to both create and fill up a new discursive space where the critics' position in the changing society was negotiated and their own notion of modernity articulated and disseminated. Among all the entrées on the discursive menu whetting the post-Mao appetite, nothing has held greater power over the imagination than subjectivity *(zhutixing)* and modernization *(xiandaihua)*. Though closely associated, sharing blurred sociohistorical and theoretical boundaries in the Chinese context, these terms seem to have had special appeal to the different social forces that remapped post-Mao China. As indicated in the state's goal of constructing a "socialist modernization," the word *modernization* was repeated like a mantra in the government-sanctioned program of reforms that swept across the country in the wake of the Cultural Revolution (1966–1976); indeed, it quickly swallowed the "socialist" adjectives in both official and public discourse as China moved swiftly to reengage global economy and society. "Subjectivity," by contrast, couched in the epistemological framework of the Enlightenment, appeared to have struck the fancy primarily of the cultural intellectuals, spicing up their debates on how to achieve postrevolutionary modernization in the late 1970s and during the well-publicized Cultural Discussion in the mid-1980s. Nevertheless, these discourses should not be seen as separate undertakings. Rallying round the

1

common objective of turning China into a rising world power, together they defined the ideological-cultural terrain of the New Era (1976–1989), making social progress and spiritual enlightenment an underlying theme of the post-Mao reconstruction.

But modernization, the programmatic center that held together its various manifestations in the discursive and nondiscursive arenas, played a cruel joke on its primary partner in the project of enlightenment and subjectivity, its fervent advocates, the post-Mao intellectuals. Although social modernization in material terms forged ahead full strength at the end of the twentieth century, the talk of subjectivity and enlightenment, loud and clear in the previous decade, all but died out. The treatises and theses that had so recently fired the zeal of thousands inside and outside intellectual circles now interested only cultural historians and the most committed scholars in the humanities. What is more, the 1980s were subjected to radical reassessments in the 1990s. Not only did its Western-oriented modernization come under severe criticism, now faulted for precipitating a national identity crisis that eventually led to the Tiananmen unrest, but the dominant discourse of subjectivity and enlightenment was also thrown into serious doubt. To give a provocative literary example, the human subject, the agent of subjectivity and enlightenment, in such avant-garde works as the fiction of Yu Hua was ruthlessly and literally mutilated and dismembered in the late 1980s. As an ancient Chinese aphorism puts it, "After the skin is gone, where would the hair grow?" (Pi zhi bu cun, mao jiang yan fu?). When it is disembodied, how can human consciousness as the locus and arbiter of the knowledge of the self (to follow the line of argument of Enlightenment philosophy) survive? Whether or not they agreed in their interpretation of the motivation behind the relentless scrutiny of the 1980s, critics concurred that the pursuit of the enlightenment and subjectivity was just another trial run—collectively engaged in by the post-Mao intelligentsia—at fulfilling a utopian dream that seemed to have been eluding China for a century.

Calling the post-Mao attempt "another" trial run was obviously a historical nod to the May Fourth project where the Enlightenment ideals debuted to become an alluring theme in China's modernization. What made matters worse for the new believers of enlightenment was that when the May Fourth project was aborted in the 1930s and 1940s because of China's domestic and international strife, there was still strong hope for its later revival under more favorable social conditions. Post-Mao intellectuals were convinced that they had finally found and created a congenial environment for the project in the 1980s, and they celebrated its coming of age. But following much hype, dreams that the lofty ideal would regain its glory were definitively shattered in the 1990s. The feverish push for enlightenment was branded "a myth of the century," a *juechang*, the last song of enlightenment *(qimeng de juechang)*, as one critic described it. This characterization captured simultaneously the heroic spirit and the tragic futility of the intellectual effort. As the same critic said, "The enlightenment project has turned out to be an extremely absurd endeavor at the turn of the century" (Meng Fanhua 1997, 192). What a difference a decade makes.

What went wrong? While modernization is still an ongoing process with attendant ambiguities and uncertainties, without sufficient historical distance, we may not see clearly the complex relationship between the enlightenment and the social modernization in the post-Mao era to explain why the latter apparently succeeded at the expense of the former. Would economic and technological development, marketization, and globalization produce conditions to eventually bring forth a full-fledged democracy, create a new form of "civil society," and result in the individual's emancipation, as some scholars argued (G. White 1994, 73–92)? Or would China's economic makeover only fashion a "self-centered consumer" instead of a "sovereign citizen," as others reasoned (Barmé 1999, 238)? It is still too early to tell. But a basic understanding of how the two major players in the social program—the state and the intellectuals—interpreted "modernization" helps us put the current discord into some perspective. In these preliminary remarks, which will lead me into the central theme of this book—the subject in crisis in post-Mao literary representations—I highlight the characteristics that distinguish the state's approach to modernization from the intellectuals'. To differentiate the state from the intellectuals is not to simplistically set them off as opponents. As I comment later in the book, their relationship, however problematic, was close and multifaceted. We must bear in mind that intellectuals have never been either completely inside or outside of the governmental structure, whether in dynastic China, in Mao's China, or after; nor should we forget that, as with any social group, they were far from homogeneous. Inasmuch as their voice in the 1980s was not officially programmed and their opinions manifested certain common inclinations, however, the intellectuals represented divergent concerns from those of the state.

The state's program of modernization clearly emphasized the development of the economy through the adoption of advanced science, technology, and contemporary management theories and practices. Prior to and following reform and the open-door policy being declared the new party line at the momentous third plenum of the Eleventh Central Committee, in December 1978, Deng Xiaoping and his supporters, in preparation for Deng's formal reassertion of power, encouraged "de-Maoization" in the realms of literature and ideology and implemented measures to shake up the administrative bureaucracies and the relationship of state and society. Yet, political reforms were not the new regime's priority. As stressed in the official slogan of the four modernizations (in agriculture, industry, national defense, and science and technology), under Deng the state shifted its focus toward boosting production and the economy. The off-and-on attempts of the Chinese Communist Party (CCP) to curb intellectual trends too liberal for its liking showed that it was very much aware that the "emancipation of thought" it had endorsed in the late 1970s was a double-edged sword that could delegitimize the center it had helped legitimize after the Cultural Revolution. Consequently, although the Deng reform regime was willing to effect drastic institutional changes to accelerate economic growth through, for example, the elimination of communes, the de facto decollectivization of farmland, and the application of the household-responsibility system in agriculture and a contract-labor system in urban industry, it was cautious about introducing political reforms that could threaten the Party's hegemony. Modernization for the state thus meant, above all, economic modernization, a pragmatic program to build up the nation's strength and prosperity through stimulating production and improving the standard of living while maintaining the central leadership of the CCP.

If the state gave weight to pragmatic considerations and everyday material life in its plan to modernize the country, the intellectuals concentrated on the cultural-ideological front, where they traditionally functioned best. To them the "emancipation of thought" was not an expediency but the essence of modernization. Though the intellectuals produced multiple interpretations, a review of the major themes in the New Era ("practice as the criterion for testing truth," the concept of subjectivity, scientism and instrumental rationality, the revival of Confucianism by the neo-Confucianists at home and abroad, and literary modernism) and the discursive venues (workshops on university campuses and academic journals) through which they were formulated and articulated shows that modernization, or modernity, in the eyes of the intellectuals was first and foremost a discursive revolution. The zeal and seriousness with which the intellectuals tackled issues of culture and ideas in China's modernization drive clearly spoke to their strong conviction that modernization in science and technology could be achieved only with, if not after, the modernization of thinking. Intellectual enlightenment was thus viewed as an indispensable prerequisite to economic modernization.

To anyone familiar with modern Chinese history, this smacks of déjà vu of the May Fourth type. Although the radically different global and domestic conditions each movement found itself in and responding to made it impossible for the post-Mao modernization to be a mere replay of the May Fourth revolution, a similar idealism—the preeminent emphasis put on the value of ideas—continued to be a hallmark of the ideological and methodological makeup of contemporary intellectuals. Despite a historical divide of some six decades, during which a significant portion of the May Fourth legacy (most notably, conceptions of the self and its subjective powers) was rejected by the Communist ideology, post-Mao intellectuals maintained faith in the self and in the power of ideas to effect social change. For many of them, this was also an epistemological and ideological rebound of the voluntaristic belief they were conditioned to operate under in the Communist era, when human consciousness was given primacy as the decisive factor in charting the course of history.

But as the intellectuals were shadowboxing with themselves in the battle of words, the economic modernization they had helped legitimize arrived with all the speed and power technology and market forces could provide. What came as an unpleasant surprise to the intellectuals deeply in love with their own modernist vision was the reality that once economic modernization had benefited from the discursive revolution (courtesy of the intellectuals, for the most part), it developed a course of its own and had no further need for the ideals dear to the intellectual heart. In fact, the commercialized popular culture that took China's cultural market by storm after the late 1980s made irrelevant many of the humanist morals I discuss in the following text, such as truth, rationality, integrity, and human dignity. In the intellectuals' blueprint of modernity, enlightenment in thought would lead to economic modernization. It did. But what then? Would the discursive and economic revolutions live happily ever after in a blissful union? Few dwelt on the possibility of a divorce. Little did the intellectuals anticipate that when the repressed productive forces were unleashed by the reforms, so would be the human desires alien to the enlightenment project they had championed. What Matei Calinescu calls "the other modernity" of "capitalist technology and business interest" won out (1987, 8). Deeply disillusioned with the Maoist socialist system, people searched for new social values, and many found them in individual wealth and personal fulfillment as exemplified in bourgeois societies. Is it then any wonder that popular culture in China today exhibits many of the symptoms inherent in capitalism, the "cult of instant joy, fun morality, and the generalized confusion between self-realization and simple gratification" (7)? To be fair, the

Communist suppression of human desires, the conditions of economic scarcity that people had endured for decades, and the political frustration in the wake of the Tiananmen crackdown, must take part of the responsibility. In the end grand idea(l)s retreated, the enlightenment vision yielding its place to popular, materialist cravings. In an ironic twist, the intellectuals relearned the Marxist principle that the economic base has a decisive say over the superstructure after all.

But in our critique of the idealism of the 1980s, we should also avoid being caught up in the same excitement and enthusiasm over conceptual schemas. The critique cannot be adequately maintained by engaging the intellectual tides of the times only on the level of theory and polemics. We should keep in mind that besides theoretical speculation on subjectivity and the Chinese modern, much of the discursive revolution was carried out through creative activities. As is traditionally the case, Chinese intellectuals often wore two hats, serving as critics and writers at the same time or in alternation. Writers critiqued, and critics wrote. Literary practice, consequently, was an integral part of the postrevolutionary pursuit of the modern. A close examination of the practice of literature and the fictional world as part of the social discourse of subjectivity and modernization would carry us beyond theoretical abstractions of the ideas of self, at which level much of the intellectual thinking in the 1980s was formulated. Anchoring the critique of idealism in the fictional world and its imaginings would also allow us to probe another side of the idealism of the era: the intellectuals' optimism about the prospect of a humanistic future for China and their central role in its reification. By turning to literature, we raise the issue whether a faith in the theory of subjectivity and enlightenment was and could be translated unproblematically into fictional realities, which, unless completely utopian (and in that case self-defeating for the social project), cannot transcend the trappings of history. We cannot assume that the age of ideas was automatically an age of the triumph of ideas. It is my contention that despite the blare surrounding subjectivity and enlightenment, the post-Mao subject was in trouble long before its final dissolution in the 1990s. Before I go on to explore that topic, however, I offer a closer look at why I use the question of subjectivity in literature as my springboard.

Why Subjectivity and Why Literature?

To answer this question requires looking back, which is abundant in contemporary criticism. Browsing through essays on Chinese literature written since the late 1980s, we are likely to come upon such descriptive phrases as *"digu"* (low valleys), *"piruan"* (fatigued and weak), *"shiluo"* (loss), *"shizhong"* (loss of gravity), and *"shiyan"* (loss of voice). Putting aside questions of whether these judgments are fair and accurate and whether we should take into consideration the complex emotions that may have prompted this kind of response (e.g., the cultural intellectuals' need to negotiate their anxiety toward a blooming popular literature, which many of them could not endorse for artistic and ideological reasons), we can agree that the negative verdict was based on the perceived existence of a prior condition. The *digu* presupposes a binary opposite, a *gaofeng* (peak) from whose glory the present has descended. Similarly, "loss," an indication of depletion, by necessity speaks to a previous state of fullness and plenitude. Behind these rather gloomy characterizations, it is not hard for us to detect a sense of nostalgia for the vanished good old days.

The "good old days" the post–June Fourth literature is often measured against came to be known as literature of the New Era *(xinshiqi wenxue)*, a golden age of creation when Chinese writers enjoyed unprecedented intellectual freedom and social prestige. Indeed, aided by Deng Xiaoping's open-door policy and the inflow of ideas from the West, post-Mao literature flourished, enlivening the literary stage with a fanfare of fresh trends and new voices. As many critics have noted, the most important feature of this new literature was its focus on the representation of the self and subjectivity, an issue at the heart of the May Fourth fiction, revisited with a sense of urgency and vengeance after the Cultural Revolution. But this was not simply a venture confined within the literary field: it had sociopolitical significance. The orchestration and exploration of the self indicated a search for a new subjectivity. In other words, the permutations in the presentation of the self and subjectivity can be interpreted as a consciously constructive process, by which means Chinese writers were seeking an alternative to the old model of the nonindividuated class consciousness imposed on the human subject by Maoist Communist ideology. The ultimate purpose of the search was to establish a new subject.

This ambitious project was initiated in an ethos of re-creation at a critical, historical juncture. The conclusion of the Cultural Revolution in 1976 marked the end of Maoist rule and the beginning of a new era. As is clear from Chinese intellectuals' fondness for the words *"zai"* and *"cong"* (equivalent to the prefix *re-* in English) in such terms as *"zai zhu"* (reconstruct) and *"cong jian"* (reconfigure), the post-Mao period was perceived as an era of extensive demolition and rebuilding. Like all former Communist states in the Eastern bloc in the 1980s, China faced profound ideological transformations, a process inevitably accompanied by ecstasy, expectations, confusion, and frustration. At the start of the radical reformation following the Cultural Revolution, society experienced an acute identity crisis. What critics called the "three-belief crisis" *(sanxin weiji)*—crisis of belief in Marxism *(xinyang weiji)*, crisis of faith in socialism *(xinxin weiji)*, and crisis of trust in the Communist Party *(xinren weiji)*—was widespread in society at large, and among young people and intellectuals—the most sensitive barometer of social sentiments—in particular (Goldman, Link, and Su 1993, 129).

No doubt the crisis was precipitated by the calamity of the Cultural Revolution, but arguably the changes implemented by the new regime also played a part. Initiated by Deng Xiaoping's supporters in June 1978, the discussion of the "criterion of truth" was carried out in the media to repudiate Mao's personality cult (Schoenhals 1991). It was soon followed by official deprioritization of the class struggle in society and the rehabilitation of hundreds of thousands of people wrongly accused of various ideological crimes. These corrective measures helped Deng Xiaoping distance his Party from his predecessor's regime, winning him tremendous support from the populace. But with all former policies denounced and new ones not yet in place, not much was left to guide the individual in the still highly politicized society. The extraordinary zeal poured into the discussion of "socialist alienation" in the early 1980s proves that despite its defiant tone, the post-Mao self found it necessary first and foremost to define itself vis-à-vis the political system.[1] If the category of class no longer served to separate "us" from "them," how would people align themselves and relate to one another? If the socialism practiced since 1949 was a moral and economic failure as often presented then by a sweeping condemnation of the Communist history in the wake of the Cultural Revolution, what could replace it as a centripetal force for the country? To those who tended to emphasize China's impressive economic accomplishments in the past two decades without the help of class struggle and Mao's brand of socialism but failed to adequately note the enormous costs exacted by the process, these may appear to be unnecessary worries. But we must remember that people had previously genuinely believed in socialism as a viable cause to lead China out of national humiliation and poverty, and that the forceful official indoctrination of class struggle and socialism since the founding of the People's Republic had enabled the three beliefs (in Marxism, socialism, and the Party) to manipulate their perception of their legitimacy in the Communist society. The political convictions on which the three beliefs rested provided the ideological moorings for individuals to regard themselves as meaningful entities in relation to the established social order.

With the ideological ground shifting under their feet after the Cultural Revolution, many felt a strong sense of disorientation.

In the late 1970s the journal *China Youth*, the organ of the Communist Youth League, launched a discussion on the meaning of life, drawing hundreds of letters in response. In one widely disseminated letter, an aspiring young writer found "the path of life narrower and narrower." Relating her disappointment with reality, she commented that altruism, the moral principle of socialism, was but a façade. Deep down everyone was selfish and would act on self-interest at critical moments (Pan 1980). In another article a young man questioned the viability of socialism. He wrote:

> So far as our generation is concerned, we have been taught, ever since primary school, how good our socialist motherland is and how bitter and hard the lives of the people are in capitalist nations. [Now] we see from television the skyscrapers, modern facilities, parks and cultural centers in foreign countries. Compared with that, our country is backward. How can you expect us to turn our thinking around to continue believing in the superiority of socialism?[2]

What is more interesting here is not the writers' recognition of the erroneousness of their former beliefs but the deep ambivalence embedded in their remarks. The anguish felt by the young people, I would argue, resulted from their unwillingness to fully accept their new convictions. The letters' negation of the whitewashed socialist reality notwithstanding, the writers still implicitly held the moral, ideological principles of socialism to be the norm. Why should attention to personal interests lead to a narrower path of life (if the idealized socialist cause was not regarded as a broader path)? Did it matter if a person believed in socialism or not? To the young man, it obviously did, or he would not have found it necessary to talk about his inability to do so. The erosion of political beliefs after Mao's death created a vacuum. It freed the individual, but for what purpose? People were consequently forced to reorient and ask themselves, "Who was I? Who am I? What will I be?" Reconstruction of the human subject(ivity) thus became an urgent task for Chinese intellectual-writers, who continued to see themselves, in the May Fourth tradition, as social reformers and spokespeople for the national conscience.

True heirs to their May Fourth predecessors, who created the *baihua* (vernacular) fiction to castigate the Confucian self in celebration of the Enlightenment individual, post-Mao writers also made literature a site of contestation, resistance, and experimentation. It was where the new human subject(ivity), often in open opposition to the former Communist ideology, was imagined and represented. Various ideas of the self and subject-positions were explored and conceptualized, their consonance and contradictions affirmed or negated in the created world. Working in close conjunction with other critical discourses of the era, literature gave concrete forms to many theoretical arguments of the day through its products and production. An important force in the postrevolutionary reconstruction, literature made a noticeable social impact in the New Era, injecting much energy into China's course of modernization. Textualizing and consequently constituting history, post-Mao literature not only is rich in "historical resonance," to use a new historicist phrase, but also has helped generate it.

Thus, postrevolutionary literature offers fascinating material for a study of the search for a new subject(ivity) in contemporary China. But in studying the works, we cannot afford to overlook their authors, those who attempted to construct China's national story. As in any act of representation, the writer's agency (or lack of it) unavoidably comes into play. An appropriative activity, representation registers, among its other aims, the representer's visions, aspirations, expectations, and anxieties. This is especially true of post-Mao literature. Wrestling with the question of the subject in literature, Chinese writers often used their own experiences of suppression (which they saw as representative of the people's experience) under Mao's rule as a reference for analysis and protest. For example, not only did many stories in the New Era have intellectuals and writers as the heroes, but also the issue of representation became a central point of contention. Liu Zaifu's theory of subjectivity in literature, which I discuss in the next chapter, stems specifically from his challenge to Mao's denial of the writer's subjective agency. The search, as a result, was as much a crusade for the Chinese people as one for the intellectuals themselves. The writers' self-consciousness in the project is clearly manifested in the directions of the search (the recall of humanism as an emancipatory discourse to counter the "socialist alienation"), its priorities (the focus on independence and autonomy), and its double objective: restoring subjectivity to literary characters and, in the process, to the writers themselves as creative agents. A decade into the New Era, the result seemed heartening. As Howard Goldblatt aptly puts it, "Chairman Mao would not be amused" (Goldblatt 1995).[3] Post-Mao writers mounted an all-out assault on the Communist principles—artistic, social, and ideological—ignoring taboos in both subject matter and techniques. It is no exaggeration to say that post-Mao literature has effectively challenged all previous traditions (which came to include the May Fourth literary realism), completely repainting China's literary landscape in the 1980s, though the writers inherited from both the May Fourth and Communist traditions the confidence in the power of literature over the human minds, the belief in literature's role in nation building, and the intellectuals' social commitment.

While I fully acknowledge, however, the achievements of post-Mao literature, the purpose of this book is not to trumpet the success of the search. In recent years post-Mao literary and cultural scenes have been the subject of a number of inquiries. From the symptoms of the "culture fever" in the 1980s, the rise of Chinese modernism in the age of reforms, to the evolving conceptions of modernity and their critiques in the intellectual discourse, from the masculinist search for the male self and the disturbing trend of misogyny in post-Mao literary practice to the individual visions of the new avant-garde writers, the critics have probed various aspects of the era, discerning and dissecting its dynamics and problematics from a variety of theoretical perspectives.[4] These studies have shed much light on the complexities of the vibrant New Era. But what David Wang names the "bizarre visage of life," a prevalent phenomenon in the New Era literature, has not received extensive attention. In 1988 Wang noted:

> Throughout modern Chinese literary history, it is difficult to find a period in which [the literary scene] is peopled by so many bizarre characters invested with such complex symbolic meaning. The range of characters that emerge from the works of the New Period mainland Chinese writers include: the blind, the mute, the crippled, the humpbacked, the sexually impotent, the bound-feet fetishist, the osteomalacia victim, the "living dead," not to mention the mentally deranged and the psychotic. Suddenly the "Socialist New China" that was once glorified by such writers as Yang Mo and Hao Ran has become a dilapidated and grotesque haven filled with souls that are maimed either physically or spiritually. (209)[5]

Possible cases to footnote the critic's terse summary come to mind readily. Both prominent and less well-known examples, which for lack of space I do not discuss in the book, are: the politically as well as sexually impotent rightists in Zhang Xianliang's novellas about life in the labor camps published in the early 1980s; a fifty-year-old man who never outgrows the mentality and physique of a child in Wang Zhaojun's story "The Man That Never Grows" ("Bu lao lao"); Cripple Ah Er, a youngster who has lost all sensitivity as a result of the abuse he suffers in the story of the same title by Wang Anyi; the tormented souls in a series of absurdist fiction on the dehumanizing political repressions written by Zong Pu, "Who Am I?" ("Shei shi wo?"), "The Humble Abode" ("Woju"), and "The Head in the Swamp" ("Nizhao zhong de toulu"); the world inhabited by the inmates of a madhouse, their warden, and the spectators, in which insanity is only a matter of degree, in "The Director and His Lunatics" ("Yuanzhang he tade fengzimen") by Xu Xiaohe. The late 1980s produced its own breed of inexplicable characters that defies logic and reason, most notably in Yu Hua's fiction—the self-mutilating middle school teacher who practices his obsession with ancient methods of torture on his own body, family members who destroy one another in senseless revenge, and friends and neighbors reveling in gruesome killings.

The "complex symbolic meaning" of these "bizarre characters" is worth further exploration. I agree with David Wang's view that this grotesque vision of life is a repudiation of embellished socialist reality; but to my mind, to confine the interpretation of such characters within the Communist past fails to recognize the full force of their representation as a historical phenomenon at the intersection of China's transition from Mao to the post-Mao era. I would argue that the problematic figures do not speak only from and about the Maoist past. As shown in many instances, the production of bizarre characters persisted well after the cathartic "literature of the wounded," which exposes the wrongdoings of the Mao era, then subsided around 1980. Distressingly resistant to closure, these characters have deeper implications that go directly to the heart of the recall of human subjectivity. While the physically deformed beings bear outward signs of their symbolic deficiencies, less obvious but equally significant to our understanding of the era and the challenges it faced are characters that appear physically unimpaired but nonetheless suffer from functional inadequacies. These apparently "normal" characters betray more insidious problems in exercising human agency and are therefore mirror images of the physically crippled. Together the two types of flawed beings form a stubborn underscore, a discordant note in the symphony of enlightenment and subjectivity.

A sharp contrast to the optimism and forward-looking ethos of the era, the problematic characters and their representation ought to be studied against the designs and desires of the age that had made the recovery of human subjectivity paramount to all its other objectives. I would contend that the imagining of the blemished characters points inevitably to the tensions very much covered up by the post-Mao urge to surge ahead. In particular, it signifies certain tensions between the writers' creative intentions— their ambition to erect a new subject in literature—and the created realities. I address these tensions through a critical reading of the problematic subject, the physically and the metaphorically impaired beings alike. I am interested in teasing out their symbolic meaning in relation to the post-Mao reconstructive project. I explore the facets of what I call the subject in crisis that has emanated from the search for a new subject, focusing on the representation of human agency in post-Mao literature. I ask the following questions about the represented as well as the representing: What are the paradigms of the problematic subject? What accounts for its deficiencies historically and ideologically? Further, what is the nature of the crisis in ontological and epistemological terms? The analyses of the fictional subject lead to questions about the meta-narrative, the national story of rejuvenation. Situating the problematic subject in the national search, I examine its potential links to the post-Mao future by uncovering the latent anxieties that informed and were embodied in its representation, anxieties about the redeemability of the subject and the writers' own creative potency muted and overlooked by the utopian longing of the era. As we reassess the euphoria of the 1980s more than a decade after it dissipated, it is time for us to recognize the prophetic role of the problematic subject and acknowledge the limit in the power of literature to transcend its own social and historical circumstances.

What Subject?

Before I spell out the details of the investigation, I must ask some questions and establish parameters in order to define the post-Mao ideal of the self, which in turn will allow us to address its absence in literature evidenced in the problematic self. I propose to locate the post-Mao subject on two spectrums outlined here in general terms, a theoretical spectrum where we can measure the Chinese model against the development of ideas in world history, and a historical spectrum where we can situate it in relation to China's own pursuit of modernity.

The formation of subject(ivity) is a well-studied category in philosophy. The twentieth century in particular has witnessed constant revisions of each and every theory of the subject. In view of the rich and vigorous inquiries, to speak of an unspecified subject becomes problematic in itself. It is generally agreed that reconceptualization of the human being in the twentieth century started with the deconstruction of the Cartesian Enlightenment subject of rationality, self-knowledge, and universality. The development of psychoanalysis and the keen interest in the function of language constitute the two dominant tendencies in the deconstructive efforts. By digging into its childhood and unveiling the repressed and distorted memories and conflictual desires in the subconscious and unconscious of the mind, Freudian psychoanalysis has successfully debunked the rationality of the self-knowing subject. Jacques Lacan, Claude Lévi-Strauss, Michel Foucault, and the feminists have further destroyed the wholeness and autonomy of the subject by locating its subjectivity in the realms of language and institutionalized discursive practices. They argue that as the subject participates in a multitude of discourses, subjectivity becomes precarious, contradictory, and ever-changing. As a result, the conscious, coherent, and rational self envisioned and idealized by Enlightenment humanism as the producer of universal meaning is radically decentered. The autonomous individual yielded its throne to the subject, whose subjectedness, according to post-structuralist theories, reduces it to being a product of language and discourse. But the story does not end there. If the subject is generated by discourse, is not discourse also generated by the subject (Weimann 1987)?[6] Thus, while acknowledging that the subject is a discursive construct subjected to the mediation and manipulation of social practices, feminists and many others chose to emphasize human agency, the being's ability to understand the condition and intention of its actions and, consequently, to effect changes. They have turned language and discursive practices into sites of resistance to carry out struggles to redefine femininity, masculinity, and both male and female subjectivity.

Where, then, does the post-Mao subject stand on this spectrum? Anticlimactic to the radical rethinking of the human being in the West, the subject idealized, glorified, and pursued by post-Mao Chinese intellectuals turns back, by way of the May Fourth tradition, to the Cartesian Enlightenment humanist model now very much out of favor in Western theories. How do we account for this anachronism? To understand the post-Mao fascination with the Enlightenment paragon, it is necessary to bring into our discussion the historical spectrum. A brief review of the genesis of the modern self, the prototype of the post-Mao subject, in pre-Communist China will enable us to put the contemporary project into historical perspective. Tracing the contours of the discursive self can also help us specify the historical roots of the postrevolutionary ideal and its salient characteristics within the modern tradition. The May Fourth endeavor that enframed the conception of the modern self and its legacies has been the subject of numerous inquires.[7] More recent scholarship in particular has examined, against the claims by the May Fourth elites, the evolution of the Chinese discourse of modernity and the cultural politics—the linguistic, rhetorical, polemic, and historiographical practices—that helped turn the project into a dominant discourse with hegemonic power in the era (Doleželová-

Velingerová and Oldřich Král 2001; Duara 1995). With full recognition of the complex nature of the movement, and the modern discourse of the self and the intricacies in its imagining and practice, I offer here a very much truncated outline of its development in the May Fourth period.[8]

The invention of a new individual has long been a central issue in China's quest for modernity. After their country's repeated defeats at the hands of foreign powers in the second half of the nineteenth century, Chinese intellectuals finally realized the need for China to emphasize ideological transformation over technological improvement in its modernization. In what Yu-sheng Lin characterizes as a "totalistic" repudiation of China's past—"an ideological commitment to a cause of total rejection of Chinese social and cultural traditions"—the May Fourth radicals advocated a complete overhaul of Chinese culture that crystallized in the creation of an antitraditional being (Lin 1972, 26).[9] Identifying Confucianism as the primary target, the critique of tradition focused on the Confucian self in personal relations, the pivot of the Confucian vision of the world. Grounding the self firmly in its relatedness to other human beings, Confucianism underlines role-playing, specifying the human being in the male position as father, son, husband, brother, friend, or subject to a ruler. Under this philosophy, self-cultivation means learning to be a ritual being, to know and observe appropriate social rules. Nevertheless, scholars of Confucianism have reiterated that the emphasis on role-playing and on the self as a center of relationships should not restrict us to seeing the self as a static, passive being (Tu 1985; Munro 1985b; King 1985). The self plays an active part in fulfilling its social duties and in developing the inner *ren*, the inborn goodness of human beings. The inherent conflicts and tensions within Confucian ethical and cultural norms[10] and the complexity of social relationships and responsibilities compel the self, with subtle efforts and initiatives, to maneuver and structure the boundaries between itself and others, to certain degrees.[11] The Confucian self enjoys some autonomy.

The iconoclastic May Fourth intellectuals, however, did not see this as their lived reality. The Confucian self in their interpretation is a totally suppressed being in submission to the authority of the father and other formalized obligations. Confucian society is, to use Lu Xun's famous conceptualization, cannibalistic, a man-eating mechanism. Putting the self and society in sharp opposition, modern intellectuals accused the Confucian system of crippling individual personality and depriving the person of choice, freedom, and independence. The catchwords of the age imported from abroad, as a result, were "individualism," "freedom," and "democracy." The words *"geren"* (individual) and *"geren zhuyi"* (individualism), now in prevalent use, rang loud and clear in literature and other intellectual writings. Though the terms did not present an essential and fixed meaning to their advocates, they nonetheless seemed to have captured the May Fourth generation's desires, hopes, and ambitions. Besides registering the confusion of an idea in the making, the indeterminacy of the terms created space for interpretation and individual appropriation (Lydia Liu 1995, 77–99). As can be gleaned from various expository essays and literary representations of the period, the tenor of the widely adopted neologisms of *individual* and *individualism* is the celebration of the once neglected and suppressed self. In broad terms, ideal individuals are beings who, free from Confucian familial obligations, have a moral right to develop their personalities to the fullest and pursue personal happiness in such basic matters as the choice of education, career, and marriage partners. This individualistic self originated in the immensely popular Western and Japanese literature introduced into China since the late Qing.[12] The foreign texts actively appropriated by the May Fourth generation provided moral examples, behavioral codes, and discursive models, which together led to profound changes in the perception of the self and the way literature was practiced in the twentieth century. The antitraditional self, scholars concur, was a synthesis of the Enlightenment humanist ideals of rationality, truth, and compassion and the nineteenth-century realist and romanticist conceptions of combative spirit and inner sensibility.

Despite the legitimization of the self and its subjective feelings, the new individual did not evolve into an isolated entity. This is best illustrated by Hu Shi's theory of *da wo* (big self or society) and *xiao wo* (small self or individual).[13] The famous May Fourth scholar explains their relationship thus: "This small self of mine is not an autonomous entity, but is joined together through direct and indirect relationship with the whole of society and of the world."[14] As a number of critics argue, the big-small dichotomy operates on a hierarchical order, allowing the state to have precedence over the individual and nationalism over personal development (Denton 1996, 44–45; Lydia Liu 1995, 91–93). In his recent reflection on the "multidimensional" and "multidirectional" nature of the May Fourth movement, Ying-shih Yu points out that there were "two contrasting projects" in it: the Chinese Renaissance and the Enlightenment. "Renaissance was originally conceived as a cultural and intellectual project" based on the notion of intellectual autonomy. "In contrast, the Enlightenment project designed by Chinese Marxists was ultimately revolution-oriented" with an emphasis on patriotism and national salvation. Given the sociopolitical condition of the May Fourth era, the Renaissance gave way to the Enlightenment and radicalization of intellectual thought (Yu 2001, 307, 308). This also sheds light on the conception of the modern individual. The privileging of the collective seems to make perfect sense when we consider the historical situations leading to the inception of individualism (however it was understood in the period). Since its birth was historically grounded in the national crisis, the design and implementation of individualism were inextricably linked with the idea of nationhood and modernity. The May Fourth individual, consequently, had a teleological purpose. It was not a simple reproduction of the Enlightenment humanist ideal that insists on the intrinsic worth of the human being independent of its social values and functions (Lin 1972, 23–58). In its commitment to the nation, the modern self did not make such a clean break from the Confucian tradition as the iconoclasts would like to think. Substituting the Confucian state with the modern society they envisioned and sanctioned, the May Fourth intellectuals relocated their loyalties and obligations and, in essence, adhered to the Confucian ideal of social service.[15]

The Communist dogma of the self is discussed in more detail in chapter 2. Suffice it to say here that it selectively preserved what it approved of in the May Fourth tradition while suppressing the elements it did not countenance. The May Fourth brand of individualism of autonomy, personal choice, and inner feelings was condemned as decadent, petty-bourgeois indulgence contradictory to the proletarian notion of selfless devotion to the collective. In both its conception and dissemination of the Communist doctrine of the self, the CCP demonstrated a remarkable continuity with the tradition it purportedly broke away from. Although in the Marxist fashion, the Party adamantly rejected all previous systems of thought, it nevertheless capitalized on the traditional belief that the individual is part of the whole, which, as I have mentioned, also became a May Fourth component.[16] What the Party effectively modified to its own advantage was the definition of what represented the whole. The Confucian *ren* as the unifying principle, the Daoist world of nature, and the Buddhist universal Void were all dismissed when the Party state was legitimized as the larger purpose to overrule all other individual concerns. Assuming a status as the new state religion, the Communist ideology granted itself supreme power to regulate the thinking and behavior of all its subjects. At the same time, the integration of the traditional faith in the perfectibility of human nature and the Marxist-Leninist belief in transforming individual consciousness provided the CCP with both a theoretical basis and an institutional approach to ruthlessly impose its orthodoxy on citizens of the People's Republic of China.[17]

Whenever they could, Chinese intellectuals protested against the Party's rigid control over the individual. Such protests, often made at great personal risk, met invariably with more severe suppression. It became increasingly obvious to the intellectuals that the socialist principle of ideological uniformity, which engendered the problem in the first place, could not at the same time be the source of rectification. When intellectual discontent with Mao's blatant disregard of personal freedom was officially encouraged by the new regime after the Cultural Revolution, it was but a logical step for Chinese writers to return to the modern tradition. Called into question by the post-Mao critiques of the Maoist practices, neither the PRC history nor the Communist ideology could offer any credible solutions to their own problems. The only model left was the May Fourth legacy. The subjectivity desired and put into unambiguous terms in the New Era refers to the familiar humanist ideal first developed in the May Fourth period: dignity and respect due to every human being, the autonomy that enables people to think for themselves as rational beings, and the inalienable rights that guarantee the individual the status of a self-determining, self-regulating entity. Similar to the May Fourth emphasis on the needs of the country, the post-Mao pursuit of individuality was also initiated as a collective venture, which, the intellectuals hoped, would lead in the end to the modernization of the nation.

Now let us come back to the question posed earlier. The post-Mao resurgence of humanism presents us with an obvious anachronism: after subject(ivity) as a humanist concept had long been discredited and deconstructed by contemporary thinkers in the West, it regained currency in the People's Republic. It seems that Chinese intellectuals were hopelessly out of step with the theoretical developments elsewhere in the world. Nearly a century after Friedrich Nietzsche's devastating statement that "God is dead" brought down the Almighty and the centered being alike, humanism was resurrected in postrevolutionary China. When individual autonomy was already proved to be unattainable fiction, Chinese intellectuals still naively believed in its uplifting power. Should we be concerned about this discrepancy? By way of answering the question, let me quote Paul Smith. In his critique of various theories on the human subject, Smith warns that "current conceptions of the 'subject' have tended to produce a purely *theoretical* 'subject,' removed almost entirely from the political and ethical realities in which human agents actually live" (Smith 1988, 29). In other words, in discussing the role of the subject and subjectivity, we must always take into consideration the sociopolitical specificities of the human condition. To apply this to the Chinese situation, it means that while making use of the powerful critical perspectives offered by contemporary Western theories, we should not lose sight of the concrete, historical circumstances that determine human existence in China. Although the post-Mao humanist notion of subject(ivity) seems almost too simplistic, naive, and old-fashioned against the modernist "dehumanization" and intricate post-structuralist speculations, the belief is nonetheless authentic to the people who had themselves gone through endless political movements and had been denied the freedom of speech, freedom of belief (political and otherwise), and even freedom of movement—the fundamental human rights people take for granted in the West.[18] This is by no means a repudiation of the relevance of Western theories in the name of cultural relativism, but a recognition that the subject in spatial and temporal realities is a historical category and that its constitution is a historical practice that responds to a specific set of conditions, raises questions, and fulfills the desires of a particular moment. When it was revived in the wake of the Cultural Revolution, humanism was used, much as it was in the May Fourth era, as a liberating discourse to challenge Mao's dictatorship and free the individual from the grip of his ultraleftism. No one can deny the great impact its *adoption* had on post-Mao reorientation. In my opinion, the intrinsic value of any theory lies in its application and the resultant social consequences and ought to be understood and evaluated accordingly. If the theory of the unconscious, or any theory for that matter, had been its author's silent, private musings, who would care?

As an emphatic protest against Maoist strictures, the post-Mao ideal of the human subject as foremost a being who thinks independently also comes close to Smith's definition of an agent. To quote Smith again, "The human *agent* will be seen . . . as the place from which resistance to the ideological is produced or played out" (Smith 1988, xxxv). The important word here is "resistance." Generated out of a desire to resist, post-Mao literature in the New Era in general was engaged in a search for such a self-governing entity, a being free to exercise resistance to Communist ideological impositions. Thus, the post-Mao discourse of the subject was not purely ontological or metaphysical speculations on the part of Chinese intellectuals. The painful reality of the Cultural Revolution, which gave rise to the need to rethink the subject, made purely theoretical considerations a luxury unavailable at the moment. The post-Mao model subject was a politicized humanist being.

Although the moral principle of the search bore more or less a humanist stamp, the way it materialized in literary representations was very much in tune with the twentieth-century fascination with language and social discourses. Let me hasten to add, lest this be seen as another instance of China's eternal catching up with the West, that this was as much a result of the writers' conscious adoption of Western ideas as a reflex action, especially in the first few years after the Cultural Revolution, when the infatuation with Western conceptions of language was still incipient. After all, no theory can claim to be prescriptive in good faith, even less so on foreign soil, where political conditions could be radically different from those in the theory's birthplace. Neither Chinese intellectuals nor the CCP needed to be taught about the discursive power of language. The Party's closely guarded monopoly over the formulation of social discourses proves that Communist ideology did not require any lessons from post-structuralist theories to be convinced of language's central role in the formation and legitimation of social knowledge.[19] The intellectuals, for their part, were victimized too many times in the Party's political campaigns, where slogans had lethal powers, to doubt the authority of words. Since language was the medium through which the official inculcation was implemented, it was also the site for launching counterattacks. The intellectual debates over the reality of "socialist alienation," the renewed interest in Kantian subjectivity, and the resurgence of humanism after 1976 were essentially fights over language, over the right to influence social discourses and, consequently, human subjectivity. Just like writers in the May Fourth era, post-Mao writers had full confidence in the discursive power of language to produce social changes.

What Crisis?

But has the recall of humanism and subjective agency been successfully played out at the textual level as was intended? The best way to find an answer to this question is to see whether the fictional subject is able to fulfill the humanistic functions expected of it. In approaching the topic, I do not take issue with humanism as a theoretical position. I am not concerned with pointing out its failure to account for the complexities of the subject(ivity) as contemporary theories have stipulated, thus proving that the post-Mao search was flawed to begin with. Even leaving aside the (de)merits of humanism, it is highly questionable that cultural transmissions could be exact reproductions of the original.[20] Nor would such duplications be desirable, had it been possible. Moreover, the question whether humanism was the right model for post-Mao China some two decades ago is moot at the beginning of the twenty-first century. So is the discussion of "could have" or "should have." Instead, I focus on the performance of the subject. I argue that the subject is problematic not because of its lack of post-structuralist sophistication and subtlety but because of a much more fundamental deficiency—its incapacity to claim agency, a constituent of any notion of active subjectivity, humanist or not.

I have chosen, primarily, works of five writers, Han Shaogong, Can Xue, Yu Hua, Mo Yan, and Jia Pingwa, to demonstrate this point. Han Shaogong and Can Xue represent two influential trends in the search for a new subject in the New Era: the *xungen* (searching for roots) approach that centralized Chinese identity and its cultural foundation in the country's modernization and an experimentalist, or more accurately, an absurdist approach highlighting existential conditions of the subject. I have selected the stories not only because the subjectivity on display there is paradigmatic of the post-Mao experience but also because the writers' representational strategies upset rather than uphold the constructive principle of the future-oriented project. Resting on a firm belief that, with intellectual intervention, temporal movement would usher in growth and re-creation, the subjectivity discourse had put a high premium on the possibilities of change. Like the May Fourth revolution, the post-Mao program of renewal was also fostered by a linear view of history. It unfolded on the conviction that history was teleological and that time should denote progression. The authors' departure from this vision is most obvious in their attempts to divorce time from its potency and evolutionary potentiality. Han Shaogong characteristically encloses his subject in a fossilized past that repeatedly generates copies of itself, whereas Can Xue fixes the self in a timeless metaphysical eternity where temporality and transformation are simply irrelevant. This making a problem of time and agency paralyzes the post-Mao project at its epistemological foundation that emphasized the self's power to analyze, intervene, and develop, unveiling difficulties in the practice of subjectivity not fully anticipated by more purely theoretical speculations. That the texts were produced in the heyday of the New Era and that they offer multilayered perspectives (cultural, historical, and existential) makes the authors' representation of the troubled subject all the more poignant and meaningful.

The fiction by Yu Hua and Mo Yan analyzed here moves us into the late 1980s and the post-Tiananmen era, when the subject, fictional and real, struggles to deal with a new set of imperatives. One such imperative affecting every individual in society was for China to speed up its modernization and continue the historical journey first set in motion in the middle of the nineteenth century. The achievements of the post-Mao reforms were undeniable and have been well documented. But not all travelers on the national journey are happy. The drastic alteration in ideological, cultural, and economic practices introduced undreamed-of opportunities as well as profound confusion and pain, making human agency and a person's ability to adjust two keys to survival and success. Yu Hua's stories of the frustrated traveler offer a somber reflection on the individual's precarious position in the collective venture, the effect of which was too often measured only in tangible, material terms. *Fengru feitun* (Large breasts and full hips) by Mo Yan (1995a) presents a unique approach to a particular aspect of the self that has piqued Chinese imagination throughout the modern era: the formation of the Chinese self in relation to its foreign counterpart. Similar to the experience of other third world countries, China's consciousness of itself as a nation-state emerged on the heels of foreign aggression. Since the country's first encounter with the Western powers in the 1840s, its position in the world and the future of its cultural tradition in the course of modernization had become recurring topics in debates. The rapid pace of westernization in the post-1989 reforms gave Chinese intellectuals further cause to worry about the erosion of the national identity. Evidently, the contemplation of the Chinese self could not be made without considering its interactions with the ever-present foreign Other. Mo Yan's inquiry into an intriguing power play between the native self and the alien Other exemplifies many of the concerns central to the configuration of the post-Mao self, such as the vitality of the national self and the authority of the foreign Other. Finally, Jia Pingwa's 1993 novel *Feidu* (The ruined capital) makes explicit the question of the writer's own agency, an issue of great urgency for the intellectuals in the early 1990s, when they were impelled to reconsider their assumptions about their profession, themselves, and their relation with the community in an increasingly commercialized society. The self-reflexivity of Jia's novel—it depicts the intellectual's experience and highlights the problem of representation—makes it a prime candidate in our study of intellectuals as historical subjects in China's transitional period *(zhuanxing shiqi)*. Together the texts will help us gauge the significance of the problematic subject and the nature of the crisis in post-Mao literature and society.

To reach this objective, careful textual analyses are essential. No doubt theoretical reflections on the issue of human agency can be carried out at a more abstract level, but in literary representations human agency can best be studied in concrete terms through the choices made or avoided, actions taken or rejected by the characters and, at the representational level, through the author's decisions to offer or withhold certain options. To reiterate the point, representation is an act consciously taken by Chinese writers in the post-Mao era for moral, political purposes. The historical mission of establishing a new being for China was reified through imagining the subject within the text. To the minds of post-Mao writers, writing had a full materiality. By describing the "real" through fiction, literature, the intellectuals hoped, would be ultimately transcribing it, making it happen as reality. Thus, the imagined world speaks equally powerfully about the creative agent and the created agent. We cannot hope to fully measure the social effect of the post-Mao search through literature, but we can discover the desires, tensions, and anxieties brought into the project by scrutinizing the texts.

Although literature provides the sources for study, my exploration incorporates both textual and extratextual dimensions of the post-Mao search. I place the literary representation against the background of major intellectual and social trends in post-Mao China: discussions of "socialist alienation" in the early 1980s, Liu Zaifu's theory of literary subjectivity and the culture fever in the mid-1980s, and post-Tiananmen marketization in the 1990s. I examine how literature concurrently produced and echoed these currents so as to lodge the literary search in its historical context. Ultimately, through a critical reading of the subject in the text against the social context in which it was created, I seek to prove that the crisis of the subject lies in the search's failure to offer a viable counter-model to the Maoist revolutionary archetype. By identifying and analyzing the phenomenal gap between what Chinese writers were seeking and what they actually produced, I hope to contribute to a fuller understanding of the intricacies of the post-Mao experience.

How is the problematic subject defined? Some of its striking features can be seen in an emblematic story written by Mo Yan, "Baigou qiuqianjia" (White dog and the swings).[21] By briefly referring to the story here, I can indicate the major thematic and theoretical concerns in my approach to the crisis of the subject. The protagonist/narrator of Mo Yan's story is a college teacher. On his visit to his hometown in the country, he goes to see his middle school sweetheart, Nuan, in her home and discovers to his dismay that the former school beauty, who is now blind in one eye, has married an uncouth deaf-mute. But even more unsettling is the grievous reality that the three children born of the marriage are all deaf and dumb like their father. On his way back to his home after the visit, the narrator is intercepted by Nuan, who waits for him in the fields with a shocking request. The woman offers herself to the narrator, entreating him to give her "a child who can speak."

Typical of the authors analyzed in the following chapters, Mo Yan traps us in a paradigm of human deficiency. The deformity in his story cuts across gender and generational boundaries: man and woman, parents and children, everyone in the family of five is handicapped. The situation, as a result, is sinister and threatens to expand to cosmic proportions. When procreation is repeatedly proven to be defective, deformity becomes a perpetuated pattern. What is more, the human subject is deformed in a most incapacitating way. The individual either has limited access to language or suffers from damaged vision. Obviously, the Party's annihilation of the subjective powers of speech and perception made post-Mao writers' obsession with their representation in and out of literature prevalent. The individual's (in)ability to be a speaking and seeing subject is consequently the central focus in my examination of the literary characters.

Mo Yan's short story also beckons us to reflect on the second group of subjects under interrogation in my study: Chinese intellectual-writers and the restoration of their agency. Little wonder that language and perception became dominant characteristics of the crippled subject in post-Mao literature. It is clear that the writers, for whom the denial of voice and vision was undoubtedly even more painful because their productivity hinged upon the exercise of these subjective powers, identified with the characters. Mo Yan's story suggests that the writer's own agency can be recovered by claiming a voice for the voiceless individual by means of creating a normal person "who can speak." Nuan's desperate plea can be answered only outside marriage, through the drastic intervention of the narrator, a college teacher who represents the intellectual. The last ray of hope, the intellectual-writer becomes the indispensable agent of healthy reproduction. The potential of the intellectual's creative power is in this way given both a dramatic representation and an existential urgency in Mo Yan's world. Following in the steps of Lu Xun's generation, post-Mao writers entrusted themselves with the task of giving birth to an unimpaired human being, a new national subject.

But significantly, Mo Yan's story is open-ended. It halts after presenting the concluding scene in the fields. The intellectual/narrator takes no action, leaving the woman's plea and her desire for repletion unfulfilled. Will the narrator do as he is asked or won't he? The lack of closure may point to a number of dilemmas facing the intellectual. He is confronted with awkward moral ambiguities. The moral duty of helping the voiceless can be achieved only by violating social codes, which would call the legitimacy of the assistance into serious question. In addition, as Yi-tsi Mei Feuerwerker cogently argues, the alienation between the intellectual and the poor peasant(s) he is supposed to represent, through which relationship Chinese writers have regularly explored the intellectual self and its role in various social and ideological programs in the twentieth century, makes his moral responsibility an "unresolvable issue" (1998, 210–213).[22] The hesitation in the story thus directs a self-conscious question at the intellectuals on the symbolic level: should they and can they shoulder the historical responsibility of creating a new subject for China? Extrapolating from Mo Yan's story, my examination of the intellectual as a subject in history centers on unpacking post-Mao intellectuals' ambivalence, doubts, and anxieties over their own creative power in China's reconstruction.

Specifically, to put the literary texts in context, chapter 2 provides a historical account of the inception of and major landmarks in the post-Mao search for a new subject. It proceeds from a discussion of the Communist representation of the self to that of its destruction by contemporary Chinese critics and writers in two areas, on the theoretical front and in literary practice. The search had been a prolonged and difficult process with diversified political, moral, and aesthetic agendas. Committed neither to a fixed orbit nor to a unified leadership, the quest unfolded with constant reprogramming and new representations. In this chapter, I examine three representative models of the subject that emerged with or in response to the intellectual debates over humanism, subjectivity, and the culture fever in the New Era: the sociopolitical being, the cultural being, and the artistic self. The examination of these models offers a literary trajectory of the search as well as an assessment of their cultural-ideological significance. Readers familiar with the post-Mao cultural and literary scene might, however, wish to go directly to later chapters.

The next five chapters are devoted to the human subject within the text. Chapter 3 focuses on the protagonists in two of Han Shaogong's *xungen* works, "Ba ba ba" (Pa pa pa) and "Nü nü nü" (Woman woman woman). Despite their different chronotopes (temporal-spatial backgrounds), the novellas have a conspicuous point in common: both have a flawed being as the central character, a retarded young man in the first and a half-deaf woman in the second. Adopting a Lacanian reading of the characters' troubled relationship to language, I argue that their lack of access to language and their manipulation by an external meaning system signify the characters' failure to be "speaking subjects," preventing them from creating new subject-positions. Linking Han's reproduction of the problematic subject with the politics of *xungen* literature, I also discuss the programmatic dilemma inherent in the *xungen* writers' vision of reinventing China through cultural exploration. I contend that by condemning China to recycle its decrepit past, the author's *xungen* practice unwittingly proves the impossibility of a cultural project that aims at simultaneously constructing both the past and the future.

Chapter 4 approaches the ineffectual self from the perspective of its relationship with the Other in Can Xue's fiction. Analyzing the antagonism between the self and the Other and, in particular, the author's fascination with "eyes" in light of Jean-Paul Sartre's theory of "the look," I point out that in the eternal struggle to be the dominating "seeing subject," the self in Can Xue's universe, who surrenders its own power of seeing to the Other, is an ultimate victim of "the look." Equally meaningful as the author's vision of life in China is her unique approach of deemphasizing overt sociopolitical factors, thereby highlighting the metaphysical nature of the situation. I am interested in exploring how, by turning the existential nightmare into a perennial present, this approach projects into the future of postrevolutionary China.

Postrevolutionary China since the mid-1980s is where the next three chapters take us. I focus here in more detail on the three writers, Yu Hua, Mo Yan, and Jia Pingwa, and their representation of the questionable subject in response to social concerns crucial to the reforms. Chapter 5 studies the image of the traveler in two short stories by Yu Hua, "Shiba sui chumen yuanxing" (On the road at eighteen) and "Xianxue meihua" (Blood and plum blossoms). Situating the lonely individual on the road in Yu's fiction against the post-Mao motif of progression and journeying, I examine the extraneousness of the traveler to the aggressive social trend of migration and movement in the post-Mao "New Long March." The self's confusion and lack of ability to negotiate its place in a new social space crowded with multiple competing discourses is the focus. I supplement the discussion of Yu Hua with that of a short story, "Ji zai pishengkou shang de hun" (A soul in bondage), by a Tibetan writer, Zhaxi Dawa. While the story shares similar concerns about the post-Mao traveler, Zhaxi Dawa's metafictional design gives, however, the journey an intriguing turn, presenting an option with which the writer can contend the autocratic paternal tradition that has debilitated the younger generation.

My reflection of the self in Mo Yan's *Fengru feitun*, in chapter 6, unfolds against the backdrop of China's constant effort to create a modern self vis-à-vis the foreign Other. It centers on issues of legitimacy surrounding the fictional conflict between the Chinese self and the foreign Other/father over the ownership of the symbolic female body. I argue that the author's preoccupation with sexual propriety and the masculinity of the Chinese self and the foreign Other is a manifestation of Chinese intellectuals' continuing anxiety over China's potency in the modern world. I also prove that by highlighting the impotence of the illegitimate child of racially mixed origin, Mo Yan questions both the authority of the foreign Other and the viability of the model of integration that has produced the weak bastard son. The novel thus constitutes another step in Chinese intellectuals' unending search for a workable paradigm to imagine and define the boundaries between the national self and the foreign Other.

The final chapter, chapter 7, deals with the subject both inside and outside the text: the intellectual self in the reform era and its literary representation in Jia Pingwa's novel *The Ruined Capital*. The chapter has a dual focus. After discussing the rise and fall of the intellectuals' representative authority in relation to various appropriating activities in the post-Mao era, I concentrate on their marginalization in China's consumerism in the 1990s. Next I examine how the intellectuals' "existential" crisis is represented and "resolved" in literature, using *The Ruined Capital* as a case study. By analyzing the artist, the mirror image of the intellectual, against the social condition in which he was created, I seek to accentuate the role of representation in mediating the complex relationship among subject, text, and history. I argue that through the appropriative act of representation, the author creates a new center to allow the marginalized intellectual to negotiate his anxiety in real history in the realm of literature.

The problematic being, in whom individual and group subjectivity and the writer's creative agency intertwine, occupies a conspicuous spot in the post-Mao gallery of subjects. A culturally and ideologically loaded complex, it aggregates post-Mao intellectual-writers' contemplation of China's past, present, and future. More intriguing than the all-powerful reformist who replaces the Communist hero and smacks of revolutionary romanticism in some of the post-Mao works, the crippled subject exposes the failure of literary imagination to go beyond the limit of its own burdened past, revealing the complexities and difficulties sometimes forgotten in the euphoria of the 1980s. The stories accounting the various deficiencies of the post-Mao subject analyzed here form a quintessential narrative of lack. Hauntingly persistent, they record moments of desire and loss. Too painful and too deeply felt to be cast aside, the lack has to be acknowledged before healing can begin. In the same spirit, I hope this study can help us recognize the full scope of the challenges confronting China's project of reconstruction, which is compelled and has endeavored to come to terms with each significant moment in the country's bumpy ride toward modernization.

2 In Search of a New Subject

In this chapter, I contextualize the search for a new subject in post-Mao literature. I approach the task by concentrating on two areas pivotal to the unfolding of the historical project: theory and literary practice. First, I discuss the efforts made on the theoretical front, focusing in greater detail on the aesthetic theory of what China's well-known literary theorist in the 1980s Liu Zaifu called "subjectivity in literature." Second, I give an overview of post-Mao representation of the subject in the New Era, examining the literary, cultural, and ideological characteristics of three models of the subject: as a sociopolitical construct, as a cultural reservoir, and as an autonomous artist. The ramifications of the post-Mao intellectual project have attracted much critical attention, where the emphasis tends to be either on conceptual interrogation of the subjectivity discourse or scrutiny of individual writers and literary trends. I attempt a synthesis here. The juxtaposition of theoretical probings with literary practice in the present chapter, I hope, will bring to light a discursive mosaic to help us understand the shifting contours that kept the investigation of the subject interactive and dynamic.

The search for the subject was motivated by Chinese writers' impulses to look inward, backward, and Westward: inward to reflect on the human subject's own role in producing its meaning; backward to renounce the Maoist subject and to explore China's cultural past; and Westward to draw inspiration from twentieth-century Western literature so that the challenge to the Communist formula could materialize in original literary forms. But ultimately, the purpose of the search was to look forward to position China in a new domestic and global scene. Although the search went through several distinct stages, these "gazes" were often concomitant movements rife with ideological and emotional ambiguities rather than neat, separate developments (though for the convenience of discussion they may appear in different sections here). As the sheer volume of post-Mao literature makes it impossible to attempt a comprehensive survey within the scope of one chapter, I analyze only trends representative of the search. Similarly, I paint the social context with broad strokes to provide a general background. The explosive cultural scene of the 1980s has been the topic of several book-length studies, for example, *High Culture Fever* by Jing Wang, *Chinese Modernism in the Era of Reforms* by Xudong Zhang, and *The Search for Modernity* by Min Lin and Maria Galikowski. I refer the reader to the critics' insightful discussions for details.

The Need for a New Definition

The "New Era literature" *(xinshiqi wenxue)*, as it was dubbed by Chinese critics, spanned the period from 1976 to 1989, the year of the June Fourth crackdown.[1] A spirit of experimentalism pervaded the times, producing much creative chaos and excitement that led to the coming and going (or lingering) of "literature of the wounded" *(shanghen wenxue)*, "literature of self-reflection" *(fansi wenxue)*, "educated-youth literature" *(zhiqing wenxue)*, "reform literature" *(gaige wenxue)*, "literature on military topics" *(junshi ticai wenxue)*, "literature of searching for roots" *(xungen wenxue)*, "experimental fiction" *(shiyan wenxue)*, avant-garde fiction *(xianfeng xiaoshuo)*, and various others that defy precise classification. There were flashes of Chinese versions of modernist and postmodernist fiction as well as revised realist fiction, such as psychological writing, fiction of mental state *(xinjing xiaoshuo)*, magical realism, symbolic fiction, allegorical fiction, neofactual or new realist fiction *(xin jishi xiaoshuo, xin xieshi xiaoshuo)*, and so on. Attempting to define the literary output of the New Era according to the point-of-view and narrative structure, still other critics grouped works under "multiple first-person-point-of-view fiction," "second-person-point-of-view fiction," "dialogue fiction," "epistolary fiction," and "nonfictive fiction" *(fei xugou xiaoshuo)* (Li and Zhang 1986; Cao Tiancheng 1986; Ding Maoyuan 1986).[2] Also popular during the period was reportage, a genre that stratifies journalism and fiction.[3]

This kaleidoscopic scene, however, does have a center. Critics and writers unanimously agree that the renaissance of post-Mao literature is characterized by a pervasive ethos of "recovery" and "return": "a recovery of once-denounced humanist values and a return to the May Fourth enlightenment projects" (Liu Kang 1993, 25). This recovery and return has two historical references: the May Fourth ideals and Maoist literature. The former provides the point of return and the latter that of departure. In order to reclaim the lost May Fourth beliefs and practices, the Maoist ideological literature responsible for their abandonment must be rejected. Post-Mao literature thus came into existence above all as a violent reaction against what Li Tuo, a Chinese critic in exile, calls the "Maoist discourse," a hegemonic "master narrative" that suppresses all other narratives (1993, 65). But the desire to regress to the May Fourth ideals only marks the inception. The trajectory of post-Mao literature shows that it has moved from a return to transcendence, from an urge to recover the familiar May Fourth model to a deeper study of Chinese culture and the human subject, which eventually resulted in the abandonment of the May Fourth model. This thematic trajectory also has an attendant technical dimension. The initial resuscitation of the May Fourth literary realism soon gave way to a hybridization of realist and post-realist experimentations.

The central issue in this development is the formation of a new consciousness that will ensure the individual the status of autonomous subject. As I pointed out in the introduction, the search for a new subject(ivity) was precipitated by a profound identity crisis experienced by the nation in general and acutely felt by the intellectuals in particular. While the blatant denial of the most basic humanist values of compassion, love, dignity, and trust during the Cultural Revolution made their retrieval a pressing task for the Chinese people as a community, a compelling motive behind the reconstructive program was the intellectuals' strong urge to redefine their own relationship with the authorities and the society after the dominant social principles of Mao's China crumpled in the wake of the Cultural Revolution. Even though the intellectuals had always been a primary target of inquisitions and political movements in Communist China, they were nonetheless made responsible for disseminating the official morals through their pens.[4] The coercive nature of the relationship between the Party and the intellectuals notwithstanding, this orthodox role, recognized and expected by society at large, was internalized by the majority of intellectuals, thus forming the basis of their self-identity.[5] When the radical Maoist principles were discredited after the Cultural Revolution, it very naturally induced a legitimacy crisis for Chinese intellectuals. On the one hand, their enforced identity as the official spokespeople needed to be shed; on the other, the intellectuals had to come up with a new role to redeem the dislocated self. To the intellectuals, a self displaced through their writing must be reinstalled by the same means. Only through their traditional function as the voice of the people's conscience could they reclaim themselves as dignified human beings deserving their place and respect in the postrevolutionary society.[6] Since this redemption hinged upon overturning the Communist model the intellectuals had helped popularize in the Maoist literature, it is necessary to start our discussion with a brief description of the human subject and its representation in the revolutionary discourse.

The Human Subject
in Communist Literary Discourse (1942–1976)

Chinese Communist literature is a familiar topic to scholars of Mao's China.[7] The most systematic treatment of the human subject in this fiction remains Joe C. Huang's *Heroes and Villains in Communist China*, which contains observations based on the author's study of full-length novels published before the Cultural Revolution (1973). Huang's study illustrates the changes in the image of the Communist hero at different stages of the revolution. Preliberation Communist heroes tend to share many traits with popular figures in classical literature, such as Song Jiang, Wu Song, and Zhuge Liang—individuals of outstanding bravery, noble character, and extraordinary resourcefulness.[8] The stringent conditions of the early years, when the Party was fighting underground with no resources to maintain regular communication with its branches, compelled the revolutionaries to rely on their own judgment in organizing the masses in the fight for power. As a result, wartime Communist heroes are not only granted a certain amount of individuality but are often allowed to develop from ignorant peasants or petty-bourgeois intellectuals into firm believers, reflecting the maturing process of the Party as it grew from a small group to a powerful ruling clique.

After the Communist takeover in 1949, there was a decisive shift in the image of the hero. Paralleling the socialist collectivization in both urban and rural areas, collectivity was strongly emphasized in postliberation literature. Portrayed now as the cadres, or leaders, of organizations, heroes lost their initiative and individuality. Their duty was to follow the Party line, trying to keep up with its volatile policies without taking the interpretation of these policies into their own hands, for indeed it was dangerous to do so. In the socialist revolution, the Party did not need a hero. As Huang phrases it, "Heroes of personal brilliance have no place in a collective society; as a matter of fact, they may be an obstacle on the road to socialism" (J. Huang 1973, 249). At that stage the Party looked for unquestioning followers to carry out its policies and transmit its will mechanically to the masses.

The disappearance of individuality was also evident in real-life soldier and civilian models held up for the people to follow: Lei Feng, Wang Jie, Ouyang Hai, and Jiao Yulu, to name a few famous ones.[9] Their outstanding quality was their selfless devotion to the Party and its grassroots representatives. The role and image Lei Feng was said to have chosen for himself were most revealing.[10] Lei Feng, the people were told, was determined to make himself "a little screw [in the machine] of the revolution." Mindless and voiceless, the screw is a necessary but insignificant part of the massive mechanisms of power. Thus, the Communist heroes "developed" over the years at the expense of their subjectivity. Radically objectified, the wartime individual of exceptional quality turns into a lifeless, unthinking "screw."

By the time of the Cultural Revolution, when literature and art fell under the control of Mao's wife, Jiang Qing, the literary stage had been set. Class struggle remained the supreme theme governing plot, characterization, and everything else. For several years, Chinese audiences were treated to only eight model plays, peopled by either staunch revolutionaries fighting the CCP's battle for power or wise, infallible Party branch secretaries, as in *Haigang* (On the docks) and *Longjiang song* (The song of Longjiang).[11] Fictionalized according to the principle of "loftiness, integrity, and perfection" *(gao da quan)*, revolutionary heroes without any human weaknesses literally occupy center stage, striking heroic poses at each entrance. The major function of the masses is to play the foil to the Communist supermen and superwomen. Much like the soldiers in a traditional military play, they charge onto the stage, make a few rounds, and vanish from sight.

The treatment of the individual as a carrier of class consciousness serving the grand collective course, however, is not of Mao's own making. It accords with the fundamental assumption behind the Marxist conception of the individual in pre-Communist society. In Marx's theory the individual is never a Hegelian single unit. Members of a specific class and, consequently, lodged in the process of history, individuals cannot stand on their own: they are a manifestation of the social relations in which they are caught. Marx holds:

> My standpoint, from which the evolution of the economic formation of society is viewed as a process of natural history, can less than any other make the individual responsible for relations whose creature he socially remains, however much he may subjectively raise himself above them. (Marx 1967, 1:10)

These social relations are, in Marx's view, inevitably class-oriented and determined by the economic conditions and positions of a particular social class
in relation to another. Therefore, Marx can only consider "individuals... in
so far as they are personifications of economic categories, embodiments of
particular class-relations and class-interests" (10). In his critique of the
Marxist concept of the individual, Paul Smith points out, "For Marx, in
Capital 'individuals' are only the ground, the resting place for certain prop-
erties which are abstract, and they attain the status of the concrete only at
the point where they belong to a class or where 'the people' can be discovered or invented." In other words, Marx does not recognize the singularity
of the individual but can only treat individuals collectively as a plural
"people" (Smith 1988, 4–5, quotation 4).

Thus, ideologically informed Marxist subjects are not called upon to
form their own subjectivity. The Marxist theorist Louis Althusser offers this
definition of ideology: "Ideology represents the imaginary relationship of
individuals to their real conditions of existence" (Althusser 1971, 162). In
Althusser's view, ideology as necessarily distorted representations plays a
crucial role in the formation of the subject's subjectivity. The notion of the
individual in Althusser's theory, as a consequence, does not exist unless
conflated with that of "subject," a being sub-jected to a certain ideology. In
Althusser's words, "ideology has always-already interpellated individuals as
subjects" (175). Subjects as such will always recognize the call of ideological discourses and, similar to Marx's view, bear the consciousness of certain
social formations.

Marx's and Althusser's theories of the subject have been vigorously scru-
tinized by theoreticians of both Marxist and non-Marxist persuasion (Smith
1988, 3–23; Hirst and Wooley 1982; Lukács 1971; Ferruccio 1990). Althusser's conception of the interpellation of the subject, as Yingjin Zhang (1993)
points out, is particularly pertinent to the situation in China (219–222). In
Althusser's system of thought, the interpellation of the subject depends to
an important extent on the operations of the state apparatus (SA)—government, army, police, prison, and so on—and the ideological state apparatus
(ISA), which are education, literature, art, media, and the like. While the ISA
functions primarily by ideology, the informing of ideas, the SA works by
force and violent means. The Communist history of China undoubtedly
proves the workings and cooperation of the SA and ISA in imposing the
Maoist ideology on the subject. Ever since the CCP established a more or
less stable base in Yan'an in 1936, it launched one thought-reform campaign after another to ensure ideological solidarity: the Yan'an Rectification

Campaign (1942), the Anti–Hu Feng Campaign (1954), the Anti-Rightist
Campaign (1957), the Socialist Education Movement (1963–1964), the
Cultural Revolution (1966–1976), the short-lived Anti–Spiritual Pollution
Campaign (1983), the Anti–Bourgeois Liberalism Campaign (1986, 1989),
not to mention those of smaller scale, such as the Bai Hua Incident in 1981,
in which individual writers were singled out for criticism for their heretical
ideas.[12] In many of these campaigns, the SA was brought in to enforce a
successful exercise of the ISA. For example, during the Anti-Rightist Campaign a large number of intellectuals who spoke out against bureaucratism
and corruption within the Party were subjected to the powerful "proletarian dictatorship": they were sent down to remote areas to reform their
thinking or were put in prison or labor camps. The most recent instance
that stunned the world was the military crackdown of June 4, 1989, and the
ensuing arrests of leading dissidents and pro-democracy activists.

In his critique of the Marxist concept of the subject, Smith (1988) contends that the existence of a variety of interpellative sources makes it hard
to produce a unified social ideology. "Thus there seems to be no reason to
suppose that there exists a correspondingly unifiable subjectivity" (18).
Although heterodoxy had always been present in Mao's China, as attested
to by the Party's perceived need to launch those unending thought-reform
campaigns, the coercive, militant nature of the political movements did on
the whole officially succeed in silencing dissidence, especially during the
Cultural Revolution.[13] The ideological uniformity was most evident (and,
in hindsight, frighteningly so) in the unvarying scenes of Mao's receptions
of the Red Guards in late 1966: hundreds of thousands of people dressed
in the same color and style of army uniform, waving the same Little Red
Book of Mao's quotations with the same expression of worship and reverence on their faces, shouting in one voice to wish Mao a long life. Drowned
in the crowd, no one stood out in the undifferentiable mass.

Given the specific sociopolitical situation in Maoist China and given
the utilitarian function forced upon literature and art and the tight control
writers and artists were working under, little wonder that the human subject, as both the creator of works of art and the character in them, becomes
a mere ideologue. Joe C. Huang's criticism that the tendency among
Chinese writers to "follow an established formula and avoid effort is also
due to intellectual lethargy" is a little too harsh (Huang 1973, 320). While
a number of writers were genuine believers of the Party line, those who
attempted any sort of individual expression were ruthlessly persecuted,
either physically or mentally or both. The authoritarian regime simply did
not tolerate any autonomous subjectivity in its subjects.

Rethinking the Subject: The Resurgence of Humanism

Open criticism, though still closely watched over by the Party, became possible only after Mao's death and the Party's admission that the ten-year-long Cultural Revolution was a mistake and a political and economic disaster. On the theoretical front, the question of subjectivity became a chief point of contention in the intellectuals' efforts at re-territorialization. The first call to arms was the much-publicized debates on socialist alienation and humanism in the early 1980s. In a series of articles published between 1980 and 1983, Wang Ruoshui, and Zhou Yang, raised the issues of socialist alienation and the presence of humanism in Marx's thinking. The "alienation school," as they came to be called, contends that alienation does not stop with the elimination of capitalism and the establishment of public ownership of means of production. It continues to exist under socialism because of dogmatic interpretations of Marxism. The socialist alienation, Wang argues, can be categorized as "the alienation of thought caused by the personal cult of Mao Zedong," "political alienation," and "economical alienation." Wang charges that ultraleftist practices in the ideological arena and bureaucratic economic policies in production alienated the people from the Party and their own labor (Wang Ruoshui 1983, 383–393). In his explication of Marxism, Wang insists that "man is the departure point of Marxism" and demands the abandonment of the cruel struggles of the Cultural Revolution in recognition of individual dignity, freedom, and creativity (Wang Ruoshui 1981). In spite of the limitations of the alienation school's position, the debate was a serious theoretical engagement that involved most of the intellectuals and opened up possibilities for future ideological discussions and resistance.[14] Though it was prematurely silenced by the Party's short-lived Anti–Spiritual Pollution Campaign in 1983, the debate brought the suppression of humanist values to national attention at a theoretical level beyond the simple emotional catharses and facile fault-finding characteristic of the late 1970s.[15] It preluded the intellectual fervor for new theories and methodologies in the mid-1980s.

At the same time, the issue of subjectivity was put forth by Li Zehou, one of China's contemporary leading thinkers. In 1979 Li published *Pipan zhexue de pipan: Kangde shuping* (A critique of critical philosophy: a study of Kant). A revised edition came out in 1984 that included his 1981 lecture on "the philosophy of Kant and the thesis on the construction of subjectivity."[16] Li's purpose in studying Kant is to "combine it with the study of Marxism" (Li Zehou 1994a, 444). Having no quarrel with orthodox Marxism, his theory cannot be said to be radically revolutionary. What Li proposes is to read the Kantian theory of human rationality from the point of view of Marxist historical materialism. Approaching Kant's ideas of universal knowledge from the Marxist perspective of practice, Li attempts to reconstruct a Marxist philosophical foundation for a notion of subjectivity. A firm believer in Hegelian historicism—though he disagrees with the formalization of human existence in Hegel's philosophy (Li Zehou 1988, 506)—Li holds fast to the Marxist stand that the economic base determines the superstructure, thus locating the formation of human subjectivity in tool-making and tool-using activities rather than in a priori principles of understanding and idealism (Li Zehou 1994a, 171–221). Still wary of the Maoist voluntarism in which the revolutionary theory prevailed in total disregard of social reality, creating human disasters, Li rejects the Frankfurt School's notion of praxis, which, in his opinion, "is so inclusive that it draws in every conceivable human activity in daily life—eating, sleeping, theoretical inquiries, and cultural activities" (211). To Li, only the classic Marxist concept of practice—labor and material production—can help us understand the origin of human subjectivity. The importance Li places on the practical activities of the subject in objective conditions leads him to emphasize social-historical dimensions of individual subjectivity and their function in the formation of cognitive knowledge. Li's book is difficult and his ideas are complex.[17] In the cultural hunger of the late 1970s and early 1980s, however, Li's study rekindled in intellectual circles a strong interest in the examination of subjectivity and Kant's philosophy, a project abandoned during China's salvation movement in the Anti-Japanese War (1937–1945) and later banished altogether by the Maoist ideology.

As Li's critics point out, in his Marxist approach to the issue of subjectivity, Li insists on the supremacy of the economic base over the superstructure without taking into serious consideration later findings of psychology and the function of language in the formation of human subjectivity (Liu Kang 1993, 40–43). The domain in which Li's subjectivity program produced the greatest repercussions is exactly where language plays a key role: literature. In 1985 Liu Zaifu, then director of the Institute of Literature at the Chinese Academy of Social Sciences, published his controversial article "Lun wenxue de zhutixing" (On subjectivity in literature). In the article and a number of further elaborations on the same topic, Liu acknowledges Li's influence on his own thinking, speaking highly of the impact Li's pioneering project had on the exploration of human subjectivity in post-Mao China.[18] In Liu's interpretation, "the central aim in [Li Zehou's] works is to replace nature-centered ontology with human-centered ontology and to reassert the primacy of Subjectivity in cosmology" (Liu Zaifu 1993, 62).

The reestablishment of human subjectivity is precisely the overriding theme of Liu Zaifu's own theory. If Li's project is to understand, from a philosophical point of view, what determines human subjectivity, Liu's less esoteric theory describes how to assert it in the realm of literature.

Subjectivity in Literature

Liu Zaifu's theory of subjectivity in literature has four aims: (1) to reassert the human=human formula; (2) to renounce the deformity of collectivity in traditional values; (3) to question the mind-matter opposition in a dualistic cosmology; (4) to challenge the current framework of popular literary theory (Liu Zaifu 1993, 59–65). The theorist's confrontational stance is forthright. It is clear that Liu's (re)construction of subjectivity in literature is based first and foremost on a destruction of the prevalent Marxist-Leninist-Maoist literary theory. And his criticism of the authoritarian orthodoxy as specified in the objectives listed is cultural, philosophical, aesthetic, and political.

The focal point of Liu Zaifu's theory is that "literature is the study of human beings" *(wenxue shi renxue)*. The realization of this highest goal lies in giving full play to the subjectivity of the human subject. Liu's definition of the "subject" and "subjectivity" is simple and straightforward: "The subject refers to the human being [*ren*] or to humanity [*renlei*]" (Liu Zafu 1993, 56); "subjectivity is the essential human force that is intrinsic to the subject's existence and embodied in the Object world" (57). The key word here is "embodied." Liu obviously subscribes to the idealist notion that the world is not inherently substance, as classical philosophy believes, but a meaningful "Object" created by the subject. As Liu puts it, "The world is an Objectification [*duixianghua*] of essential human forces, a world of meaning" (58). The subjectivity of human beings is realized "by creating an Object world and turning the external world into evidence of their own Subjective powers" (58). Therefore, objectification of the world is the only way for the subject to establish and prove its subjectivity. Liu Zaifu's agreement with Li Zehou's Marxist viewpoint of humanized nature is unmistakable. When the object is fully integrated into the subject as part of itself, this complete realization of objectification will result in the total elimination of the distinction between object and subject. "Literature and art," Liu holds, "represent attempts to approach this ultimate state" (58). What is clear in Liu's theory of literary subjectivity is that, first, as an object created by the human being, the world loses its "thing-in-itself" quality; second, literary creation, which Liu regards as the most complete and comprehensive

of human activities, transcends its epistemological function and is of ontological significance in human existence.

As the title of his article indicates, Liu Zaifu is concerned mainly with
the manifestation of human subjectivity in literature. This subjectivity has
three ramifications: (1) the subjectivity of the writer as the creative agent;
(2) the subjectivity of human characters in the fictional world; (3) the subjectivity of readers and critics in their reading experience of literature. Liu
puts forth his explications of each of the categories by dismissing Maoist
practices. He starts his discussion with the most approachable and most
obvious: the subjectivity of literary characters. Literature can deal with
nature, history, and society, but, "only human beings are the fundamental
object for literary creation" (Liu Zaifu 1986a, 273). In their own social
environment, characters function as subjects with independent consciousness and self-worth. But self-determination is largely denied in previous
Communist literature dominated by the theory of "environment determinism" *(huanjing jueding lun)*. Characters are seen not as interacting forces
that create as well as are influenced by their environment but as manipulated like "pitiful creatures" *(kelianchong)*, totally controlled by external
forces. Subsumed under the abstract notion of class nature, individuality
disappears. Ordained to obey the needs of class struggle, characters lose
their ability to act on their own and their value as free subjects. As a result,
"literature is no longer literature of human beings but degenerates into a
study of class 'semiotics'" (276). The remedy Liu proposes is that writers
should treat their characters with respect, grant them individual souls, and
let them be self-governing beings with free agency, even against the wills of
the writers themselves.

Under the subjectivity of writers, Liu discusses primarily what he
calls the "spiritual subjectivity" of writers *(jingshen zhutixing)*, the writer's
dynamic role in literary creation. To give a free rein to the writer's creativity will lead to self-realization, defined by Liu as "the full demonstration of
the spiritual world of the writers." Liu divides this self-realization into two
levels. The first is superficial, the conscious realization of the writer's personal vision of life in the created works. Writers should not be forced to
write any "command literature" *(zunming wenxue)* to meet the functional
standards but should give full play to their independent observations. The
more profound level of self-realization is the "externalization of the deep
formation of the writer's spiritual subjectivity" (Liu Zaifu 1986a, 286). This
deep formation consists of the writer's will, moral character, capacities, and
creativity. In the creative operation, writers will not simply achieve complete freedom in representing themselves but will form selves in the very

process. But yoked by the deep-rooted philosophy of the golden mean and later by the politicization of literature, both traditional intellectuals and the writers of Communist China share the same mentality of self-suppression, as a result of which the self is constantly on guard against its own creative impulse in order to comply with the demand for uniformity.[19]

The inclusion of the subjectivity of the reader in Liu's treatise touches on a topic seldom explored in Communist literary theory. Because of a high illiteracy rate among the populace and the moral weight traditionally placed upon the words of the literati, the subjectivity of the reader has been habitually overlooked.[20] Receivers of art are seen as passive reflectors who can only register the content of an artistic work in the manner of a mirror. Liu Zaifu contends that, first, to treat readers as mindless receivers is to deny them the ability to subjectively create and critique during the reading process. Second, overlooking the reader's subjectivity reduces artistic works to mere transmitters of knowledge, ignoring their aesthetic function in perfecting human nature and satisfying readers' emotional needs. In real life, Liu states, people live under various social inhibitions and are often alienated from themselves. In their aesthetic reading experience, readers can shake off these restraints and enjoy a freedom unattainable in their everyday lives. Through this they can rediscover themselves, repossess the emotions suppressed in the real world, or release their pent-up frustrations. The aesthetic process of reading thus replenishes readers by restoring to them the alienated part of their humanity, making them fuller human beings (Liu Zaifu 1986a, 295–304).

Liu Zaifu characterizes his theory as efforts toward "recovering the human being's status as subject in literature" (Liu Zaifu 1986a, 241). By naming it a "recovery," thus emphasizing the precedence of similar endeavors, Liu acknowledges his indebtedness to the May Fourth writers and the affinity between the post-Mao zeal over the human subject and the May Fourth celebration of individualism. Liu credits Zhou Zuoren with the authorship of the slogan that "literature should be literature of human beings," the premise on which he builds his theory of subjectivity. Liu points out that despite Zhou's overstated chastisement of traditional literature, he was the first who championed the inclusion of the common people in literature on a theoretical basis (257). It is clear that Liu treats his subjectivity project as a revival of a prior engagement canceled by the Communist practice.

Liu's emphasis on the writer's inalienable right to creative subjectivity, on the other hand, has a historical echo in the suppressed voice of Hu Feng (1903–1985), who had always been at the center of literary dissent in

Communist China.[21] In his confrontations with Communist authorities, Hu Feng is strongly opposed to the subordination of the creative mind to authoritarian theories, be they literary or political. A staunch realist, Hu Feng considers the depiction of "the truth about the human condition" in Chinese society the ultimate purpose of literature.[22] The writer's "subjective fighting spirit," Hu Feng's term for the writer's individual understanding, personal feelings, and emotions, is the only guarantee for the success of a truthful representation of human reality. The archenemies of Hu Feng's "subjective fighting spirit" are what he calls "subjectivism" and "objectivism." The former is a departure from true reality, resulting in the creation of formulaic stereotypes; the latter manifests itself in the utilitarian view of literature, the demand that literature be the means to certain political ends. During the early 1950s, when Hu Feng was singled out for criticism, his greatest "crime" was his resistance to the Party's leadership and to thought reform in accordance with the Maoist doctrine. Though his critics constantly misrepresented Hu Feng's views, they were basically correct in saying that he tenaciously opposed unitary control of literature.[23]

There is yet another source of inspiration behind Liu's project. The famous maxim from Fan Zhongyan (989–1052) that an intellectual should be the "first to worry about the world's troubles; last to enjoy the world's pleasures" *(xian tianxia zhi you er you; hou tianxia zhi le er le)* obviously underlines Liu's blueprint of subjectivity. A true descendant of the Confucian literati, Liu Zaifu is a traditional intellectual deep at heart. His call for the realization of the writer's subjectivity resounds with a strong note of moral responsibility. The subjectivity of the writers has a string attached. The aesthetic subject serves a higher purpose than merely proving its ontological freedom through literary creation. As Liu puts it, "The realization of the subjectivity of the writer lies not only in a sense of freedom, but also in an acute sense of mission" (Liu Zaifu 1986a, 291). In a narrow sense, the writers' mission resides in fulfilling their duty to uphold public ethics and cultivate social morality; in a wider sense, writers must connect their souls with the pulse of the times, shouldering the worries of humanity and the spiritual burden of history (286). This "sense of anxiety" *(youhuan yishi)* forms the center of the writer's subjectivity Liu advocates (291–294). Devoid of its traditional responsibility toward society, Liu's subject may become a nonentity.

The alienation theory, Li Zehou's reintroduction of Kant, and Liu Zaifu's literary subjectivity share certain impulses and concerns. Products of the times, they are manifestations of the post–Cultural Revolution historical consciousness. Coming out of an age when words carried enormous political power, the critics all showed a high awareness of the capacity of language and discourse in forming human subjectivity.[24] They not only located the revolutionary discourse as the object for contention, but in so doing they simultaneously opened up space for the introduction of other discursive possibilities. The contestatory nature intrinsic to the theories makes it clear that the post-Mao subject envisioned by the scholars is a political being. Despite the era's general aversion to ideology and political systems, the call for depoliticization and the efforts to aestheticize the subject are inevitably caught up in politics. For instance, Liu Zaifu's emphasis on self-expression independent of prescribed political standards has an unmistakably depoliticizing tendency. But his demand that literature be segregated from the class stand is also an open and direct challenge to the sacrosanct Leninist-Maoist theory of functionalism. A summation of Liu's own critique of and resistance to the Maoist ideology, his aesthetic subject has to depart from purely aesthetic values the moment the project is conceived. The political origin of the post-Mao discourse makes a neutral, self-centered subject impossible and useless to the search. Born out of a program of resistance, the subject bears a clear ideological-political birthmark.

This birth was undoubtedly expedited by the intellectuals' belief in humanism, in which the political resistance found an expression. Induced into being by an intellectual and historical nostalgia for the enlightenment project of autonomy and individuality suppressed by the Communist ideology, the post-Mao subject is not a new creation but a rehash of the May Fourth model. The subjectivity Liu Zaifu sets out to restitute to his literary subjects—the writer, the character, and the reader—is their freedom to construct their own meaning. What he stresses is apparently the sovereignty of human subjects as self-determining beings working toward their own fulfillment. Even though Liu avoids the politically sensitive term "socialist alienation" after the debate was silenced, his project is in fact a continuation of the criticism of socialism and the call to return to humanism (Jing Wang 1996, 205–206). In the post-Mao resurgence of humanism, the revolutionary father replaced the Confucian patriarch as the object of erasure. By negating the Communist past, the intellectuals attempted to close the fissure it introduced into China's cultural terrain and reconnect the contemporary with the modern to continue the crusade of enlightenment.

But despite the intellectuals' championship of the enlightenment ideal, similar to its May Fourth prototype, the post-Mao subject does not have a free subjectivity. It remains a communal being at the nation's service. Li Zehou's emphasis on socialization leads to "the subjugation of the senses to reason, the natural to the sociocultural, the individual to the community" (Jing Wang 1996, 104), whereas Liu Zaifu replaces the Communist imposition with a traditional Confucianist social responsibility. Indeed the world outlook of both Li and Liu is holistic and teleological. Having a hard time imagining a private space for itself, the post-Mao subject stays firmly tied to the psychological and political needs of the collective. It has not only an immediate battle to fight with Maoism in the past but also a historical mission to fulfill for the future beyond individual concerns. Thus, the post-Mao discourse of the subject is infused with tensions that have dogged China's pursuit of modernity, tensions between the individual and society, autonomous subjectivity and collective existence. Not until the end of the 1980s did a being unmoved by sociopolitical, humanist, and moral concerns appear. By then, disillusionment with political participation, the growth of a market economy, and a flourishing pop culture idolizing material achievement would join force to relegate the discussion of the enlightenment subject(ivity) to memories and history books, finally putting an end to Chinese intellectuals' utopian dreams. But history evolves in stages. The explosion of the humanist subject would not have been possible if such a dream had not existed in the first place.

The Rise of the Sociopolitical Being

Even before the critics engaged the issues of humanism and subjectivity on the theoretical front, literary practice had already made its own move. "Literature of the wounded" and "literature of self-reflection" constitute the preliminary steps. The first came into being as a direct response to the catastrophic decade of the Great Cultural Revolution, when tens of thousands of human lives were lost and millions of people suffered torture of one form or another. As the name of the trend indicates, the dominant theme of the literature of the wounded is to bare the "wounds" and denounce the Gang of Four and its followers for the atrocities committed against the people. Since the Cultural Revolution was of unprecedented magnitude, touching the lives of all, everybody had "wounds" to redress. Catharsis, as a result, was the basic mood. When the publication of Liu Xinwu's "Banzhuren" (The class teacher), in 1977, and Lu Xinhua's "Shanghen" (The wounds), in 1978, had lifted the floodgates, the writers' irresistible desire to display their scars met with ready identification from enthusiastic readers. Literature of the wounded turned into a lamentation on a national scale. Saturated with tears of rage, frustration, and pain, this form of literature is a political expression via an artistic channel. The victim's cry, the underlying tone of the literature of the wounded, is that of anger, indignation, and accusation. Notwithstanding the official encouragement the trend received and the help it gave the new regime to legitimize its rule, the sentiments were genuine and the outpouring spontaneous.

Literature of the wounded also reveals injury in a different sense: it becomes the manifestation of a "wounded literature" (Michael Duke 1985, 64). Though "wounds literature" started as a revolt against the Cultural Revolution and the revolutionary literature, it fell back on the Maoist model, following its conventions in the depiction of the human being. Characters continue to be black-and-white, helpless victims or iniquitous followers of the Gang of Four. External and descriptive, plot absorbs the attention of writers and readers alike.[25] The political naiveté and artistic inferiority of wounds literature are understandable when we consider that China had just stepped out of a literary desert created by the Cultural Revolution's blanket condemnation of literature of both Chinese and foreign origin. But immature as it is, such literature was an inevitable first step. Only after this initial emotional outburst could a deeper interest in a new subject be developed.

Literature of the wounded as a distinctive trend subsided after 1979. The next step in the recall of humanist values materialized in what is known as "literature of self-reflection." This reflective literature has a wider thematic scope and a longer historical stretch. Reaching back to the first major political movement of the Anti-Rightist Campaign in 1957 and moving forward to the present, it explores a wide range of social topics, the people's sufferings, bureaucracy, dogmatism, corruption, as well as topics relating to individual lives, such as love, personal responsibility, self-worth, and self-alienation.

The two most controversial and most representative works are Bai Hua's *Bitter Love* (1979) and Dai Houying's *Oh, Humankind* (1980), both of which are extensively treated by Michael S. Duke (1985) in his *Blooming and Contending* (123–181).[26] As suggested by the title, *Bitter Love*, which was later made into a controversial film, depicts the betrayed love of Chinese intellectuals for their country. The protagonist, Ling Chengguang, is a patriotic intellectual who returns to China upon the founding of the PRC after spending years abroad to escape persecution by the old regime. The Cultural Revolution forces him into a second exile in his own homeland. The intellectual's similar experience before and after the liberation highlights the theme of betrayed loyalty. The story ends with an ironic tragedy. When Ling's friends and family come to look for him upon the downfall of the Gang of Four, Ling, seeing people approaching, flees higher into the hills for fear of being arrested. He freezes to death on a mountaintop after tracing in the snow a huge question mark, his curled-up body forming the period. The question mark and the recurring scene of the wild geese forming the Chinese character *ren* (for "human") in the sky present the fundamental question: Why cannot human beings be treated as human beings and have their dignity and individual worth recognized and respected? In many senses *Bitter Love* continues the theme of wounds literature, but it locates the origin of the devastating Communist policy in its earlier years. Thus it goes beyond the officially encouraged scapegoating of the Gang of Four as the root cause of all evils. When Bai Hua steps into the forbidden area of implicating the socialist system, it was more than Deng Xiaoping was willing to countenance. *Bitter Love* was sanctioned and the writer was ordered to perform self-criticism.

Dai Houying's *Oh, Humankind* shares with Bai Hua's *Bitter Love* an interest in humanism. A self-conscious rationalist, Dai Houying presents the theme of her novel and the motivation behind its production in clear terms in the postscript. By her own account, she was an undoubting advocate of the class-struggle theory and had vehemently and openly denounced and rejected humanism as a valid universal human experience. Having witnessed the senseless annihilation during the Cultural Revolution, Dai tells her reader that "I was like one just awakened from a bad dream. . . . And I wanted to proclaim my awakening to my fellow man. So I set about writing fiction." The awakening crystallizes in one word: "A single word in capital letters quickly appeared before my eyes: 'HUMANISM!' A song long ago forgotten and cast aside arose in my throat: human nature, human feelings, humanism" (Dai Houying 1992, 29).

Oh, Humankind primarily portrays the inner lives of a group of university teachers as they are involved in various political movements. Not strictly written in the stream-of-consciousness technique as the author professes, *Oh, Humankind* does succeed in creating monologues by different types of intellectuals: independent thinkers, the credulous, the disillusioned, cynical Party functionaries, and the young and rebellious who challenge the orthodox interpretation of Marxism. Through the characters' confessions and reflections, the author not only seeks to reaffirm human dignity and the individual's right to intellectual freedom but also strives to examine the individual's moral character through truthful descriptions of both positive and negative human experiences such as love, faith, betrayal, cowardice, and painful disillusionment. The author's ultimate belief is that "Marxism and humanism are one and the same" and that the arbitrary, erroneous interpretation of Marxism by Chinese authorities is responsible for banishing humanism from Marxist thinking and socialist practice (Dai Houying 1992, 29).

Bai Hua's and Dai Houying's works indicate two distinctive features of reflective literature: the shift of attention from the external to the internal and the conscious experimentation with new literary techniques. When the description of collective events yielded to individual reflections, the writers paid more and more attention to the use of Western modernist techniques, such as symbolism, dream sequence, stream-of-consciousness, and nonlinear narrative structure, as a means to probe into the depth of the human soul.[27] Reflective literature thus marked a turn in the emphasis from social experience to individual beings, from the immediate and superficial to the deeply felt. The irrepressible outrage replete in wounds literature cooled down, and the strong sense of "us against them" was waning. No longer satisfied with censuring previous Party policies and the Gang of Four, the writers devoted more attention to various elements leading to the alienation of human values. By scrutinizing not just sociopolitical causes but also economic, moral, and ethical factors, literature of self-reflection arrived at more objective appraisals of society and the human subject.

One example from among a host of writers and numerous stories is Zhang Xianliang, an ex-rightist well known for his series of novellas on life in the labor camp based on his own firsthand experience. Instead of focusing on the injustices that condemn the wrongly accused intellectuals to the harsh life of the penal colonies, Zhang Xianliang examines in detail how the dire living conditions make normal human emotions and physical functions aberrant, reducing the individual to trickery, thievery, cruelty, and deceit to stay alive. As well-educated intellectuals, Zhang Xianliang's characters are highly self-conscious and thus in constant struggle with themselves, torn between their intellectual contempt for their moral debasement and the physical instinct for survival.

Compared with wounds literature, reflective literature was more concerned with the human soul. The introspection in most such works, however, continued to be firmly bound to historical particulars. The individual was seen above all as a sociopolitical construct operating under the influence of sociohistorical forces. Similar to the literature of the wounded, the moral values the writers sought to recover in reflective literature—rationalism, trust, love, independence, dignity, and compassion—obviously originated from the May Fourth humanism. The urge to return to the May Fourth paradigm speaks to the optimistic view in the immediate post-Mao years that it is possible to reestablish and re-present a self familiar and known but lost and suppressed as a result of fallacious political interventions. As Duke comments, the Marxist ideology "inspir[es] Dai Houying (and Liu Binyan and Bai Hua as well) to reemphasize the goodness and worth of the individual in an oppressively collective society." But this source of inspiration has its drawbacks. For "at the same time this ideology seems to bind them, or at least severely inhibit them from probing the genuine evil that springs from human nature and seems to require more than a merely secular humanistic explanation in terms of materialistic determinism." Duke further reflects that "perhaps only a generation of writers younger than Dai Houying can reach beyond the boundaries of Marxist ideology (humanistic or not) and realist poetics to probe deeper into the psychological depths of the individual and produce something closer to the poetry of prose" (Duke 1985, 181).

The "Culture Fever"

The younger generation of writers Duke places his hopes on belongs to what Li Zehou and Vera Schwarcz characterize as the sixth generation of modern Chinese intellectuals, the Cultural Revolution generation (Li and Schwarcz 1983/1984, 42–56). This generation was born and grew up in New China and lived through every stage of the Cultural Revolution. "They have experienced rebellion, search for power, factional strife, armed struggle, physical labor, unemployment, crime. Every conceivable kind of hardship has shattered their souls."[28] Unlike the generation of writers such as Wang Meng and Dai Houying, who, having seen the contrast between the last years of the corrupt Nationalist government and the golden days of the People's Republic in the early 1950s, had true faith in the Communist ideals, the younger generation's knowledge of the doctrine remained more of a theoretical notion. But this abstract concept did not stop members of this generation from participating fanatically in the Cultural Revolution. The severe blow to their revolutionary enthusiasm dealt by the concrete, ugly reality of the movement disillusioned them more thoroughly than the middle-aged generation of writers.[29] While the Dai Houyings, Wang Mengs, and Liu Binyans could still be nostalgic about the lost true Marxist practice, the younger generation harbored no such illusions. Less encumbered, they tended to be more skeptical in their political beliefs and more iconoclastic in their artistic pursuits. Like the May Fourth generation represented by Lu Xun, Chen Duxiu, Hu Shi, and Li Dazhao, the Cultural Revolution generation was "bent upon a rediscovery of the quest for truth. They are consumed by a search for a new vision of the world and of the self" (Li and

Schwarcz 1983/1984, 52). Notably different from the program set by the middle-aged generation, the quest of the writers of the Cultural Revolution group transcended the May Fourth model in terms of both moral principles and literary techniques.[30] Theirs was a search for the unfamiliar, a process fraught with self-doubt and difficulties, as I go on to show.

The strongest manifestation of this new stage in the post-Mao imaginings of the subject is the obvious tendency to move away from politics and social history toward culture and aesthetics.[31] This literary tendency was formed amid a surging interest in Chinese culture in the intellectual circles in general. In the mid-1980s, China was gripped by a "culture fever" saturated with contradictions and ambiguities. Various factors contributed to the revival of attention to the indigenous culture. Jing Wang argues that it came into being as a result of the intellectuals' realization that China's modernization program failed to deliver, and because the intellectuals were prevented from attributing the cause of the failure to Deng's Four Principles,[32] they used the critique of Chinese culture as an "alternative outlet" (Jing Wang 1996, 55). Pang Pu, the editor in chief of the Chinese Culture and Cultural China series launched during the Cultural Discussion, offers another motive. In Pang's view Chinese intellectuals' group identity is underlined by their social mission, a historical responsibility to envision the future for society. But in the past three decades or so, Chinese intellectuals' sense of mission was suppressed and left undeveloped. The culture fever is "a manifestation of the intellectuals' self-awakening" to their inalienable right to represent and chart the blueprint of social progress (Pang Pu 1988, 65–66). The phenomenon suggests two things: (1) Toward the mid-1980s, at the inception of the Cultural Discussion, Chinese intellectuals had definitely got over the self-pity and lamentation characteristic of the literature of the wounded and literature of self-reflection. (2) Ready to leave their image as helpless victims behind, they were now geared up to resume their elite position as the vanguard and spiritual leader of society. As Pang pronounces, "The intellectuals are the primary force in the cultural studies" (66). Fully confident in their discursive potential, Chinese intellectuals were eager to realize it by finding a way for the nation to move out of stagnation. By the mid-1980s, the entire intellectual world was caught in the fever. Various research centers and organizations of cultural studies sprang up, conferences and workshops were held on the mainland and in Hong Kong, and numerous articles were published, giving voice to a divergence of views ranging from the radically iconoclastic to the conservationist.[33] The central issues of the discussion are what social and aesthetic modernity means for China and where Chinese tradition stands in relation to modernization.

On these issues intellectual opinions are generally divided along two lines, those who claim that Chinese culture is inadequate in meeting the challenges of modernity and those who pin their hopes on its revival for the development of a modern consciousness. Although it is too simplistic to name the camps "traditionalist" and "antitraditionalist," the attitude toward China's traditional culture does form some sort of watershed. To Gan Yang, a young research fellow in the Institute of Philosophy at the Chinese Academy of Social Sciences, modernity boils down to the modernization of Chinese culture. He maintains that the "cultural conflict" unfolding in China's modernization is not external, between China and the West, but internal, between its age-old tradition and the fledging modern culture. As Gan puts it in uncompromising terms, "There is an unavoidable historical conflict between traditional Chinese culture and China's modernization" (Gan Yang 1989, 4–5). As a result, it is a war that China must fight on the home front. To resolve the conflict, Chinese tradition, which should not be carried as "a tremendous cultural burden," must be reformed and thoroughly reconstructed. It is imperative for China to find a replacement, a new "national structure of culture and psychology" (22). Jin Guantao, the director of the department of philosophy of science in the Research Institute of the Academy of Natural Sciences, in contrast, regards social modernity specifically as technological development. Like Gan, however, he sees traditional culture, with its "superstable structure," as an obstacle to modernization. To enable modernization to take hold, China needs what is lacking in its tradition—a new system of epistemology that privileges scientific rationality *(kexue lixing)*, the basis on which the West developed its modernization. The reason scientific rationality failed to develop in China is that in emphasizing ethics and empiricism, traditional culture imposed its order of ethical values on natural phenomena, preventing China from taking a crucial step in turning its early scientific discoveries into a modern science, thus curtailing the development of true science (Jin and Liu 1989, 400–428).[34]

If thinkers such as Gan Yang and supporters of scientism were critical of China's Confucian tradition, others were in favor of using it as a foundation for a modern culture. This resulted in a renewed interest in Confucianism and neo-Confucianism, the writings propagating Confucianist ideals by contemporary scholars on and outside the mainland, such as Xiong Shili, Zhang Junli, Tang Junyi, Mou Zongsan, and Xu Fuguan.[35] Session after session of discussion on Confucianism was organized, in the media and on university campuses, drawing academicians from home and overseas. The Confucian scholars recognize and concede that the ultrastable Confucian hierarchies and family-centered system hindered progress and led to centralized power and bureaucratic inefficiency. But they contend that Confucianism and modernity may not be totally incompatible.[36] Pang Pu shares Gan Yang's view that modernization means that of Chinese culture but argues that "development does not simply mean total rupture. It also means continuation" (Pang Pu 1988, 53). To ensure the continuity between the past and the future, China should critically inherit its Confucian tradition, retaining the cream (*jinghua*) and discarding the dregs (*zaopo*). The moderates reason that the rational elements in Confucianism can be salvaged and put to use in China's modernization. Reevaluation and transformation of Confucianism in turn will provide a new ideology for China to survive the transition. Many of them also hope that the Confucian renaissance, the revival of Confucian ethics and neo-Confucianism, will aid China in establishing a new spiritual civilization with which it can counteract the alienation and materialism that modernization inevitably brings.[37] This will enable China to have an alternative modernity outside the confines of the Western experience.[38] Thus, paralleling the government's slogan of building "a socialist modernization with Chinese characteristics," these cultural critics advocate the construction of "a modernized culture with Chinese characteristics."

"Searching for Roots"—Digging Up the Cultural Being

Echoing as well as developing the major themes of the culture fever (tradition vs. modernity, China vs. the West) in concrete, creative forms, the "searching for roots" (*xungen*) literature constituted an active voice in the Cultural Discussion.[39] But literary critics and writers were more concerned with defining and exploring the "authentic" in Chinese culture and its aesthetic expressions. If, as Gan Yang holds, the essence of the Cultural Discussion is tradition versus modernity (*gu jin zhi zheng*) and not China versus the West (*zhong xi zhi zheng*), the anxiety about adverse consequences of achieving aesthetic and literary modernity via westernization (though China and the West were not seen as an antagonistic pair) certainly seems to have fanned much of the furor of the *xungen* literature. While avidly adopting Western literary isms and techniques in an attempt to break free from the Communist dogma and secure membership in the world club, Chinese writers were also troubled by the specter that Chinese literature might lose its uniqueness in the international community. Thus, compared with the May Fourth period, when Western literature was held to be the national idol, the intellectual mood in the 1980s was much more diverse. No doubt critics and writers greeted Western trends with an awed fascination and a sense of belatedness, but the excitement was also accompanied by an uneasy realization that nonidentification and overidentification with Western literature would produce the same result—the obscurity of the self. How to create a new, non-Maoist literature that was accredited as both modern and Chinese was what most concerned writers in the mid-1980s.

Indeed, if Western modernism is assumed to be the ultimate model for measuring literary and aesthetic modernity, it will certainly lead to the denial of the indigenous. And if literary modernization entails total westernization, that would make modernity another kind of totalitarianism, another formula absorbing individuality and creativity, not to mention that thorough westernization also hurts Chinese writers' sense of national pride. The attitude voiced by Li Tuo during the debate on pseudomodernism *(wei xiandai zhuyi)* in 1988 was already in place in the mid-1980s. He asks, "Why must we be modernists? Why must we run after the others [Western modernists]?" (Li Tuo 1988, 8). To be sure, Chinese literature in the twentieth century lagged behind modern developments. But many writers felt that China's rich literary tradition, dating back more than two thousand years, was a match for any national literature and deserved recognition.

With these sentiments strong among the writers, Gabriel García Márquez's winning of the Nobel Prize in 1982 served as timely inspiration. It is true that all major modern Western literary schools have left their marks on post-Mao literature, but Latin American literature had a special appeal to Chinese writers, not only because, like Chinese literature, it, too, remained marginal to the Eurocentric Western literary tradition, but also because Chinese writers saw in Latin American literature a solution to the problem haunting them. The accomplishments of Latin American literature convinced them that it is possible to achieve modernity and international fame and at the same time retain one's own national characteristics. A prominent contributor to the modernization of world literature, Latin American literature successfully challenged and redefined the boundaries of what was marginal or central in the literary canon. The secret of its success, Chinese writers believed, lay in Latin American writers' presentation of the indigenous reality soaked in its own cultures. Magical realism, the trademark of Latin American literature that offers a perfect blending of the modern with the local, is the ultimate proof. Chinese literature should, thought Chinese writers, follow suit. Rather than denouncing wholesale traditional Chinese culture and literature, as in the May Fourth era, post-

Mao writers decided that a distinctive Chineseness could only be located in and established by tapping China's own rich cultural and literary resources.

With regard to the exploration of the human subject, the birth of *xungen* literature also had an internal impetus already clear in the self-critical mood of the reflective literature. In 1979 Ba Jin published his first volume of *Suixiang lu* (Random thoughts), his retrospective on the political movements in Communist China. In his book, the veteran writer did some relentless soul-searching. He analyzed his own behavior and deeply regretted having succumbed to political pressure and written articles, against his own better judgment, criticizing and denouncing several writers, including Hu Feng (Ba Jin 1979). In his comments on *Random Thoughts*, Liu Zaifu hails Ba Jin's self-criticism as starting a new period in Chinese literature, a period of self-reflection *(ziwo fansi)* and self-repentance *(ziwo chanhui)* (Liu Zaifu 1988a, 172–174). Liu calls on the Chinese people to follow Ba Jin's example and examine their own contributions to the Cultural Revolution so that a political catastrophe of the same magnitude will never happen again. The significance of this self-reflection is not simply for everybody to shoulder his or her responsibility but to understand how such a senseless movement was able to take place in China and how, as a nation, the people themselves played a complicitous role. What was it within themselves that made them susceptible to the propaganda, made them follow the Party line blindly to inflict pain on one another or act so indifferently toward the sufferings of their fellow human beings? These thoughts prompted the *xungen* writers to explore the worldview and philosophy of the Chinese people and, like Lu Xun during the May Fourth era, question their shared national character.

"Searching for roots" literature got its name from Han Shaogong's article "The 'Roots' of Literature" ("Wenxue de 'gen'") published in the fourth issue of the literary journal *Writers* in 1985.[40] This article was later held to be the manifesto of the new trend. By no means a unified camp, *xungen* writings took different directions.[41] Han Shaogong himself cautions his reader that "the writers who favor a 'roots' approach differ from each other in a thousand ways, so putting one label on all of them is a little awkward" (1992b, 148). Not only are the writers highly idiosyncratic in their approaches to the assessment of Chinese culture, but, as Yi-tsi Feuerwerker and Jing Wang have noted, there is also discrepancy between the theory and practice (Feuerwerker 1998, chap. 6; Jing Wang 1996, 213–224). The following statement from Han Shaogong nevertheless points out some general characteristics of *xungen* writers and their pursuits:

They were searching for "roots," and their endeavors were beginning to bear fruit. In my opinion, this [roots searching] is not motivated by cheap nostalgia or a preference for one's native region. Nor is it a shallow fondness for dialectical expressions. This is a rethinking about our nation, an awakening to the historical factors deep down in our aesthetic concepts and a concretization of the efforts to come to an understanding of the infinity and eternity of human existence. (1985, 3)

As indicated here, the "roots" the writers were searching for are cultural and aesthetic: culturally, to discover the essence of the Chinese nation, to understand who the Chinese people are and what gave them their national identity; aesthetically, to reevaluate and utilize the rich resources of China's literary tradition. The "roots" analogy makes it clear that the cultural essence (the aesthetic is seen as part of it) needs to be excavated. The temporal past and the geographically remote are consequently the preferred sites for the dig. Deep mountains, the hinterlands, and the backwaters of the country are where the *xungen* writers hope to find the authentic Chinese culture and the mythic, aesthetic origins of the race. The inhabitants of these places, the mountaineers, fishermen, herdspeople, and minorities, are the writers' favorite objects of analysis. These inhabitants' primal desire to love and hate, their intense and spontaneous responses to life become the cultural ground for discoveries, explorations, and self-expression. The writers' fascination with the marginal can also be found in their attention to China's native religion, the Daoist vision, which has been more or less absent from the theoretical Cultural Discussion. In contrast, a number of writers, such as Feng Jicai and Lu Wenfu, zoom in on the alleys and marketplaces of traditional towns to explore the textures of urban culture. Their "cultural fiction" *(wenhua xiaoshuo)* with its vivid local colors complements the rural stories in the xungen writings.

In a sense the culturization of literature in the mid-1980s can be seen as the product of the "anxiety of out-fluence," to use one critic's coinage, which accompanied the hunger for Western ideas.[42] But this "anxiety of out-fluence" did not end in a rejection of the modern, as simple logic would lead one to think. The strategy of *xungen* writings is competition through assimilation. This results in an interesting array of styles: the bifurcation as well as convergence of traditional, realist, and modernist modes of representation. Such traditional forms as *biji xiaoshuo* (literary sketches), episodic fiction, and a literary diction unmistakably tilting toward classic Chinese resurfaced with a vengeance.[43] At the other end of the spectrum, there are works experimenting with modernist techniques. What we should note is that the two kinds of writing do not form opposite camps, as was the case with the modernist and nativist schools of literature from Taiwan in the 1960s and 1970s.[44] Not only is there no clear-cut timeline separating the advent of modernist and more traditionally flavored writings, but also these two types of writing coexisted peacefully, often freely crossing each other's borders in a single piece of work.[45]

In this culture fever highlighting Chinese culture and its national psyche, the study of the human subject takes yet another turn. First, the roots-searching consciousness bespeaks a transhistorical vision. The insistence on the existence of a national essence allows such essence to outlive history. Though the *xungen* writers were often faulted for delving into the past, history is not their destination. The purpose is to go beyond historical contingencies to bring to light the "roots" that speak to the "infinity" and "eternity" of the Chinese experience. As a result, even though in some stories characters still operate in recognizable social situations, historical specificities are no longer presented as decisive factors determining human behavior. History and the sociopolitical, in this approach, are twice depowered. They not only lose their potency as determinants of the individual's action, but because of it, they are also denied as the potential site of resistance. The battle is fought elsewhere. Transcending the immediate surroundings, *xungen* literature is a further step along the path of depoliticization toward aestheticization.

Second, the comparison of Chinese characteristics to "roots" works on the assumption that these characteristics are collective, revealing the Chineseness of the people as a group. The divergence in the "branches" and "leaves" sprouting from the roots is only superficial; deep down there is a shared substance in the nation's cultural and psychological structure. Thus, the interest of the *xungen* writers is not in examining the individual as a unique being but in mapping out the Chinese people's collective subjectivity, or their cultural unconscious. The *xungen* practitioners are intent on identifying, isolating, and ultimately eternalizing what they consider the constant in the psychological makeup of the Chinese nation. Seen as the ground for discoveries, the individual's psyche, behavioral codes, and relationships to the environment and to fellow human beings are approached and analyzed as reflections of Chinese culture. From a sociopolitical being, the subject turns into a cultural construct. Obviously, just as the sociopolitical being is a collective expression of anger, rage, and historical introspection, the cultural subject of the *xungen* project is also a group image. Precluded from being a purely individual manifestation, it is foreordained to be a generic symbol.

Lu Wenfu's story "Well" can serve as an example. The story is built upon the title image. On the realistic level, the well is the world of the womenfolk in a small southern town, where they gather every day to wash clothes and exchange gossip. It is their gossip that finally kills the protagonist of the story, Xu Lisha. Because of her capitalist family background, Xu is assigned to work in a pharmaceutical factory after college. She marries Zhu Shiyi and suffers daily abuse from both her husband and her mother-in-law. After the Cultural Revolution, Xu is given the title of technician in recognition of her successful research. She is interviewed on TV and her name often appears in newspapers. Xu's accomplishments incur her neighbors' jealousy, making her the object of their slander. Unable to stand it, Xu drowns herself in the well.

In its roundness the well symbolizes women and may be associated with their gossiping mouths. On a deeper level, the well points to the narrow-mindedness, the irrational jealousy and malice in the dark corners of the human soul characteristic of Chinese small-town mentality. Arguably, this imperfection in the Chinese national character is neither related to a particular historical period nor induced by specific political conditions. The protagonist's life before, during, and after the Cultural Revolution provides what the Russian formalists called the "realistic motivation" for the story, but the environment cannot be held solely responsible for the insularity of the mean-spirited crowd. We find a similar throng against an entirely different sociohistorical background in the Taiwan writer Li Ang's novella "The Butcher's Wife." The malignancy comes from sediment in the nation's deep cultural formation. It is such inveterate traits of the collective unconscious that some *xungen* writers are trying to bring into critical limelight through their literary examination of Chinese culture.

The culturization of the subject unavoidably raises the question of agency (Jing Wang 1996, 215–224). If the subject is completely informed by culture (no matter how many ways it is interpreted and imagined), it closes off the possibilities of self-determination and in consequence the possibilities of resistance. Thus, the very purpose of the cultural discovery is problematized. The impetus and dynamics of the Cultural Discussion reside in its resolve to meet variegated challenges in the experience of modernization. Whether the battle is envisioned on the home front over self-transformation or in the international arena between a Western modernity and a Chinese alternative, active agency is a precondition if the cultural subject is to rise to the occasion. The celebration of the indigenous is predicated on its capacity to function as a source of empowerment. The subject must somehow transcend its immersion in the cultural reservoir. The solution, as Jing Wang puts it, is found in a "romanticization" of the subject. Nature is brought into the configuration, providing an activating landscape for the otherwise entrenched cultural subject. "What culture constrains, nature sets free" (218). The unbridled human instinct, the primitive strength, the raw courage of the creature of nature are eulogized as the repository of virility, action, and resilience. A being pulsating with the unspoiled world of nature, the *xungen* subject will, ideally, take China back to the future.

The image of digging for roots should not obscure the fact that this is not mechanically retrieving what already exists. The "roots" are not there to be recovered; they are to be constructed through fictional exploration. For all their sincere belief in the existence of a Chinese essence, such an essence can take shape only through the writers' interpretation and intervention. "The search for roots...is concomitantly a search for the writing self" (Feuerwerker 1998, 225). Like all acts of representation, the search for roots is an undertaking of appropriation and self-projection: the cultural subject is imagined and created. The *xungen* terrain and its inhabitants are Chinese writers' symbolic investments in the revamping of China. The journey into the past is fundamentally an expression of anxiety about the present and the future.[46] The backward glance of *xungen* literature is thus forward-looking in intention. The cultural being is another projection of the national subject on the representational screen transcribed by post-Mao intellectual-writers.

The New Artistic Self

It should be clear from my preceding discussion that the evolution of the post-Mao subject concurs with a revolution in literary representation. The ideological restructuring materializes through an artistic carnival, a process combining the subjectivity in the text with that outside it. The growth of the artistic self made the representation of the post-Mao subject possible; at the same time, representation provided space for the development and deployment of the artistic self. The search for a subject for the nation has thus simultaneously brought into existence an autonomous, artistic being: the writers as free-willed agents. The pursuit of new narrative choices in post-Mao literature was part and parcel of the formation of a new subjectivity. The national subject found another mirror image in the independent writers in the extratextual arena.

The ontological significance of technical innovation in literature is made clear by Liu Zaifu's essay on literary subjectivity. That Liu finds it necessary to emphasize artistic freedom as part of the writer's subjectivity makes the lack of it a lamentable reality in Maoist China. Mao's literary policies not only prescribed behavioral codes for fictional characters but also stipulated specific literary avenues for their concretization.[47] The favored mode was revolutionary realism, complemented in the Great Leap Forward campaign (1958–1960) by revolutionary romanticism. In Maoist thinking, techniques were labeled either revolutionary and correct or reactionary and bourgeois. The obvious fact that realism was imported from the West in the May Fourth era in the first place and that its advent was commonly associated with the rise of the bourgeois class was conveniently overlooked in this simplistic logic. Because of its political import, the adoption of new techniques in post-Mao literature was a very self-conscious act, aiming at toppling the submissive self-identity established for the writers by previous literary authorities (Leo Lee, 1985a). The question here is not to turn the tables to condemn one technique in order to endorse another. The demand for the freedom to use new (or traditional) techniques and different narrative modes is to confirm the writers as self-regulating subjects. The post-Mao zest for new techniques in the late 1970s and early 1980s should first be understood in this light, though the subversive edge became dulled in later years when the state's tolerance made it less of a political issue.

Because of its conspicuous ideological, psychological, cultural, and emotional connotations, the introduction of the techniques and perspectives categorized under the phrase *modernist school* was a noisy and stormy process, sparking debates in literary circles on and off throughout the 1980s. In the early 1980s (1980–1983), the battle was fought around whether Western modernist techniques had a legitimate place in contemporary Chinese literature. The mid-1980s saw a shift in focus from form to content. The skeptics now questioned whether the sentiments expressed in Chinese modernist writings such as alienation, sense of loss, and absurdity were authentically Chinese and, even if they were, whether the portrayal of these tendencies would produce a positive social effect. When the existence of a Chinese modernism became indisputable fact, the nature and interpretation of Chinese modernism (i.e., according to what standard it should be judged genuine or fake) dominated the controversies toward the late 1980s (1987–1989).[48] The most relevant for my purpose here is the first round of debate in the early 1980s, during which the relation between the adoption of modernist techniques and the assertion of a new subjectivity is clearly articulated.

The debate was provoked by a booklet Gao Xingjian published in

1981, *Xiandai xiaoshuo jiqiao chu tan* (Preliminary discussions on the techniques of modern fiction), brief impressionistic reflections on a number of Western and Chinese literary trends and techniques. At a time when the Chinese literary field was just beginning to experiment with ways to break free from the officially promoted realist mode, the booklet's appearance became a much-needed catalyst. Articles both for and against "modernism" (*xiandai pai*, a term used loosely at the time to include any modern Western trend) were carried in newspapers and literary journals.[49] Those in favor of modernism saw it as a necessary stage in the evolution of literature, thus linking literary modernism with the concept of social modernity. They held that as China modernized, its literature, too, would go through a transformation. The opposition considered modernism a product reflecting the decadent capitalist society in the West, thus denying its applicability to the socialist reality in China. Both sides clearly used their own interpretations of Western modernism to justify or disqualify the attempts at producing Chinese modernist writings already under way.[50] In doing so, neither side treated modernism purely as a technical matter but politicized it within the Chinese context.

The crucial point of contention for the writers is the issue of artistic autonomy. The question whether China needs literary modernism boils down to whether the writers have freedom to choose what to represent and how to represent it. All promodernists recognize in Chinese modernist writings an attempt to create a new, unprescribed self. In his controversial essay "Jueqi de shiqun" (A flourishing group of poems), Xu Jingya locates in the new poetry known as *menglongshi* (misty poetry) the emergence of a new sense of self, a self entirely different from what the reader is accustomed to seeing in Maoist poetry (Xu Jingya 1983).[51] This self, in Xu's opinion, has an independent consciousness undictated by any existing doctrine. It is a consciousness that privileges the interiority of the poet, both conscious and unconscious. The self ascending from this consciousness expresses and sings for itself.

Another critic, Sun Shaozhen, makes this point even more clearly in his essay "Xin de meixue yuanze zai jueqi" (The rising of a new aesthetic principle), a commentary on the works of the same group of young poets. The new aesthetic principle Sun discerns in their poetry is manifested in their disobedience to the orthodox pragmatism. "They disdain to be the trumpet of the spirit of the times, and they are not interested in singing the praises of great deeds external to their own emotional world." They avoid writing on conventional themes of heroic revolutionary struggles or socialist construction; they do not concentrate on superficial reality; instead, "they are going after the secrets deep down in the human heart" (1984, 325). As is generally the case with dissident voices, both articles brought down a shower of criticism loaded with quotations from Marx and Engels, harping on the trite view that poets should never detach themselves from the collective cause and that the poetic self must be connected with that of the people.[52] The rebellious gesture and the political significance of adopting new techniques aside, we should also recognize that the polymorphic Western literature solved practical problems of representation for Chinese writers. It offered a panorama of unheard-of and undreamed-of literary techniques through which the autonomous self could be given new representations. During the more relaxed mid-1980s, artists joyously complied with the creative imperative.[53]

If the autonomous, artistic self in the early years after the Cultural Revolution was nourished by the spirit of humanism, its coming of age during the economic reforms also brought an end to its benefactor. The ardor to claim artistic independence and the insistence on maintaining literature as an individual aesthetic experience eventually led to the start of self-reflexive literature in the mid-1980s. Initiated by Ma Yuan, this kind of metafiction, as I have commented elsewhere, takes the creation of literature as the object of its description, openly displaying itself as an artifact of human imagination, deporting social, political, and moral concerns from the "house of fiction." Recognizing only the writer's absolute authority over literary maneuvers, self-reflexive fiction thoroughly negates the Maoist functionalism, which persisted to a large degree in the mainstream post-Mao literature in the 1980s in spite of its anti-Mao, humanist stance (Cai 2002).

This exclusive devotion to formal matters of writing and the ahistorical perception of literature inherent in such a position ushered in what Chinese critics called "a discursive revolution" (huayu geming), in which the emphasis on the performative quality of language replaced the humanistic interest in ethics and morals. After Ma Yuan (temporally, technically, and conceptually), the "new-wave writers" (xinchao zuojia), such as Yu Hua, Su Tong, Ge Fei, and Sun Ganlu, further explode the myth of the self-regulating subject in the text, offering on a linguistic altar their own fictional construct that thrives or decomposes at the stroke of the pen, free from any humanist imperatives.[54] Thus, metafiction finally and formally declared its independence from politics and social concerns. Put in ontological terms, the rejection of the teleological and utilitarian perception of literature locates the act of narration as the locus of subjectivity, allowing the writing self to evolve with the performance of narration outside the social, moral arena. This autonomous, discursive self presents an alternative to the Enlightenment subject that dominated Chinese intellectual imagination throughout the twentieth century. Stepping over the boundaries of humanist subjectivity, metafiction offers a cultural critique whose power of resistance resides, in the final analysis, in its ability to form and inform counternarratives on its own terms.

From the revival of humanism to its abortion, post-Mao literature has traveled a long way on a journey of replenishment. This was clearly a journey sustained by the writers' full faith in the power of language—what the Communist discourse had destroyed through the use of words, they hoped to reconstruct by the same means. Together with other intellectual endeavors of the day, literary imagination assumed the historical task of rebuilding China's social foundation by restoring agency to the post-Mao subject. But were there limits to literary imagination that Chinese writers overlooked in their optimism, confidence, and utopian urge for plenitude? And to what extent did the burden of history interfere with the representational goal set by the writers? In the following five chapters, my examination of the human subject seeks to answer these questions.

3 The Spoken Subject

Han Shaogong's Cripples

Despite the changing perspectives in the theorization and representation of the subject in the 1980s, and despite the multifarious roles the subject was called upon to perform in the post-Mao era, one thing remained constant: the emerging new subject was expected to be an empowered being fully competent to exercise its formerly inhibited agency. Anticlimactic to the eager anticipation and passionate theoretical pleas for the autonomous subject, however, postrevolutionary literature produced an unprecedented contingent of deformed beings, as David Wang notes.[1] That a problematic subject should dominate the cathartic "literature of the wounded" and "literature of self-reflection" in the wake of the Cultural Revolution is understandable: the soul needs to be purged after decades of forceful ideological imposition. But the creation of the problematic being continued into the 1980s. When the crippled subject develops into a persistent pattern beyond the landscape of Mao's China, it becomes a portentous projection into the future, defying our attempt to confine it to history and memory. Speaking from a position of lack induced by the Communist suppression, the post-Mao imagination, it seems, could only succeed in voicing the lack it desperately wanted to rid itself of.

Two unforgettable images among a host of troubled beings produced in post-Mao literature are Bing Zai, a mentally retarded boy, and Aunt Yao, a half-deaf woman who regresses to a primitive stage, in Han Shaogong's "Pa Pa Pa" and "Woman Woman Woman." Both of these works were published in the mid-1980s, when the *xungen* fever celebrating the stalwart native champion was at its height. Because of the sharp contrast between Han's antihero and the larger-than-life, victorious *xungen* subject, Han's creation, the boy in "Pa Pa Pa" in particular, proved perplexing. Li Qingxi expressed the puzzlement all his fellow critics felt: "The mischievousness of Han Shaogong lies in the fact that he presented us with a nondescript, an idiot. We're at a loss what to make of him" (1986, 50). But critics soon got over their initial bewilderment and rose to the challenge. All invariably recognized the symbolic import of the novella. The benighted Bing Zai is considered brother to the famous Ah Q, thus a representative of the Chinese national character. Some placed the work against the backdrop of Chinese culture in general, seeing in its description of barbaric rituals, primitive beliefs, and the lack of mental power in the protagonist a "symbol of the primitive, defective aspects in the nation's cultural consciousness." In others' views the mentally impaired young man is universalized to stand for the blemished state of human existence.[2]

All these readings are highly pertinent. We can press the issue further, however, and ask what particular cultural defects Bing Zai and Aunt Yao symbolize and how these defects jeopardize the post-Mao reconstruction of the subject. I suggest that at the most fundamental level, through the characters' physical disabilities, the novellas reveal an ongoing crisis of the subject. This crisis is manifested, above all, in the subject's problematic relationship to language and the attendant absence of self-representation. Han Shaogong's subject is either denied access to language or is appropriated by an external discourse to such an extent that its ideologically constructed subjectivity becomes self-destructive and self-alienating. The exclusion of the subject from the formation of its own subjectivity, I argue in this chapter, has robbed it of self-awareness and hence autonomy. I further contend that even more disturbing than the author's drastic undermining of the humanist, rational subject is his pervasive sense of crisis, which is evident not only in his refusal to kill off this crippled subject but also in its relentless reproduction. Situating Han's subject against the historical mission of the *xungen* literature, of which the author is often cited as a representative, I also discuss how his duplication of the flawed being frustrates the *xungen* mission as a futuristic endeavor whose purpose is to find an alternative Chinese modernity. The subject's troubled relationship to language and the historical implications behind the recycling of the questionable subjectivity are the issues I explore in this chapter.

One of the young writers who captured national attention during the culture fever in the mid-1980s, Han Shaogong (as mentioned in the preceding chapter) is known for attaching the name "literature of searching for roots" to *xungen* literature. Born in January 1953 in Changsha, Hunan, Han Shaogong had a typical teenage experience to which many in his generation could relate. The second year of his middle school saw the start of the

Cultural Revolution. Credulous and undoubting like many of his peers, Han participated enthusiastically in the Red Guard movement, passionate in the belief that he was contributing to a revolution that would decide the fate of socialist China. In time Han was swept by the tide of "reeducation" of the intellectual youth to a people's commune in Miluo County, Hunan, where he stayed for the next six years. The mysterious hinterland, with its untraversed, thickly forested mountains where primitive customs still prevailed, amazed and fascinated Han Shaogong and became the setting for many of his stories. In his review of Han Shaogong's fiction pre- and post-1985, Joseph Lau concludes that "given less governmental interference over a sustained period of time, a gifted writer can perform many wonders in self-transcendence" (1993, 21). In many ways Han Shaogong's literary path epitomizes the development of post-Mao fiction writing in general. Written in the vein of "wounds literature" and "reflective literature," his early creations centered on topical, sociopolitical issues, depicting in detail the wretched existence of the country folk suffering from the perversities of the leftist policy. The author's more mature work of drastically different thematic and artistic inclinations came out in the mid-1980s with the publication of his novellas "Pa Pa Pa" and "Woman Woman Woman" and five short stories.[3] An intriguing blend of realistic details, imagination, symbolism, and allegory, these stories break free of the rigid realist mode. Typical of the *xungen* literature, they are not so much involved with "a particular issue, a specific social group or individuals, but [with] a spiritual state, a psychological state," and ultimately with Chinese culture (Xu Zhaohuai 1989, 62).

The novellas "Pa Pa Pa" and "Woman Woman Woman" are the literary manifestation of Han Shaogong's roots-searching urge, his trenchant inquiry into Chinese culture, past and present, and his vision of its future. To assess the burden of tradition and the underlying forces stalling the nation's growth, Han Shaogong chooses the human subject, the bearer of the collective unconscious, as the focus of his investigation. What he resorts to amounts to a kind of shock therapy. Contrary to the romanticized, resilient subject of nature who invariably transcends his surroundings teeming in other *xungen* stories, the subject Han Shaogong presents is a crippled being who is equipped neither with self-knowledge nor any power to act independently. An eternal victim whose incapacity to realize its own position precludes the possibility of agency, this crippled subject is endowed with a larger and profoundly disturbing allegorical significance for China and the post-Mao reconstructive efforts.

Han's Roots: Mute and Stultified Youth

"Pa Pa Pa" has a simple plot. Bing Zai, a severely mentally retarded boy abandoned by his father, lives with his mother alone in a remote, stagnant mountain village. A year of severe drought causes a series of bloody fights between Bing Zai's village and a neighboring one over a particular superstition. Defeated and devoid of hope, the villagers set out to look for another place to settle as their legendary forefathers did hundreds of years ago.

In taking as its central figure a mentally deficient boy, Han Shaogong's "Pa Pa Pa" immediately recalls a more famous work in world literature, William Faulkner's *The Sound and the Fury* (which Han did indeed read).[4] What Han's text shares with the modernist novel is his narrative focus on the enigma of human subjectivity. Hauntingly suggestive, Bing Zai's intriguing deformities challenge the reader's imagination. On the immediate level, the character's debilitation is manifested in his alienation from his own body. The misproportioned and clumsy Bing Zai is burdened by his oversized head; simply moving it involves enormous labor:

> It was no easy job for him to roll his eyes: it seemed as if he had to mobilize all the muscles of his neck, chest and abdomen before he could manage it. Turning his head was an equally laborious job. His neck was weak, and his head had to roll like a pepper grinder, tracing a big arc before steadying into the turn. But running took the most effort. He stumbled and staggered, and had to thrust the weight of his head and chest forward to drag the rest of him along. (Han 1992a, 36)[5]

What is routine for a normal person is a constant struggle for Bing Zai. He is a being at odds with his own body as a physical link between him and the external world.

If Bing Zai's difficulties in controlling his body are not evidence enough of his awkward relationship to himself, Han Shaogong further condemns the character by plunging him into an abyss where no light of self-consciousness ever penetrates. The bizarre exterior of the subject is matched with an equally devastating interior. Paralleling his physical abnormality is Bing Zai's mental retardation. Except for his natural instincts to sleep and eat, Bing Zai does not seem to recognize any meaning in his existence. In fact, from the very beginning, he lives in an existential limbo between living and dead. We are informed that at his birth, "he showed no sign of life for two days. His eyes remained closed, and he refused to feed, scaring his folks out of their wits. It was not until the third day that he started to cry" (Han 1992a, 35). Bing Zai's slow response to the world indicates his marginality, heralding the unlikelihood of his ever being integrated into that world. Indeed, despite the villagers' efforts to teach him to talk, Bing Zai manages to utter only "Papa" and "F—— Mama." Bing Zai's marginality is also shown in the failure of his body to grow with the passage of time. "One after another, the lads [who were born at the same time as Bing Zai] found bristles growing on their chins; slowly, their backs began to arch. Another batch of snot-nosed kids grew into lads. Bing Zai, however, was still no taller than a pack-basket, and he still wore a child's red-floral open-crotch pants. For many years, his mother had been telling people he was 'only thirteen'" (39). Time, a human invention to measure development and progression, thus endowing life with meaning, is irrelevant to Bing Zai's existence. Dislodged physically and mentally from time, he is frozen in his condition. Ageless, with both past and future closed to him, Bing Zai becomes, in one critic's description, "a living fossil," the residue of a tradition that created him and that he himself nonetheless has no memory of, as the reader finds out (Li Qingxi 1996, 50).

Not only has Bing Zai started his life with lack, but it is filled with a loss that has become a source of misery for him: the absence of his father, who is said to have been driven away by his shame and anger at Bing Zai's condition. Even though Bing Zai does not seem to have ever been aware of the presence of his father, he experiences the latter's absence daily. The lack of a father leaves Bing Zai to face the world's cruelties unprotected, all by himself. Treated as a bastard, he is forever at the mercy of the village youngsters, who are constantly making him the butt of their malicious jokes. Fatherless, Bing Zai has no one to turn to; defenseless, he bears his pain silently.

Thus, absence in its various forms characterizes Bing Zai's life. Yet absence does not necessarily constitute misfortune. It is such for Bing Zai because of another important void in his life, the lack of a voice. Besides his two famous utterances, Bing Zai cannot say anything else. He is enclosed in a world with no outlets, emotional or verbal. Beaten up by others, all Bing Zai can do is cry. Unable to articulate, Bing Zai cannot tell his mother about his bullies when she is summoned by his cries. Finding him alone with no visible bruises, Bing Zai's mother blames Bing Zai for fooling around and hurting himself. "At times like this, Bing Zai would fly into a rage. He would roll his eyes until the pupils disappeared, the veins on his forehead all stood out, and he would bite his hands and tear his hair as if he had gone mad" (Han 1992a, 49–50). Bing Zai's wordless protest is futile. He has to internalize the anguish, aggravating it with self-destruction.

Bing Zai's lack of speech is neither simply caused by his physical deformity nor an intentional act. The character's muteness could have been compensated for by the use of a nonverbal language. But without sufficient consciousness, Bing Zai cannot make recourse to it. The philosopher Bernard P. Dauenhauer's study of silence and its implications can help us define this voicelessness. At the root of Dauenhauer's theory is the distinction between muteness and silence:

> Silence is neither muteness nor mere absence of audible sound. The difference between muteness and silence is comparable to the difference between being without sight and having one's eyes closed. Muteness is simply the inarticulateness of that which is incapable of any sort of signifying performances. A man cannot be absolutely and permanently mute unless he can be completely and permanently unconscious. Unlike muteness, silence necessarily involves conscious activity. (Dauenhauer 1980, 4)

Obviously, Bing Zai's lack of voice is not silence but muteness. That Bing Zai is physically conscious, a condition that should have made permanent muteness impossible, only makes its presence in the subject's existence even more poignant.

Jacques Lacan's theory of self and language can offer us a more detailed explanation of the ontological significance of Bing Zai's privation. The most relevant part of Lacan's intricate explication to my discussion here is his observation that the maturation of the subject can be seen as a development in which the infant-subject moves from the imaginary order to the symbolic, from a sense of self to subjectivity. Visionary, involving perception, hallucination, and their derivatives, the imaginary order refers to the mirror images that give rise to identifications and reciprocities in what Lacan calls the *stade du miroir*, the mirror stage.[6] It is where the ego comes into existence through its identification with the Other, be it the infant's mother or its own mirror image.[7]

If the imaginary is concrete and perceptual, the symbolic is conceptual. Simply put, the symbolic is the realm of language and the unconscious. Lacan (1968) defines the unconscious as "the discourse of the other" (27), and as "that part of the concrete discourse insofar as it is *transindividual*" (Wilden 1968, 265).[8] Intersubjective and social, the unconscious is always collective and operates through rules, taboos, and law, in particular, the law of the father. Anthony Wilden sees Lacan's symbolic as "exactly equivalent to Lévi-Strauss' notion of the 'world of rules' and the 'symbolic relationship' into which we are born and to which we learn to conform, however much our dreams may express our wish for a disorder or counterorder" (270). James A. Mellard (1991) further notes that "the register of the Symbolic is characterized by mediation rather than immediacy" and that "here in its mediating role, is where language becomes dominant" (16), for "the unconscious speaks through conscious discourse" (Wilden 1968, 263). Thus, language ultimately governs the unconscious.

The child's accession to language provides a passage for the ascending movement from the imaginary to the symbolic, thus opening up the possibility of the child's development of subjectivity. We can best illustrate the point by citing the same anecdote that Lacan uses to formulate his "myth of origins," the beginning of human subjectivity. This is the anecdote that Freud reported concerning his grandson, the "Fort! Da!" game, which I quote in full:

> This good little boy...had an occasional disturbing habit of taking small objects he could get hold of and throwing them away from him into a corner, under the bed, and so on, so that hunting for his toys and picking them up was often quite a business. As he did this he gave vent to a loud, long-drawn out "o-o-o-o," accompanied by an expression of interest and satisfaction. His mother and the writer of the present account were agreed in thinking that this was not a mere interjection but represented the German word: "fort." I eventually realized that it was a game and that the only use he made of any of his toys was to play "gone" with them. One day I made an observation which confirmed my view. The child had a wooden reel with a piece of string tied round it. It never occurred to him to pull it along the floor behind him, for instance, and play at its being a carriage. What he did was to hold the reel by the string and very skillfully throw it over the edge of his curtained cot, so that it disappeared into it, at the same time uttering his expressive "o-o-o-o." He then pulled the reel out of the cot again by the string and hailed its reappearance with a joyful *"da."* This then was the complete game—disappearance and return. (Freud 1964, 16–17)

What Lacan sees in this anecdote is "the birth of symbols." The spool stands for the mother, and through his game the child gets momentary satisfaction from the desired return of his mother. It also proves to Lacan that absence is at the origin of language and that language, consequently, is a presence created to fill the gap of absence. It is through his discovery of the lack, the absence of the mother, that a desire is generated in the child, which then gives rise to the use of language: "The moment in which desire becomes human is also that in which the child is born into Language" (Lacan 1968, 83). The child's use of language to satisfy the desire in turn starts his subjectivity. Once the sounds "o" and "a," which Freud identifies with the German words *"fort"* (off, gone, or away) and *"da"* (there or here, to mean "here it is"), are vocalized, they can replace the spool to evoke the fantasized presence and absence of the mother. This obviously is evidence that the child is starting to master reality through language, and this constitutes the beginning of his subjectivity. Even though at this stage the child cannot yet speak, he has discovered the power language gives the human subject. "He sustains as subject means that Language permits him to consider himself as the engineer, or the *metteur en scène* of the entire Imaginary capture."[9] Now the picture is clear, *"absence* constitutes the subject of the Fort! Da!, who has previously known only the asubjectivity of total presence. The lack of object is then what enables the child to progress to the subjectivity of 'I'" (Wilden 1968, 191), and the accession to language is the final attainment of the "I." In other words, the accession to language allows the infant-subject to enter the symbolic order in the capacity as a signifying subject.

Let us return to Bing Zai. The absence in his life is perpetual—he is mute and can never utter his *Fort! Da!* There is no presence of language in his world with which Bing Zai can replace the absence. His existence starts and continues with absence. In light of Lacan's theory, the lack of a voice indicates for one thing that Bing Zai is irrevocably arrested at the preverbal stage and remains Lacan's infant-subject. This helps to explain the boy's infantile fascination with people who, unlike him, are skilled and move in harmony. Whenever a craftsman visits the village, Bing Zai always follows him around. But being divested of a voice has much more sinister consequences. The importance Lacan assigns to the acquisition of language in the *Fort! Da!* game further makes evident Bing Zai's hopeless plight. Since language both dominates the symbolic order and is the subject's means of entry in the capacity of a meaning-producing subject, the lack of voice ultimately denies Bing Zai passage into the symbolic. And his banishment from it consequently equals a denial of subjectivity.[10] Thus devoid of subjectivity, to use Wilden's mathematical metaphor, Bing Zai is condemned to the status of being a not-nothing-not-something zero, in whose nonrelationship "identity is meaningless."[11]

As a "zero," a void in essence, Bing Zai becomes an empty signification for himself. His troubled relationship with language reduces him to a linguistic construction, a signified with no signifying power of his own. The only two phrases Bing Zai has ever managed to utter do not perform their nominal functions.[12] When he is happy, Bing Zai addresses everyone in the village as "Papa" indiscriminately. The second phrase, the narrator tells us, "was a vulgar expression but coming from a toddler, it didn't really mean anything and could simply be taken as a sign, a symbol, what you will" (Han 1992a, 35). This "sign" or "symbol" is no other than Bing Zai himself, a created being in others' meaning system who is drawn into the game of words precisely because he is alienated from the words, as I focus on shortly. In the same nonchalant tone, the narrator informs us how Bing Zai got his name. "He had to be given a name—for use at formal celebrations and for his tombstone. And so he came to be called 'Bing Zai'" (36). We are not even told about Bing Zai's namer. When the namer has relinquished his naming power, Bing Zai's name becomes simply another sign that carries no individual significance for its bearer.

Like his two expressions, Bing Zai himself is also out of the discursive convention. As protagonist of the story, Bing Zai is a drastic subversion of the autonomous hero. He does not act; he is acted upon. Or to put it in Lacanian terms, he is not a speaking subject; he is spoken. This is especially evident in the way his two expressions are manipulated by others against him.

> Sometimes, the lads would poke fun at one another. Laughing, one would seize Bing Zai by the arm and point a finger at his mate, coaxing him, "Say Papa. Come on, say Papa." If Bing Zai hesitated, the lad would sometimes press a few slices of sweet potato or a handful of baked chestnuts into his hands. After Bing Zai had obliged them they would, as usual, laugh heartily and Bing Zai would, as usual, be rapped on the head or have his ears boxed. If he paid them back with an angry "F—— Mama," the world would spin before his eyes, and his face and head, already smarting, would burn. *The two expressions seemed to have different meanings, but as far as Bing Zai was concerned, they produced the same effect.* (Han 1992a, 38; emphasis added)

Excluded from the discourse and fixed at the receiving end, Bing Zai is no interlocutor. He is used by the words he cannot command. As I have said, the loss of language prevents Bing Zai from entering the symbolic order as a subject, but he does not have the freedom to live outside it either. He is brought into the system at the mercy of others. In this light, that Bing Zai is mute but not deaf is highly significant: he takes but cannot give.

Bing Zai's lack of signifying power leaves him no choice but to take on any signification assigned to him. His mother enjoys talking to him at night. But

> staring at this motherly mama, at her gleaming dead-fish eyes, Bing Zai wet his lips with his tongue and, finding the droning all too familiar, spat out the words excitedly, "F—— Mama." But the mother had heard the expression too often to feel offended. She went on rocking to and fro, and the bamboo chair creaked softly.
>
> "Will you still care about Mama when you've found yourself a wife?"
>
> "F—— Mama."
>
> "Will you still care about Mama when you have kids?"
>
> "F—— Mama."
>
> "Will you look down on your Mama and treat her like dog shit when you become a high official?"
>
> "F—— Mama."
>
> "You have a sharp tongue, don't you? . . . " (Han 1992a, 39–40)

Bing Zai's mother easily dismisses her son's offensive words as no more than empty sound. Although she is perfectly aware that Bing Zai understands none of her words, she is not discouraged. Thoroughly wrapped up in her illusions, the mother paints a rosy picture of Bing Zai's future, his marriage, his starting a family and even becoming an official. Insisting on fitting Bing Zai into her own vision, the mother derives great psychological satisfaction from the game of self-delusion.

Thus, elevation and degradation are both totally beyond Bing Zai's comprehension and control. He is only a free-floating sign to be arbitrarily interpreted. This is further dramatized in another incident. After their repeated failure to win a dispute with the neighboring village, the villagers begin to see Bing Zai in a new light. They recall that on the day they gathered to predict the outcome of the dispute, Bing Zai uttered his famous obscenity, and its significance seemed to have been illustrated by their ensuing defeat. "Everyone found Bing Zai most mysterious. Just think: he could only say 'Papa' and 'F—— Mama.' Could it be that these two expressions are actually the divination symbols for *yin* and *yang*?" (Han 1992a, 76). Deciding to consult this living divination, the villagers carry Bing Zai on a door board to the front of the ancestral hall. Calling him "Bing, our lord," "Immortal Bing," they prostrate themselves before Bing Zai, gazing at him expectantly. Pleased with the twittering of the sparrows, Bing Zai points his finger in the direction of the birds resting in the eaves and mumbles an indistinct "Papa." After some discussion, the villagers finally agree that Bing Zai has pointed to the eaves. But since the Chinese character for eaves *(yan)* has more than a dozen homophones, understanding what Bing Zai is trying to "say" becomes a matter of pure interpretation. Some suggest that it stands for *yan* (talk), therefore negotiation; others insist that it stands for *yan* (scorching), meaning to attack by fire. Just like Bing Zai, who has become an arbitrary sign, so has his utterance, into which the villagers are simply reading what they would like to find. When the village suffers yet another defeat after the fire attack, Bing Zai is blamed and again returns to his former status as an idiot.

Han Shaogong said, when asked about the novella "Pa Pa Pa," that he wanted to depict the decline of a race (Han 1992b). Lau (1993) comments that "we could not be reading 'Ba Ba Ba' properly if we took Bing Zai as an isolated syndromic manifestation of China's cultural malaise" (33). Bing Zai is more than an individual idiot; his deficiency has a larger significance. Like a mirror, Bing Zai faithfully reflects the obsessions, fear, stupidity, ignorance, and cruelty of the people around him. It is in his receptive and reflective role that Bing Zai becomes the symbol of the collective subject bearing all the burden of the negative values in Chinese tradition. Although Bing Zai does not remember his absent father, Delong, he is unwittingly the latter's living memory. Like one's image in the mirror, which is an exact yet opposite copy of oneself, Bing Zai's dumbness serves as a foil to Delong's skillful use of his voice. Born with an effeminate voice, Delong is famous for singing songs of amorous affairs and heroic deeds of their legendary ancestors. But he fails to carry out in his own life the feats he so expertly sings about. Delong's adroitness with his voice is, therefore, but a cover for his fatal lack of substance. Singing and playing with a blue snake are what he does all day long. After singing for some ten years, Delong disappears, supposedly because of his disappointment in Bing Zai. The man does not realize that his son's incompetence is simply an intensified form of his own inadequacy. Bing Zai is a poignant mockery of Delong's romantic disposition and an indication of his unworthiness as an offspring of his fantastic ancestor Xingtian, who separated the earth from the sky with his ax. A true son, the good-for-nothing Bing Zai is proof of his father's intrinsic weakness.

Indeed, nonaccomplishment seems to be the primary characteristic of the entire family. Bing Zai's cousin Renbao, meaningfully nicknamed Idiot Ren, shares with Bing Zai many of the latter's deficiencies. Renbao is the only one in the village who frequently travels to the other side of the mountains. Motivated by only a superficial interest, however, Renbao's contact with the outside world brings no positive results. If he introduces "freshness" into village life, what he brings home from his excursions are insignificant, discarded objects—"a glass bottle, a broken barn lantern, an elastic band, an old newspaper or a small photograph of somebody or other" (Han 1992a, 51). Nonetheless, this garbage serves Renbao's purpose well enough. "As he strutted about in a pair of oversized leather shoes, the clack-clack of the shoes added to his air of familiarity with new-fangled ways" (51). In addition to the refuse he brings home, Renbao has picked up bits and pieces of phrases unfamiliar to his own people. These he brandishes to give himself a sense of self-importance. When the youngsters in the village go to see him, he complains that the village is too conservative. "The lads did not understand the meaning of 'conservative,' and so the word shot up in value; and so did Idiot Ren" (52). An identity sustained by false language, Renbao lacks genuine self-expression as much as Bing Zai. Like Bing Zai, who amuses himself by poking earthworms or rolling chicken droppings in his palms, Renbao occupies himself all day long with senseless activities. His favorite expression is "This is the beginning," which he utters with extreme solemnity. But nobody, not even Renbao himself, understands what is beginning. Devoid of concrete action, Renbao's prophecy is mere sounds, empty and meaningless. Thus incapacitated by his purposelessness, Renbao's life is no more productive than Bing Zai's.

But Bing Zai is more than a reflection of the inanities of his kinspeople or a symbol of a single dwindling family line. The title character, Bing Zai's "papa," calls for closer scrutiny. In the context of Chinese culture, the patriarch is considered the most important figure in the family history. Yet once Delong disappears, he becomes inconsequential. Bing Zai's natural father assumes no importance because Bing Zai belongs to a larger family, that of the whole community in which "the emphasis seemed to be on unity—the unity of a large family—for there was a deliberate confusion of the distinctions between close and distant relatives" (Han 1992a, 43). In this big family, Bing Zai's father, Delong, is dispensable because his paternal responsibilities are taken over by the village as a whole. "When he [Bing Zai] could crawl, the villagers often played with him, training him to be a man" (35).[13] In time Bing Zai learns to call everybody "Papa," and his mother is not particularly concerned with it as long as the one addressed does not take offense. Thus, as the title "Ba ba ba" indicates in a way, Bing Zai has one "ba" too many. He is inappropriately raised and collectively owned.

A child of all, Bing Zai is a faithful replica of his cultivators and their world. The tragic irony is that the villagers fail to realize that they are looking at a duplication of themselves when they tease and abuse him. The boy's isolated mind points to the sequestered world of the village, and his timelessness the inertia of village life:

> The village perched high in the mountains above the clouds. When you left the house, you often found yourself stepping into rolling clouds. Take a step forward, and the clouds would retreat, while those at your back would move in behind you, bearing you up on a solitary island without end, floating. (Han 1992a, 40)

Not only are the clouds a visual obstacle barring communication with the outside world, but the image of moving forever in clouds also speaks to the lack of self-perception. The lack of contact and clear vision results in a stagnation aptly reflected in the language. The local dialect has kept many archaic words. "They said 'watch' instead of 'see' or 'look', 'speak' instead of 'say', 'lean' instead of 'stand', 'lie down' instead of 'sleep'" (43).

In such an arrested world, the future does not exist, and the present is but reproduction and extension of the past. Immersed in the memories of their ancestors, the inhabitants punctuate their existence with rituals commemorating the past, making their lives a recycling of predictable patterns. Whenever there is a funeral, a wedding, or a holiday, people gather to sing about ancient times and their ancestors, from father to grandfather to great-grandfather, all the way back to the origin of the race. Contradicting true history, the legend passed down to the villagers is one of peaceful migration without violence and strife. Year after year the same story is repeated; generation after generation the old way lives on in the self-contained world of the village. As David Wang states, "Han Shaogong invests the temporal sequence of his narrative with a dimension of mythical recurrence *and* hiatus" (Wang 1992, 299). In spite of the cyclic motion inherent in the act of recurrence, recurrence precludes development. History freezes in Bing Zai's village. In the stasis of the world, time has lost its significance as life moves in endless circles. Temporal movement, both in the fictional world and in its narration, has become a meaningless mechanical replay of recognizable elements. As a result, there is an unresolved tension between the imperative of progress underlying the flow of time and the stagnant village life. We are never told in what time the story is set, or given a chronological point of reference, such as "yesterday" or "tomorrow." Having been denied their specificity, events in the story are reduced to routine repetitions. The trees that grow and die in the mountains thus become a powerful emblem of the world of the village:

They grew in majestic splendour, competing for sunlight and rain and mist and then died quietly in the mountains. The branches fell and rotted on the ground, the layers thickening year by year. When trod upon, they oozed black slime and a few air bubbles, exuding a pungent smell of damp and rot that hung so heavy in the air it enveloped the wailings of generations of wild boars. (Han 1992a, 43)

This entrapped, deteriorating world is eventually destroyed by the villagers' feud with their neighbors. When the lack of grain is not alleviated, the villagers decide to blow away the chicken-shaped ridge, thus angering the people on the other side of the mountain. The dispute results in a series of skirmishes, and each time Bing Zai's village is defeated, with heavy casualties. Finally abandoning all hope, the villagers decide to move. After poisoning the old, the babies, and the sick, the villagers set fire to their houses and start on their way, singing in chorus the same song that accompanied their ancestors hundreds of years ago in their exodus. The journey will lead to a predictable end. Just like the futile temporal movement, the spatial relocation can only change the physical setting of the village and not the cultural, psychological texture of its life.

Through Bing Zai, then, Han Shaogong has delineated "the decline of a race" and has shown that "the rational and nonrational have both become absurd, and all ideas, old and new, lack the power to save the situation" (Han 1992b, 151). The situation depicted in "Pa Pa Pa" is indeed beyond redemption. The only characters who have some mobility in the world of the novella are Renbao and Bing Zai's parents. While Renbao is incapable of introducing substantive changes, the case of Bing Zai's parents is even more disconcerting. Bing Zai's mother married into the village from outside the mountains, yet she fails to be the force of transformation, and the union between the world outside and inside produces a defective being. His father leaves the village not for help but to shirk his responsibilities. If the parents present a hopeless situation, the disabled son further aggravates it. The mother's last words to Bing Zai, "You must kill him [the father]," sound hollow and feeble. Her son does not even know who his father is. No agent can be located either externally or internally in the novella.

The full extent of Han Shaogong's despair shows itself as much in making Bing Zai the epitome of a deteriorating subject as in the boy's uncanny ability to endure and survive. After his mother's death, Bing Zai wanders into the mountains and people assume that he is dead. But after an indefinite period, he again emerges in the village to everyone's surprise. Later, as the villagers prepare to leave, Bing Zai is the first they try to get rid of. Some time after the people have vacated the village, however,

> Bing Zai had surfaced from no one knew where. Believe it or not, he survived. What's more, the running sore on his head had stopped festering and a scab had formed. He was sitting naked on a low wall and stirring the water in a half-full earthware jug with a twig, stirring up eddies of reflected sunlight. Listening to the song in the distance, he clumsily clapped his hands once and, mumbling in a very soft voice, he called again and again the man whose face he had never seen—"Papa." (Han 1992a, 90)

The eternal Bing Zai is not going to die. A composite product of the collective papa, he is tradition that persists and a story that continues, as emphasized by the potent image of the whirling currents of sunlight he stirs up in the preceding passage. The swirling lights prophesy a protraction that goes in circles, producing repetitions, an omen already being fulfilled as the novella ends:

> Although he [Bing Zai] was skinny, his navel was the size of a copper coin, and the kids [from the neighboring village] hovering round stared at him with wonder and amazement, with admiration too. They glanced at that admirable navel and offered him a handful of pebbles, smiling, looking friendly. Then they clapped their hands, like he'd done just now, and shouted, "Pa Pa Pa Pa Pa!" (Han 1992a, 90)

Thus, the novella begins with the birth of an idiot and ends with the possible births of several others. To further bring home the message, Bing Zai's lack of reproductive power is compensated for by a woman from the neighboring village. She comes over to Bing Zai and takes away with her the boy's jug filled with the ominous whirling currents. A capable agent of reproduction, the woman will continue to duplicate the image of Papa.

Han's Woman: Locked in Silence

In January 1986 Han Shaogong produced another novella, "Woman Woman Woman." Han defines its perspective, in contrast to the "social history" in "Pa Pa Pa," as "individual action—the fluctuations of good and evil within the individual, the shifts between bondage and freedom, and the danger to human survival." Han concedes, however, that "these are not final opinions" (Han 1992b, 151). The author's exegeses are no doubt significant pointers for the interpretation of the novella. But the disturbing question is: Why should the individual oscillate violently between two extremes, good and evil? Why is there an absence of self-moderation, which could have enabled the female protagonist to be a self-restrained, constructive being? I believe "Woman Woman Woman" shares similar thematic concerns with "Pa Pa Pa." Not only does Han Shaogong's vision of the blemished subject persist, but the troubled relationship to language again underlines the being's precarious status as a subject without agency.

"Woman Woman Woman" portrays the mysterious metamorphosis of Aunt Yao, the narrator's youngest aunt, who lost most of her hearing early in life. After the death of the narrator's father, Aunt Yao comes to live with the narrator and his wife, devoting all her attention to the care of the family. One day Aunt Yao suffers a stroke while taking a bath and, following her recovery, changes into a completely different person, difficult and petulant. Unable to put up with her, the narrator sends her to live with her sworn sister, Aunt Zhen, in the country. There she gradually loses her human characteristics, degenerates, and dies.

While the primary concern over the questionable subject remains, the novella approaches it from a different angle. In "Pa Pa Pa" we have witnessed the formation of the subject(ivity); in "Woman Woman Woman," we are presented with both its (in)formation and deformation. Similarly, tradition, now more specific in its historicity, plays an important role in the informing process of the subject. The burden of tradition in "Woman Woman Woman" is accentuated through the deafness that has beset the narrator's family for generations. Besides the protagonist, her father is also hard of hearing, as are two of her granduncles. "In fact, the whole clan had to scream and shout, shout and scream" (Han 1992a, 92). The family characteristic is, however, only a symbolic heritage from a larger tradition. Aunt Yao once had a baby, who died during the difficult birthing. The special emphasis the local custom placed on the procreative role of the woman greatly deepens Aunt Yao's natural grief over the loss of her baby. Those who fail in this role are ostracized so that they either have to commit suicide or leave their native place. Under the pressure, Aunt Yao cried herself deaf and left her hometown to live in the city. The protagonist's deafness, therefore, is indicative of her victimization by a long-standing tradition.

But Aunt Yao is a double victim, not only crippled by an old ideology but also indoctrinated by the prevalent official discourse of Maoist thinking, which penetrated every sphere of life in the PRC. A model worker in a small factory who has little formal education, Aunt Yao is nevertheless keen on reading newspapers, retaining the habit even after the Cultural Revolution, when other people had in disillusionment given up their subscriptions. What Aunt Yao has learned from the newspapers regulates her behavior. Her role model in life is Jiao Yulu, the much-publicized, late Party secretary of Lankao County, Henan, who is known for his selfless devotion to the welfare of the people and his honesty in performing official duties. Time and again, Aunt Yao expresses her admiration for Jiao's selflessness: "One mustn't be selfish, Jiao Yulu's own chair had fallen to pieces, yet...If everyone was unselfish, the world would be a wonderful place" (Han 1992a, 111). The woman certainly practices what she says. Aunt Yao has lent a considerable amount of money out of her meager wages to her fellow workers, but when the narrator suggests that she remind her debtors to pay her back, she is horrified by the idea. "She uttered a long drawn-out 'Well,' her chin drawing back, her lips quivering, and mumbled, 'No, I can't, I can't.' Then she laughed, 'It's too embarrassing! I must learn to be Jiao Yulu'" (104).

Aunt Yao's submergence in the official discourse is evident in her obsession with setting her clock whenever she has a chance. The announcement of time on TV always sends her to her old alarm clock, and she is enormously relieved if her clock tells the exact time. Recognizing only the homogeneous public time, Aunt Yao attaches a great importance to it, staying willingly within its structure and boundaries. The media, the newspapers, and the TV thus establish for Aunt Yao a decreed world, a formulated existence of regularity. When she is mechanically "on time," Aunt Yao feels safe and assured; otherwise she becomes disoriented. As a result, the character has a monolithic existence in which there is no separation between public and private worlds, both governed by the same ideological, moral principles. This is exactly the outcome intended by the Party's strategy of publicizing, through controlled media, the Communist models such as Aunt Yao's idol Jiao Yulu, who made their lives a nonsegmented extension of their official obligations.

Aunt Yao's susceptibility to a prescribed discourse is also symbolized by her peculiar hobbies, her morbid passion for two things, bottles and paper.

> Apart from cooking, mending clothes, and grumbling about this one or that, she loved to hoard all sorts of junk. Bottles, for example. She wouldn't throw away even an ink bottle, let alone wine bottles, oil bottles, pickle bottles and glass jars. Tucked away under and behind her bed, they formed a dusty forest of bottles, a tribe of bottles a century old. She was fond of

paper, too. Whenever I crumpled up a piece of paper and threw it into the dustbin, she would pick it out as soon as my back was turned, smooth it out, and stealthily add it to her collection of newspapers, wrapping paper, used envelopes that had been opened up...etc., and then fold them into a square parcel which she stuck under her pillow. (Han 1992a, 101)

What the bottles and paper have in common seems to be their storability and containability. Yet what they contain is more often than not things no longer fresh: outdated information in the newspapers and leftovers from a factory meal in the bottles. In fact, Aunt Yao's belongings all bear a sort of trashiness. Her towel is a piece of cloth cut from old pants; the lid of her teacup is made from used cardboard, and the tea leaves in her cup have already been used by some guest; her black umbrella, all patched up, can neither close nor open fully. Once the narrator even overheard Aunt Yao's fellow workers joking about selling her spoiled rice, knowing that she would invariably accept it. For Aunt Yao herself has become a symbolic container, indiscriminately taking in whatever is doled out to her, and her existence consequently becomes as stale and outmoded as the discards she treasures.

Aunt Yao's situation is made incorrigible by her resistance to other alternatives, a trait well illustrated by her refusal of assistance from the narrator. When he buys her a new hearing aid, Aunt Yao complains that the gadget is useless, upon which the narrator finds that Aunt Yao has deliberately either not turned it on or kept the volume at zero so that the set will not work properly. The hearing aid finally ends up buried deep in her trunk. Aunt Yao chooses to turn a deaf ear to the device capable of introducing new sounds to her. Emblematic of her rejection of other social expressions, the character's self-enforced deafness indicates her willing enclosure in a fixed world whose exits are intentionally blocked, resulting in a lack of effective communication. Aunt Yao constantly misses the narrator's questions when he tries to talk to her. The fixedness of Aunt Yao's world is further evident in her immobility and agoraphobia. Nervous on the streets, Aunt Yao tends to lose her bearings once she is in a diverse crowd. To forestall unpredictability, she never ventures out if she can help it. When there is nothing happening at home, Aunt Yao prefers sitting inside doing nothing to going out to the park or visiting her neighbors. Shying away from interactions that may bring changes to her life and so shatter her established routine, Aunt Yao stays indoors even in summer, when the room temperature is unbearably high. Although Aunt Yao is not mute like Bing Zai, her relationship to language is no less problematic. Deaf to heterogeneous discourses and totally informed by the official language, Aunt Yao is no speaking subject either. Lacking individuality and, consequently, its expressiveness, her language becomes a mere echo of the orthodox ideology. With no desire for dialogue with others, the character has isolated herself in a world of silence.

The voluntary and unquestioning consumption of a totalizing ideology reduces Aunt Yao to a "subject" without independent subjectivity. Loss of self thus comes to mark the existence of the woman. Symbolic of the absence of a self-sustained center, Aunt Yao wanders from place to place, never able to settle anywhere. She is spurned by her hometown because of her barrenness; she has stayed in the factory dormitory as a temporary shelter; she later moves in with the narrator's family primarily as a housekeeper; she finally ends up living with a sworn sister, who takes her in out of charity, and dies there without ever having a home or having lived a life of her own. All this points to the inability of the subject, having no self-determining power, to establish a solid, sovereign position to stand and function on its own.

Self-destruction, therefore, becomes Aunt Yao's dominant tendency, which is vividly reported in the narrator's strange experience. One day as he is reading in his room, the narrator hears a suspicious sound. Thinking that Aunt Yao has cut herself preparing dinner, the narrator rushes into the kitchen. Finding nothing wrong, he returns to his room. But

> the sound rose timidly again. But it was no longer a simple slicing sound. . . . I pricked up my ears and seemed to hear the sound of things snapping and hissing and squeaking. That couldn't be the sound of ginger being sliced, it had to be the sound of a finger being chopped into pieces, of cartilage snapping, skin and flesh being torn off, and the knife catching in the joints. Yes, that was what it had to be. But why didn't she cry out in pain? All of a sudden, a round of almighty thumps exploded in the kitchen, so loud that the windows and doors trembled. I concluded that she must have got such a thrill slicing and cutting just now that she decided to do it on a grand scale. Was she slashing at her shoulders now? When she'd done her shoulders, would she hack at her legs? When she'd done her legs, would she go for her waist and then lop off her head? Bits of bone must be flying, blood streaming; and the blood, hot, thick and steaming, must be trickling down the table legs onto the floor, stealing its way into the corridor and, finding its way blocked by a plastic bucket full of chestnuts, turning, heading for my room. (Han 1992a, 93).[14]

Though a hallucination, the narrator's illusion accurately pins down the masochistic nature of Aunt Yao's being. The imaginary dismemberment alludes to the sacrifice and self-abuse in the character's existence. In real life Aunt Yao often willfully neglects her welfare. Once she insists on eating some rotten eggs and, unhappy with the narrator, who has tried to stop her, stuffs herself with all sorts of leftovers, even scraps of food dropped on the floor. As a result, Aunt Yao gets seriously ill, and this leads to further fights between her and the narrator over how she should take care of herself. As the narrator tells us, "It amazes me no end that she should be so clear in her mind when it came to judging what was good or bad for her, and that she should opt so instinctively for that which would harm her" (114). Thanks to her stubbornness, Aunt Yao wins the argument every time. Her life, as a result, constitutes a continuous process of self-annihilation.

The emaciated body of Aunt Yao signifies metaphorically the consequences of this self-destruction. Dashing into the bathroom after Aunt Yao has had her stroke, the narrator is struck by her naked, withered body: her ribs bulge out of her flat chest, her arms are all bones covered with a layer of loose skin, and her sunken temples and eye sockets, contrasted by a protruding chin, give the head a skeleton-like appearance. What is horrifying about Aunt Yao's white shadow of a body is its hollowness: it is devoid of substance. This erasure of the body is the ultimate message that the subject receives from Maoist indoctrination. Significantly, few official Communist models of war heroes and civilians the people were called upon to emulate were alive. In many cases the fame came posthumously. The exemplary figures' death and gross negligence of their health when they were alive were often glorified and celebrated as proof of their altruistic devotion to the collective cause. Revolution demands body and soul. The Communist sublimation is realized with the displacement of the body.

The despair of the situation lies in that the author descries no positive models to relieve the ineffective subject. On the face of it, Old Black, Aunt Yao's nominally adopted daughter, is everything that Aunt Yao is not. As her name suggests, Old Black appears to be a sharp contrast to the pallid Aunt Yao.[15] A complete hedonist, Old Black maintains a couldn't-care-less attitude. She thumbs her nose at the tradition that reveres the procreative role of the woman. She has no qualms about either getting impregnated or having an abortion. Kidnapped and forced into a marriage with a bandit, Aunt Yao nonetheless remains single when the marriage is terminated after liberation. Old Black, on the contrary, sleeps around, treating her admirers as playthings. Aunt Yao has been a model worker; Old Black quits one job after another. Opposite of the frugal Aunt Yao, Old Black is a spendthrift. Aunt Yao saves every bit of paper she can find; Old Black enjoys tearing paper to pieces and, when there is no paper at hand, rips up paper money for fun. Aunt Yao has lived in her fixed world blind to the changing reality around her, whereas Old Black has followed every passing fad of the day. "She'd done lots of things for kicks. She'd taken part in the [cultural] revolution and sported an old military uniform, got married and got divorced, she went disco dancing and played with cassette recorders, cosmetics and the like, and fags and booze gave her a jolly good time. Everything she had on was imported, no domestic products for her" (Han 1992a, 99). The mechanical time so important to Aunt Yao means nothing to her adopted daughter. Old Black dances late into the night, mistaking morning for evening. In a word, Aunt Yao stands for a being in bondage, and Old Black seemingly represents a figure totally free of restraint.

In spite of these apparently striking contrasts, however, Old Black shares an essential weakness with Aunt Yao—the lack of power as an agent to create her own subject-positions. Just like Aunt Yao, who has eagerly swallowed the pre–Cultural Revolution discourse, Old Black stomachs everything fashionable in the post-Mao period. This, too, leads to a damaged constitution. "Everyone knew that that dainty mouth of hers with its sweet smile opened onto a pair of lungs ravaged by cigarettes, and insides that reeked of half-digested or undigested tidbits" (Han 1992a, 158). Thus, Old Black's wanton intake of new trends similarly calls her subjectivity into question. Lacking self-control, her mind is as easy to manipulate as Aunt Yao's. Despite her superficial fluidity, Old Black is likewise locked paradoxically into a fixed identity, that of a "free signified" constantly mutating under the influence of external forces.

Obviously, Han Shaogong views the amiable Aunt Yao as only an ideologically constructed façade to a much more sinister inner layer, which surfaces following Aunt Yao's visit to Old Black one day. Worried that the girl might marry one of her boyfriends, of whom Aunt Yao strongly disapproves, the woman goes to see her adopted daughter and seems to become contaminated by her contact with the girl. Back home after the visit, Aunt Yao complains of feeling itchy, goes to take a bath, and suffers a stroke. Somehow the water washes away the Aunt Yao on the surface, disclosing the one underneath. "Aunt Yao seemed to have changed. The person who had emerged from those clouds of steam was someone who only looked like Aunt Yao" (Han 1992a, 120). Joseph Lau argues that "psychologically... [Aunt Yao's] inhibitions are removed when her nakedness is exposed. An invalid, she might feel that she is no longer answerable to the claims of social civility to which she has been a slave for the better part of her life. When taboo fails to restrain, instinct rules" (Lau 1993, 41). The character's sudden psychological breakdown carries various implications. It challenges the authority of the Communist ideology by deflating its alleged invincibleness. As soon as other social languages are given a chance to operate, the Communist ideology proves a feeble competitor when the support from the state machine is weakened. A short visit to the modern girl is lethal enough to neutralize the effect of decades of interpellation. Aunt Yao's change also debunks the myth that Communist thinking could transform human nature for the better. The suppression of normal human instincts seems only to have strengthened the more nefarious impulses. Moreover, Aunt Yao's transformation presents the serious consequences of the iron-fisted ideological imposition. Because the previous absolute control has deprived the individual of any ability and power to negotiate and achieve a healthy balance between good and evil, once the taboo is lifted, the individual can but slide from one extreme to the other.

This is what happens to Aunt Yao. The formerly neglected body becomes her center of attention. After the stroke, she develops an insatiable appetite for pork, which she used to avoid in the past. Her attitude toward spending is drastically reversed, and she squanders her savings on unnecessary items. The most conspicuous change occurs to her character. Aunt Yao has been a nurturing type, giving her all to the care of the narrator's family following the death of the latter's father. The narrator still remembers fondly the basket Aunt Yao carries with her on her visits to the family:

> That basket was for us a direct access to the market. It was a large mouth that poured out eggs, vegetables, fruit, clothing, new sports shoes, and things bought with her latest wage packet, and they soon turned into our sustenance, into an answer to our dreams. Out of that basket poured years of our lives. It was a magic basket, an inexhaustible supply of precious things. (Han 1992a, 110)

The negative side of this selflessness, as I have pointed out, is self-destruction. But if self-denial characterizes Aunt Yao before her fatal stroke, the Aunt Yao who has survived has turned to destroy those around her. The quiet, unassuming Aunt Yao now wants constant attention, making excessive demands on the narrator and his wife, asking for this and that to eat and invariably complaining about the taste after the first morsel. Confined to bed, Aunt Yao soils her bedding on purpose, keeping the narrator and his wife busy bathing and taking care of her. Feeling overlooked, she beats continually on a table with her scrawny hands, soon making a depression in the tabletop. The stubborn tapping not only ruins all peace of mind for the narrator and his neighbors but also damaged their apartment building, making it unsafe to live in. The state soon pronounces it a condemned building, vacating all the residents.

The sabotage continues when Aunt Yao is sent to live with Aunt Zhen, in the country. Aunt Zhen's sons take great trouble to provide the hare meat and rice-field eels she demands and then refuses to eat. To relieve Aunt Yao's boredom, the brothers carry her around in the village on a bamboo bed after their day of backbreaking labor in the fields. Prevented from pursuing her own life, their mother suffers even more. Aunt Zhen no longer has time to visit her neighbors but spends her days washing clothes for Aunt Yao, bathing her, and helping her turn over in bed to prevent bedsores. Aunt Yao eventually tears the family apart: to save their mother from total exhaustion, one of the brothers arranges for a boat to take Aunt Yao away without his mother's knowledge. When she finds out the plan, Aunt Zhen threatens to commit suicide, and her angry son runs away from home. In a way Aunt Zhen is a mirror image of her sworn sister, Aunt Yao.[16] She is doing for Aunt Yao what the latter has done all her life for other people: completely suppressing her personal interests. Aunt Yao's sojourn in the countryside is therefore an encounter between the protagonist's former self and her transformed self. Without a mutually beneficial middle ground between the excesses, the result is the destruction of both.

Aunt Yao's total self-centeredness at the expense of others signifies her degeneration and loss of humanity. The dehumanization of Aunt Yao is given a physical manifestation in the novella. The woman feels neither cold nor hunger. She wears very little clothing in winter, but her palms are still warmer than the young men's. Moreover,

> there were other mind-boggling things which even the local doctors could not explain. Aunt Yao began to shrink, her wrists hung down and curled inward more and more, and her skin became drier and coarser until it finally cracked into patches of furrowed, delicately interwoven lines. Her nostrils began to flare and the narrow ridge between her nostrils and her upper lip grew longer and longer. One day, it suddenly occurred to people that she was like an ape. (Han 1992a, 145)

The retrogression goes on:

> She continued to shrink until her hands and legs were short and thin, as if they were about to crawl back into her body. If you just cast a casual glance at her, you'd only see a bare smooth body, puffy eyelids, and a pair of dull

expressionless eyes in which the white of the eye was dominant. And then one day, people hit upon another discovery: she was like a fish. (145)

When the human-monkey-fish metamorphosis is complete, Aunt Yao has fully abandoned the habits of a human being. The outer layers of cultural and ideological coverings are sloughed off to expose the natural instincts. She feeds on raw meat and even eats grass and earth. Aunt Yao gradually fades out of the life of the community altogether and is no longer counted when a census is conducted. Significantly, it is her contact with the humans that finally kills Aunt Yao. Curious about the creature in Aunt Zhen's house, the children in the village slip in one day and, after moving Aunt Yao out of her cage, give her a thorough cleaning. Dehumanized and unable to stand humane treatment, Aunt Yao dies soon after.

Through the death of Aunt Yao, Han Shaogong has depicted for us the dissolution of a human being, the undoing of a subject. Swinging between excessive selflessness and self-indulgence, the subject fails to function properly as a productive, autonomous, and psychologically stable being. Incapable of negotiating a compromise between the two extremes, neither model will prevail. "Woman Woman Woman" is thus also laden with the same kind of misgivings about the future found in "Pa Pa Pa." The loss of humanity is shown to be irrevocable. When the old being dies, there is left a staring blank. The apparently "new" Old Black hardly has the power to survive either. As the narrator reveals to us, the girl's appearance bears unmistakable similarities to that of Aunt Yao: "The more I [the narrator] looked at her, the more I felt that there was something strange about her pallid skin and her puffy eyelids—she too looked like a fish!" (Han 1992a, 159). Clearly, the self-serving, irresponsible Old Black is but another version of the degenerated human subject.

Han Shaogong strongly suggests that just as Aunt Yao bears the "birthmark" inherited from her ancestors, the defect in her character has also been passed down to the next generation. The presence of Aunt Yao lingers long after her death in that her deafness has already affected the speaking habit of the narrator, who catches himself shouting unnecessarily all the time in spite of himself. In addition, his rearing by Aunt Yao proves to be a troubling thought for him; in his dream vision Aunt Yao's basket reappears laden with ambivalent implications. Summoned by a telegram from Aunt Zhen informing him of Aunt Yao's death, the narrator hurries to the country. That night he has a distressing dream in which scenes at Aunt Yao's funeral alternate with those of an earthquake. In the dream the crowd of mourners is intermixed with troops of rats fleeing the earthquake, leaving the narrator to wonder if the earthquake is not caused by Aunt Yao's thumping fist or by the noise of the firecrackers and the steps of the mourners at the funeral. Amid the river of rats hurrying toward an unknown destination appears a boat, which, immediately occupied by the rats, becomes a rat island. The narrator soon realizes that it is not a boat but Aunt Yao's straw basket. The basket as a boat seems to emphasize its lifesaving quality. Just as for years Aunt Yao's basket provided sustenance for the narrator's family when they faced financial difficulties, it is the only solid object for the rats to cling to in the fast-flowing river. Yet, at the same time, the image of rats as the beneficiaries also suggests the negative view the narrator has kept in his subconscious of the lives the basket saves and nurtures. They are a degraded form of life, defective and flawed. Thus, in essence the same message delivered through the image of the idiot boy Bing Zai is reiterated: the posterity is debilitated and indelibly marked with the blemishes of the parent generation.

Yet the quake seems to hint at the possibility of shattering the status quo, heralding a new beginning. For a while, the narrator does sound elated and expectant. Back from the funeral, he finds the city exuberant and bustling:

> I stamped on the accelerator of my motor bike and saw in the rear mirror one fast-moving lorry after another, while the display shop windows on either side of the street reflected a continuous stream of traffic. I felt as if I was in a big, noisy, busy square. Rows of tall buildings were waiting to be finished, it looked as though they were struggling to emerge from a chrysalis of scaffolding and safety net to soar into the sky upon their beautiful wings. (Han 1992a, 160)

It appears that not only a new world is under construction but a new being might come into sight:

> I swept past a young man who, laughing and shouting, was pedaling a pedicab loaded with fruit and a young woman. His bulging muscles were so tanned and so beautifully flexed that I couldn't help but turn round to look at his face. I felt that this body, so full of life and vitality, was a good omen for me. . . . Perhaps I would, after that turning at the junction ahead, meet a certain person, one whom I'd never met but had long been waiting for.

> I was getting nearer and nearer the junction.
> What would I see? What had I been waiting for? (160)[17]

The new subject, however, is only a will-o'-the-wisp, a fleeting fantasy. The hopeful tone is suddenly dropped, and the novella comes to a disappointingly anticlimactic stop:

> In the end, I didn't take the turning and I didn't backtrack, I just drove on. I didn't have much time. When I got home, I'd get something to eat, then I'd do the dishes, then I'd ring Yuan for an appointment. . . .
> There really was no point thinking too much about things. The days had to be spent like this, should be spent like this—after you've eaten, you do the dishes; when you've done the dishes, you make a phone call. . . . Get that and you've got the simplest and most profound truth about life. (Han 1992a, 161)

This "most profound truth about life" is repeated at the end: "When you've eaten, you do the dishes. That's all" (161). After heightened expectation comes deflation. The mundane daily routine triumphs over a flash of idealism and hope. The death of a crippled being fails to lead to the birth of a hero. The novella then concludes with an archaic character *xu*.[18] As in "Pa Pa Pa," we have now come full circle: the story ends where it begins. The repetition of "Woman Woman Woman" in the title is echoed by "xu," an obsolete character used in every woman's name. As he is overcome by chagrin, the narrator's search closes in dejection.

Thus, through the novellas, Han Shaogong offers the reader a vista of the historical, cultural, and ideological moorings of the human being. More than an individual, Han Shaogong's subject expands to an allegorical scope. The collective papa in "Pa Pa Pa," as Chinese critics were quick to realize, stands for the tradition of the Chinese nation, an interpretation amply supported by what David Wang calls the "allegorical landscape" of the novella. The stagnant, secluded village links readily with the until recently isolated China; the absurd holocaust recalls the senseless bloodshed during the Cultural Revolution; and the villagers' coldness and apathy evoke for many their painful experience in Communist China. The pathetic, detestable Bing Zai, as a consequence, is not to be looked on with indifference. Just as the detached village is identifiable with China, Bing Zai, the victimized descendant, is linked in disquieting fashion with every Chinese. No one is more straightforward about this association than the veteran writer Yan Wenjing, who wrote an essay addressing the question, "Am I an Old Bing Zai?" (Yan Wenjing 1985). Liu Zaifu, too, recognizes in the backward boy "one of us":

> What's intriguing is that after reading "Pa Pa Pa," I kept thinking about myself, about my past. I feel that Han Shaogong has helped us discover human existence and ourselves.
>
> I realized I, too, was once a Bing Zai. I think many honest readers will acknowledge that they were also once Bing Zais. We not only had some Bing Zaiesque shadows [in ourselves], but we could also say that in terms of our mode of thinking, our existence as well was once as dumb, crude, and vulgar as Bing Zai's. (Liu Zaifu 1988c)

By means of the mighty earthquake, the individual being in "Woman Woman Woman" is likewise endowed with a national significance. The quake in the novella parallels an emotional outburst of the narrator, which takes form in a lyrical rhapsody vibrant with images, quotations, and allusions to China's creation myth, history, philosophy, and literature. It is in this powerful passage (freed from the shackles of punctuation marks and grammar rules) that the allegorical nature of the individual subject, implicit so far, comes to the surface. Through the mosaic of birth and death, beginning and progression, bloodshed and salvation, a mosaic of the legendary, historical, and literary moments in the history of the Chinese people, the individual is linked to the shared existence of the nation. It is, at the same time, also a mosaic of complex emotions, of wonder, fascination, distress, grief, remorse, compunction, anxiety, expectation, and frustration. Each emotional surge invariably leads up to the at once hopeful and apprehensive query: Where would you go?

Mission Unaccomplished

"Where would you go?" This is the quintessential question transformed into art in Han Shaogong's novellas. It is also a question of programmatic import to *xungen* literature. Han and his fellow writers collectively put this question to their characters, their readers, themselves, and their compatriots. But raising the question is only the preliminary step. The ambition of *xungen* literature is to search for an answer, thereby imagining a new cultural subject for China's post-Mao reconstruction. The *xungen* project is a literary endeavor with a historical purpose. It has a mission that Han and the *xungen* writers took on eagerly and with utter sincerity. As Jing

Wang suggests, to understand the *xungen* school's unyielding sense of mission, we must first understand its advocates (Jing Wang 1996, 219–224).

Like Han Shaogong, the majority of *xungen* writers were *zhiqing*, sent-down youths of the Cultural Revolution generation, who grew up in the Communist euphoria and were accustomed to being crowned "the sun in the early morning," the future and hope of socialist China. Imbued with a sense of importance and purpose, they had learned to embrace their patriotic responsibilities. But their delusions of grandeur were relentlessly spoiled during the Cultural Revolution, when they woke up to the cruel reality that they were no more than dispensable pawns in Mao's game of power. Giving up ten years of their prime youth to total waste and victimization was not easy; the psychological need to somehow find meaning in their Cultural Revolution years remained strong and urgent. The experience of the *zhiqing* protagonist Chen Xin in Wang Anyi's story "Ben ci lieche zhongdianzhan" (The destination) is a revealing case. Finally returning to Shanghai after toiling in the countryside for many years, Chen is elated with high hopes for the future in his native town. Soon he realizes that he has become an outsider treated with pity and indifference by the people in the city. The character's superfluity is symbolized by the discord his homecoming triggers among his family over his right to a room in the family's apartment. Chen no longer has a place in the city he used to call home. The *zhiqing* character's reintegration into urban life after his exile is a humiliating and painful process. Tired of the mundane reality in the city, Chen decides to make the countryside the final destination of his life. The same kind of romanticized nostalgia for the *zhiqing* past is echoed in Kong Jiesheng's "Nanfang de an" (The riverbank in the south), in which a group of sent-down youths, doubtful about their self-worth after returning to the city, make a similar choice. Even though Kong's characters are more successful financially thanks to a small business they run, they miss their idealistic past and the excitement of life on a rubber plantation in south China. Giving up a more comfortable life and a promising future in the city, the characters choose to go back to the farm, casting the anchor of their life in the frontier.

What the *zhiqing* characters, and the *xungen* writers, who identified wholeheartedly with them, miss in their past is certainly not the hardships and difficulties they have endured in the countryside and frontiers.[19] It is their zeal, idealism, and a sense of personal fulfillment. These sentiments had helped them transcend their individual loss and sacrifice, giving their materially deprived lives in the countryside a deeper meaning. The trajectory of the development of *zhiqing* fiction proves how difficult it was for this generation to let go of their idealism. The writers' initial, thorough negation of their life as *zhiqing* in the late 1970s was quickly replaced in the early 1980s by much more upbeat stories emphasizing the positive influence life in the countryside had had on their moral development and maturation. All was not lost.

The culture fever in the mid-1980s, with its strong utopian bent, offered the *zhiqing* writers a second chance to return to the mainstream, thus reasserting their presence in society. No wonder the *xungen* writers invariably identified the "roots" of authentic Chinese tradition and an alternative route to cultural modernization in the remote countryside. Having been first centralized and later marginalized by Communist politics, the *zhiqing* writers turned their peripheralized experience into the center of the cultural exploration through the *xungen* project. In his article on the "roots of literature," Han Shaogong, besides locating as part of China's cultural roots the *chu* culture in Hunan, where he spent six years, also mentions the Temple of Qu Yuan and Qu Yuan's famous poem "Li sao" (On encountering sorrow). We can sense psychological identification with the archetypal figure of *huai cai bu yu* (with talent and no position to use it) in Chinese history.[20] To Han and the former sent-down youths, the idealism and sense of mission that fired them into enthusiastically participating in the "rustication movement" (at least in its early stage) remained a salvageable element that could help them reposition themselves in the New Era. Though cultural exploration replaced socialist construction as the goal of the *xungen* project, the motivation of the writers stayed the same. The Cultural Revolution destroyed their faith in Maoism, but it did little to assuage their sense of duty as intellectuals to their nation and their people. Having had their lives intimately intertwined with the ups and downs of social development, the *zhiqing* writers, like other Chinese intellectuals, could not separate their individual fate from that of the nation. To their generation, involvement in the welfare of China had an existential significance. The realization that ideological monopoly was a social mechanism of power contributing to Mao's dictatorship made them all the more eager to have their voices heard. What makes the *zhiqing* writers different from the non-*zhiqing* writers in their exploration of Chinese culture is that the former's idealized memories of the countryside, where they had spent their adolescence, led them to reinvest the hinterlands and backwaters of China with a grand new promise and purpose.

The new purpose projected onto the familiar landscape in *xungen* literature is the reinvention of China through discovering and retaining its cultural characteristics. Played out through an imaginary return to the wilderness, the *xungen* project not only redeemed to some extent the writers' *zhiqing* experience, but it also provided them with a point of entry into the future. Their generation was not to be passed over as unfortunate victims of the past; it still had a role to perform in post-Mao China. In David Wang's words, the "'search for roots' indicates a historical endeavor, assessing what is happening now in the light of what happened in the past" (Wang 1993a, 2). Han Shaogong hopes that the exploration of the past will "release the energies of modern ideas, recast and broaden the self among our people" (Han 1992b, 149). Thus, the establishment of a new cultural subject who embodies both the past and future topped the *xungen* agenda. The cultural essence the new subject absorbs from China's rich tradition is supposed to enable it to ensure the nation's progress as well as its triumph over an overbearing Western model of modernity.

It is precisely on this point that Han Shaogong's two stories discussed here defeat the *xungen* promise, revealing some dilemmas inherent in the strategy of looking back. Making tradition yield patterns for the future operates on the premise that the tradition is capable of meeting expectations. But Han's stories paint an uncomplimentary picture in which both the immediate past, Maoist China, and its remote past, entrenched tradition, prove to be deficient. The questions then arise: how can a defective history be the source of a resuscitating energy, and how will delving into this yesterday lead to constructing a new self for tomorrow? Han's novellas seem to have demonstrated the impossibility of conflating the past and the future in the same cultural subject. Admittedly, his defective being cannot be read in the same light as the transcendental and virile heroes of nature hailed by other *xungen* writers such as Wang Anyi, Zheng Wanlong, A Cheng, and Zhang Chengzhi. It could be argued that by presenting the crippled subject, Han aims at destroying it, thus paving the way for the birth of a truly competent being. Indeed, exposing the weaknesses of the individual had been a recurrent theme in modern Chinese literature. Han's creation of Bing Zai has often been compared to Lu Xun's exploration of the Chinese national character. Highlighting certain aspects of the two authors' treatment of the typical Chinese, therefore, can help us understand Han's vision of crisis.

There is no doubt that both Lu Xun and Han Shaogong have offered scathing critiques of their protagonists, Ah Q in "The True Story of Ah Q" and Bing Zai in "Pa Pa Pa." But the amount of self-consciousness allowed the characters and their outcome are vastly different. A number of critics have pointed out Ah Q's "lack of spirituality."[21] Although Ah Q often fails to comprehend and has intentionally deluded himself into forgetting his troubles by resorting to a past spiritual victory, he does have an epiphany. In a lucid moment on his way to execution, he panics. Recalling his previous experience with a hungry wolf, Ah Q identifies the spectators on the streets with the animal. The momentary nature of the epiphany and his last comic-tragic attempt at heroism notwithstanding, Ah Q realizes his impending death: his head will roll. Lu Xun allows no illusion. He leaves the reader without any doubt that Ah Q will die. Through the execution of Ah Q, Lu Xun pronounces unequivocally that the national failings symbolized by Ah Q and the representative Weizhuang will inevitably lead China to destruction. Ah Q's decapitation is therefore both a condemnation and a stern warning to Lu Xun's contemporaries, a call to arms. On the metaphorical level the decapitation in Lu Xun's writing also signifies "a mutilated condition of the meaning system that makes reality what it is not." The decapitation offers Lu Xun a chance to isolate the mind as a focal point in his search for a cure for the ailing nation (David Wang 1993b, 175–179, quotation 178). His story illustrates that as in Ah Q's misuse of his intelligence, this will invariably result in a separation of mind and body, that neither will survive.

Han Shaogong, in contrast, completely denies his subject self-reflective ability. The crippled being is an unpenetrable totality, the inextricably united mind and body resisting fragmentation. The "wholeness" of the subject makes it futile to even imagine any possibility of agency. What is more, Han is unable to envision the demise of the diseased body. Defiantly potent, it lives on in various guises. Bing Zai threatens to proliferate; Aunt Yao's funeral leads to depressing sound and fury and the survival of numerous rats. In Duke's assessment Han's fiction "is a highly problematic critique [of Chinese culture] fraught with tension, doubt, and confusion about the value of China's historical past for the present day and the future development of Chinese culture and society" (Duke 1989a, 41). Han sees no future. Post-Mao China has developed by leaps and bounds materially and technologically, as attested to by the rapidly changing city skylines and the narrator's fashionable motorcycle in "Woman Woman Woman." But modern progress seems to have ushered in an age of ennui saturated with a spirit of irresponsible self-indulgence of the kind represented by Old Black. When the past meaning systems, traditional or Communist, are cleansed away, the phoenix fails to rise from the ashes. The new subject promised by the *xungen* logic is nowhere in sight. Ultimately, history and culture in Han's vision become an infinite stretch. They have shed their "pastness" and turned into a continuum that can neither be safely contained within yesterday nor ruptured to allow the advent of tomorrow.

They are at once past, present, and future. On the level of representation, the prevalent problematic relationship to language and the characters' difficulties at self-expression also betray the author's deep-rooted anxiety at his ability to reinvent China after his tirade against Chinese society and culture, a task he and other *xungen* writers proudly entrusted to themselves. The contemporary writer has trouble speaking across the cultural terrain to a new China and the world. The stubborn memory of the problematic subject threatens to construct not only the present but also the future.

Having witnessed the ordeal of Han Shaogong's subject(ivity), we can now recapture the sense of crisis we have discovered in the author's investigation by focusing on the titles "Pa Pa Pa" and "Woman Woman Woman." On the one hand, the repetitious titles point to a shared group identity and an unusually burdensome tradition that disables the subject and denies it all sovereignty in the composition of its own subjectivity. On the other hand, the repetition also indicates that even after the questionable subject(ivity) is deconstructed, the blank remains unfilled. Without an empowering interiority, the subject lacks creative agency necessary for a negotiation between itself and ready-made meanings, for the agency to start anew. This in turn results in the perpetual duplication of the flawed parental culture, a continuous re-creation of the crippled subject. The author's profound sense of despair is also evident in the fact that the Chinese *Ba ba ba* strongly suggests the homophonic expression *bababa* (罢罢罢), a sigh filled with sadness, fatigue, frustration, and resignation.

4 In the Madding Crowd
Self and Other in Can Xue's Fiction

While Han Shaogong and his fellow *xungen* writers dug into the collective, cultural foundations of the subject from a historical perspective, others chose to face the present, lodging the subject in its daily, individual reality. When the Cultural Revolution and previous political movements were openly repudiated in the late 1970s, people had a chance to look honestly into the real conditions of their existence without the officially imposed, and sometimes self-exercised, ideological sanctions. As a result of the candid scrutiny, a new trend in the representation of the subject appeared: "absurdist fiction" *(huangdan xiaoshuo)*, which presents life as irrational, illogical, and bizarre from the individual's subjective point of view. This chapter focuses on the absurdist fiction of the mid-1980s by a woman writer, Can Xue.

Can Xue's work falls into the absurdist category because of two distinct characteristics with regard to her themes and techniques. Unlike the *xungen* literature, her fiction does not seek to appeal to the collective unconscious; it is fiercely individualistic. Preoccupied with the innermost recesses of the human mind, Can Xue devotes her fiction almost exclusively to exploring the being's subjective feelings of its existence. Although the feelings she analyzes are doubtlessly rooted in China's sociopolitical realities, she allows external events to remain subterranean, accentuating instead their devastating effects on the self. Isolated from any identifiable social context, the ultimate reality felt by the individual appears fantastic, hallucinatory, and absurd in her world. Moreover, Can Xue has done away with rationality not only in her themes but also in their presentation: she conveys the nightmarish quality of the absurd reality in a nontraditional mode. Such conventional elements as characterization, plot, morals, and development are noticeably absent. Often twisted out of shape, the mindscape unfolding under her pen defies realist literary principles.

Occupying the center of Can Xue's uninhibited display of individual consciousness is the self's obsession with the threatening presence of the Other: in her stories they are forever locked in battles. Intermingled with the issue of antagonism between the self and the Other is that of self-identity. Always at war with the belligerent Other, the self in Can Xue's work is often agonized, fearful, and confused. In this chapter I explore these two related themes in Can Xue's fiction—the tormented relationship between the self and the Other and the being's futile search for self-identity. My task here is twofold. First, I identify some recurrent patterns of the relationship between the self and the Other. I argue that alienation, failures in communication, and the individual's persistent fear of persecution invariably characterize the interactions Can Xue dissects. Second, I isolate a prominent motif in the author's work, in particular in her 1986 novella "Canglao de fuyun" (Old floating cloud): the motif of seeing and being seen by the Other. Analyzing the scopophilia (the urge to see) and the attendant scopophobia (fear of being seen) characteristic of this motif in light of Sartre's theory of "the look," I seek to prove that the struggle to be the dominating seeing subject underlines the eternal conflict between the self and the Other in Can Xue's universe. Losing the battle to the seeing Other, the self inevitably fails in its attempt to create an independent identity. In the course of discussion, I also examine the historical significance as well as the implication of Can Xue's unique approach to the problematic of the self. I contend that by turning antagonism between the self and the Other into an existential pattern, Can Xue reveals a metaphysical truth of life beyond Mao's China. Thus, from a different angle, she joins Han Shaogong in demonstrating the difficulties involved in the post-Mao search for a new subject.

The Absurdist Echo

The emergence of Chinese absurdist literature with existential concerns after the Cultural Revolution was driven by both external and internal factors. When China reopened its doors to the outside world in the late 1970s, Western literature of various absurdist and existentialist persuasions was among the first wave of foreign ideas to surge into the country.[1] According to one source, one of the only three essays concerned with modern Western literature nationwide in 1978 was an introductory commentary on the theater of the absurd by Zhu Hong (1978, 98–133). From 1979 onward, the number of articles dealing with absurdist literature grew substantially. Names of writers and playwrights such as Franz Kafka, Albert Camus, Eugene Ionesco, Jean-Paul Sartre, and Samuel Beckett were mentioned frequently in essays and lengthy discussions of the theater of the absurd, existentialism, and human alienation.[2]

The interest in Western absurdist literature among Chinese readers, writers, and critics should not be seen as simply a rush to embrace a new fad. The response was serious and genuine. The being's existential anguish, the central theme presented by the Western absurdists, found a ready echo in the hearts of millions of Chinese. As the ugly truth of the Cultural Revolution came to light, Mao's orderly house of cards crashed. The sharp contrast between repeated official claims of success and the tremendous amount of human suffering people witnessed daily in their lives was staggering, making reality seem absurd and surrealistic. Reality seemed absurd not only because it gave the lie to Communist ideology but also because after Maoist thinking was stripped of its privileged interpretative power, people had no other meaning system to help explain the absurdity they were confronted with. Reality thus became doubly absurd. Baffling and unspeakable, it turned into a shattered entity defying explanation and description. In the utter confusion, life and individual existence appeared meaningless, bizarre, and grotesque. Within this post–Cultural Revolution environment, the human condition portrayed by the Western writers—one of anxiety, fear, helplessness, and alienation—had a direct emotional appeal to the Chinese public. These feelings were not images created by a distant, foreign fiction: they were close to home and easily identifiable.

Before entering Can Xue's world, I should first comment on a pioneering work in post-Mao absurdist writing by Zong Pu. In the late 1970s and early 1980s, before Can Xue's debut with her profoundly disturbing stories in the mid-1980s, Zong wrote a series of short stories in the absurdist vein. Zong, who had published in the 1950s, created her first post-Mao absurdist story in 1979, "Wo shi shei?" (Who am I?) (Zong 1987). Against the background of the Cultural Revolution, the story records the delirious thoughts of a college professor, Wei Mi, before her suicide. When she and her husband become targets in the political campaign, Wei Mi is rejected and shunned by her colleagues and neighbors, left deserted in the collective madness. Shocked out of her mind by the sight of her husband's dead body, the character stumbles out of her house and wanders around campus in a state of total confusion. To her troubled consciousness, the world has turned into a strange place infested with demonic beings and objects. During her mental roaming on this fatal trip, Wei Mi asks herself over and over the question in the story title: "Who am I?" Her memories of a happy life with her husband before the Cultural Revolution are interspersed with those of the struggle sessions, in which she and her husband were physically and verbally abused. Each time the character is close to finding an answer to her question, her mind is bombarded by the accusations flung at them by the "revolutionary masses." Distraught, Wei Mi begins to wonder if she is indeed an "ox demon and a snake monster" *(niugui sheshen)* and even pictures herself crawling on her belly like a "poisonous worm." The intellectual's futile search for identity ends when the character throws herself into a lake.

Zong Pu's story highlights two issues of grave importance to the post-Mao self: the identity crisis and the realization that this crisis was caused by a totalizing official language. The existential anxiety pungent in these issues is summed up by the title, "Who Am I?" The entire story is Wei Mi's vain effort to conceptualize a self against Communist ideological characterizations. With her self alienated and disengaged from her being, she is unable to complete the sentence "I am . . .". The "I" is indefinable because it can neither cling to its former identity nor accept the new one parceled out in Cultural Revolution parlance. The character imagines herself a "little white flower." But *white*, which connotes innocence and purity to her, means "counterrevolutionary" and "poison" in Maoist language. When only the official language is given the power to signify, the self loses that resource and, consequently, that recourse. In the absence of alternative meaning constructions, self-definition outside the Communist system is impossible. Much as the character tries to reject the identity imposed on her, she has nothing to replace it. The space after "I am" stays blank. The self has no identity besides the assigned political label. If the character can suspend the physical abuse by wandering out on her own away from the crowd, the political accusations dog her consciousness wherever she goes. Backed up by the "proletarian dictatorship," the ideological label sticks, and stinks. The signifying Other is able to completely overwhelm the silenced self.

Although Can Xue, too, explores the absurdity of life in Communist China, she has her own perspective. To shed some light on the difference between Zong Pu and Can Xue, we can borrow the distinction that Martin Esslin, who coined "theater of the absurd," makes between the playwrights of the theater of the absurd, such as Beckett, Adamov, Ionesco, and Jean Genet, and other writers who also comment on the absurdity of the human world. Esslin points out that what sets writers of the theater of the absurd apart from writers like Sartre and Camus is that the former have "renounced arguing *about* the absurdity of the human condition; [they] merely presen[t] it in being" through concrete, irrational dramatic images and situations, whereas the latter use highly lucid, rational arguments to prove the irrationality of human existence (Esslin 1973, 6). In other words, the difference lies in form, not theme. Zong Pu's approach bears more affinity with the latter group. Her world is absurd, but the logic woven into its presentation is not. It is easy for the reader to understand the plight of the self by juxtaposing her character's train of thought against the historical reality of the Cultural Revolution. Moreover, in Zong Pu's vision, alienation and absurdity are temporarily induced by erroneous practices. When Wei Mi throws herself into the pond, a flock of wild geese fly overhead in the formation of the character *ren* (human). The ending suggests optimistically that a wholesome being will arise under the healing power of humanism. Can Xue, in contrast, grants no such illusion. She probes deeper into the subjective consciousness beyond the immediate sociopolitical reality, ruling out possibilities of closure. Her fictional world, as a result, is more challenging and more difficult to decipher.

Can Xue's Universe

"Can Xue is an anomaly in Chinese literature," Charlotte Innes states in her foreword to the English translation of the novellas "Huangnijie" (Yellow mud street) and "Canglao de fuyun" (Innes 1991, 9). Can Xue's Chinese readers and critics recognize this distinction as well. Her peers tend to react to her work with puzzled dismay; most acknowledge its newness but nevertheless find it hard to appreciate. "Nightmarish," "mad," "hysterical," and "unreadable" are the epithets most frequently used to describe it. Labeling it "dream-imitation fiction" *(fangmeng xiaoshuo)*, Li Jie holds that the reader must approach Can Xue's fiction in the same way a psychoanalyst decodes a patient's dreams. This dreamlike fiction, Li goes on to say, is characterized by "random and sloppy narration" like "hors d'oeuvres with a pig's trotter here and a chicken foot there" (Li Jie 1988, 123–124).[3]

As Li Jie's amusing culinary image suggests, in both its subject matter and its form Can Xue's fiction is considered some kind of narrative monstrosity. Can Xue seems to have committed a double offense. Not only does her surreal portrayal of an illogical human world upset the reader's (and the critic's) conception of what fictional reality (or human reality in fiction) should be, but her unconventional presentation, which neither follows any clear temporal or spatial order nor offers any closure in terms of plot development, breaks the writer's contract with the reader and threatens people's customary idea of how human reality should be narrated.[4]

But these criticisms are justifiable only when the principles of literary realism, amorphous as that concept may be, are used as the ultimate yardstick. True, in Can Xue's writing such essential elements of realist fiction as plot, characterization, and, frequently, even common sense are kept to a minimum. As a result, her stories are indeed surrealistic and difficult to read. But it is just this cultivation of an oneiric world that Can Xue consciously seeks. In her own words:

> I can't deal with realism, and may not even in the future. I have to enter a kind of supernatural state to write anything creative. I have to raise my spirit to a certain indulgence in the wildest fantasy. All my characters and happenings are my creation. They don't need to coincide with the reality ordinary people can understand. I deliberately make them run counter to that reality. I'll gather all my emotion and ideals to fight against iron-strong reality.[5]

Rationality and believable characters and events are not Can Xue's concerns. Readers and critics often complain about her unreadability because logic has lost much of its guiding power in our reading experience of the young woman writer. Lacking understandable motivation, Can Xue's characters and their actions resist conventional appropriation by the reader.

The refusal to conform to any customary notion of reality supposes a program of both conscious destruction and audacious creation. In its non-realistic form, Can Xue's fiction is an original response to the havoc caused by incessant political movements in mainland China that left hundreds of thousands dead or psychologically and physically scarred. What distinguishes her works from writings devoted to the same subject is her unique approach to the oft-explored "wounds" topic. Reaching beyond the immediate historical conditions that have provoked its appearance and deemphasizing realistic details, Can Xue places the social debris of Maoist China under an unorthodox fictional microscope. In her works the damage the Maoist campaigns have done to the most basic family ties takes center stage. And she dwells on this subject with a sort of unshakable obsession. Ruined interpersonal relationships seem to permeate Can Xue's literary imagination. As a result, her fiction offers a limited range of topics, which she treats in a consistent but remarkably idiosyncratic manner. Instead of highlighting the sociopolitical factors responsible for the twisted human connections, as other writers do, Can Xue focuses on the grotesque relationships themselves. By making the sociopolitical causes peripheral, thus forcing the reader to concentrate on the naked consequences, Can Xue's fiction represents new efforts that explore the metaphysical rather than the political and historical aspects of individual existence in contemporary China.

Can Xue, whose real name is Deng Xiaohua, was born in the same city (Changsha) in the same year (1953) as Han Shaogong. One of six children of a veteran Communist intellectual who had once been chief editor of the newspaper *Xin Hunan ribao* (New Hunan daily), Can Xue experienced the ever-present political movements in the new China much earlier than did Han Shaogong. Like many intellectuals, Can Xue's parents were branded ultrarightists in 1957. Two years later her entire family was forced out of the newspaper's residential area to a tiny hut of about ten square meters at the foot of Mount Yuelu. On the couple's meager monthly income of less than ten yuan per person, the family struggled on the brink of starvation. With the start of the Cultural Revolution, in 1966, Can Xue's father was locked up and her mother was dispatched to a May Seventh Cadre School to go through additional reform.[6] Can Xue's delicate health spared her the reeducation by the peasants in the late 1960s when the rest of her siblings went down to the countryside. Their house having been taken away, Can Xue lived alone in a small, dark room assigned her under the stairs. Because she was the only one left behind in the city, Can Xue took it upon herself to visit her jailed father, bringing him the things he needed. After the Cultural Revolution, Can Xue quit the job she had had in a neighborhood workshop for ten years and started a tailor shop with her husband.

It is clear from this short account that Can Xue was no stranger to hostility and hardship. Alienation, solitude, frustration, torment, and constant struggle to survive marked Can Xue's childhood, and therein lie the seeds of the recurrent themes that fill the pages of her fiction. When the nightmare of the Cultural Revolution was over, "ten years of youth had slipped by in struggle" (Can Xue 1989b, 11).[7] Those ten years left an indelible mark on the conscious and, perhaps more deeply, on the subconscious level of the sensitive girl. Can Xue began to publish in 1985 because, she says, "I believe that I have something to say about these ten years, and about the future…, something beyond ordinary consciousness, beyond ordinary talk. I want to say it in the form of literature and imagination. Something abstract, something emotional condenses itself in me" (11).

What Can Xue has to say is filtered in her fiction primarily through the individual's subjective feelings. One conventional idea of reality Can Xue resists is the distinction between inner and outer worlds. In her vision what is ultimately real is what the individual consciousness experiences. To a large extent, her fiction is a recording of the mind's wanderings and wonderings as it encounters a human world whose official ideology turns out to be alienating and intimidating. The world registered by a mind focusing on itself, free from conscious inhibitions, is sustained in her works by vivid, unforgettable images that are most often sordid, uncanny, and repulsive. These images aim at evoking a direct experience of life unburdened by abstract, transcendental values. When rationality and social and moral issues are marginalized, left at the core of the subjective consciousness are basic human relationships marked by indifference, apathy, senseless persecution, and hatred. Through their repetition in her texts, these situations become existential patterns in which Can Xue portrays hostility between the self and the Other as a general, fundamental condition of human existence.

The Lonely Self in Private Obsessions

The most frequently occurring relationships in Can Xue's fiction are those of the couple and the family. With few exceptions, Can Xue's characters, whose social positions are either not mentioned or play no part in each of the little dramas, are confined within these family ties.[8] Even though familial relationships are the only ones operating in her individual's life, they are without exception failures. Family thus becomes a site of contestation between the self and the Other, the stage on which this problematic relationship unfolds.

The prevalent narrative point of view representing the self on this central stage is the first person. The dominant use of "I" indicates that the "I" is acutely aware of itself as a different entity from the rest of the world—the Other personified in the members of the family. The "I" sees itself principally as a lonely being. We encounter this lonely "I" again and again: in the girl who embarks on an imaginary date with a kindred spirit, a solitary sleepwalker, in "Yuehui" (The date); in the speaker who waits patiently every night for a tuberose in "Tiantang li de duihua" (Dialogues in paradise); in the narrator at a midnight meeting with an old cremator in "Tianchuang" (Skylight). Each of these scenes occurs at night, but whether the nightly rendezvous with the phantomlike characters have actually taken place is highly ambiguous. The apparitional partakers of these encounters strongly suggest that these are merely meetings with the protagonists' projections of their inner selves. The encounters therefore remain the mind's wanderings within itself. These internal excursions are infused with a strong sense of longing, desperate searching, frustration, and anguish. The dark settings, where no light can penetrate to create openings, however, already imply the failure of these inner searches. The eternal dilemma is that when conferring with its alter ego, the mind is locked within itself, forsaking the possibility of reaching beyond its own boundaries.

In these stories we as readers are not so much asked to ascertain what really happens as to be called on to understand why these imagined meetings take place. It is loneliness, the failure to draw comfort and sympathy from one's fellow beings in the external world, that drives the mind into taking an inward journey that ends where it starts. In Can Xue's fiction the troubled relationship between the self and the Other is only too evident in the apathy between what should be the most intimate members of the family, the husband and wife. Despite their physical presence in the relationship, husband and wife in Can Xue's world do not share their lives. They remain strangers to each other. Ah Mei, the protagonist in "Ah Mei zai yige taiyangtian li de chousi" (The gloomy mood of Ah Mei on a sunny day) calls her husband "Old Li" because she "couldn't remember any other name for him" (Can Xue 1989b, 16). In fact, love is not the cause of the union. The most important reason Old Li gives for proposing to Ah Mei is that since Ah Mei's mother has an apartment, he can be spared the trouble of finding a place to live after the marriage. True to his words, the second day after the wedding, Old Li starts to build a separate attic for himself in the couple's bedroom. What is more, three months after the marriage, he moves back to his parents' home for no reason at all.

In another story, "Zai kuangye li" (In the wilderness), a couple who lives in a huge deserted apartment building is engaged in a similarly indifferent relationship. Every night they roam the forlorn building, though not together: "To avoid bumping into each other in the dark, both stepped more heavily" (Can Xue 1989b, 80). Even in their dreams, husband and wife stay apart: "She went to the wilderness. Frozen rain was falling. The icy dregs shuttled from the trees. All her body was swollen. Water oozed from her swollen fingers. She wanted to sleep, but she heard someone groaning in the swamp. Clumsily, she moved toward the sound while dozing, muddle-headed" (83). Meanwhile, the husband is dreaming about his bitten toe: "He really had stepped on a scorpion. The toe swelled. The red, swollen spot expanded toward his knee. The puddles rippled in the wind. His leg stuck in the mud and refused to come loose. In the solitude he heard the horrifying step come near" (83). The woman's efforts to move closer to the sound of groaning may be interpreted as a gesture to reach out, but the husband prefers to suffer in solitude. His wife's footsteps sound threatening to him, and he cries out to forestall her: " 'This is only a dream, a voluntary dream!' he protested. He was afraid of her approach" (83).

Thus, more than a physical state, the dank "wilderness" denotes a mental state in which alienation, loneliness, anguish, and horror dominate for no clear reason. In this psychic wasteland, no affection can be produced, as symbolized by the husband's inability to grow plants in their apartment. The dead plants are evidence of accumulated frustration caused by the lack of passion and love between the young couple. The story demonstrates eloquently that it is impossible to share or have any meaningful interaction beyond the self.

In other cases the breakdown of communication comes as a result of the individual's private obsessions. The short story "Gongniu" (The ox) presents a typical situation. The story has two characters, the narrator ("I") and her husband, Old Guan. There is no true conflict in the story, because the couple does not have any real contact. The story starts presumably with the woman's reflection on a day in her married life:

> It was drizzling that day. In the wind, mulberries were falling from the old tree into the crevices between the tiles. In the big mirror on the wall I saw a purple light flashing outside the window. It was the rear of an ox which had just passed slowly by. I ran to the window and poked out my head. (Can Xue 1989b, 71)

Whether she has really seen the ox now occupies the woman's mind. She mentions her encounter to her husband Old Guan again and again, anxious to get him to verify her experience. But all of her attempts fail because Old Guan is preoccupied with his own problem, the decay of his teeth caused by his habit of having a midnight snack of crackers. Every morning Old Guan is in a hurry to brush his teeth to get rid of the cracker residue, complaining that "all night the field mice were scurrying between [his] teeth like mad" (72). While the wife talks exclusively about the ox, the husband grumbles constantly about the mice and his dental problem.

In spite of the "dialogues" that fill up the space of the short story, then, no real communication takes place. The dialogues exist in form but not in essence, because each party talks but never listens. The following is a sample:

> "I've seen something," I told him vaguely. "A strange purple color. This seemed to have first happened long ago."
>
> "Look here," he was showing me his black teeth. "These holes could have been dug by field mice."
>
> Our bed stood against the wooden wall. When I was about to fall

asleep, the horn [of the ox] poked in through the hole. I reached out to caress it, but what I touched was the back of Old Guan's head, cold and hard; it shrank and wrinkled.

"You tossed and turned in your sleep," he said. "All night the field mice were scurrying between my teeth like mad. Did you hear? I couldn't help eating a couple of crackers again. Then I was done for. Why couldn't I stop myself..."

"That thing [the ox] keeps circling our house day and night. Don't tell me you haven't heard it even once."

"I've been urged to have my bad teeth pulled out. Then all my troubles would be gone, they say. I've thought about it for some time but have decided to keep things as they are, lest some other trouble should set in. I guess I'd better put up with it." (Can Xue 1989b, 72–73)

The futility of communication between the couple can be analyzed on two levels. First, the passage is full of Freudian sexual symbolism. The "horn" and the "mice" (because of their ability to go into holes) stand for the penis; the images of losing teeth or having them pulled represent, for a male, masturbation and sexual repression; and the hole obviously refers to the female organ.[9] What ties the symbolism in with the theme is the frustrated sexual contact. When "the horn poked in through the hole," the woman tries to "caress it," but "it shrank and wrinkled." In contrast, the husband seems to have given up on physical intimacy and is content with self-eroticism (as shown by his constant reference to his teeth).

Second, the intercourse also fails on the discursive level. With each of them concentrating on his or her private worries, husband and wife are disengaged. The dialogue, in consequence, disintegrates into interwoven monologues. In her characteristic grim humor, Can Xue allows the futile babbling to continue into the night, making the monologues erode further into somnologues. Even in his dream talk, Old Guan's worrisome teeth dominate. He talks about the withered berries falling from the chinaberry tree, and the white sheet hanging on it, which is later used to wrap his mother's dead body. In other words, Old Guan continues to be obsessed with decay and death. Without realizing what she is doing, the wife joins in, her thoughts not far from her daytime fixation either. In the woman's talk, physical deterioration is more closely linked with her frustration at not being able to communicate. She relates how she wants to get to the store so she can buy a bottle of ink to write a letter to a friend, how she fails because of the slippery road, and how dust blinds her eyes so that she cannot make out the house numbers. Doubtful of the accuracy of her vision at night just as she is during the day, the woman is dismayed by her foiled attempt at establishing contact.

No more productive than the daytime monologues, the nocturnal ravings are a more dramatic manifestation of the failure to communicate. The narrator tells us pathetically, "We talked all night. By morning we had blisters the size of soybeans on the tips of our tongues" (Can Xue 1989b, 74). The grotesque "dialogues" do not function because they violate what the philosopher Paul Grice calls the "cooperative principle" in conversation (Grice 1989, 26). The couple's irrelevant rejoinders are inappropriate responses: they move in different directions, robbing the "conversation" of any coherence.

The bankrupt communication may, however, result ultimately from the private and therefore unsharable nature of the individuals' obsessions. This is suggested by the recurrent motif of the mirror in Can Xue's stories. As used in "The Ox," the mirror has multiple significations. Catching sight of a purple light flashing outside the window in the mirror, the woman takes it to be the hindquarters of an ox. Because of its unlikely link with an ox, the mirror symbolizes the private nature of the vision: it produces a reflection only for the eyes of the beholder and the vision of which anyone who does not behold cannot share. Nor does the mirror automatically reflect everything: it can reflect only certain objects when adjusted to a particular angle. The person using the mirror chooses the kind of reflections she or he wants to see and consequently chooses to see those images in a certain light. This may explain why Old Guan is offended when he discovers his wife looking at him in the mirror. At the same time a reflector of a real object, thus removed from it, the mirror also suggests the unverifiability of the vision originating from it: the mirror produces but an illusion of an external thing. The ox, a symbol of private vision and private obsession, comes in purple light in the mirror, and the woman, skeptical of its existence, never succeeds in finding out the truth. Moreover, the person who is glued to a mirror is no doubt self-obsessed. The woman's fascination with her own image in the mirror lends itself to a Lacanian reading. As I discussed in chapter 3, in Lacan's view in order to become a subject, the child must pass through the mirror stage and enter an interpersonal relationship with the Other through the mediation of language. The woman obviously has trouble taking this vital step. Old Guan's resentment at his wife's habit of viewing herself in the mirror is thus in a sense justifiable.

The exclusiveness of the individuals' visions and the intensely private nature of their obsessions prevent them from reaching each other, causing much frustration on both sides. Unable to confirm the existence of the ox, the woman is finally resigned to the fact that the ox might either forever turn around them or never come again. For the husband, the couple's disjointed conversation means the loss of the hope of getting any sympathy for his eternal dental problem. In this light the man's decaying teeth signify the decay of what should be an intimate, supportive relationship, a process husband and wife alike have contributed to. The deterioration is clearly self-inflicted. One day the woman discovers Old Guan filling the cracks between his teeth with arsenic in an attempt to poison the field mice scurrying there. As a result, "his lips turned black; his eyelids drooped heavily. He swayed and his skin suddenly wrinkled up like that of an eighty-year-old" (Can Xue 1989b, 75). Involved in an inescapable (non)relationship, the woman also suffers from declining health. Her hair is parched like hay and, when she combs it, clumps fall out.

The last reflection the woman sees in the mirror is a scene of death: "I could see far, far away in the mirror. A huge beast had fallen into the water and was splashing and writhing in the throes of death. Black smoke was belching from its nose; dark red blood spurted from its mouth" (Can Xue 1989b, 76). Is this dying beast the ox, therefore the death of the woman's private vision? Very possibly. In any case, Old Guan seems to have recognized the mirror as the source of the problem. In the concluding scene, the woman turns away from the mirror in surprise and sees Old Guan "raising a big hammer high above his head and swinging it toward the mirror" (76). The husband's action nevertheless comes too late, since husband and wife are already consumed by their private obsessions in their mutually closed worlds.

The Self under Siege

The relationship between the self and the Other becomes a problem not simply because individuals shrink from intimate contact: Can Xue also believes that close ties are impossible because when interrelationships do exist, they are marked not only by apathy but also by suspicion, distrust, and, above all, the individual's omnipresent fear of persecution. In a polarized world made up of tormentors and tormented, victimizers and victims, relationships between individuals are always tense, torturous, even murderous. "Wushui li de feizaopao" (Soap bubbles in the dirty water) enacts a short but intensely built drama of this kind between a mother and her son.

San Mao, the protagonist, lives with his nagging mother, who wants to marry him into her section chief's family as a live-in son-in-law so that she can curry favor with the chief. When San Mao complains about her plot, the mother flies into a rage, accidentally knocking over a cup of tea and splashing it into her own face. When she tries to dry off her face, the rubbing produces bubbles, leaving hollows in the spots that were wet. This gives San Mao an idea. He coaxes his mother into taking a bath, hoping that she will melt in the water like a piece of soap. She does. Stunned at what has happened, San Mao sits there with a lowered head, not knowing what to do. Suddenly, his mother's voice comes out of the soap bubbles in the washbasin, urging San Mao to deliver some presents to her section chief. The story concludes with San Mao's running into the street, pursued by his mother's voice. There he turns into some sort of animal, barking ferociously and attacking an onlooker in the crowd that gathers around him.

In this short, well-handled story, the contact between mother and son is characterized by unending abrasion and wariness. Suspecting San Mao of bearing her ill will, the mother never has a warm word for him. The old woman prefers to sleep in the kitchen, shutting both windows and the door to keep her son out. Physical separation, however, does not stop the mother from constantly humiliating her son. She shouts and scolds him from the kitchen, calling him an unfilial son if he protests even a little. In their undisguised mutual hostility, there is no hypocrisy, for each openly acts as the source of pain and torture to the other. Driven to his wit's end, the son resorts to murder. Yet the mother is no less a murderer herself. Her marriage plan for San Mao and her continual rebukes are meant to destroy her son's independent identity and create a being after her own will. The consequences of this kind of slow torture and deprivation can be seen in San Mao's drastic metamorphosis. His loss of human form signifies the irrevocable devastation of his very being as a result of his mother's harassment and abuse. Although she has melted into the water, the mother's domineering will lives on in the disembodied voice, through which the mother's persecution of the son persists, precipitating his final breakdown. It is significant that the abuse is verbal rather than directly physical. But the scathing effect of the language on its victim and the vulnerability it introduces into the young man's existence are so potent and palpable that they are able to induce his grotesque physical transformation.

The son's sense of endless persecution is further deepened by the crowd that watches him being turned into an animal barking furiously yet helplessly in their midst. Among the throng is an old man pushing his way here and there with an idiotic smile on his face. San Mao obviously identifies this old man with his pushy and sarcastic mother. By attacking the old man, the son carries on his battle with his tyrannical parent. But San Mao does not realize that he has already been defeated, for, having lost his humanity in the metamorphosis, he has lost what he is fighting for.

"Soap Bubbles" demonstrates one of the most characteristic techniques of Can Xue's writing, the deliberate conflation of objective and subjective realities. In stories such as "In the Wilderness," "The Date," and "Skylight," we have reason to believe that what is described are nightmares and dreams (and even dreams within dreams). Despite the mother's irrational behavior toward her son, however, "Soap Bubbles" is presented in what is for the most part a realistic setting. As a consequence, the disappearance of the mother into the water and the dehumanization of the son are more conspicuously unreal against our conventional sense of reality. The murderous act by the son presents no great surprise, considering the mounting tension between the characters. But we would be at some difficulty to separate objective reality from fantasy. Has the mother really melted, leaving a bodiless voice behind to haunt the son? It is most likely, on the realistic level, that the voice is coming from the mother very much alive in the kitchen and that the son is merely fantasizing about her disappearance. But to Can Xue what counts as true is the individual's subjective feeling: the son finds himself losing his mind because of his mother's nagging, and in his bitter antipathy, the son wills that his abusive mother turn into soap bubbles. This subjective experience becomes the only authentic truth for the individual. When the superficial reality is discarded and genuine, suppressed emotions are freed from the bondage of conventional morality, the grotesque nature of the deadly relationship comes into the open. This is the aim and the force of Can Xue's bizarre stories.

Another excellent piece that spells out the individual's painful and frustrating experience in a grating relationship is "Shanshang de xiaowu" (The hut on the hill). The story is so experiential that it defies plot summary. We are not even sure of the narrator's gender, and the ambiguity, I would argue, serves to strengthen the power of the story by making the experience depicted in it universal rather than gender specific.[10] The hut parallels the ox in the story "The Ox" in that it represents an exclusive, subjective experience unsharable with others. Whenever the narrator mentions the hut in an attempt to confirm its existence, her family either pretends not to have heard her comment or regards the narrator's insistence on finding out the truth about the hut as "some sort of disease."

The emotional involvement in "The Hut" is much more intense than it is in "The Ox." While in "The Ox" the woman's attempts at communicating her vision to her husband meet with indifference, in "The Hut" the narrator's efforts to convey her thoughts arouse common animosity among her family. In order to decode the image of the hut, we must start with another image closely associated with it, the narrator's drawer. The narrator's daily routine consists of trying to clean up the drawer and contemplating the hut on the hill. Both projects somehow deeply upset her family, who seize every chance to thwart her plans. One day when the narrator makes a trip to the hill, they throw her drawer into disarray. The narrator tells us that "I discover that they took advantage of my absence to tip up my drawer and made a big mess out of it, dumping several dead moths and dragonflies onto the floor; they know very well those are my favorite things" (Can Xue 1991b, 42).[11]

The drawer, in which the narrator stores her "favorite things," clearly stands for her private world. When she finds several things missing from it as a result of her family's interference, the narrator's mind is in a "turmoil." The narrator's constant efforts to tidy her drawer, then, are obviously an attempt to understand herself, to face and sort out her mental confusion. The hut on the hill, in this light, can be interpreted as an external projection of the narrator's confused inner world. The narrator insists that she can hear someone moaning in the hut, and its occupant, according to her description, is identical in appearance to the narrator herself. Once, coming back from a trip to the hill, the narrator looks at herself in the mirror and sees that "her eyes were ringed with two black halos" (Can Xue 1991b, 41). Later, the narrator tries to tell her mother that "there is really someone crouching in there [the hut], he's got two big purple smudges under his eyes, too, from staying up all night" (42). The hut dweller's exhausted mien recalls the narrator's tiring nightly project of straightening out her drawer. The family's unremitting sabotage of the narrator's plan to rearrange her drawer constitutes an intrusion upon her privacy, an act aimed at preventing the narrator from ever coming to an understanding of herself. The narrator's little sister tells her that "they [her family] helped you clean up your drawer when you weren't here" (42). Apparently, her family considers the narrator's "favorite things" worthless, dead objects to be abandoned. The narrator informs the reader that over the years she and her family have been engaged in an ongoing battle over the narrator's chess set: time and again her family buries it and she digs it up. At issue in the struggle between the narrator and her family is without doubt the narrator's right to her own world of self. Her family's "help" not only amounts to denying the narrator a right to have a private world, but it also seeks to impose their own on her. As a result, even in her bedroom the narrator constantly feels threatened and persecuted. She tells her mother that "there are so many thieves pacing around outside our house in the moonlight. I turned on the light and saw that someone had poked countless holes in the window" (41). Through the countless holes, the narrator's private world is being spied on and encroached upon. What makes the situation particularly lamentable is that the eyes behind those holes belong to her family. Extremely conscious of the stares from her parents and sister, the narrator becomes nervous whenever she is looked at. The intense feeling of insecurity has made the narrator hypersensitive; the menacing looks from her family have a magical power to inflict physical damage to her body, as I discuss shortly.

The family's hostility and the narrator's unceasing vigilance have made it impossible for the narrator to have any individual sense of self. Thus, the narrator's search for the self inevitably fails, as symbolized both by her aborted plan to clean up her drawer and her inability to determine the existence of the hut. On one trip up the hill, the narrator has trouble seeing: "I climbed for a long time, the sun beat down making me dizzy and blurring my vision, every pebble shimmered with tiny white sparks" (Can Xue 1991b, 41). Because of her blurred vision, the hut becomes an illusory object, forever eluding her. The character's problem with her eyesight points to the narrator's failure to make sense of her self or create a world of her own. After repeated fruitless ascents, the narrator finally admits defeat: "When I climbed up the hill, all I could see were the sparks from white pebbles; there were no wild grapes, there was no hut" (44). Under persistent attack from her family, the narrator's hope of creating an identity for herself is completely crushed.

The Self in the Sartrean Look

Throughout Can Xue's works, as in "The Hut," there is a recurring situation that becomes one of the primal patterns of the self's relationship with the Other. This is the individual's existential struggle to see and the agony of being seen by the Other. As Sartre's theory of "the look" provides a theoretical framework for my analysis in this section, a brief discussion of the philosopher's reception in post-Mao China is in order. Existentialism, especially that of Sartre, was part of the interest in the absurdist literature in the late 1970s.[12] In 1980, when Sartre died, the philosopher and his existential philosophy were spotlighted. The Chinese Academy of Arts and Sciences sponsored a collection of studies on Sartre that was published in 1981.[13] In his elaborate foreword, Liu Mingjiu, the editor, quite boldly (given the bias and suspicion Chinese authorities have always reserved for any Western ideas except Marxism) declared Sartre "a towering monument in the development of twentieth-century ideas" (Liu Mingjiu 1984, 427). Essays on the interpretation of Sartre and his existentialism, a critical reading of *Nausea*, as well as an article commemorating his death appeared in various literary journals throughout 1980.[14]

The appeal of Sartre's existentialism to Chinese readers in general lies in its emphasis on choice and responsibility in human life. As I have shown in chapter 2, the keynote in post-Mao grievances was the individual's lack of autonomy. In the environment of discontent and protest, the existentialist credo of individual freedom provided both a theoretical possibility for the critics to challenge the ossified Marxist ideology and a cathartic outlet for the people to denounce the communist denial of personal choice. At the same time, the stress on the being's responsibility over its existence added force to the reflective mood that had begun to take hold at the end of the 1970s. One outcome of this reflective mood was the examination of the individual's own role and accountability in the Cultural Revolution. It was felt that a human disaster of such magnitude as the Cultural Revolution could not have occurred without the participation of millions of people. To prevent a similar catastrophe from happening again, it was necessary for each individual to reflect on his or her contribution to the political movement. Sartre's philosophy struck a responsive chord in the hearts of those who insisted that the individual should take responsibility.

But Sartre and his existentialism did meet with some controversy. Although Sartre's emphasis on individual subjectivity and self-determination made him a potential ally to alienation theory, its advocates were wary of blending Sartrean humanism with the Marxist stand (Jing Wang 1996, 27–31). Some Chinese critics applauded Sartre's exposure of the human reality in the capitalist world but took him to task for seeing alienation, loneliness, horror, and absurdity as universally valid human experiences (Ou Litong 1984; Liu Fangtong 1984). In their view, these experiences do not apply in a socialist society. Ironically, as I have commented above, Can Xue's work proves the opposite of what these critics claim. Her portrayal of human life in Mao's China shows many of the aspects that Sartre explored in his philosophy and literary creations. In particular, Sartre's perception of the significance of the act of "looking" between the self and the Other lends a powerful perspective for understanding the self's mournful experience with the spying Other, as I discuss in the following pages.

The archetypal pattern of the battle between the self and the seeing Other in Can Xue's fiction is established through her fascination with eyes. The eyes in her writings fall invariably into two groups, the eyes of the narrative "I's" and those of the Other. And these two groups of eyes exhibit two distinct qualities. The eyes of the "I" always experience pain and suffering. In his book review of Can Xue's *Dialogues in Paradise,* Jon Soloman comments, "As with many of the images in Can Xue's writing, these actions [of seeing and being seen] are associated with great pain" (Soloman 1988, 241). In the story "Skylight," the narrator's "eyeballs are always swollen and pained" and she is plagued by sties. In the narrator's dreamy world, other eyes also feature prominently: "Under every tea bush there was a gray eyeball, which blinked constantly, giving out clear, dewlike tears. I picked up one of them, but immediately it turned into powder and a puff of smoke in my palm" (Can Xue 1989b, 115). Similarly, the woman in "The Ox" finds "a green secretion . . . oozing from the corner of [her] eyes" (73); the narrator in "The Hut" complains that "everything is so glaring that my eyes blear from the pain" (Can Xue 1991b, 42). The monologist in "Dialogues in Paradise" tells us that "I tried to flow away from this body [of mine], but it only resulted in my eyes turning a strange color. Now they can no longer distinguish day from night" (Can Xue 1989b, 140).

As shown in the last quotation, ailing eyes always suggest the individual's failing vision. The narrators constantly worry that they cannot see clearly. Examples abound in "The Ox," "The Hut," "The Fog," "The Date," "Skylight," and other works. As I have argued in my analysis of "The Hut," the problematic sight in Can Xue's intensely subjective world is highly symbolic. The object the eyes of the "I" are trying but fail to discern is the "I" itself. Thus, the troubled vision bespeaks a self bewildered and in deep anguish, a self that, unable to make sense of itself, feels afloat in a meaningless world devoid of warmth, care, love, and understanding.

The eyes of the Other, in contrast, are inevitably depicted as malevolent and threatening. Lacking any human quality, they appear ominous and abhorrent. The most telling examples again can be found in "The Hut." The narrator's little sister always has a blank stare, and at one point her left eye suddenly turns green. Often the gaze from the Other not only has the power to induce unnameable fear and anxiety in the gazed upon but is even capable of inflicting physical damage. In the same story, the narrator is more than simply aware of the look from her family; she experiences it with her body: "I can feel her [the narrator's mother's] hostile stare on the back of my head, the point on my scalp she stares at tingles and swells" (Can Xue 1991b, 42). The little sister's stare produces a similar reaction: "Little sister's gaze is always a perfect blank; it pierces through me and makes the back of my neck break out in little red bumps" (43). The character's father is no exception either: "My father glares at me suddenly with one eye, a very familiar wolf's eye. I have a sudden revelation: every night

my father turns into one of those wolves that run around our house howl-
ing mournfully" (42). Readers of modern Chinese literature would recognize the wolfish eyes as a re-creation of the chilling image first presented by
Lu Xun in his stories "Diary of a Madman" and "Ah Q, the Real Story."
Ironically it is reproduced six decades later by a young writer under the
socialist system Lu Xun's generation had fought for and helped bring into
being, a system the May Fourth writers hoped would guarantee the
oppressed individual emancipation and equality. Little would Lu Xun sus-
pect that his lamentable loner should outlive the removal of the old social
order.

If the existential conflicts of seeing and being seen, or, to use the
Sartrean dichotomy, of looking and being looked at, are to varying degrees
the undercurrent in many of Can Xue's short stories, her novella "Old
Floating Cloud" foregrounds the metaphysical implications of these conflicts. "Old Floating Cloud" manifests many of Can Xue's literary predilec-
tions. It has a nightmarish quality built up by grotesque characters and
numerous nocturnal scenes. The story is set in no particular historical period,
nor does the passage of time play any significant role in the development
of events. The story "evolves" insofar as there is an increasing sense of
degeneration, but nothing is resolved. As a result, one has the feeling that
the ending is only the inevitable outcome of an eternal situation, a pattern
created not by any particular individuals but by the mode of existence itself.
Involved in this existence are not what we would normally call productive
members of society, for the characters are not engaged in any socially
meaningful activities. The major characters in the novella are the two protagonists, Xu Ruhua and her neighbor Geng Shanwu, and their families.
Apart from Xu Ruhua and Geng Shanwu, the other characters' occupations
are not very clear. But their preoccupation is—they are engrossed in other
people's affairs. The characters' daily pursuits in the novella clearly divide
them into two categories, the seeing and the seen.

Xu Ruhua, a shop assistant in a small grocery store, and Geng Shanwu,
a clerk in some kind of government institution, are the seen. The novella
begins with Geng Shanwu's dream:

Geng Shanwu dreamed all night under the influence of their [the fallen
mulberry flowers'] irritating fragrance, an odor inducing dizziness like the
stench of sewer water that sends one into wild spirals of delirium. He saw
red-faced women squeeze their heads in through the window. They had
long, asthenic necks, and their heads hung down like poisonous toadstools. (Can Xue 1991a, 177)

The telltale image in the dream is that of heads crowding to look into the window. Geng's aversion to the heads (the "poisonous toadstools") and their huddling to look into the house indicate that Geng Shanwu is inside the house and therefore the object of the gaze. The dreamy vision soon becomes reality. Geng Shanwu starts his day in a good mood, expecting "a rebirth, a new beginning." His merry mood does not last long. Annoyed with the white flowers strewn on the ground in the courtyard, Geng tries to bury a flower in the mud with his foot. But "while he was stealthily patting down the mud, the thin face of a woman in shock flashed past the window and disappeared into the darkness of the room" (178). The realization that he has been seen greatly upsets Geng Shanwu. "He rushed to the street out of breath, but a pair of eyes seemed to gaze on his narrow back" (179). The eyes have become etched into Geng's consciousness. No matter how hard he tries, he cannot forget that he has been seen.

This is not the only look Geng Shanwu receives. Like Old Guan in "The Ox," Geng is in the habit of snacking on crackers. Ashamed of his habit, he steals only a few mouthfuls when there is no one around. Once when Geng is eating crackers in an alley, he is surprised by his father-in-law, who sneers at him, showing Geng that he knows his little secret. Geng Shanwu realizes that "his father-in-law, too, was a spy" (Can Xue 1991a, 190). The most aggressive prier, however, is his neighbor, Ma Laowu. For no apparent reason, Ma Laowu pursues Geng Shanwu relentlessly, going out of his way to make Geng aware of his presence.

Xu Ruhua, the other protagonist, is primarily also the seen, although at the beginning of the story she appears to Geng Shanwu to be among the seeing. Xu Ruhua is subject to the look from everyone around her, her parents, her in-laws, and her neighbors. During the course of the story, their look drives Xu Ruhua more and more into herself until she physically isolates herself from the world behind locked doors. This isolation is complete at the end of the novella, when the woman loses her ability to consume and excrete, the self having totally blockaded itself from the external world.

The other characters in the novella are people who give the look. Geng Shanwu's wife, Mulan, who holds a job in a factory, makes it her daily business to spy on her neighbor Xu Ruhua. An innovative spy, she puts up a large mirror on the back wall so that she can catch her neighbor's every move. The single-mindedness of Mulan and the monotony in her life are indicated by her unchanging diet of stewed spareribs. When Geng Shanwu complains about it, she admits that she "can't think of anything else." The only "spices" Mulan adds to her daily menu are what she discovers: her neighbors clean house one day and install a fish tank another. She resents, however, that although she has lived next door to Xu Ruhua and her husband, Old Kuang, for eight years, she "can never guess their next thought."

The parents of Xu Ruhua and Old Kuang are also veteran spies. With no affection whatsoever for her daughter, Xu Ruhua's mother does not visit Ruhua to offer her love and comfort; she comes to "see." She hides behind trees and, whenever there is a chance, imposes her "advice" on Xu Ruhua. She pastes notes on trees, leaves them outside her daughter's door, or throws them into her room if the door is open. Finally, she sticks an ultimatum on the door, warning Xu Ruhua, "Cling obstinately to your course; the cobra will take revenge tonight" (Can Xue 1991a, 202). The mother's choice of the cobra as avenger is not accidental. Since the word *cobra* in Chinese is *"yanjingshe"* (literally, "the spectacled snake"), the snake is a metaphor for the mother, who, having exploited her eyes to the point of exhausting her vision, admits that she "truly regret[s] having used them [her eyes] too much" (262). The cobra thus both stands for the mother herself and points to her vicious and venomous criticism of Xu Ruhua.

Xu Ruhua's mother-in-law is no less ardent in interfering with the couple's life. Whenever she comes, "she cast her eyes around the room suspiciously, even peering cautiously behind the door" (Can Xue 1991a, 195). Like Xu Ruhua's own mother, her mother-in-law enjoys writing instructive notes to the couple. Every two or three days, she sends a bald niece of hers to deliver them a note bearing a nonsensical message such as, "Looking into the distance can cure the fatigue of the lower limbs." These dicta, however, sustain Old Kuang. When they stop coming for a while, Old Kuang is so distracted that he has to move back in with his mother.

By far the most tenacious pursuer in the novella is Geng Shanwu's neighbor Ma Laowu, a mad sadist. Part of Ma Laowu's everyday routine is to chase his white rooster, pelting him with stones until he develops welts. With the same indefatigability, the old man preys on Geng Shanwu. Ma Laowu despises Geng Shanwu for no discernible reason. Whenever he meets Geng on the street, he gives a snort of contempt, calling him "idiot" and making sure that Geng hears it. Geng Shanwu tries all kinds of ways to escape Ma Laowu, but he never succeeds:

Ma Laowu was so determined that he became yet more diligent when he saw through Shanwu's evasions. He calculated the young man's office hours and waited patiently on the street. As soon as Shanwu approached, the old man would come forward to greet him, and after Shanwu passed he would utter the curse that made Shanwu so angry.[15] This had become Ma's greatest enjoyment. Even in snow or rain, he would stand at the door under an oilskin umbrella waiting for Shanwu's arrival. (Can Xue 1991a, 212)

Though disgusted with him, Geng Shanwu is afraid of Ma Laowu. His fear is noticed by all his neighbors and greatly puzzles his wife, who asks Geng Shanwu bluntly why he is afraid of Ma Laowu and what their relationship is.

Why should the two protagonists be terrified of the look from the Other? Sartre's explication of the being's relationship to the Other and of the influence of the look from the Other on the existence of the being is highly relevant to our understanding of Can Xue's vision. "Old Floating Cloud" may well be seen as a dramatization of the self caught in the Sartrean look. In Sartre's philosophy two terms are essential in decoding the relationship between the being and the Other: *"pour-soi"* and *"en-soi."* Human as consciousness is *pour-soi,* "for itself." For Sartre, consciousness must have an object, and what consciousness is conscious of is the *en-soi,* the "in itself." Sartre tells us that consciousness knows itself as a negation of the *en-soi.* For example, the table, the chair, and the tree are all *en-soi,* objects in the world. Consciousness is able to distinguish itself from these objects by negating them: "I am not a table"; "I am not a chair"; "I am not a tree"; and so on. The power of negation allows consciousness, the *pour-soi,* to be free, to be a subject with all possibilities. The negation between the *pour-soi* and *en-soi,* between consciousness and the objects in the world, also applies to human relations. The "I" knows itself as the negation of the Other: "I am not John, not Mary, not Richard."[16] I constitute myself as negative, as a void, a *pour-soi,* and the Other as *en-soi,* an object known. In other words, subjectivity is "nothingness," free to choose anew at any moment, hence Sartre's statement that "insofar as I am my possibles, [I] am what I am not and not what I am" (Sartre 1956, 263).

The Other-as-object and me-as-subject is not the only relationship between the I and the Other. In order for the I to negate the Other, to distinguish myself as not-the-Other, I see the Other as one of the objects in the world. At the same time, however, there is always the possibility that the Other seen by me may turn into one who sees me. In other words, the relationship between the I and the Other is dynamic, the status of the I shifting between the seeing and the seen.

Then how does the look from the Other affect my being-as-subject? The classical example Sartre uses to illustrate the meaning of the Other's look is that of shame. Motivated probably by jealousy, I listened at the door and peeped through the keyhole. Alone and not self-conscious, I am a pure consciousness of things, of a spectacle behind the door to be seen and a conversation to be heard. "My attitude, for example, has no 'outside'; it is a pure process of relating the instrument (the keyhole) to the end to be obtained (the spectacle to be seen), a pure mode of losing myself in the world" (Sartre 1956, 259). Therefore, I am pure activity, that is, pure consciousness. But suddenly, I hear footsteps in the hall and, startled, I realize there is someone looking at me. "What does this mean? It means that I am suddenly affected in my being and that essential modifications appear in my structure" (260). One of the essential modifications is that I immediately become self-conscious. To be self-conscious means that I have now acquired an outside, a self. But the self is presented to my consciousness as an object: I now view my self through the eyes of the Other: "This means that all of a sudden I am conscious of myself as escaping myself, not in that I am the foundation of my own nothingness but in that I have my foundation outside of myself. I am for myself only as I am a pure reference to the Other" (260). Alienated from myself, my self becomes a given object. Without even acting on me, simply by the upsurge of its being, the Other has conferred on me an outside, a nature.

The Other's look has thus brought my self into being, and in the process I am no longer nothingness: I become something. The Other has killed my possibilities but has retained its own. In other words, I have lost my power of negation and attained an objectness, for by looking at me the Other has turned itself into the Other-as-subject. The relationship between I and the Other is now between the Other-as-subject and my being-as-object. Consequently, I am reduced to being an object-in-the-world, an *en-soi*. Alienated from all my other possibilities and limited to those imposed by the Other, I am now known.

The incident in which Geng Shanwu tries to bury a flower in the mud is a revealing example of the shame Sartre discusses. The realization that he has been seen embarrasses him: "Shanwu's face felt hot. Lowering his head, he stumbled away, tramping a flower at every step. He dared not look around but fled like a thief" (Can Xue 1991a, 178–179). Even though he curses "indignantly," Geng Shanwu is nevertheless affected. He is now very self-conscious. At work, finding himself the object of everybody's look, Geng Shanwu again feels awkward. "They stared at him intently. 'I—I'm saying... I mean to say—I'm extremely self-conscious.' He looked at the mob timidly, not daring to continue" (220). Although Geng Shanwu is not clear about what the others may find wrong in him, that he is looked at is enough to disconcert him. His self-consciousness shows that he is aware of being judged. In Sartre's words, "A judgment is the transcendental act of a free being. Thus, being-seen constitutes me as a defenseless being for a freedom which is not my freedom" (Sartre 1956, 267).

As I have mentioned, the relationship between the I and the Other is an unstable one. It is either me-as-subject confronting the Other-as-object or me-as-object submitting to the Other-as-subject. In order to maintain my being-as-subject when the Other is looking at me, Sartre states, the I must return its look. In other words, the I can refuse to be objectified by the Other's look; the I must look back to turn the Other's look into a look-looked-at. By looking back at the Other, the I asserts freedom, negating the Other's possibilities. To look or to be looked at, in Sartre's view, becomes a constant battle and, in consequence, constitutes the fundamental relationship between the I and the Other.[17]

Without the ability to look back, though, the two protagonists of "Old Floating Cloud" can only be the victims of the look from the Other, yielding unresistingly to its power. Well aware of the existence and purpose of the mirror Mulan has hung up, Xu Ruhua nevertheless does not even protest. At home she mechanically follows her husband's instructions to spray pesticide several times a day. When her mother intrudes by pressing her notes upon her, she simply tries to avoid her.

Similarly, much as he loathes being looked at, Geng Shanwu is powerless to initiate a look himself. This is clearly shown in the little drama between Geng Shanwu and his wife. One of the veteran priers, Mulan takes great pleasure in discussing what she sees. She reports and keeps count of how many times an old man called Lin in her factory defecates in his pants. Geng Shanwu understands that "his wife was trying to distinguish herself from Old Lin. They always tried to laugh at others out of their inner fear of exposing themselves" (Can Xue 1991a, 211). People like Mulan obviously seek to maintain their own subjectness by fixing others at the end of their look. Geng Shanwu learns this from his own experience:

> There used to be an old man who fried cakes. One day she [Mulan] called Shanwu to the old man's door in a mysterious way. She invited him to peek in through a crack to see an "excellent performance." He bent over and peeked in for a long time but saw nothing. Standing aside, she bent over with laughter. "I could die laughing!" she had said. So she was laughing at him? He only realized that a long time afterward.
> "Why did you laugh at me?" he asked later.
> "Because you're a fool."
> "And you?"

"How can I be a fool? I couldn't discover your foolishness if I were a fool." (211)

In this incident, Geng Shanwu for a short while seems to be looking. In fact, he is only playing a role Mulan has designed for him. He himself is giving an "excellent performance." In other words, Geng's "look" fails to be a look-looking but is turned into a look-looked-at. As a result, Geng Shanwu is "fallen into the world in the midst of things" (Sartre), becoming an object among other objects within Mulan's vision.

Victims of the look and unable to look back, Geng Shanwu and Xu Ruhua have each tried different strategies to exist under the look from the Other. Geng Shanwu's strategy is what Sartre terms "a project of absorbing the Other": acknowledging the Other's subjectness, the I adopts the point of view of the Other, taking it as its own and accepting the me-as-object that the Other's look has created for the I. As Sartre puts it, "I want to assimilate the Other as the Other-looking-at-me, and this project of assimilation includes an augmented recognition of my being-looked-at. In short, in order to maintain before me the Other's freedom which is looking at me, I identify myself totally with my being-looked-at" (Sartre 1956, 365).

But Geng Shanwu is unsuccessful in his attempts to do this. Geng Shanwu has an acute sense of being looked at. He tells Xu Ruhua that even when he goes to the bathroom, "someone peeks through the crack in the door" (Can Xue 1991a, 199). At first Geng Shanwu tries to avoid being watched, by standing at the office window, pretending to be looking at something outside like everyone else. But he is soon isolated. Once the director of his institute hints to Geng Shanwu that he wants Geng to find him a rare breed of parrot. Absentmindedly, Geng Shanwu asks the director if he raises cats. As the anecdote quickly circulates in the institute, Geng becomes a laughingstock. Feeling the increasing pressure from the director and his colleagues, "Shanwu made up his mind to remold himself completely" (220). He goes to the director's house, promising to find him the bird he wants. Significantly, that bird is a parrot that imitates whatever it is taught to say. This rare bird may well be Geng himself, for now Geng Shanwu tries to behave exactly as everyone else. When a butterfly flutters into the office, everyone leaps into frantic action, some beating at it desperately with feather dusters, others jumping and cheering them on. "To cover his stealth, Geng Shanwu also started yelling and followed the others in acting like a madman" (192).

Trying to adopt an identity the Other creates for him does not bring

Geng Shanwu any peace. Instead, he degenerates further. He has trouble recalling his experience on a geological team. The geological team, where Geng Shanwu worked before his marriage, represents his youthful past. In his attempt to assume a false identity, however, the memory of his former energetic self is quickly fading. Geng Shanwu confesses his dilemma to Xu Ruhua:

> "Too hard! I'm almost an idiot." He stopped, worried and indignant. "Everyone, every word they say, everything they do, is fixed. But I, I'm nothing. I can't change into them, no matter how I rack my brains to imitate another's walk, no matter how I pretend to be thinking as I stand at the office window until my legs break. In fact, I, too, am fixed. I can only be nothing." (Can Xue 1991a, 217–218)

Of course, Geng Shanwu's "nothing" is totally different from Sartre's concept of nothingness. For Sartre, nothingness as the very essence of consciousness means absolute freedom and infinite possibilities. Geng Shanwu's "nothingness" denotes a dislocated being denied his subjectness, a being for whom the "nothingness" is a source of horror. For, rather than indicating unlimited possibilities for himself, the "nothingness" turns Geng into infinite possibilities for the Other to make him a known object that is nevertheless unknown to Geng himself and therefore inassimilable. All Geng is sure of is that he is "fixed" in his object status as a "being-for-others" (Sartre) and that others are "fixed" in their role as subjects for him.

Xu Ruhua's strategy toward the Other, in contrast, has some of the characteristics of what Sartre calls "blindness." Acting as if the I were alone in the world, the I becomes blind to the Other's existence. "I brush against 'people' as I brush against a wall; I avoid them as I avoid obstacles" (Sartre 1956, 380). Sure enough, Xu Ruhua does her utmost to shun society. She stays at home as much as possible to avoid meeting her mother. She runs home from work and pulls down a dark shade as soon as she is in the house. Finally, Xu Ruhua asks her husband to put up iron bars on the windows and doors, thinking that once the room is turned into an iron cage she will be able to have some peace.

But Xu Ruhua's reaction cannot be called total "blindness." To be blind to the Other means that the Other's subjectivity expresses what it is but not what the I is. "In a sense I am assured, I am self-confident; that is, I am in no way conscious of the fact that the Other's look can fix my possibilities and my body" (Sartre 1956, 381). Although later in the story Xu Ruhua seems to have ignored the Other's look by refusing to take advice or to play the role set out for her (she throws away the notes her mother smuggles into her house and finally stops spraying insecticides), her self-confinement is not a blindness to the existence of the Other. On the contrary, it is a heightened awareness of it. In Can Xue's fictional world, the stronghold the self desperately clings to is the character's house, his or her room, or a drawer and a hut. Although these dwelling places provide a certain space for the self, they are nevertheless limited enclosures in which the self hides in an attempt to ward off the hostility of the Other. But frequently this stronghold is assailed. In "The Hut" the narrator finds numerous holes in the window screens of her room; in "The Gloomy Mood of Ah Mei," Ah Mei's neighbor is digging a hole in the wall and earthworms are making their way into the room wherever there is a crack. In "Old Floating Cloud," even behind her barred doors and thick curtains Xu Ruhua does not feel safe:

> At night, Ruhua shut the iron-barred door and propped trunks against it. . . . The blanket [she covered herself with] was so light it flipped up and down in the wind. Even when anchored with bricks, the blanket was of no use. Long-horned beetles appearing from nowhere clattered onto her pillow and crawled toward her face. (Can Xue 1991a, 197)

In Can Xue's fiction, the rampant insects in the house obviously symbolize the constant harassment and attacks from the Other that the self cannot escape; meanwhile, the flipping blanket testifies to Xu Ruhua's sense of vulnerability and her morbid fear of being exposed to the look from the Other.

This intense self-consciousness demonstrates to the fullest extent the objectness in Xu Ruhua. If her efforts at blocking the Other's look by shutting herself in the house are motivated by defiance and her refusal to be fixed and have her possibilities taken away from her, they unfortunately result in exactly what she tries by all means to avoid: she is fixed as an object trying vainly to escape her objectness. In other words, Xu Ruhua's self-confinement becomes her only possibility. By locking herself up and pretending to be free from the Other's look, Xu Ruhua has renounced her other possibilities, the possibilities of putting the Other to the test, of transferring the Other into an object by returning the look, thus building her subjectness upon the destruction of that of the Other. The relinquishment of her subjectness then becomes tantamount to self-destruction and self-erasure.

The seeing and the seen in the world of "Old Floating Cloud" form two distinct groups, those of we-subject and us-object. Similar experiences of being the seen draw Geng Shanwu and Xu Ruhua together. In spite of his initial dislike for Xu Ruhua, Geng Shanwu soon realizes the communion between them. Unable to sleep at night, Geng Shanwu can hear Xu Ruhua, too, tossing and turning in the neighboring house; in the daytime he is the only one who can hear Xu Ruhua talking to herself about her worries (his wife apparently catches nothing). Likewise, Xu Ruhua identifies herself with Geng Shanwu as a fellow victim. When Geng comes over to share his anxieties with her, "she didn't feel surprised by his words at all, but listened as though to her own voice" (Can Xue 1991a, 187). More significant, the two of them share a dream vision:

> During the night amid the remaining fragrance, Geng Shanwu and the woman next door had the same dream. Both saw a turtle with bulging eyes crawl toward their house. The front yard had turned into a mudhole. The turtle crawled and crawled along the edge of the wall on its muddy feet but couldn't reach its destination. (184)

To both, the turtle with bulging eyes may stand for the seeing Other haunting them. The image of the turtle crawling but unable to reach its destination may express the characters' wish to be free from the Other's objectifying look as well as their fear of the impending danger. In their unremitting anxiety, Xu Ruhua and Geng Shanwu often suffer from insomnia. The insomnia indeed signifies the hopelessness of their situation. For, through the cycle of sleeping and waking up, human life is divided into past and present, history and new beginning. Unable to maintain the cycle means that, for the two victims, persecution becomes the perennial present, the very mode of their existence.

Without a common goal to tie them together, however, the union between Xu and Geng does not last long. Lacking courage to look back, they are consumed by their own endeavors to fend off the Other's aggressive look. Xu Ruhua eventually not only shuts her door to her persecutors, but she becomes tired of Geng Shanwu's visits as well, though at times she both longs to hear him talk and feels repulsion for his presence in her house. Of interest to us is that the final severance of the short-lived bond is induced by Xu Ruhua's seeing Geng Shanwu. Once Xu Ruhua starts to see, she becomes aware of Geng's thin back, his dirty shirt and its sour smell, and grows increasingly bored by his talk. Unable to tolerate the intimacy any longer, Xu Ruhua shields herself behind her iron cage, sealing up every crack in the doors and windows. Thus wedded to their own anxiety and loneliness, the seen cut themselves off from each other as well. The total seclusion of Xu Ruhua, as I said earlier, is conclusively indicated by the cessation of her bodily functions. She stops sweating and has no bowel movements for days on end. The contact between the inner and the outer worlds completely stopped, the self will ultimately be smothered within itself.

The seeing, in contrast, band together with a collective interest—to impose their look on the seen. Though Xu Ruhua's mother despises her ex-husband for having an affair with a cigarette vendor, it does not prevent her from enlisting his help in dealing with their daughter. The old woman even draws Mulan into the alliance, advising her to place a mirror on a tree to make it easier to spy on her daughter. Finally, everybody is mobilized. Day and night Xu Ruhua is haunted by shadows stealthily walking around her house. She does nothing to the outside world, but this is her very crime. In isolating herself, she is obstructing the look. Without an object to distinguish itself from, the Other is suspended and its being-as-subject is, as a consequence, put in danger. This is at the root of the ruthless persecution.

Under their intense hatred, Xu Ruhua quickly shrivels. She feels like a piece of dried fish, her body "thin and transparent, containing nothing but the shadows of the reeds" (Can Xue 1991a, 267). In her own calculations, she has locked herself up in the room for three years and four months and has not eaten anything for two months and twenty days. Meanwhile, the world around her is completely disintegrating: "Termites had eaten a whole cane chair, leaving a bunch of veins at the corners; crickets had frozen to death even without insecticide. The floor was littered with stiff corpses" (267).[18] As in Can Xue's other stories, the proliferation of insects and worms is symbolic of the ceaseless attacks and hostility plaguing the individual. The death of these hateful creatures in the closing scenes, then, also indicates the demise of the plaguers themselves. Losing each other as the reference to define themselves, neither the self nor the Other can survive. Thus, not only is Xu Ruhua consumed by the enmity, but her persecutors meet their end as well. In her last vision, Xu Ruhua sees her father running wild in circles, vomiting leeches, and hears "the millstone grind her mother's body. Her horrifying screams split into broken pieces. The cracking sound may have been her mother's skull. The millstone turned; the corpse became a thin layer of paste, oozing slowly down the edge" (268). In this way the novella concludes with an unrelieved topography of madness, decay, and death. In overwhelming its target, the Other has also brought about its own destruction. A world ruled by antipathy, hatred, fear, and horror has lost its raison d'être and cannot continue to exist.

As observed in the preceding text, existential and experiential, Can Xue's world is crazed, ugly, and deeply disconcerting. As absurd as the world seems in her fiction, it is no idle figment of the imagination. The truth of human existence uncovered by Can Xue is unmistakably about the world she lives in. Even though she dehistoricizes her writings, references to life in Maoist and post-Mao China abound and are easy to identify. For example, the lazy workers and government employees we find in "Old Floating Cloud" were a prevailing phenomenon across all sections of the society, especially before China's new policy spurred on the country's productivity in the 1980s. It is common knowledge that a typical office clerk's daily routine consisted of gossiping over a cup of tea and a newspaper. The practice was so widespread that a contemporary writer wrote a scathing story to satirize it: in Lu Wenfu's 1983 prize-winning story "Weiqiang" (Wall) the protagonist, Ma Erli, a clerk in the department of administration of the Institute of Architectural Design, is distrusted and criticized precisely because of his efficiency in getting things done. When the enclosing wall of the institute collapses, Ma manages to have it rebuilt in one day while the rest of the institute, those in favor of the traditional style and those who prefer modern Western style, are engaged in meaningless squabbles over the design of the wall. Ma is first reproved for building the wall without consulting his superiors, and later, when the wall is praised by some distinguished visitors, the director of the institute takes the credit.

Reading "The Gloomy Mood of Ah Mei," the Western reader may find it absurd that his future mother-in-law's apartment should be the primary motivation for Old Li's proposal to Ah Mei. The acute housing problem is, however, only too real for China's urban residents. In big cities, especially major cities like Shanghai, Beijing, and Nanjing, many young couples lived separately in single-person dormitories after marriage, waiting for their work unit to make a room available to them. The waiting period could span several years. Another way of obtaining housing was through the family of the bridegroom (preferably) or the bride. As a result, whether the prospective groom could provide a room for the couple topped his fiancée's list of desirable qualities.[19] Housing problems also feature frequently in fictional writings in the 1980s. In Wang Anyi's "The Destination" (which I discussed briefly in chapter 3), the *zhiqing* character Chen Xin is pressured by his elder brother and his wife to marry a woman whose only appeal lies in her family's spacious apartment. The couple wants Chen Xin out of the way so that they can secure the only bedroom in their mother's apartment. Because of tight housing, living conditions were poor. Families were crammed together in state-run housing projects with less-than-adequate sanitation and very little space to themselves. The fetid, musty houses in Can Xue's stories are as much the characters' subjective experience of their environment as realistic descriptions of living conditions for many ordinary Chinese people in the early 1980s.

But more pointed and more powerful are Can Xue's commentaries on the mentality of a society ravaged by arbitrary, man-made social upheaval that has irreparably destroyed people's ideals, confidence, and trust in one another. Beneath the irrational, insane surface of Can Xue's stories, we can discover the truth about human relationships after nearly four decades of Communist ideological campaigns. Those endless political movements ruined the innocence of human relationships of every sort and hopelessly politicized them to the extent that one feels safer in one's isolation, for by venturing any communication, one runs the risk of receiving it back in the form of a self-incriminating political bullet. The scopophiliac crowd in "Old Floating Cloud" reenacts the training the Chinese people were given over the years: under the Party's slogan of carrying out criticism and self-criticism, they were required to spy on one another. As Foucault's study of various disciplinary apparatuses—prisons, schools, medical clinics, and army camps—proves, observation or surveillance is an efficient technology for the authority to exercise power and control over society and particular groups (Foucault 1977, 146–165; 1979, 170–177). Under Communist rule the centralized system of observation was channeled through each individual's calculated gaze on his or her neighbors for maximum effect. Unaided and, as a result, unrestrained by such physical institutional structures as towers and wards, the indoctrinated gaze was ubiquitous, limited by neither spatial nor temporal boundaries. Deriving its power from its seemingly absent presence, it put the gazed-upon on constant high alert. The surveillance of one another as a trend was brought to a head during the Cultural Revolution, when distrust and betrayal were the order of the day. The intense hatred between neighbors and among family members and the universal pleasure the characters take in hurting one another in Can Xue's fiction may seem morbid and inexplicable. They are, however, a version of the ten years of nationwide madness during the Cultural Revolution, whose origins can be traced to even earlier political movements.

The whole range of the literature of the wounded (no matter how artistically wanting the stories are), personal memoirs, and numerous newspaper reports on people's experiences during the political campaigns attest to the truth exposed by Can Xue's stories. To cite a few well-known literary and real-life stories: the daughter in Lu Xinhua's "The Scar" disowns her mother during the Cultural Revolution because the mother is attacked as a counterrevolutionary. Nien Cheng's *Life and Death in Shanghai* (1986) records in chilling detail her six and a half years of prison life, from 1966 to 1973. Nien was "convicted" for the "crime" that her late husband was a diplomat in the Guomindang government and that she worked for a foreign company in Shanghai. Another profoundly ironic memoir is Wang Ruowang's *Hunger Trilogy*, which retells the veteran Communist's experience of starvation during the 1930s as a prisoner under the Nationalist regime, during the Anti-Japanese War, and in the Cultural Revolution. In 1966 Wang found himself imprisoned in the same jail where he had been housed thirty-two years previously for his Communist ideals. There he met an old jailmate who had suffered the same fate. Though on the whole Can Xue's stories are limited to family relationships, these relationships become the epitome of diseased social relationships in general. By concentrating on the most basic human relationships within the family and desocializing and dehistoricizing them, Can Xue reveals to her reader the intensity of the destruction done to the foundation of human existence by Mao's dehumanizing ideological practices.

A representative player in these practices, the mother in Can Xue's stories, deserves special attention.[20] Much like the May Fourth writers' obsession with the patriarch, the insistence on the matriarch in Can Xue's fiction makes her writings a forum for the young. The word *mother* not only brings to the Chinese reader's mind the notion of the motherland, a politicized entity after 1949, but also that of the Communist Party and its "great helmsman," Mao Zedong. Year after year the people were told to be grateful to Chairman Mao and the Party (constantly referred to as the "mother of the people") for saving them from the miseries of the old China, for giving them a new life as masters of their own country. Against the political image of the mother, Can Xue's presentation of a querulous, vicious, domineering matriarch is a vigorous and subversive demythicization of the Party and its former chairman.

The political allegorical significance of the mother image in Can Xue's work is made clear in that the fictional mother bears unmistakable resemblance to the Party and its dictator, Mao. The mother as a central authority figure, the ultimate Other, is crazy, ill-tempered, and forever fond of handing down orders to her children. Likewise, Communist history has been dominated (by and large) by the caprice and whim of Mao, who issued one directive after another to the people of the country, involving them in meaningless, destructive movements that pitted citizen against citizen. In Can Xue's fictional world, the mother is the primary adversary of the children; she sets out to destroy their sense of self, preventing them from establishing their own identity. The mother in "The Hut" comes up with one scheme after another to sabotage her daughter's efforts to straighten out her drawer; Xu Ruhua's mother swears that she is "going to destroy that little house [belonging to Xu Ruhua]." Mao and his Party played the same role in the life of the Chinese people. For many years, weekly political studies of the Party's policies and Mao's works were mandatory throughout the country, and rectification campaigns and purges were regular headline news. The purpose of these activities was none other than to impose the official ideology on the people and to crush whatever individuality and differences there may have been in people's thinking. In this light the bodiless voice of the mother harassing San Mao in "Soap Bubbles" may well point to the tenacious influence of Mao and his thought on China even after his death, in 1976. This is indeed an influence hard to come to terms with. Can Xue's characters are engaged in irreconcilable conflict with the mother and always have trouble uttering the word *mother*. In "Old Floating Cloud," Xu Ruhua tries to call to her dying mother: "'Mother...' She suddenly had a strange feeling in her throat and had a fantasy of calling out. She held her breath and gave out a funny, clumsy imitation" (Can Xue 1991a, 268–269). The narrator in "Skylight" has a similar experience: "Moving my lips, I was thinking of shouting something, but suddenly my vision was obscured by a vast haziness" (Can Xue 1989b, 109).[21] It is her friend the cremator who articulates her thoughts, telling her that she wants to say "Mother." The difficulties Can Xue's characters have with the word *mother* speak eloquently to the disillusionment of a whole generation of young people who felt deceived and betrayed by the "mother" they were taught, and learned, to love.

But this is a "mother" not easily disowned. Can Xue's existential approach to the problem between the self and the Other proves that the damage inflicted by the Communist ideology has not only penetrated basic interpersonal relationships, the core layers of the social fabric, but has also reached the most fundamental level of human existence, that of social and individual psychology. While structural changes are relatively easy to bring about, transformation of social mentality is much harder to effect. Can Xue's refusal to historicize and personalize the conflict between the self and the Other emphasizes the fact that mutual suspicion and hostility have become a permanent, metaphysical reality beyond Mao's China. It has outgrown its historical origin and turned into a perennial present. Even though the social condition that had given rise to the belligerence may have been eliminated, it will not disappear. It is a kind of Frankenstein's monster that, once created, takes on a life of its own. The lack of logic and understandable motivation behind the human conflict in Can Xue's fiction defeats any hope for resolution. When there is no cause, there can be no solution.

Under the reign of this unnamable antagonism, the weakened self is completely debilitated. It has lost its subjective seeing power and is cemented into an object position. Can Xue's stories illustrate that the construction of a new identity free of the evil influence of old is a formidable process. The exhaustion the narrator in "The Hut" suffers from is symbolic of the fatigue of a whole younger generation that, worn out by abnormal and malignant human relationships, has trouble imagining a self outside the Other's look. After lifelong suppression by powerful authority figures, people have become incapable of creating a self. With no positive models to follow, they cannot transform themselves for the future. Mao once said with regard to China's poverty and backwardness that on a clean sheet of paper, people can draw the most beautiful picture. But the Communist patriarch (or matriarch, in Can Xue's perception) did not give China a piece of blank paper. He left a stubborn legacy that threatens to forever confine the post-Mao self in the destructive Communist shadow.

5 The Post-Mao Traveler on the New Long March

In the preceding two chapters, I concentrated on a number of works published by Han Shaogong and Can Xue in the heyday of the New Era, the mid-1980s. The two writers' visions of the physically and symbolically deformed being are anything but congruent with the optimism of the age that had invested much of its energies and desires in the recovery of the *ren*, the human being writ large. Despite differences in their subject matter and artistic sensibilities, Han Shaogong and Can Xue are products of the times. Embodying as well as contributing to the ethos of the 1980s, their explorations have a strong philosophical bent characteristic of the intellectual disposition of the generation of writers who, gnawed by vivid memories of the Cultural Revolution, the movement that had both instilled in them a sense of mission and frustrated that sense, retained the zeal and ambition to intervene. Anxious to identify the causes and consequences of the human and political disasters of the Communist era to prevent them from recurring, Han Shaogong and Can Xue adopted a sort of macro-approach in examining the problematic subject. They transcended textual idiosyncrasies and specificities to go after meanings on a grand scale—the metaphysical state of the Chinese existence and the historical, cultural foundations of the nation. This sort of intense fascination with ideas and cultural formations and their generative and explanatory powers was also in line with the intellectual climate of the post-Mao age that had taken shape under the heavy influence of Western theories and methodologies, which, for all their conceptual divergences, shared a spirit of interrogation and an expectation that, through incessant critiques of ideas and their social formulation, we may be able to get to the bottom of things.

How did the subject fare in the raw realities of the reforms? What new social, historical, economic, and national concerns have informed its construction and expression since the mid-1980s? And how has literary imagination negotiated and accommodated the complex desires through the act of representation? These considerations form a broad exploratory backdrop for the rest of this book. In chapters 5 and 6, I focus primarily on two other influential writers in contemporary China, Yu Hua and Mo Yan. Noted for their innovation in both the art and the subject matter of representation—innovation that often tests the limits of the reader's aesthetic and moral sensitivity—the authors have been a Dionysian delight for critics at home and abroad. Translated widely into several foreign languages, their works have been regular items on college syllabi in the West, showcasing the wild, rebellious post-Mao literary spirit. The writers' popularity enjoyed a further boost with the release of cinematic versions of Mo Yan's *Red Sorghum* (1987) and Yu's *To Live* (1994), both directed by Zhang Yimo, who has received wide international acclaim. Both films became instant hits at a number of international film festivals.

I have selected from the authors' fiction the image of the traveler and that of the foreign Other as a counterpart of the Chinese self to reveal the multiple dimensions in the imagining of the post-Mao self. Responding to a variety of imperatives, which I spell out later in the analyses, the formulation of the self must pluralize to address concerns of present and past, national and international alike. Unlike in Han Shaogong's and Can Xue's worlds, where the subject often operates against a dehistoricized background, thus becoming an idea of the self at a more abstract level, the images in Yu Hua's and Mo Yan's creations have much more concrete connections with history. Closely associated with the country's continual journey forward and its constant concerns about its position in the world, the traveler and the foreign Other are discursive categories deeply embedded in the historical imagination of both modern and contemporary China. Consequently, my interpretative strategy in these two chapters is to accentuate the images' ties with both the post-Mao context and long-standing issues in modern literary and intellectual traditions. The traveler and the foreign Other were no doubt generated by the authors to respond to the challenges and exigencies of the reform era, but neither the images themselves nor the impulses that animated them were unique to the post-Mao period. We can trace their emergence to the eventful late nineteenth century, after China entered the modern era. Having been worked and reworked by Chinese intellectuals at pivotal moments since then, the images have accrued meanings that, echoing their own discursive history with variations, reach beyond their individual moment of deployment, becoming part of a historical continuum. The current chapter explores the image of the traveler on the post-Mao journey. Focusing on Yu Hua's "Blood and Plum Blossoms" and "On the Road at Eighteen" in more detail, I also bring Zhaxi Dawa's prize-winning story "A Soul in Bondage" into the discussion.[1] Concerns about the postrevolutionary traveler apparent in Yu's stories also inform "Bondage." More important, the metafictional strategy adopted by Zhaxi Dawa introduces an intriguing dynamic into the politics of representation, allowing the author to address the anxieties about the writing self voiced by his colleague Yu Hua.

The Lonely Traveler Revisited in Yu Hua's Fiction

To put the trope of journeying into historical perspective, let me start with its transformation. Travel literature *(youji)* that shares borders with prose and poetry is a distinctive genre in Chinese tradition. Unlike ancient Western legends of explorers' encounters with the mysterious and unknown, narratives of travel in premodern China do not feature heroes and adventures or focus on individual actions and achievements. Rather, the natural scenery is the exclusive subject matter. Guided by the traditional cosmological view emphasizing harmony of the universe and the continuity between a person's subjective consciousness and the objective world, the traveler in *youji* seldom intrudes into his composition. The traveler's narrative attention is devoted to recording the environment and the natural wonders of the world in minute detail; he allows neither himself nor social vicissitudes any presence in his meticulously constructed account of the geographic characteristics of the natural landscape (Leo Lee 1985b, 282–283).

It was not until the beginning of the twentieth century that narratives of personal journeys highlighting the traveler's subjective experience in the social space became prevalent. The shift of representational interest to the fictional traveler and his travail, I would argue, had much to do with China's traumatic entry into the modern world. The realization of the country's weakness after repeated defeats by foreign powers forced China into undertaking a journey toward modernity in the late nineteenth century. But this epochal move could not be, and indeed was not, smooth. The rejection of the Confucian tradition, prolonged internal and external strife, and finally the repressive and volatile Communist rule since 1949 have combined to make the national journey tortuous and unpredictable. In times of such dramatic reconfiguration of national identity and social values, the individual was the most profoundly affected. The radical reorientation brought both hope and frustration, joy and pain to the sojourner on the national journey, whose position and moral responsibilities in the rapidly changing world were anything but clear-cut and stable. Nation building and personal growth, as a result, became intertwined. Indeed, nothing could better capture the chaos and confusion emanating from China's collective venture than the trope of traveling, with its intrinsic emphasis on disloca-tion, change, and the attendant possibilities of danger and ambiguity. In the hands of modern Chinese writers, journeying became a symbolic action of progression that gauged the individual's vertiginous experience. Thus, a study of stories of the traveler can reveal to us the trajectory of development of the modern self at various stages of the national journey.

Leo Ou-fan Lee's 1985 essay "The Solitary Traveler: Images of the Self in Modern Chinese Literature" is such an inquiry. Taking examples from semi-autobiographical and fictional travel stories produced from the late Qing through the Communist era, Lee perceives certain patterns in the portrayal of the traveler, dating the dawning of the traveler's self-consciousness from Liu E's *Lao Can youji* (Travels of Lao Can, 1903–1906). A doctor by profes-sion and a knight-errant by disposition, the itinerant scholar roams both the natural and social landscapes of his time, interspersing lyricist pursuits with chivalric feats. Helping the poor and battling injustices and government cor-ruption along the way, the late Qing traveler engages the human world as much as he explores its natural surroundings. If Lao Can feels comfortable in his social, cultural milieu, the hapless traveler in May Fourth literature is culturally and ideologically alienated from society after he has destroyed its Confucian idols. Represented by the agonized and sentimental "I" in Yu Dafu's stories, the solitary soul on the road projects his individual personal-ity and inner chaos onto the objective reality, turning his journey into a record of his futile attempts to cope with modern life. In the travel accounts by Shen Congwen and Ai Wu in the 1930s and 1940s, the search for the meaning of life and society extends from the person's internal turmoil to external realities. While Shen pours out his anxieties about modernization and the erosion of innocent rural culture in his nostalgic memories of the hinterland of western Hunan, Ai vents his anger and indignation in his harsh indictment of the social vices he witnessed on his trips to the south. The antagonism between the subjective self and a hostile environment even-tually disappears in Communist fiction by Ai Wu, Hao Ran, and Wang Meng. Ideologically conformed, the self-effacing traveler now embarks eagerly on "the pilgrimage along the road to socialism" (Leo Lee 1985b).

Since Lee's study, the lonely individual on the road has continued to appear on the contemporary literary scene. The stories by Yu Hua and

Zhaxi Dawa—"Blossoms," "On the Road," and "Bondage"—offer us a glimpse of the experiences of the postrevolutionary traveler. All three stories portray young travelers on a mission imposed by parental authority. The journey as a result not only becomes a quest the youngsters either do not understand or are estranged from, but it also turns out to be an assignment with grave consequences. Examined together, the stories constitute a meaningful allegory of Chinese youths' frustrating relationship with the post–Cultural Revolution journey they were obligated to take but for which they were ill-prepared. I start with Yu Hua's stories. I focus on the new traveler's incompetence in a carnivalesque era when the Communist ideology faced serious rivalry from other emerging nonorthodox social expressions. This incompetence, I contend, is induced by the self's confinement within an imaginary reality superimposed on its consciousness by a fixed discursive system. As a result, the self on the contemporary journey becomes a solitary soul who is precluded from a negotiation for social space. In order for us to grasp the historical specificity of this experience, I situate the fictional hiker within a pervasive ethos of impatient progress, agitated geographical movement, and a growing multiplicity of social trends in the postrevolutionary world. During the course of my discussion, I also hope to identify a shift in narrative energy from recording immediate social realities, such as the poverty, hunger, and social alienation characteristic of the modern stories analyzed by Lee, to a heightened post-Mao awareness of the essential role of discourse in the construction of individual subjectivity.

Yu Hua was born in 1960 and began writing fiction when he was twenty-three. His first story, "Stars" (Xingxing), appeared in the January issue of *Beijing wenxue* in 1984. Since the publication of "On the Road," in 1987, he has attracted considerable attention, owing mostly to his rejection of literary conventions in his creation of an insane human world. Critics in general have been intrigued by Yu Hua's penchant for portraying violence done to the human body.[2] The writer has penned a collection of the goriest and most disquieting images in post-Mao literature: human butchery turned into a meat market, uncanny family murders, anatomical dissections, cruel and yet curiously unfeeling self-mutilation, to list a few. What is even more shocking is that, divorced from the usual elements that give structure and meaning to human experience (including violence)—history, politics, ideology, love, and romance—the desire that propels much of the internal destructive acts in Yu Hua's narratives is often gratuitous and unintelligible. (*To Live*, a family story entangled with the social upheavals of modern China, is one of a few notable exceptions.) It seems as if before the century could run its course, all the turbulence, devastation, and rage that the Chinese had experienced in the previous hundred years and that had been rationalized and justified in terms of morality and ideology were determined to come out in their most naked form in Yu's writing, to protest the normative values that made them signify in the past.

Critics have also noted that the disembodiment of the human being in Yu's fiction works hand in hand with a textual dismemberment, a dissolution of representational conventions at all levels, in structure, point of view, logic, and semantics (Li Tuo 1990; Zhu Wei 1990; Chen Sihe 1992; Guan 1994; Jones 1994; M. Wagner 1997–1999). They have identified the power of Yu Hua's writing in its probing into subjective truth through memory and its questioning of the relationship between language and verifiable reality. As Yiheng Zhao puts it, "Yu Hua is most interested in the meaning constructing systems in Chinese culture, and [is] also the one who shows the strongest awareness in subverting them" (Yiheng Zhao 1991, 419). As a result, past and present, history and fiction, truth and concoction, reason and unreason coil around each other in Yu's fiction, confounding our expectations of certainty and decency. The two types of violence, physical and meaningless in the characters' daily lives and representational in the disorder (or new order) of writing, pair up in a grotesque dance to puzzle, horrify, and fascinate us. Yu Hua's radical approach to such normative categories as history, memory, human desire, language, and reality is not just a subversion of the Maoist discourse; by simply banishing its principles from the territory of human action and denying them interpretive privileges, it poses a great threat to the Enlightenment philosophy that has argued vehemently for the rationality and dignity of the human being and its place in history. Confronted by the joint insurgence of corporeal and representational violence, the orderly humanist vision that relies on a rational mind and a predictable language to both make sense of the world and make claims about the world collapses.

The critical response to Yu Hua's fiction has done much to unravel his disconcerting and enigmatic world. But critics tend either to subsume individual experience under the author's experimentation with and challenge to familiar literary traditions as a writer with a (post)modernist stance, or attribute the ineffectuality of the self to an all-encompassing chaos accompanying social progress. In their comments on "On the Road," Xiaobing Tang and Wendy Larson place the character's perplexing experience in a modernizing and "illogical" post-Mao world in which "all existing language and meaning systems are shown to be incapable of explaining and containing individual experience" (Xiaobing Tang 1993, 14).[3] In my reading of the two stories, I emphasize the self's own failure in creating new subject positions, thereby expanding my discussion of the issue of agency in the representation of the post-Mao self. I argue that Yu Hua is not simply vigilant about literary conventions as a writer facing narrative choices but lands his characters in the interactions between competing value systems. The sense of frustration aptly pointed out by Tang and Larson thus testifies to the inability of the self to exercise its active agency for survival in the age of reforms.

The New Long March

Both "Blossoms" and "On the Road" are about a young man's journey. Yu Hua's choice of travel as a defining motif in exploring the experience of the self in the post-Mao era should not be seen as the mere adoption of a convenient literary device. His travel stories produce a powerful social resonance when placed in the prevalent discourse of journeying in contemporary China. If the May Fourth belief in an inevitable national journey was individually expressed by various pioneering thinkers and writers, the post-Mao version of the Great Leap Forward mentality was officially cultivated.[4] As discussed in my introduction, in the aftermath of the open renunciation of the Cultural Revolution and many previous leftist positions, the Party was faced with an ideological vacuum of its own creation and an ensuing legitimacy crisis. When class struggle, with which the CCP justified its leadership, was declared to have been a grievous miscalculation of social reality from 1949 onward, the Party lost the ideological center it had relied on to rally the people. It needed to relocate its sphere of operations and redefine its role. How to overcome the accumulated popular cynicism and rechannel social energy presented a fresh challenge to the new regime. At the historic third plenum of the Eleventh Central Committee (1978), the Party announced a "shift in focus" from class struggle to economic modernization, a project cast in the official language as a "New Long March."[5]

The ambitious journey ahead required the cooperation of every individual. To ensure devotion and reaffirmed trust from the people, the new Central Committee adopted a series of corrective measures ending in a large-scale reversal of verdicts. As a result, the symbolic, political journey took on concrete forms involving an amazingly large percentage of the population. Hundreds of thousands of people exiled for ideological reasons came back.[6] The initial travelers who benefited from the political readjustments were soon succeeded by those who took advantage of the Party's new economic policies, which, for the first time in Chinese Communist history, encouraged the pursuit of wealth and family life, deemphasizing egalitarian goals. Inspired by the much-publicized official slogan "Some will get rich first," the more enterprising among the populace quickly took to the road. The loosening of the household registration system also helped make geographical relocation possible in the 1980s.[7] The busy travelers included private business owners, new settlers to the booming coastal regions[8] and the surplus rural workforce, estimated at over two million in 1995, which flooded urban centers in search of jobs in factories, construction, and small enterprises and private homes.[9] The "floating population" of China reached one hundred million by the mid-1990s (Zhao Yibing 1995). In other words, one in every twelve Chinese lived away from his or her place of permanent residence.

Geographical mobility in post-Mao China extended beyond the country's borders as well. Along with the introduction of modern technology and the relaxation of restrictions on foreign travel, official exchange programs with universities and institutions in the West and Japan resumed. At the same time, many college graduates chose to further their education abroad at their own expense or on scholarships provided by foreign universities. The outward flow, however, did not consist solely of students and scholars. It included movie stars, artists, and scientists, as well as legal and illegal immigrants from all walks of life. According to official statistics, between 1979 and 1995 more than 3.33 million people were permitted to go abroad for various reasons.[10]

On the ideological level, these multifarious comings and goings involve a rupture with the past, a reconsideration of moral principles and collective and individual priorities. They have greatly added to the social dynamic, unleashing repressed desires, generating various forms of resistance, and producing a proliferation of independent expressions through which new values vie to assert themselves. A sensitive discursive practice, literature not only constitutes a potent voice in itself but also brings to a head, within the dialogic text, the interaction of social thought in the individual's experience. The two stories I analyze in the following pages are a significant case in point.

The Disengaged, Involuntary Avenger

The protagonists in both "Blossoms" and "On the Road" are young men. Yu Hua's selection of a youth as the fictional hero, as a number of critics have noted, is symptomatic of the youth mentality in contemporary China: upon the disintegration of the paternalistic social order, people were left to survive on their own (Wang and Xiao 1989; Xiaobing Tang 1993, 12–13). The self portrayed in the two stories thus best represents those of more or less the same age as the protagonists, young people in their late teens or early twenties who grew up in the social turmoil of the Cultural Revolution and the confusion of the reform era. In order to clarify the unique experience of the post-Mao traveler and its literary representation, let me first briefly comment on the modern creation of the traveler discussed by Leo Ou-fan Lee.

The travelers Lee analyzes have some common features. First, in spite of different postures in relation to society, each self is nonetheless situated in the immediate social environment—for example, that of acute poverty, chaos, and social injustice in Yu Dafu's and the young Ai Wu's stories and socialist construction and post-Mao retrospection, respectively, in Hao Ran's and Wang Meng's fiction. Second, to varying degrees the road stories are fictionalized accounts of the authors' real-life experiences (*Golden Road* by Hao Ran is an exception). Yu Dafu traveled a great deal in the 1920s; Shen Congwen's *Xiangxing sanji* (Random sketches on a trip to Hunan) and Ai Wu's *Nanxing ji* (Accounts of a southern journey) are products of the authors' visits to the region; and Wang Meng returned to Beijing after being exiled to Xinjiang for nearly twenty years. The narrative emphasis of these writers' travel stories is on their personal encounters. The authors' attitude toward language, the means by which they retain their memories of the journeys, tends to be innocent in the sense that whether they focus on their own subjective thoughts or the more objective documentation of society, they treat language as a competent instrument that enables them to keep track of their educational experiences. Language, therefore, is not a primary reality deserving comment in its own right but a tool for the writer to reach and present the social reality in which the self is lodged.[11] These two characteristics serve as my reference point in discussing the new direction in Yu Hua's treatment of the traveler.

Similar to those modern literary travelers cited in Lee's essay, the youth in Yu Hua's contemporary fiction remains a lonely figure. But he is lonely not because he is on the road by himself or because he is emotionally alienated from society, as had been the case with most of his fictional precursors. The earlier traveler's realization of his alienation, one can argue, comes as a result of the self's involvement in the social world, whereas the loneliness of his contemporary counterpart is induced by his disconnection from society.

This is most immediately obvious in "Blossoms," a story ostensibly written in the form of *wuxia xiaoshuo,* knight-errant fiction. At the age of twenty, the hero, Ruan Haikuo, is sent on a journey by his mother to avenge his father, Ruan Jinwu, a martial arts master who mysteriously died fifteen years before. The story's journey takes place in a purely natural world of rivers, mountains, and jungles cut off from any social activity. Only four people with some significance to the development of the plot cross Ruan Haikuo's path; his encounters with them are brief and limited to the exchange of a couple of sentences. In the end it turns out that two of them, the Lady of the Rouge and the Black Needle Knight, are seeking revenge on the same people who murdered Ruan Haikuo's father. But the essential reason for their animosity is not mentioned. Also missing from Yu Hua's world are human feelings. The protagonist seems to be living in an emotional void, neither eager to fulfill nor nervous about his mission. When he finds out after three years of wandering in the wilderness that his father's enemies have died at the hands of the Lady of the Rouge and the Black Needle Knight, all he feels are confusion and puzzlement. As a consequence, the moralistic stance, the interest in human affairs, and the righteous indignation at social injustice rife in modern stories are entirely absent. The traveler and his journey in "Blossoms," then, cannot be fully understood and analyzed within the same humanistic framework that has accommodated their predecessors.

To read "Blossoms" we need to move to the metafictional level. Yiheng Zhao holds that "Blossoms" is a generic parody of martial arts fiction. It satisfies the conventions by sending the protagonist on a knightly journey to avenge his father. Yet the metalanguage—the noble sentiment behind the mission—is totally absent from the young man's emotional makeup. Thus, "revenge without hatred, executed via conventions but without motivation turns the story into a dejecting process of desemanticization" (Yiheng Zhao 1991, 419). We can add to Zhao's list of parodied conventions that of the bildungsroman. The trope of journeying as a quest and an educational experience requires development and closure. The writer, however, denies the character any moral maturation and the reader the satisfaction of seeing the revenge rightfully achieved through the great show of kung fu usually expected in such a potentially sensational story involving murder and retribution. Without even having to face his father's enemies, Ruan Haikuo has his mission preempted. The journey is a wasted effort, since neither temporal nor spatial movement has been able to impart any meaning to it. By virtue of their very absence and vacuity, the generic principles are paradoxically made even more conspicuous as sets of ethical and narrative conventions.

To pursue the issue further, we need not limit the collapse of humanistic concerns and the preoccupation with conventions in the story to a writer's formal approaches to literary representation. We should also consider the fictional character's own participation in the process of meaning production. Through his characters' experience, Yu Hua pinpoints the practice of discourse as the site of self-constitution for post-Mao youth. Inevitably involved in the journey theme is the question of identity, which Yu Hua examines through the individual's relationship with existing meaning systems. His traveler characteristically bears a false identity and is consequently alienated from it. Ruan Haikuo in "Blossoms" lives in an imagined relationship to himself, for although his sole identity is as a traveler, he is not the initiator of his journey; he is a reluctant wayfarer packed off totally unprepared. Ruan Haikuo as a traveler with a mission is rooted in his mother's memory, itself deeply entrenched in the past. For fifteen years, the mystery surrounding her husband's death has preoccupied Ruan Haikuo's mother, who has been unsuccessful in unraveling it. Not only does the mother refuse to let go of the past, but she insists on her son's participation in it. To instill her memory into Ruan Haikuo's mind, the mother "described to him the moment [she discovered her husband's body] fifteen years ago in a voice of the past" (Yu Hua 1996, 183).[12] The old woman's purpose in adopting the "voice of the past" in telling Ruan Haikuo about his father is to intensify the hold of her memory on his consciousness, compelling him to share her imagination with her. The moment Ruan Haikuo is led into the talk of revenge, he starts to fulfill a preconceived role in his mother's scheme.

The mother's tormented imagination thus becomes Ruan Haikuo's present, his lived reality. Walking along the road, Ruan Haikuo often has the feeling that "he had walked through another memory" (Yu Hua 1996, 185). The journey by means of which Ruan Haikuo should develop his genuine self is ironically turned into proof of his projected identity, locking him into a single, permanent subject-position. The protagonist has great trouble constructing his own memory. When he tries to recall what he has done on the journey, "there was only empty space where the memory should have been" (186). The "empty space" of his own memory taken up by his mother's obsession with revenge, Ruan's relationship to himself and to the world is foreordained and hard to escape. Whenever he runs into people on the road, the young man is forced to keep his mission fresh in his mind. On his chance meetings with the Lady of the Rouge and the Black Needle Knight, they invariably ask him where he is going, invoking in his mind's eye the scene of the blazing cottage in which his mother burned herself to death after seeing him on his way.

Even though Ruan Haikuo is forced into this imagined role, his integration with it is highly problematic. The character's alienation from his created identity is evident in a series of ironies underlying the execution of his mission. We are told that "without so much as an inkling of the skills required of a swordsman, Ruan Haikuo shouldered the celebrated Plum Blossom Sword in order to find and take his revenge on the men who had killed his father" (Yu Hua 1996, 184). The young man is neither psychologically nor physically prepared for the task assigned to him. The absurdity of the situation, in addition, lies in the tension between the formal assumption of the theme of journeying and its realized content. The apparent urgency and seriousness of the goal-oriented pursuit are canceled out by the protagonist's confusion and aimless wandering. The constant use of such words as *wu bian wu ji* (boundless), *kongkong dangdang* (empty), *xuwu* (illusory), *manyou* (roaming), and *bu you zi zhu* (helpless) points to the journey as an utterly purposeless project whose moral and emotional underpinnings are unassimilable to the traveler. Ruan Haikuo has no control over where he is going and often forgets "which direction he had planned to take" (185). He feels "like a leaf floating helplessly across the surface of a pool" (188). When he finally has a chance to discover the identity and whereabouts of his father's enemies from a Daoist priest, he misses the opportunity by putting other people's questions before his own.

Thus, Yu Hua's traveler is set on a journey with an imposed identity to which he cannot relate. The final fulfillment of Ruan Haikuo's mission, according to his mother's design, is for him to add to the sword one more bloodstain from his father's enemies, thereby bringing the number of bloodstains to a hundred and proving himself his father's successful avenger. Ruan Haikuo is aware that the hunt for his father's foes is "tantamount to going in search for his own funeral" (Yu Hua 1996, 199). The completion of the mission could lead to a total destruction of the traveler himself, enclosing the young man as part and continuation of the legendary memory of his father. Such an outcome would have perpetuated his imagined relationship to himself, physically eliminating all possibility of establishing a true identity of his own.

Taken on its own, the story might be seen as an instance of a writer's experimentation with literary conventions. But when the story is located against the background of the New Long March, the grand discourse guiding all social movements in the post-Mao era, its allegorical thrust becomes apparent. That the writer invokes the trope of journeying only to simultaneously subvert it by distancing the traveler from the moral and emotional motives of the pursuit is particularly poignant. The traveler's detachment from the imperatives of the trip he is destined to take and his inability to meet its expectations place him in an ironic relationship to the journey, whose success is predicated on his meaningful participation. The hiatus between the post-Mao journey of great social urgency and the traveler's detached, opaque self-consciousness inevitably throws doubt on the effectiveness of the journey and the competence of the young traveler to complete it.

The Disillusioned Traveler

The fascination with the self in the grip of an alienating preconception likewise underlies Yu Hua's "On the Road," the story of a misadventure of "conventional logic" (Larson 1993, 185–187). Like Ruan Haikuo in "Blossoms," the traveler here emerges as an unsuspecting victim of predetermination. As a result, he is unable to make sense of the world when his only means of self-expression is destroyed. This misadventure reveals the young traveler's limited choice of self-representation and, ultimately, the author's distress at the paralysis of the self in a changing reality because of its lack of exposure to the divergent social languages active in post-Mao China.

"On the Road" describes an eighteen-year-old's first day on a journey his father has sent him on to experience the world. The title of the story, "Shiba sui chumen yuanxing," immediately juxtaposes *chumen* (leaving home) and *yuanxing* (going on a long journey)—home and the world. It is a journey from the known to the unknown, from adolescence to adulthood. The trip, then, is one of self-discovery. Though the young man in "On the Road" has no preset goals, he is by no means a free wanderer: he soon discovers that his interlocutive incompetence to operate outside his familiar beliefs turns the journey into a disaster.

The youth's language and mentality are dominated by conventional logic that is manifest in the images through which he regards himself and the world. Carefree and in high spirits when he leaves home in the morning, he compares the undulating mountain roads he walks on to waves of the sea and himself to a sailboat. Such clichés (sea, boat, and voyage) are the only means of expression the young traveler is comfortable with, and his way of dealing with reality is to trim it to his own terms. The youth associates the clouds and mountains he sees with his acquaintances, amusing himself by calling out to the natural objects the nicknames of those they remind him of. By giving himself a naming power with interpretive authority, thus creating a comforting connection between himself and the unknown world, the young man is trying to familiarize the unfamiliar. He resorts to the same strategy when he actually meets people: using the hackneyed term *laoxiang* (people from the same area) to address them, the traveler attempts to draw the strangers into an imagined and desirable fellowship with himself, falsifying the new reality as an extension of his previous environment.

But the traveler's self-sufficient world is disrupted as soon as he comes into close contact with other people, and the limit of his communicative ability becomes apparent. Each time he puts his language to work, he encounters totally unexpected results. Spotting a truck loaded with apples, the traveler thinks happily that it can take him to a hotel. He starts his conversation with the truck driver (a *laoxiang* to him) and offers the man a cigarette in an effort to establish a relationship. When the driver finally takes the cigarette, the youth eagerly lights it up for him, confident that the driver's acceptance of his cigarette will guarantee him a ride. To his great surprise, the driver pushes him aside rudely when he asks for it. The traveler then forces his way into the truck and yells at the driver, fully prepared for a fight. Yet the driver smiles at him in a friendly manner and starts to chat with him, telling him anecdotes about himself. Later, a group of local people come and loot the truck when it breaks down, making off with the apples after taking the truck apart. While this is going on, the driver, though the owner of both the vehicle and the truckload of apples, looks on with indifference and amusement.

As Xiaobing Tang (1993) comments, Yu Hua's story offers "a historical experience that constantly brings to crisis all given traditions and expectations" (12). To the young man's logical mind, the world operating on principles incomprehensible to him becomes illogical. What is notable here is, first, that the world appears irrational only to the youth; the rest—the peasants and the driver, the robbers and the robbed—seem to accept one another readily: when his truck is being looted, the driver strolls nearby as if nothing unusual is taking place. Second, the world further defies conventional reason because the traveler's attempts at producing meaning simply lead to violence: when the peasants start to load the apples into their baskets, the youth tries to stop them and is hit in the face and has his nose broken. Then more people arrive with tractors to get their share. Despite his surprise at the truck driver's lack of concern, the youth, guided by his own morals, throws himself at the mob, calling them bandits. This time he is severely beaten. But what angers the young man more than the physical violence done to him is that when he shouts at the driver to call his attention to the robbery, the driver, amused by the sight of his bleeding nose, responds with hearty laughter. As the last group of peasants is leaving after picking the truck clean, the driver jumps onto their tractor, taking the youth's red backpack with him and keeping up his loud, derisive laughter. The series of incomprehensible actions essentially demonstrates a dissolution of the traveler's language. Its failure to generate a "signified" that can be shared by both him and his "addressees" reduces it to an empty sign system with meaningless symbols.

Thus, on his short journey, the youth is rudely deprived of his false confidence in himself. At the end of the day, the formerly buoyant boy does not "even have the strength for anger" (Yu Hua 1996, 9). His experience on the road proves not only the young man's limited options and his gross ignorance of the world but also his inability to mingle with a changing crowd. As absurd as the day's events may appear to us, they have strong social and historical resonance. Xiaobing Tang (1993) has noted the different modes of transportation represented in the story—the truck as the most advanced technology as opposed to the lesser means, the tractor and the bicycle. What is obvious in this "distinct historical moment of incomplete modernization" (19) is that all the characters are on the move, fitting embodiments of the frenzied migration of the 1980s. The story also captures the distinctive mood of the social journey. The spatial movements here are confused and directionless. The protagonist is unconcerned about where he is heading. He catches a ride on a truck going in the opposite direction from which he has been walking, but he does not care because all he and the driver have to do is "keep driving" (Yu Hua 1996, 6). Similarly, all others in the story seem not to know where they are headed. When the youth asks the pedestrians what lies ahead, they invariably reply, "You'll see when you get there." This uncertainty and indifference, which tend to reduce all physical motion to the blind imperative of the journey, stand witness to the pervasive fluster and hesitation along the New Long March in post-Mao China. The Party's blueprint of a "socialism with Chinese characteristics" is at best a sketch using the most general terms. As Deng Xiaoping put it in vivid though not very elegant terms *"mozhe shitou guohe"* (feeling your way over the river stone by stone), neither the policymakers nor the people can be fully prepared for the complexities of the onrush of modernization. The introduction of Western ideas, the weakening of central political control, and the practice of a market economy brought about not only tremendous progress but also complicated problems, such as accelerating inflation, high consumption, low economic efficiency, a decline in public morals, and widespread government corruption.[13] In the face of rapid social transformation, official policies have had to be constantly adjusted to accommodate unforeseen possibilities and new developments. The future for many people remains a matter of "you'll see when you get there."

The different forms of transportation in the story and the restless movement also point to a detotalizing tendency in contemporary China. Communist ideals, though still nominally endorsed as the official guideline, can no longer monopolize social thought.[14] Older and newer institutions and practices clash with each other. Post-Mao journeys are no longer infused with the kind of idealistic comradeship the Communist hero Gao Daquan (in Hao Ran's *Golden Road*) fosters in his collective venture. For many travelers, the goal seems to be the pursuit of self-interest at the expense of others. In the story the peasants' tractors are transformed from farm machines to a means of transferring the truck driver's property to the new owners. What is more, the youth and his so-called *laoxiang* are not fellow travelers. The mob's demolition of the truck, taking its tires off in particular, can only be understood as a plan to destroy its mobility, to exclude it from the journey. Selfless camaraderie is a thing of the past along this route.

"On the Road" suggests that its young traveler's conventional understanding of the world belongs to an outdated ideological position. When the youth leaves home, his father gives him a red backpack, which can be interpreted as the youth's cultural and ideological heritage from the older generation—all his instruction and training, his language, his manner of thinking, his knowledge of the world, and his strategy for dealing with it. The color red alludes to the revolutionary nature of this heritage (Xiaobing Tang 1993, 14 n. 8). The youth's identification with this red bag is clear not only in his realization that the backpack is his sole personal possession in the world but also in that his memory of the sunny morning when his father sends him on his way invokes a certain comfort and nostalgia in his mind. The youth's day on the road, however, shows the deficiency of such a system to interpret and survive in the symphony of discordant social voices. In the story, as I have mentioned, the truck driver snatches away the young man's knapsack, apparently without his knowledge.

Confronted by a reality outside his interpretative possibilities, the youth is totally powerless. Since he only has a fixed monodiscourse under his command, he is unable to function beyond his exclusive system. The youth is reduced to silence. The second time he is beaten up by the mob, he opens his mouth to cry but finds that "nothing came out" (Yu Hua 1996, 9). The loss of his red backpack further symbolizes the destruction of the youth's "voice." Left alone with the dismantled truck in the mountains, the traveler has to admit to himself that he has nothing left. Significantly, during the robbery no exchange of words is heard or attempted (Xiaobing Tang 1993, 15). When newly surfaced heterogeneity has rendered all extant orthodoxy obsolete, verbal communication is no longer attainable between parties sharing no common discursive ground. As a result, unnameable violence becomes the radical means of human contact. Moreover, the young man's red baggage seems to be the ultimate object of the attack. During the violence, the suggestive "red blood" is twice mentioned in relation to the traveler's bleeding nose, the repeated target of the blows. But instead of rousing any sympathy, the red blood flowing from the young man's smashed nose gives the truck driver much pleasure. Thus, through the driver's mocking laughter, the absurdity and fragility of the traveler's outmoded revolutionary ideology are ridiculed.

The solitude of Yu Hua's traveler on the immediate level is physical. When everyone is gone, the young man crawls back into the truck, which he now identifies with himself. Just as he is badly battered, the truck is also a wreck, its windshield, running boards, and tires stripped away. Like the young man himself, stranded on his journey, the truck is unable to move anywhere. The youth finally realizes that the hotel he has been longing to find is right there in front of him, in the immobile truck.

On a deeper level, the youth's solitude is semantic and spiritual. The dysfunction of his language, the unconditional loss of meaning in his signifying system, shuts the traveler off from the world. Without a common language, he cannot even enter into a dialogic relationship to negotiate with the rest of the world. He and the world are therefore mutually exclusive. What is more, Yu Hua's traveler's possible channels of support are blocked. In "Blossoms," as soon as Ruan Haikuo is on the road, his mother sets fire to their house and throws herself into it. It dawns on the character that "in the months and years to come, there would be no home to which he could return" (Yu Hua 1996, 184). Similarly, having handed the youth the backpack, the father in "On the Road" fades out of the protagonist's consciousness until he has fully experienced meaningless violence. By then the happy home, where the father lives, becomes an insubstantial memory. The traveler is left absolutely alone in an incomprehensible world. The series of identifications in "On the Road"—the self with the truck, the truck with the hotel, therefore the self with the hotel as the sole source of warmth and protection—confirms the utter loneliness of the young man. He can find shelter only in himself.

Yu Hua's demonstration of the self ensnared in an alienating discourse is indicative of both post-Mao writers' alertness to the power of meaning systems in constructing individual consciousness and their anxiety over how much signifying authority they can claim in a society that is quickly becoming a site of conflictual social interests. The fervent literary activity in China in the 1980s was the burst of creative energy newly freed from the restrictions of the Communist ideological codes. The imperative to be innovative, however, was caused by the writers' desire to prove to society and to themselves that they could produce literature independent of official guidelines. But the need to prove their productivity can also be seen as stemming from the writers' apprehension that their limited discursive options under Communist rule may have indeed crippled their creative ability and limited their vision. This is, of course, a legitimate concern of greater urgency for writers of Yu Hua's age. Yu Hua was only six when the Cultural Revolution began. During the impressionable early teens of Yu Hua's generation, the dominant social ideology was the leftist extremism of the Cultural Revolution, whereas writers ten years older than Yu Hua had a somewhat richer literary experience. They had opportunities to read classical works and books from the Western and Russian critical realist traditions before they were thoroughly repudiated. Besides, for creative materials, they could (and many did) draw from their own eventful lives during the disastrous ten years of the Cultural Revolution. But all the younger generation inherited was an impoverished literary tradition and a postrevolutionary world ravaged by a decade of senseless destruction.[15]

The awareness of the paucity of previously available choices, the influx of modern Western literature, and reflections on their own complicity and gullibility during the Cultural Revolution prompted Chinese writers to focus on language and its predetermined discursive nature, making this an overarching characteristic of post-Mao fiction in general and of Yu Hua's writing in particular. The morals, ideological interests, and social involvement of the earlier travelers are displaced in Yu Hua's fiction by a deep consciousness of institutionalized language as an ultimate force shaping the individual's social identity. Consequently, an outstanding difference between Yu Hua and the modern writers discussed by Leo Lee is the narrative and thematic priorities Yu Hua gives language and its constructive power in his treatment of the traveler. Without a doubt, to challenge the cultural and philosophical tradition of old China was a clear objective of the rejuvenation project by modern intellectuals such as Liang Qichao, Chen Duxiu, Li Dazhao, and Lu Xun. But the May Fourth wariness of linguistic conventions gradually weakened under the pressing task of national salvation in the 1930s, when a large number of intellectuals joined the Communist camp. After Mao's 1942 "Talks on Literature and Art" dictated the foundation of the Party's literary policy, the authority to influence social perceptions was reserved as a "divine right" of the Party, whose numerous stringent political campaigns made literary dissent increasingly impossible and dangerous to pursue. Creative freedom had to wait until the postrevolutionary thaw.

Against the panorama of popular distrust for the official system in the 1980s, it becomes clear that the specific social reality Yu Hua's young traveler grapples with is the domination of a totalizing language over his subjectivity and the disintegration of his signifying power. Because his language is disturbingly inadequate, the youth appears in a conspicuously disadvantageous relationship to the discourses that condition his existence. He claims no agency and is not the organizing center of his own experience: he either lacks sufficient preparation to successfully perform the role he is assigned, or he is so restricted by his training that he becomes a dysfunctional outsider in the interplay of social forces. In Yu Hua's vision, the post-Mao self is in dilemma. It is a solitary being in an inevitably advancing social movement whose motivations, governing principles, and practices prove extraneous to its own ideological makeup, threatening to make it irrelevant to the latest stage of the national journey.

The Politics of Form:
The Double Journey in "A Soul in Bondage"

My preceding discussion reveals Yu Hua's serious concerns about the manipulative power of the dominant ideological tradition and its detrimental effect on the welfare of the young traveler on the post-Mao journey. Similar motifs appear in Zhaxi Dawa's "A Soul in Bondage." The Tibetan writer's story, however, has an interesting twist. Through a series of metafictional moves that create a story within the story, Zhaxi Dawa engages the authoritarian tradition in its major field of operation, that of discursive representation, refuting the official fiction on its own terms. This politics of form with contestatory power is what I explore in the following text, in addition to the image of the traveler.

Zhaxi Dawa, who was born in Chongqing, Sichuan province, to a Tibetan father and a Han mother, in 1959, spent most of his childhood with his mother's relatives in the city, traveling now and then to join his parents, working for the government in Tibet. After junior high school, he studied painting at the Tibet Exhibition Center and, at fifteen, started to work as a stage designer for the autonomous region's Tibetan theater. Zhaxi Dawa became a playwright of Tibetan drama at nineteen and later took a one-year course at the Chinese Opera Institute in Beijing. To his own recollection, he began to read fiction when he was only nine years old (Zhaxi Dawa 1989a). All Zhaxi Dawa's creations are about Tibet in the whirlpool of social changes in the modern era. His first story, "Reticence," appeared in the journal *Tibetan Literature* in 1979; he has been a member of Tibetan Writers' Association since 1986.

The story I discuss, "A Soul in Bondage," was published in *Tibetan Literature* in 1985. The plot develops with the help of a typical metafictional device popularized by the French *nouveau roman*—the *mise en abyme*, a structure involving a frame and an enclosed narrative (in other words, a text within a text or a story within a story) that accentuates the fictional nature of the narrative.[16] In the framing story of "Bondage," the narrator, a reporter and writer by profession, goes to Pabunaigang, a mountainous area in Tibet, to interview a ninety-eight-year-old Living Buddha. On his deathbed, the dying saint informs the narrator that two youngsters from Kangba have gone on a pilgrimage to find Shambhala, the legendary Ideal Land. To his great amazement, the narrator realizes that the Living Buddha is actually reciting word for word a story he once wrote but did not complete because he was not sure of his protagonists' destination when he drafted the story. Intrigued, the narrator goes home, retrieves the manuscript from his files, and makes it the centerpiece of "Bondage." The embedded centerpiece is a story of adventure. Jade, a Tibetan girl often home alone when her father goes on his storytelling tours, decides to run away with a stranger, Tabei, a young man on a journey. After months of aimless roaming, Tabei meets an old man in a village wine shop and admits to him that he does not know where he is heading. The old man assures the young traveler that he knows his destination—to look for Communism across the snowy mountains. After the meeting, Tabei sets on his way, leaving Jade behind to be the old man's daughter-in-law, as he has requested. The framing story resumes from here. After his interview with the Living Buddha, the narrator makes up his mind to travel into the mountains to look for his protagonists. He finds Jade there; the girl leads him to Tabei, who is dying in the so-called Palm-Print Land, allegedly made by the palm print of Padma-sambhava, an ancient Buddhist monk from India. Realizing his mistake in sending his characters on the disastrous journey, the narrator determines to start anew, bringing Jade with him out of the mountains.

In her analyses of Zhaxi Dawa's fiction, Lu Tonglin (1995) highlights the author's vision of Tibet as "an agglomeration of different value systems, such as Tibetan religion and tradition, Han culture, Communist ideology, and Western influences" (104). In the writer's search for a cultural identity of contemporary Tibet, Buddhism "gains its identity by negating the cultural and ideological domination of Communist China." The critic, however, also points out that religion is not exempt from the author's playful treatment and is on occasion identified with its counterpart, Communism (114, 115). It is this identification, or conflation, of these two ideological systems that I would like to emphasize in my reading of "Bondage." I would argue that in the author's metafictional design, Communism becomes a discourse of religion, a master-narrative with hegemonic, prescriptive power over its followers. In this light, I see the Living Buddha as an incarnation of autocratic, parental authority responsible for sending the young travelers on a journey of destruction and death, an echo of Yu Hua's vision of the post-Mao traveler, as I have pointed out in the previous section.

The Living Buddha is thus a central figure in "Bondage." Although he only appears in the frame, he dominates both parts of the narrative and plays a decisive role in the quest in the embedded story: he is the only person with definitive knowledge of the destination of the journey while neither the narrator who produces the story nor Tabei who embarks on the quest has any idea about the goal. The Living Buddha's power over the planning and completion of the journey is enforced by his literary double, the old man in the wine shop. The identification between the Living Buddha and the old man is proven by the fact that the saint insists in his talk with the reporter that it is he who had a conversation with Tabei in the tavern. Sure enough, after receiving directions from the old man, the frustrated young man heads for the Kalong mountains to look for the Ideal Land. Furthermore, at the end of the journey, it turns out that there are 108 knots on the leather cord used by the characters to keep track of time, the same number as the Buddhist rosary beads on the dying hero's wrist. In this way, the leather cord is linked to the Living Buddha as the spiritual leader, and the journey becomes, specifically, a pilgrimage under his guidance.

The fruitless quest in the embedded centerpiece, however, is not the only journey in the story. Examining carefully, we can find a parallel one, a literary quest carried out by the narrator-writer in the embedding. The narrator's statement that "I decided to return to Pabunaigang.... Perhaps I would encounter my protagonist again" (Zhaxi Dawa 1989b, 427) indicates that the framing narrative is written in a nontraditional, nonrealist mode. This self-reflexive statement in fact recalls another one made earlier by the narrator. On his way home after talking with the Living Buddha, the narrator tells us that he begins to "muse on the source of inspiration in creative writing" (417). As Wallace Martin (1986) points out, "when a writer talks about a narrative within that narrative, s/he has put it in quotation marks, so to speak, stepping beyond its boundaries. . . . Everything normally outside the narrative [is] being reproduced within it" (181).

When we put the narrator's two statements together, we can see that the framing story begins to take shape as an adventure of a story, a story in the making. Thus, the indeterminacy and dislocation of time and space noted by Lu Tonglin could also be read as an open display of the creative process, in which the producing agent, the writer, wonders aloud about the time, place, and identity of the characters in his story, a process ending with his admission of failure. Read in this light, the young travelers' frustration on the journey mirrors the uncertainty of their literary creator, who is unsure of his source of inspiration and the denouement of his story.

But, if "Bondage" were only to describe a botched literary attempt, would it not have been better if the author had kept it to himself? The act of publicizing what the narrator-writer considers a literary mistake therefore becomes significant, forcing us to take a closer look. Under scrutiny, some peculiar relationships emerge. Rereading the story, we realize that we are only partially correct in assuming that the narrator is the only author of the enclosed story of quest. There is another author—the Living Buddha, whose claim to authorship is made clear by his being the first person to narrate the story word for word to the narrator. The Living Buddha's knowledge of the narrator's unpublished story puts his status as a character into serious doubt, for he transgresses the boundaries of a character, intruding into the territory of the creative agent.

The special working relationship between the authors comes to light in the following passage where the two authors and the manuscript are mentioned:

> The Living Buddha began to recall the story of the young man and the woman who had come to Pabunaigang mountains, and the things they encountered on the way. As the story unfolded, I realized that I was listening to a tale I had written some time ago, and locked away in a trunk, without showing to anyone. Yet he seemed to be reciting the story word for word. The place was a village named A on the road to Pabunaigang. The time was 1984. There were only two characters: a young man and a young woman. *The reason I never showed the manuscript to anyone was that I did not know how to end the story. Now that the Living Buddha enlightened me, I knew.* The only difference was that at the end of my story the young man meets an old man in a tavern and it is the old man who tells him where he must go. I did not describe the way ahead. I could not because I did not know it at the time. *Yet, the Living Buddha claimed that it was he who showed the two*

young people the road they must travel. There was yet another coincidence: both the old man in the story and the Living Buddha spoke of the lines in the palm of the Lord of the Lotus' hand. (emphasis added, 417)[17]

As indicated here, the Living Buddha identifies the destination of the journey while the reporter repeatedly admits his ignorance. A few sentences later we are told that, taking leave of the Living Buddha, the narrator begins to meditate on the inspiration in literary creation. The relationship between the coauthors is thus clear: the Living Buddha supplies the "inspiration," and the reporter the "literary creation." In other words, the Living Buddha specifies the ultimate goal for the creative project and the reporter is to materialize it in a story. The actual manner in which the two authors produce the story attests to this hierarchical relationship: the Living Buddha dictates it (prescribing through saying), and the reporter writes it down.

The ultimate goal defined by the Living Buddha is the Ideal Land of Shambhala he tells the reporter about in the frame; it turns out in the centerpiece to be Communism, "the way ahead" pointed out by the old man in the tavern. This supreme goal apparently holds power over both the protagonist and his creator. After his encounter with the old man, Tabei seems to have finally gained a lucid idea how to continue the journey. Similarly, after being enlightened by the Living Buddha, the reporter produces his final draft of the embedded story. When the reporter first mentions it, he informs us that "I did not describe the way ahead. I could not because I did not know it at the time." But in the actual centerpiece, "the way ahead" is identified as Communism. The embedded story, as a result, appears to be an edited version of the manuscript locked away in the reporter's trunk. Thus, the enclosed eventually emerges as a story created under the instruction of the Living Buddha. Dictating what the writer should write and how his characters should act, the Living Buddha sends the narrator on a literary journey and the characters on a literal one.

The literary mode in which the narrator presents the centerpiece—a story of pursuit of Communism—in a way confirms his subjection to his designated mission: he adopts the realist form privileged by the Communist ideology and honors its fundamental organizing principle, the temporal imperative. Realist fiction, Patricia Tobin points out, "has Time at the center of both its inner process and outer form." Because we often think of human existence as a progress through action to knowledge, "Time inaugurates, sustains, and augments this movement toward completion" (Tobin 1978, 4–5). In the embedded account of quest, the linear movement of time is conveyed through the image of the leather cord used by the characters as a measurement of progression; each knot represents a day on the journey. By the time the characters have reached the village A, "The leather thong around Jade's waist was a mass of tight little knots" (Zhaxi Dawa 1989b, 424).

Yet this temporal imperative is not totally innocent. In the high order of literary realism, "merely chronological succession becomes informed with the operation of cause and effect," and "events in time come to be perceived as begetting other events within a line of causality similar to the line of generations" (Tobin 1978, 5, 7). As a result, the temporal imperative, Tobin argues, becomes closely associated with the genealogical power of the father and in the end turns into the "genealogical imperative," both metaphorically and literally, in realist fiction (3–28). Thus, in obeying the temporal imperative, realist fiction at the same time complies with the generational power of the father.[18]

In "Bondage" we indeed see such a parental power exercised in both parts of the story: through the old man in the wine shop in the embedded, and the Living Buddha in the embedding. The old man guides Tabei into resuming the search for Communism, a project the villagers failed to realize some twenty years before, not to mention that he wants Jade to be his daughter-in-law, literally assuming the role of father. Similar to the experience of Yu Hua's travelers, the grand objective set by the father figure informs the young man's very being. Tabei devotes himself to the endless journey without even knowing where it leads; he insists on Jade's participation when she tries to run away. Later, when the narrator is surprised to find Jade—whom he has left in the village A in his manuscript—in the Palm-Print Land, the girl tells her perplexed creator, "he [Tabei] took my heart and tied it to his belt. I can't live without him" (Zhaxi Dawa 1989b, 429). The "tied it to his belt" is too obvious for us to miss the reference to the leather cord with 108 knots, an image with Buddhist association. The leather cord that gives a concrete form to the temporal imperative in this way becomes a symbol of parental power, a symbol of bondage. The Living Buddha consequently turns into the very incarnation of Communism, a master-narrative of control that binds the younger generation to the high purpose laid down by the father.

The journey to realize the lofty goal is, however, a total disaster. In order to escape suffocating solitude in her life, Jade embarks on a seemingly promising journey with Tabei. But instead of living alone at home, Jade now travels through a deserted world with a reticent companion. For days she and Tabei would walk without spotting any human trace and without exchanging a word. Not knowing his destination, Tabei is also haunted by indescribable frustration. The farther they walk, the more lost he feels. "The village ahead would lose their original tranquility more and more; they would become noisy and clamorous. There would be the roar of machines, laughter, music, voices raised in joy and anger. He wanted none of those things. He wanted to get to . . ." (Zhaxi Dawa 1989b, 423). The truth is that the youngster does not know where he is heading. Tabei's blind commitment in the end leads to his death in the Palm-Print Land of Buddhist origin; the character literally dies in the hands of an authoritarian power that dispatches him on a journey of self-destruction.

In contrast, it is paradoxically through the very act of seemingly heeding the imperatives demanded by the master-narrative that the narrator-writer frees himself from the bondage. After observing closely the temporal, genealogical imperative, the narrator defeats it at its very core by denying the completion and maturity the movement of time should bring and by frustrating the "prospective design of the father" (Tobin 1978, 7). The story of adventure in the embedded section ends with no end, and the adventure of a story in the embedding concludes with the narrator's realization of his mistake and his resolve to restart his narrative. Thus, the narrator has appropriated the rules dictated by the master-narrative and turned them into a representational strategy, whereby he undermines its control, subjecting its supreme power to an ironic interpretation.

The *mise en abyme* technique is the very means by which "Bondage" achieves this subversive power. By producing for us in the embedded story a world destitute in its landscape and barren of meaningful human interaction, the narrator exposes the suppressive nature of the master-narrative that informs the journey: it is intolerant of heterogeneity and allows no dialogue. Moreover, through the metafictional "story-within-story" structure, the narrator deliberately draws our attention to the embedded text as a constructed "ideological narrative," in which "all actions of the characters can be presented as the products of a few very simple and very abstract rules" (Todorov 1971, 42)—blind faith in pursuit of Communism in the current story. This in turn enables him to spell out the context of the creation of the enclosed in the enclosing. Through this self-contextualization, in addition to a story within the story, the narrator has produced a story of the story (a story about the creation of a story). It is eventually in the story of the story, i.e., the frame, that Zhaxi Dawa exposes the fictive and arbitrary nature of the master-narrative responsible not only for imposing the quests on the narrator and his characters but also for the failure of the journey, as I will comment on momentarily.

The author makes it unequivocal that the journey in the story takes place in 1984. "Bondage" is thus invested with a profound skepticism about the "New Long March" under way in post-Mao China. By making Tabei retrace the steps of a calamitous journey attempted two decades before, a social project "no one cared to follow, no matter how hard things got" (Zhaxi Dawa 1989b, 426), the author seems to make no distinction between the pursuit of the official dream in the Mao and post-Mao eras. Thus juxtaposed, the young travelers' quest in 1984 becomes a reenactment of the failed endeavor of 1964. The old man who sends Tabei off into the mountains has to admit that "Everybody was talking about communism, but nobody knew what it was. They said, it was some kind of paradise" (425). He repeats the lack of assurance at the end of his talk with the young man, "That is only a legend. I don't really know whether it's true" (426). The renewed journey may well end in an empty "paradise" that allured Tabei's predecessors into misplacing their zeal in Communism in the mid-1960s.

In the conclusion of the story, Zhaxi Dawa envisions for us what the old man is unwilling to disclose about Communism. Despite its grand status, the doctrine is shown to be essentially a fiction or fantasy with no basis in real life. Not only does the Ideal Land originate in "a legend recorded in an ancient scripture," but the fictiveness of the master-narrative is laid bare by the nonrealistic world it is associated with. The snowy mountains beyond which the Palm-Print Land lies are the boundaries between the real world and the illusion of the "paradise." Once he has gone over the snowy mountains, the narrator discovers that the hands on his watch begin to "reverse... five times faster than normal" (Zhaxi Dawa 1989b, 428), a fact pointing back to the legendary source of the Ideal Land. The abnormal movement of time echoes the transformation of the landscape: it is no longer the familiar world of Tibet. There are peepul trees, elephants, and hot springs. The narrator is now in a world of fantasy.

But the fantastic world is only ephemeral. Waking up one morning, the narrator finds himself in the Palm-Print Land, a land of total desolation. It is here that the narrator meets his dying protagonist, Tabei. Regretting his mistake in sending the young man to such a land, the narrator makes his last revelation to Tabei, and to us: "I pressed my lips close to his ear and tried to tell him in words that he could grasp that the place he sought all his life did not exist any more than Thomas More's utopia" (Zhaxi Dawa 1989b, 429–430). The narrator finally makes it evident that this Ideal Land promised by the master-narrative has its roots in a work of fantasy created in the sixteenth century by Sir Thomas More, one of the beliefs that inspired Karl Marx's Communist theory.

In the final analysis, it is deeply ironic that Tabei, the unquestioning and most committed traveler, is destroyed by the very journey he faithfully undertakes. The skeptical reporter survives by challenging the discursive foundation of the hegemonic system. A post-Mao writer aware of both the manipulative power of official representations and his newly gained options, Zhaxi Dawa lodges the dominant fiction in a metafictional maneuver of his own design, laying bare its imaginative nature. By displaying itself as a story constructed under the imperatives set by the master-narrative, thereby turning itself into a narrative within the master-narrative, "A Soul in Bondage" makes clear that "the primary narrative is also (only) a sign, as any trope must be—but with added power, according to its stature: *I am literature, so is the narrative that embeds me*" (Dällenbach 1989, 57).

6 Mirror of the Self

The Foreign Other in Mo Yan's *Large Breasts and Full Hips*

The image of the traveler I analyzed in chapter 5 reveals the frustration and confusion experienced by the ill-prepared youth on the post-Mao journey of reforms. But this journey does not only involve the Chinese self. Just as in the initial stage of the national journey in the late nineteenth century, the post-Mao move toward modernity has also been designed and implemented under an acute awareness of the need to position China in an increasingly globalized environment. Opening its door to the outside world to establish strategic and economic ties with the West was at the basis of China's post-Mao reforms. Not only did international trade, foreign capital, and technology prove to be vital to China's economic growth, but the inflow of Western social theories and cultural practices has profoundly changed the society as well. As foreign investment and technology were redrawing the skylines of virtually every city in China, pop culture streaming in from the West and its Asian neighbors was redefining the country's ideological orientations. In this extensive transfer of technologies and ideas, the foreign Other, for better or for worse, became China's permanent travel companion in its advance toward the future.

But ever since its disastrous encounters with the foreign Other in the late imperial years, China has had an ambivalent and tumultuous relationship with it. For more than 150 years, the question of how to situate the native self vis-à-vis the West has preoccupied Chinese intellectual minds of various persuasions. The task was necessarily complicated because the foreign Other took on multiple identities. In the modern period, it was seen as both an aggressor inflicting shame and humiliation on the nation and a representative of a historically progressive force whose Enlightenment philosophy and advanced scientific knowledge could facilitate China's belated modernization. The alien Other, as a result, was to be simultaneously admired and feared, emulated and contained.[1] The complexity remained in the post-Mao era, when the rush to modernize and the influx of Western ideas and practices induced both appreciation and apprehension. The problem of how to configure the foreign Other in relation to the Chinese self, therefore, continues to be a subject of intellectual speculation.

In 1995 Mo Yan published a novel of nearly seven hundred pages, *Fengru feitun* (Large breasts and full hips). A conspicuous feature of this gigantic work is that its I-narrator is an illicit child born to a married Chinese woman and a Swedish missionary. Not only do the adultery and the birth of the bastard centralize the theme of legitimacy,[2] but the involvement of an alien man also intensifies the significance of this culturally and morally sensitive topic. Cutting across racial and national boundaries, individual indiscretion acquires a symbolic import in the novel, pushing the conflict between the native and the foreign Other to the forefront. An analysis of a complex, panoramic novel the length of *Fengru feitun* might explore many different themes. My focus in this chapter is on how the sexual transgression in *Fengru feitun* turns into an issue of national sovereignty and subsequently develops into a violent and intricate confrontation between the Chinese self and the foreign Other. I argue that this preoccupation with sexual propriety is informed with some latent anxieties toward the Chinese self. In particular, I discuss how the nationalist urge to disempower the foreign Other evolves when male sexuality is equated with self-identity, national dignity, and paternal authority to become the center of contention. My examination of the sexual politics underlying the conflict aims at bringing to light representational strategies that allow the author to contest the alien power over the symbolic female body while negotiating his ambivalence toward both the Chinese self and the foreign Other.

But first, Mo Yan's literary exploration of the relation between the native and the alien should be seen as part of a modern tradition. In their fascination with the West, represented by the European countries and the United States, Chinese intellectuals have proposed various formulas to understand and cope with the foreign Other. The self-strengthening movement in the wake of the calamitous Opium War yielded the famous slogan by Zhang Zhidong, *"zhongxue wei ti, xixue wei yong"* (Chinese learning for the fundamental principles, Western learning for practical application). In keeping with the movement's conservative position, the *ti-yong* (substance-application) configuration privileged China's traditional value system while acknowledging the superiority of the West in science and technology. Even though more radical reformers, such as Kang Youwei and Tan Sitong,

rejected the Confucian principles of "three bonds" (*san gang:* the relationship between prince and minister, father and son, husband and wife) and
"five constant virtues" (*wu chang:* benevolence, justice, politeness, wisdom,
and faithfulness), by radically reinterpreting ancient Confucian works and
painting Confucius as a champion of reform, they nevertheless clung to the
Confucian models of moral perfection of self and society and the "unity of
Heaven and man," hoping to find in them a foundation for China's social
modernization. Having witnessed the defeat of the self-strengthening
movement in the Sino-Japanese War, the abortion of the Hundred-Day
Reform at the turn of the century, and the disappointing republican revolution, the May Fourth intellectuals, on the contrary, completely lost faith
in the efficacy of the Confucian tradition. Identifying it as an obstacle to
the country's modernization and survival, the iconoclasts called for fundamental changes in people's thinking beyond pragmatic applications of
Western technology. The May Fourth intelligentsia opened up the suppressed Chinese self to the Western model, seeking to replace it with an
Enlightenment and romantic being of independent thinking, inner sensibility, and self-fulfillment.

Never absent from the Chinese consciousness since the modern revolution, the relation between China and the foreign Other once again
became a prominent issue in the mid-1980s, when Chinese intellectuals
were confronted with the urgent task of mapping out the possibilities of
the Chinese modern for the post-Mao reforms. Centering on the potential
of Chinese tradition in the modernization, the debates during the Cultural
Discussion in the mid-1980s generated an array of diversified positions. As
I discussed in chapter 2, while the majority maintained the traditional
approach of locating China's modernization in the dichotomy of China
versus the West, others proposed to view the modernizing process on a linear trajectory of China versus China through a reevaluation and rejuvenation of Chinese culture. Nevertheless, it could be argued that the desire to
re-present the dynamics was conceived as a result of a heightened awareness of the need to deal with the potent influence of the foreign Other in
China's quest for modernity. Of special interest to us here is Li Zehou's
reworking of the *ti-yong* theory, which merged the different emphases of
previous thinkers. Criticizing Zhang Zhidong for his simplistic separation
of *ti* (the substance of ideology) and *yong* (the application of science and
technology), Li extends *ti* to cover everything in people's social existence,
not only their way of thinking but also material production and daily life.
Since science and technology introduced from the West play an important
role in modernizing people's social existence (the *ti*), they do not belong to

the category of *yong,* as Zhang Zhidong proposes; rather, Li reasons, they fall into that of *ti,* substance (Li Zehou 1994a, 4:276). *Ti* having been thus redefined, *zhongti xiyong,* the critic concludes, should be reformulated as *xiti zhongyong: xiti,* social modernization via westernization; *zhongyong,* Sinificizing of Western thought and technology to meet China's own needs and wants (3:332, 337).

If visions of the modern in the 1980s privileged westernization, domestic changes in China and global politics a decade later subjected the approach to critical scrutiny. The mid-1990s saw the surge of a new nationalism characterized by a strong sense of national pride accompanied by equally strong anti-westernization and anti-U.S. sentiments. As scholars point out, many complicated reasons lay behind the rise of nationalism in the 1990s (Gungwu Wang 1996; Zheng 1999). The rapid growth of the Chinese economy after 1992 not only added to China's national strength, raising its status in international affairs, but it also built up the average citizen's sense of well-being and confidence. Making full use of the situation, the state encouraged and periodically appealed to the people's nationalist feelings, promoting patriotism as a strategy to command allegiance and enhance its legitimacy in an increasingly diversified society. Beyond its borders, China's rise to power, however, also led to misperceptions and growing tensions between China and the foreign powers (Tucker 2000; Cumings 2000). On the one hand, some in the West, in the United States especially, viewed China's growth as a threat to U.S. interests in East Asia and the balance of power in the region and advocated policies to contain China.[3] On the other, suspicious of the West's willingness to see China develop into a world power and resentful of foreign interference in China's domestic affairs over such issues as Taiwan, Tibet, Hong Kong, and human rights through what they saw as anti-China technological embargoes and economic sanctions led by the United States, many Chinese were convinced of U.S. intentions to antagonize and demonize China (Li Xiguang et al. 1996; Song Qiang et al. 1996a, 1996b). The simmering anger eventually erupted in May 1999, when hundreds of thousands of people held violent protests in front of the U.S. embassy over the U.S. bombing of the Chinese embassy in Belgrade.

In this general atmosphere of tension and misgivings, the decline of national identity became part of the nationalist concerns. Wary of similar economic and political chaos that plagued the former Eastern bloc states after the collapse of European communism, Chinese cultural critics argued against adopting radical changes after the Western model to China's political and economic systems, insisting that China must follow its own path and design its own economic strategies to ensure its strength as a nation-state in the international community. Lamenting the erosion of China's cultural identity brought about by the worship of Western culture among the people, especially the young, more conservative intellectuals like He Xin (1991) pushed for a revival of a Confucianism-centered national identity. Responding to Samuel Huntington's vision, which sees the clash of civilizations as a new pattern in global conflicts after the Cold War, these intellectuals believed that a solution to the competition could lie in adopting the philosophy of Confucianism.[4] The social Darwinism–based Western civilization would inevitably introduce conflict, aggression, and expansion, they contended, whereas Confucianism, with its emphasis on personal relations, would lead to harmony and peace in the world and is thus superior. The rebirth of Confucianism, they hoped, would help China solve its moral crisis, providing an internal solidarity for the people to stand up to the encroachment of the West.[5] Thus, unlike the total rejection of Chinese tradition in favor of a wholesale westernization in the radical May Fourth era, in the 1990s a growing sense of national pride and confidence, concerns about the decline of China's cultural identity, resentment towards the "contain China" policies spearheaded by the United States, and the fear in the aftermath of Tiananmen of the fate of the former Soviet Union—loss of central state—contributed to a much more sober perception of Western ideas and practices.

It is beyond the scope of this chapter to evaluate in detail the different approaches to the foreign Other, but the preceding synopsis should make a few points evident. The continual reimaging of the foreign Other proves that, treated as a permanent reference point to make the reflection and discussion of the national self more meaningful, the alien Other has never stopped haunting and teasing the Chinese imagination. Furthermore, though China's dealings with the foreign Other involved many countries besides the United States and its European allies, their position of power in international politics in general and their role in China's modern history in particular made the West represented by them loom large in the Chinese awareness of itself and the world. When viewed diachronically, however, the foreign Other, by turns wooed and rejected, did not have a fixed identity. It has been subject to recurrent reinterpretations each time China reassessed its imperatives and positions in global and domestic politics. The foreign Other, in consequence, tends to be concretized and assigned significations that reflect the contingencies of a historical moment. Guided by its own needs and desires, the social imagination constructs the meaning of the foreign Other to respond and react to the considerations and challenges of its own era—hence the seeming contradiction between the transformability of the foreign Other as a historical image and its fixed identity as a historicized entity in a particular instance. The fluidity of the foreign Other in discursive practices thus leaves room for individual representation, which in essence often registers the desires and anxieties of the appropriating consciousness toward itself and its foreign counterpart. Mo Yan's novel is an example.

National Authority over His Dead Body

Mo Yan, pen name of Guan Moye, is one of the best-known post-Mao writers both in China and abroad. Born in 1956 to a peasant family, Mo Yan spent the first twenty years of his life in Gaomi, a rural community in Shandong province, before joining the People's Liberation Army in 1976. He began writing fiction in 1981 and was formally enrolled in the Liberation Army's School of Arts to study literature in 1984. True to his pledge to "plant [his] roots in the rich soil of [his] hometown," Mo Yan has devoted his literary talent to portraying the lives of Chinese peasants, creating dynamic stories of their gallant struggles to live and survive.[6] Also noted for his predilection for displaying violence, Mo Yan has produced many memorable scenes of gruesome injustice, ruthless torture, and bloody slaughter. But the will to violence behind the epic tales in Mo Yan's world is more recognizable in terms of morality, ideology, politics, and history than in Yu Hua's fiction. Woven into the background of China's national journey in the twentieth century, the primordial passions powering the actions in his narratives—love, hate, corporeal pleasures, vengeance, and bravado—nonetheless often bear social and communal significances. This can be readily seen in *Fengru feitun.*

Fengru feitun was first serialized in the literary journal *Dajia*, in mid-1995. Later that year it claimed a handsome literary prize in a contest cosponsored by the journal and the Honghe Tobacco Company, winning a hefty 100,000 yuan for the author. The title of the novel, however, created some controversy. Although they voted in favor of *Fengru feitun*, the judges nevertheless voiced their reservations.[7] In reply to the charge that he had chosen a vulgar and sensational title in order to attract readers, Mo Yan published an article in the influential *Guangming Daily* to defend his decision. He explains that his creative urge came from his deep admiration for his mother and that the inspiration of the title was derived from his experience of seeing an ancient stone sculpture of a female figure with protruding breasts and buttocks. He assures the reader that he made the choice after careful and serious consideration. "*Fengru* and *feitun* symbolize mother and the earth," he observes. The author further notes that his purpose in creating the novel is to explore the essence of humanity, to glorify the mother, and to link maternity and earth in a symbolic representation (Mo Yan 1995b).

The author's exegesis sounds rather trite and conventional, but taken at face value, it offers little one can quarrel with. *Fengru feitun* is a story about a peasant household over the span of some ninety years, from the late Qing to the post-Mao reforms in the 1990s. One of the protagonists of this family saga is Shangguan Lu Shi, a mother of nine children. In a Japanese attack during the War of Resistance in the 1930s, the male members of the family, Shangguan Lu Shi's husband and her father-in-law, are slaughtered along with many villagers. Shocked by the massacre, her mother-in-law loses her mind, leaving Shangguan Lu Shi to become the matriarch who helps the family survive the social turmoil of more than five decades. The prominent role Shangguan Lu Shi—"Mother," as she is called—plays in the novel undoubtedly makes her a central figure in the fictional world.

But to treat Mother merely as a symbol of universal maternal virtues of endurance, love, resourcefulness, and self-sacrifice, qualities she certainly personifies, would miss an important theme of the novel. To underscore this theme, let me first start with the author's acclaimed novel *Red Sorghum* (Mo Yan 1993). In their reading of the novel, critics have applauded Mo Yan's narrative experimentation with such fictional techniques as point of view and temporal sequence, linking the author's formal innovation with his exploration of the nature of history and historical memory. More pertinent to my focus here are the discussions on issues of gender and sexuality sparked by the novel's untamed protagonists, the narrator's grandparents, who obey no prescribed ideological principles. Focusing on the free-spirited female character Grandma Fenglian, Lu Tonglin argues that even though this character defies both Confucian ethics and Communist moral values in her pursuit of independence and sexual freedom, female sexuality is still made to submit to the dominance of masculine authority and violence. Grandma's wild energy and desire are nonetheless guarded and monopolized by Grandpa, Yu Zhan'ao, the novel's most powerful male figure. Identifying the female body with the sorghum field where the story's dramatic actions (the initial violent sexual intercourse between Grandma and Grandpa and the battle against the Japanese) take place, Lu asserts that by turning the female body into a site of actions, the author makes it "highly improbable, if not impossible" for the woman to participate because her body is the stage and not the agent of the actions (Lu 1995, 59–63, 68–73; quotation 71).

Also interested in the author's celebration of masculinity exemplified by his unconventional, larger-than-life bandit hero Grandpa, Xueping Zhong centers her analyses on the male narrator "riddled with a strong self-contempt." Psychoanalyzing his intriguing self-debasement, Zhong treats the novel as an example of post-Mao male writers' search for a strong man to replace their weakened identity as a result of political oppression and to fill the void left by the removal of the officially established Communist male image. She locates this search in the antithesis set up in the novel between the pure red sorghum, whose dazzling color and tall straight stalks symbolize the narrator's forefathers, who are capable of heroic feats of legendary proportions, and the weak "bastard sorghum" *(zazhong gaoliang)* emblematic of his own debilitated generation. The narrator's self-loathing comes to a head when he finds himself paralyzed in a field of hybrid sorghum, unable to break free from its "snakelike leaves" and "pervasive green poisons." Hearing a collective voice from his predecessors beseeching him to cleanse himself and find one "stalk of pure-red sorghum," the young man yearns for the red sorghum with "extraordinarily rich, extraordinarily majestic colors," the "epitome of mankind" and his courageous ancestors (Mo Yan 1993, 358–359). Zhong contends that the narrator's self-contempt in the end leads to his identification with Grandpa as the desirable model of masculinity, the "manly man" (Xueping Zhong 2000, 119–149).

Fengru feitun shares many characteristics with *Red Sorghum*. Like the previous story, it is a family history related by an "unworthy descendant." Similarly, it is set in Mo Yan's much-mythologized northeastern Gaomi county, partly against the background of the War of Resistance against Japan. No less colorful, the family in *Fengru feitun* boasts legendary local heroes full of raw energy and sexual prowess and rebellious females with unrestrained libidos. Though the identity of the I-narrator in *Fengru feitun* is unambiguous, as in *Red Sorghum* the narration characteristically switches between first and third person, interweaving layers of narration and imaginary construction.[8] Even the representation of adultery and bastardy is not really new. The relationship between Grandma and Grandpa in *Red Sorghum* starts as an illicit affair, and after her husband's death, Grandma is not formally married to her lover, Yu Zhan'ao. This makes the narrator's father, Douguan, a product of Fenglian and Yu's lovemaking in the sorghum fields, a bastard in a conventional sense.

But what makes adultery, bastardy, and the "unworthy descendant" complex different in *Fengru feitun* is the participation of a foreign man and the existence of an alien bastard with blond hair, blue eyes, and fair skin.

Yi-tsi Mei Feuerwerker points out that *Red Sorghum* is an "exploration of the relationship between the writing/intellectual self and the peasant 'Other,' transposed to a personal level, brought close to home...by being located within the family" (Feuerwerker 1998, 214). While the self-Other relationship is retained in *Fengru feitun*, the presence of an alien intrusion in the form of an illegitimate sexual affair redefines the dichotomy as that between the Chinese self and a foreign Other. Consequently, the themes in *Red Sorghum*—masculinity, male and female sexuality, and the anxieties over the purity and vitality of *zhong*—are reformulated and take on a different set of significations in *Fengru feitun*. In both works these themes come down to the idea of *zhong* and its healthy reproduction. "*Zhong*" is a word of multiple meanings even in its more formal usage. In different contexts it can be translated as "seeds," "species," "breed," and "race," all denoting an origin that can pass on its genetic characteristics in procreation. Although female participation is necessary, the idea of *zhong* in Chinese patriarchal tradition stresses the male's identity and re-creative authority. Delineated along a lineal order of forefathers versus offspring, the notion of *zhong* in *Red Sorghum* is domestic, generational, and temporal. That the "hybrid sorghum" the narrator detests is transplanted from Hainan Island outside the local area points to the radical dislocation imposed by the revolution, limiting the misplacement within the geopolitical space of China. The foreign involvement in *Fengru feitun*, in contrast, carries the questions of authority and authenticity essential to the reproduction of *zhong* over national and racial boundaries, adding a new dynamic and complexity to masculinity and sexuality as gender categories. This broadens the ramifications of the self-Other conflict, allowing it to address a collective, historical concern about foreign intervention beyond the confines of familial and individual experience.

The collective nature of the conflict in *Fengru feitun* is supported by the use of modern China as the fictional setting of the novel. The saga of the Shangguan family unfolds against major milestones in the country's twentieth-century history: the war against Japan, the civil war, the Communist revolution, and the post-Mao economic reforms. The male members introduced into the family through matrimony represent a cross section of significant players in these social events: Japanese corroborators, nationalists and their American allies, and Communists. Because of this unusual composition, the discord among the family members comes to epitomize social antagonism between contending political forces. Mother's first son-in-law, a supporter of the Japanese, is captured and killed by her fifth son-in-law, a Communist, whose comrades later hunt down and execute the second son-in-law, a nationalist. The males' political positions have also created rifts among Mother's daughters, who in general share their husbands' convictions. At the heart of the family and yet remaining neutral in the ideological strife is Shangguan Lu Shi, the mother. She treats all her descendants with unconditional love, no matter how unworthy they may be. Despite her complaints about hardships, Mother opens her home and heart to her daughters, sons-in-law, and her grandchildren when their parents are too busy with their political pursuits to care for them. Transcending politics, the female protagonist is deindividualized to stand for China, a figure of magnanimity, forbearance, and resilience. The Shangguan family consequently is emblematic of the nation. In this light, Mother's hometown, the northeastern Gaomi county where the historical drama of struggle and survival is staged, rises above individual importance to represent the homeland of the Chinese nation.

This symbolization enriches the family saga with a national significance and, through the development of the story, turns the female body into a site of a nationalist battle against the foreign Other, a battle where the loss of the native's dignity is redeemed through male sexuality. The foreign Other in *Fengru feitun* is personified by an obvious outsider from an alien culture, who enters the scene in a most dramatic and traumatic fashion. Lu Xuaner, a delicate beauty with a full bust, is married to Shangguan Shouxi, son of a local blacksmith. Unable to conceive three years after the marriage, she is blamed and abused by her husband and mother-in-law for her failure to provide a son for the family. A medical examination arranged by Xuaner's aunt confirms, however, that it is her husband who is infertile. Finding it impossible to tell the Shangguans the truth, Xuaner suffers in silence. In growing desperation for a son, she becomes promiscuous, but her affairs with her uncle, an uncouth dog butcher, an itinerant artisan, an amorous monk, and her rape by bandit rapists produce one daughter after another, seven in all. The person who finally answers the prayers of Xuaner and her family is ironically a foreigner, a Swedish missionary from a local Catholic church. Tortured almost to the brink of death by her husband, Xuaner drags herself to the church in search of consolation. The relationship that develops between Xuaner and the foreign priest leads to the birth of twins, a boy and a girl.

The message presented in this plot twist is multifarious and, on a metaphorical level, suggests Chinese intellectuals' ambivalence toward the alien Other and the indigenous self. Represented in the most humiliating terms, the success of foreign intervention is a bitter joke at the Chinese patriarch's expense. He is chided and ridiculed for his inability to satisfy the imperative of his own tradition. His incapacity to produce a male heir threatens the continuation of the ancestral line and in consequence challenges the very essence of his raison d'être in the patriarchal system. What is more, this is not an individual disaster limited to the Shangguan family; it is a group failure. The men Mother has had sexual contact with voluntarily or involuntarily hark back intertextually to the morally ambiguous but nonetheless heroic figures of the author's earlier stories, the peasants-turned-bandits who fight the Japanese in Red Sorghum, for instance. When the inadequacy is extended to the collective and national level, the inability of Chinese men to father a son in their own image for Mother China seriously questions the vitality and productive power of the natives. The easy—double—victory scored by the priest, in contrast, confirms both the superiority of the virile foreign Other and the vulnerability and inviability of the Chinese tradition. Apparently, the sexual failure of the Chinese male has national implications. The conflation of male potency with China's survival in this way adds international significance to the love affair. Not only does the missionary engage in cultural penetration, but his trespassing, physical and sexual, violates the symbolic female body and is therefore an affront to China's national dignity and pride. As a result, even if foreign assistance appears to be desired to save the situation, it is vehemently counteracted, as I discuss shortly.

If the question of legitimacy is already embedded in the clandestine affair between Mother and the foreign priest, the birth of the twins brings it into the open. It is true that all Mother's children are born out of wedlock, but the illegitimate status of her daughters is easily dismissed. Unaware of the truth of their paternity, the Shangguan family accepts them without doubting their origins. Neither is there evidence in the novel that anyone in the village suspects transgression. In fact, the reader does not learn about the girls' illegitimacy until the last chapter, when the circumstances of their conception are revealed. Blended smoothly into the lineage of the family, the girls' unnatural births are "naturalized," consequently posing no threat to the normative social structure. The alien nature of the twins, however, receives so much narrative attention that it carries special thematic weight.

In contrast to the succinct account of the girls' births, the twins' arrival occupies a salient position in the narration—it is the event that begins the novel. To accentuate the twins' otherness from the "legitimized" illegitimate children, their bloody and difficult birth is given an extended and graphic description. Mother and the family's black donkey go into labor at the same time. The parallels are obvious as the narration goes back and forth between the two events. Like Mother, the donkey is in great agony. The human female, however, is in a more wretched situation: the adults of the family assist the donkey, leaving Mother by herself. The double labor opens up a range of interpretive possibilities. At the most immediate level, reminiscent of Xiao Hong's *Field of Life and Death*, it demonstrates the miserable existence of the human female. But a more significant link lies in the identity of the babies. The baby animal is a mule, a hybrid between a horse and a donkey; the twins are products of an adulterous liaison between a Chinese woman and a foreign missionary. The juxtaposition, infused with racial overtones, condemns the sexual relationship as a base, animalistic mismatch by labeling the human babies as aberrant creatures like mules.

But the similarities end here. If producing a mule is a common practice and therefore acceptable (as the family's concern for the donkey suggests), illicit crossbreeding between a native woman and an alien man is not to be brushed off, for begetting a mule is domestic business and that of the bastard twins an international affair. This is dramatized not only in that both the foreign priest and Shangguan Lu Shi's lawful husband are present during the labor, but also in a Japanese rampage in the village that happens simultaneously with the birth of the twins. The Japanese attack serves two thematic purposes. First, it further stresses the alien nature of the bastard children by attributing their survival to a Japanese doctor in the invading army. He cuts their umbilical cords, pats the unbreathing babies into life, and gives Mother an injection to stop her hemorrhaging. The affinity between the bastard children and the aggressors is also established by the family's fate at the hands of the Japanese: the soldiers kill Shangguan Shouxi and his father but spare the lives of Mother, the babies, and the Swedish priest, a fellow alien on Chinese soil. Second, the slaughter of the male members of the Shangguan family brings into relief the grave consequences of the seemingly innocuous love affair. Coinciding with the death of the native father(s), the birth of the twins is full of patricidal implications. By closely associating the birth of the bastards with the physical violence against the local inhabitants, the author casts the adultery and the foreign attack in the same light: the sexual violation of the symbolic national body is as serious a threat to China's sovereignty as the military invasion.

Obviously, various representatives of the foreign father—the priest and the Japanese soldiers, the doctor in particular—have collaborated in bringing the illegitimate children into being. The I-narrator informs the reader that a picture of him and his twin sister cradled in the arms of the army doctor appeared in newspapers in Japan during the war for propaganda purposes. Decades later, in the 1980s, the Japanese doctor comes back to China and locates the narrator much like a parent searching for a lost child. Precisely because the sexual affair and the existence of the bastards involve national authority, patriarchal power must be restored to the native father. As in many war stories, this metaphorical struggle is carried on over the female body, the signified of the Chinese nation in her weakness and humiliation in the nationalist discourse. Very often the rape of a Chinese woman by a Japanese soldier during the war against Japan was seen as the rape of the nation. In her study of Xiao Hong's *Field of Life and Death*, Lydia Liu demonstrates how the woman writer challenges this nationalist discourse by depicting a Chinese man as the rapist instead of a Japanese soldier. Refusing to bury women's suffering under the unified nationalist expression, Xiao Hong highlights the female's experience of life through her battered body, unrecognized and unrepresented by the male-centered nationalist consciousness (Lydia Liu 1994).

But the rape of a woman by a Chinese man during the Anti-Japanese War is not always a subversion of the nationalist discourse. In the context of Mo Yan's novel, it is put in the service of the very discourse Xiao Hong sets out to undermine. In *Fengru feitun* Mother is raped by a group of Chinese guerrillas soon after giving birth to the twins. In a conventional sense, the author's description of the Japanese doctor who saves lives and the behavior of the anti-Japanese heroes who loot and rape are contrary to the stereotypes in standard war stories. Indeed, Mo Yan has been berated for glorifying the invaders and vilifying the Chinese soldiers (Tao 1996; Wang Derong 1996). But to insist on an orthodox interpretation would be to miss the symbolic significance of the rape. Just as the Japanese doctor's assistance to the twins must be evaluated in the conflict between the native self and the foreign Other/father, the rape of the woman acquires a new dimension of meaning when anchored in the same thematic schemata. Because of the circumstances of the rape, it becomes a means of contestation against foreign authority, as I show in the following text.

After the deaths of her husband and father-in-law, Shangguan Lu Shi assumes control of the family. At the celebration of the twins' first hundred days, which coincides with the Mid-Autumn Festival, she takes the babies to visit the foreign priest in the church. The priest eagerly gathers them into his arms, kissing Mother and calling the babies "My dearest." When the baby boy starts to cry, Mother tries to comfort him, saying to him, "Don't cry. . . . You are afraid of him, right? Don't be afraid. He is a good man. He is your real . . . godfather" (Mo Yan 1995a, 68). Mother obviously wishes to acknowledge the priest's parentage. Without any doubt, the reunion pre-

sents a rare moment of familial bliss in a novel full of misfortune and turmoil. Mother sits down to help grind wheat flour, and when that is done,
the priest shows off the domestic skills he has learned during his long
sojourn in China by making fine noodles. After the meal, the priest pre-
pares to choose names for the twins and baptize them.

The mother, the birth father, and the twins form a picture of a harmo-
nious household, a sharp contrast to the daily battery Mother has endured
for years in the Shangguan family under Chinese male authority.
Significantly, this gathering takes place on a day of double importance—
the Mid-Autumn Festival, a major family occasion in Chinese custom, and
the twins' hundredth-day "birthday," when children receive their names
and are entered into the family tree. Against this cultural background, the
assembly in the church on this momentous day would legitimize both the
priest's claim over Mother and the twins and his irregular relationship with
them. Furthermore, the reconstituted family is not a simple replacement of
the disintegrated Chinese model. Mother's family is being transplanted
into a foreign culture via an alien religion. The ritual of baptism would
immerse the babies physically and spiritually in the foreign father's tradition, where the natives have neither representation nor control. In addition,
the baptism would have granted Mother and her bastard children unconditional acceptance into a new religious order through which Mother's infidelity and sin against the Chinese father would be forgiven and forgotten.
By the authority and power conferred on him by his alien belief, the foreign father would also help eliminate the marginal status of his bastard
descendants.

However, this alien power is arrested at a critical moment. Just when
the priest is about to name the twins, Chinese guerrillas storm the church.
Through the naming, an ultimate confirmation of paternal authority and
identity, the foreign father would openly declare his victory, mocking the
authority of the Chinese patriarchy. The timely intervention in the naming
ceremony defies and delays the foreign father's attempt. In this light, it is
not accidental that the priest is confronted by a group of bandit soldiers
who are carrying out guerrilla warfare against his symbolic ally, the
Japanese invaders. Equally significant is that the bandit commander soon
marries Mother's eldest daughter, infiltrating the family by reasserting a
native male presence. Finding the priest there with his "family," the bandit
soldiers surround him and start to make fun of his appearance, calling him
"a monkey." When the priest protests, a soldier says to him, "Let me tell
you. You're a bastard from a screwing between a man and a chimp" (Mo
Yan 1995a, 81). This is no ordinary name-calling. By singling out the

priest's alien identity for ridicule, in essence challenging his *zhong*, the Chinese soldiers are trying to dehumanize and consequently delegitimize the foreign father, reducing him to be an Other that can be easily dismissed. The verbal insult is quickly followed by physical violence. When the soldiers make advances toward Mother, the priest tries to stop them and is shot in the legs. After witnessing the rape of Mother by the bandits, the priest drags himself to the top of the church tower and jumps to his death.

On the symbolic level, the fierceness and brutality with which the peaceful family gathering is interrupted turn the incident into a contention over national authority. Through the death of the foreign father and the rape of the woman, the native patriarch reclaims his right over the symbolic female body. Mother is punished for adultery, which becomes a double offense since it involves an alien man and is therefore an added insult to the masculinist nationalist sensibility. The intruder, the foreign father, pays for his sexual invasion with his life. What is more, before his death, he must first acknowledge the surrender of his authority by witnessing the repossession of the female body by his Chinese counterpart. He has to face the humiliation and accept his defeat by committing suicide.

But the foreign Other has undeniably produced a stubborn presence. Before putting an end to his life, the priest writes the names he has chosen for the twins on the wall with his blood. The existence of the twins therefore constitutes what Paul Ricoeur calls "a historical trace," which cannot be erased simply by violence and physical elimination of the foreign father. The naming right exercised by the Swedish priest marks the children off as a hybridized entity for the Chinese self to deal with. Those names, and not just their foreign paternity, indicate the twins' hybridization: although chosen by the alien father, the names he picked—Jintong (Golden Boy) and Yunü (Jade Girl), which Mother later uses—are undoubtedly Chinese. The question, then, is how to interpret and evaluate this crossbred product. Having established the alien connection of the twins, the author goes on to exploit their difference to examine the viability of the model of intimate integration. Comparing his portrayal of the bastard to representative images elsewhere in world literature can help us see more clearly his own strategy.

Her Body and His Otherness

Because of the stringent codification of female sexual behavior and a double standard toward male sexuality, unwed motherhood and illegitimacy do not seem to be a serious social problem in Chinese tradition and consequently have not received much attention.[9] In world literature, however, bastardy has long been a topic of immense interest.[10] Representations of illegitimate children appear in all literary genres—in myths, poetry, legends, drama, and fiction.[11] Among authors of bastard characters are such noted figures as Homer, Shakespeare, Chaucer, Malory, Stendhal, Dickens, and Dostoyevsky.[12] Studies on the subject conclude that birth out of a normal social order that privileges the authority of the father makes the bastard a surplus in society.[13] Alison Findlay's analyses of bastardy in Renaissance England and the drama of the time provide an interesting array of historical and representational possibilities. Displayed as "object lessons," as powerless and unhappy beings controlled by the legitimate subject, the illicit children were murdered at birth, disinherited, and persecuted. They are the "necessary Other" to the sanctioned self that allowed the state to regulate public behavior and demand conformity (Findlay 1994, 28–44). At the same time, the bastard is used under patriarchal systems as a demonstration of destructive female sexuality. He is portrayed as an incarnation of evil in literature, full of negative energies, a walking example of all sorts of undesirable human character traits, who disrespects authority, breaks up family unity, and often fails to govern his own sexual impulses, thus inducing incestuous relationships and rendering patriarchal authority precarious. Moreover, the bastard's unnatural domestic behavior carries over into his public role as a subject. He transgresses social rules, usurps power, rebels against the state, and creates national disorder (106–128).

On the other end of the spectrum, viewed as a positive condition, the out-of-the-ordinary genesis of the illegitimate child makes bastardy a convenient prop in the delineation of heroism. As Otto Rank's discussion of the characteristics of the hero myths illustrates, one of the hallmarks of the hero's exceptionalness is his birth as a result of secret intercourse between his parents (Rank 1952, 61). Findlay concurs that illegitimacy can be the bastard's source of strength: "The bastard's status as outsider makes him particularly suitable to explore the paradoxical relationship between qualities of glorious individualism and service to society which make up the archetypal hero" (Findlay 1994, 170). Indeed, many European mythic and legendary heroes are bastards. Bequeathed with a preexisting individuality, bastard characters possess superhuman power and resourcefulness, and their rebellious nature transforms into a positive quality in their challenge to corrupt authorities. Thus, while the bastard's innate irregularity isolates him as unnatural, the alienation makes bastardy "potentially an ideal characterization for a quintessential theme of literature: the quest for self-definition within, and in opposition to, the family, society and the universe at large"

(Goscilo 1990, 3). An active pursuer of individual goals and a high achiever who is able to overcome his disadvantages, the virtuous bastard strives to construct a self beyond the confines of social regulations. A fertile testing ground for complex social, cultural, and historical concerns and values, the bastard serves as a useful Other in the writer's quest for unorthodox expressions. His difference allows him to operate outside traditional boundaries, turning him into a conduit of aspirations and unconventional meanings, so much so that bastardy is often adopted as a narrative strategy in questioning and subverting existing social orders. Whether upheld as a superlative being or denigrated as a deviant to be despised, the bastard comes across as a man of action, a man with free agency to fashion himself.

Placed against historical and literary precedents, the bastard in Mo Yan's world is a unique type. The element central in the character development of the bastard, the conflict between the illegitimate child and society, which often stimulates him into action, does not seem to play a significant role in *Fengru feitun*. The death of the native father(s) and the insanity of her mother-in-law give Shangguan Lu Shi full authority at home. If this conveniently relieves domestic tension otherwise unavoidable, the villagers' nonchalance toward the children's dubious roots makes social pressure virtually nonexistent. Over the five decades recorded in the novel, the bastard twins suffer with their family, but on no occasion are they singled out because of their foreign paternity. The lack of discrimination and unfavorable conditions requires the reader to abandon the conventional approach of analyzing the bastard character in terms of the opposition between the underprivileged self and a conformative society. Instead, the absence of social adversities directs our attention inward to the inherent quality of a tainted bastardized self.

Unlike the typical villain or the noble hero, Mo Yan's bastard characters neither suffer from moral depravity nor aspire to recognition. They are predestined to be weak. While the double birth of a boy and a girl, an ideal combination in the common belief, appears to testify to the strength of the foreign father, the author makes a mockery of the seeming superiority in number. Born blind, Jintong's twin sister contributes little to the plot. Ignored by everyone, she spends most of her time on a brick bed and eventually commits suicide at twenty during a great famine. In a moment of deep remorse for neglecting her, the I-narrator calls her his "dearest sister." What the twins have in common is their characteristic passivity. Just like Yunü, Jintong accomplishes nothing. He follows orders all his life and is manipulated by those around him, including his own unscrupulous relatives. The girl's blindness, consequently, is a symbolic birthmark of the bastard children's inadequacy inherited at least partially from an alien stock. In particular, Jintong's deficiency is given a full representation in his failure to achieve normal growth, which eventually leads to his impaired sexuality. The character suffers from a severe eating disorder. He is breast-fed by Mother until he is seven, and it is only after much coaxing that he is able to drink goat's milk from a bottle. Jintong does not have his first morsel of solid food until he is eighteen. If he is given solid food, he throws up and falls physically ill. Mother has tried all means to wean him, but Jintong clings to his mother and resists desperately, going so far as to attempt suicide. The bastard character's dependence on his mother is conclusively demonstrated in his fascination with her breasts.

In time Jintong's fascination develops into a lifelong obsession with women's breasts. He considers himself an expert on the subject and for a short period makes a living designing bras for women. While the bastard character's fixation on women's breasts has strong sexual overtones, which would indicate a psychological development that could offset his attachment to his mother, the author frustrates its potential, thereby refusing the character growth and maturation. Ambiguously caught between infantile needs and adult masculine cravings, Jintong's passion is problematized, keeping the character in a developmental limbo. This is clearly illustrated when he is finally cured of his eating disorder at eighteen through psychotherapy and is admitted into a local junior high school, where he excels in his studies and becomes the secretary of the Youth League. To further his mastery of Russian, a subject he is particularly good at, his instructor arranges for him to be a pen pal with a Russian girl, Natasha. The youngsters start exchanging letters and pictures. In a photo she sends to Jintong, Natasha appears in a revealing, low-cut dress. At the sight, "Jintong's heart beat wildly and he felt blood rush to his head" (Mo Yan 1995a, 399). With tears in his eyes, the character envisions the girl's breasts and weeps in happiness.

Jintong seems to be sexually aroused and soon lapses into delirium. He loses sleep and mumbles constantly in Russian at night. In his imagination Jintong sees Natasha approach him provocatively, feeling himself falling hopelessly under her spell. But the normal sexual attraction of a girl for a pubescent young man appears to the bastard character as "a terrible trap." In order to free himself from it, Jintong purposely offends Xiao Jin'gang, a Communist soldier-turned-cadre in his school, hoping that Xiao's anger can help him get rid of his obsession with Natasha. Consciously resisting feminine attraction, the bastard character refuses to enter the adult world to establish a grown-up relationship with the opposite sex, which would entail responsibility and independence. The prospect of a possible sexual relationship produces such a trauma that it triggers a recurrence of Jintong's eating disorder. His aversion to solid food returns, and when he tries to force himself to eat, he only sees two breasts rising from the bowl. Severely disturbed, the character has to abandon school and return to Mother and his former familiar and secure environment. At home Jintong continues to hallucinate, seeing the image of Natasha everywhere. In his fantasy the character alternates between trying to run away from the Russian girl with bloody breasts and pursuing her. He vacillates between a desire to give in to his awakened libido and an urge to avoid the autonomy and growth a sexual relationship inevitably demands.

The bastard character is obviously pulled between opposing psychological forces, between sexual maturation that requires action and self-sufficiency and an infantile regression that seeks certainty and protection. The former has generated so much excitement and at the same time such intense fear in the character that it precipitates a mental breakdown. In Jintong's impasse the breast signifies the clashing expectations, ultimately confusing the character. When he is drawn toward the breast as a sexual symbol, it simultaneously invokes his attachment to his mother and his primordial need for milk. The regressive tendency triumphs in the end: Mother has to buy a goat to feed him. Jintong is able to regain his sanity only after witnessing his brother-in-law's sexual abuse of his sister. The sight of his sister's swollen breasts and badly bruised body seems to convince him of the violence and danger inherent in carnal desires, dispelling completely his nascent sexuality. The crisis is thus passed and Jintong retreats safely to a "babyhood" sustained by milk from his surrogate mother, who reminds him of the goat he grew up with.

This incident marks the beginning of the bastard character's disastrous relationships with women and his suppressed and troubled sexuality. His first sexual experience, with his Communist supervisor who has just shot herself because of her failure to seduce Jintong, lands him in jail for fifteen years. Seriously ill after serving his time, Jintong, now in his forties, returns home and is once again brought back to health by a surrogate mother and her milk. Seeing Jintong at the brink of death, Mother understands his yearning for breast milk and sends for the malformed One-Breast Jin to feed him.

One-Breast Jin, whose name underscores her malformation, seems to mirror the lack of wholeness in the bastard character. A new mother in her fifties, One-Breast Jin is another figure in the novel that registers the bastard character's problematic relation with the female's breasts. Calling Jintong in turns "my brother" and "my son," she hovers ambiguously between being a mother and a lover. When she stands over Jintong after being summoned by Mother, Jintong "lifted his head and searched for her breast anxiously with his lips like a new-born puppy" (Mo Yan 1995a, 504). At the same time, it is hard to miss the sexual excitement both feel. "While Jintong's mouth was searching for the nipple, it was also searching for him. When he closed his lips over the breast, and when she entered his mouth, they were both trembling. As if scalded by boiling water, they started to moan in ecstasy" (504). However, when Jintong is called on specifically to separate the breast as his infantile need-satisfying object from the breast as a symbol of femininity, he again falls into a paralysis. On Jintong's recovery, Mother realizes her mistake and calls off One-Breast Jin's visits. She challenges Jintong to go and sleep with the woman to turn their mother-infant relationship into a sexual one, thus growing out of his eternal childhood into manhood.

But Jintong has tremendous difficulty overcoming his attachment to the breast as his baby love object. Despite One-Breast Jin's tricks to arouse him, he "failed to embrace her like a man" (Mo Yan 1995a, 513). "He felt extremely thirsty, like a dried well. His upper body was on fire, but his lower parts were cold like the water in a dead pond" (516). The character thus continues to be caught in a psychological split. Exhausted by wrestling with Jintong to stop him from nursing, the woman gives in and lets him suck her breast like "an old baby." The sexual relationship is eventually consummated when One-Breast Jin puts on a cotton-padded jacket, which she secures at the waist with a belt, leaving the rest of her body naked. Only by blocking Jintong's access to her breast is the woman able to temporarily lure the character out of his infantile self. But the success is short-lived. Although sexuality is momentarily restored, it fails to correct Jintong's intrinsic weakness. Realizing that he is of no value to her in her business, One-Breast Jin soon becomes tired of Jintong and turns him out of her house. This brief affair terminates Jintong's sexual relationship with women for the rest of his life. Thus, the bastard's otherness is fully registered in his problematic encounters with the female body.

The development of the self-Other dichotomy in *Fengru feitun* makes it clear that the standoff evolves around a masculinity that privileges sexuality. It is within this matrix that both the self and the Other, as well as their confrontation, are imagined and defined. The self and Other assume a masculine identity in *Fengru feitun* not simply because the fictional representatives are male—the priest on the one side, the bandit soldiers and the male members of the Shangguan family on the other, and the hybrid Jintong in the middle—but, in more meaningful terms, because their strengths and failings are explored and expressed first and foremost through male sexuality, the context in which the clash between the self and the Other invariably occurs in this novel. The alien assault on Chinese authority takes the form of a forbidden love affair that flaunts the virility of the foreign father and challenges that of the native male. The counterattack is mapped out and mounted on the same battleground by subjecting the foreign Other to a sexual defeat. The nationalist struggle against alien intrusion is reified by an outburst of violent sexual activities by Chinese soldiers, through which the native male reclaims the ownership of the female body, the object of desire of the foreign Other, thus recovering the loss. A similar sexual politics governs the description of the bastard son. His difference and inadequacy as a descendant of a nonnative father are demonstrated through a troubled sexuality that degenders him, reducing him to a neutral being and therefore a direct opposite of the "pure" Chinese sons in the family, his brothers-in-law and nephew, whose masculinity without exception resides in their unbridled sexual energy. Opposing ideological beliefs may set Mother's sons-in-law apart, but their insatiable sexual desire, on which they never fail to act, nevertheless gathers them together in a shared male identity.

The dominantly masculine nature of the self in *Fengru feitun* inevitably makes us ponder the position of the female, Mother in particular, and her thematic role in the novel. Zooming in on the woman's breasts and hips in the title, the novel clearly emphasizes the function of the female body in procreation and child rearing. In this line of thinking, female sexuality has no legitimacy outside human reproduction, especially, in Chinese tradition, the reproduction of males. Mother's promiscuity may be an act of defiance and self-preservation in some instances, but as it is kept from public knowledge, it serves to honor the patriarchal demand for a son, losing its subversive potential. Although in the end mothering is indispensable in the universal order of things, female fecundity becomes more significant in *Fengru feitun* when channeled into the nationalist contest with the foreign Other. Peripheral to the contest, the births of Mother's daughters are non-events and denied narrative attention. Their illegitimacy can be ignored because it does not challenge the authority of the native father (the men all share the Chinese *zhong*, after all) in the more important international conflict. Even between the foreign twins, the girl, Yunü, is placed in a subordinate position as a muted reflection of their weakness. Since the loss of male sexuality is the mark of the weakness, her body assumes no meaning in this design and cannot signify, precluding her participation. The most prominent female figure in the novel, Shangguan Lu Shi, is not given the privilege of representing the combative self in spite of the narrative space she occupies. Undoubtedly, Mother embodies many of the traditional female virtues of diligence, tenacity, selfless love, and devotion to her family. These qualities, however, do not set the terms of struggle between the Chinese self and the foreign Other. She helps define the self but enjoys no autonomous agency in her own right. Her body provides the site where the native and his opponent engage each other and match their sexual strength, a site for the Chinese male to face his ineffectuality and regain authority. In a similar fashion, it is used to problematize the masculinity of the bastard son, accentuating his otherness from the indigenous Chinese self that can possess and conquer the female body. The bastard character is defined by his foreign heritage instead of his maternal Chinese connection. Even if his alien paternity affects him in a negative way, it nonetheless has differentiating power, while his unwillingness to separate from the mother is proof of his weakness, an obstacle to his growth and development.

The sexual politics can be located in China's modern history in general and the post-Mao worries about the future of Chinese tradition in the country's modernization in particular. Mo Yan's fascination with male sexuality and its tug-of-war between the Chinese self and the foreign Other over the symbolic female body seems to be another manifestation of Chinese intellectuals' anxiety over the country's potency in the modern world. The complicated relationships among nationhood, womanhood, and the nationalist rhetoric have generated many studies in recent years. Critics have focused in general on how the idea of the new woman was inscribed by national concerns in various historical periods (Barlow 1993; Gilmartin et al. 1994; Larson 1998). It is widely recognized that in the discourse of modern nation building in the early twentieth century, the frail female body became a signifier of China's weakness and vulnerability. For example, the inhumane treatment of women, such as footbinding and female infanticide, was taken to be evidence of China's backwardness in contrast to the more civilized and vigorous Western culture. Drawing a relation between the strong female body and the strong nation, the reform-oriented intellectuals promoted women's physical education "as a form of personal cultivation with national implications" (Larson 1998, 112).

The shaping of the female body and issues of women's emancipation were thus incorporated into China's modernization and growth as a nation. But where does this woman-China equation leave the Chinese male? And how does the foreign Other feature in this gendered imagination of nationhood and femininity? After all, national identity, which involves boundaries (social and physical) and vigilance against foreign incursion, becomes more pertinent in an international environment. In my present context, what contributes to but often remains subterranean in the analogy is important. The powerful and bullying foreign Other that "feminized" the nation was assigned the superior masculine quality, hence the persistent use of rape as a trope to represent national humiliation. The admission of the "female" weakness of the nation put the Chinese male in an awkward position. Not only did China's feminization make evident his moral failure in fulfilling his responsibilities to the country, but it also led to the symbolic loss of his own male identity, on which China's patriarchal tradition had constructed its cultural priorities.

The engendering of China was given an interesting twist by the socialist ideology and women's liberation under Mao's rule. In the Communist promotion of sexual equality, women were called upon to "hold up half the sky." But the half of the sky allotted to women duplicated the other half, a male space occupied by an idealized image of strong revolutionary heroes devoted to the Party's cause at the expense of personal matters such as love and family. By denying gender differences and thus turning the entire nation into masculine Communist fighters, the Party finally enabled China to stand up and face the imperialist Other "man to man."

The sexual politics in the novel has an intriguing *mise en abyme*, an internal "mirror" within the text that reflects aspects of its own narrative design, a different type from that used by Zhaxi Dawa.[14] The fiancé of Mother's third daughter, Han Dingshan, nicknamed Bird Han because of his superb skills in using slingshots to kill birds, is captured by Japanese troops during the war and taken to Japan to do hard labor. He escapes from the camp and spends thirteen years hiding in the foreign wilderness. Enduring unspeakable hardships, Han develops a habit of constantly covering his private parts with his hands to shield them from the severe cold of the wintry days. In his valiant struggle to stay alive, preserving his manhood seems to be preeminent in Han's consciousness. The character's fear of losing his sexual ability fully exemplifies his sense of humiliation and subjugation in a foreign land. Significantly, the Japanese woman who participates in hunting Han down wears a man's uniform, while the piece of clothing the fugitive uses to cover his naked, vulnerable body is a woman's blouse. The symbolic transfer of sexual identity crystallizes the victimization suffered by the Chinese man. The character's unremitting efforts to protect his sexual organs are thus suggestive of the Chinese male's fear of castration at the hands of foreign powers. Han is only gradually able to relinquish his fear and move his hands away from his crotch after he returns to China. What is more, his reinstallation in his native land not only removes the character's anxiety but soon rekindles his sexual desire, in which he indulges with a vengeance by engaging in a frenzy of adulterous sexual activity with Mother's eldest daughter. The threat to his masculinity having lifted upon his emancipation from the pernicious foreign Other, the character regains his maleness and wholeness via the female body.

Mo Yan's handling of masculinity, sexuality, and national authority bears out Cynthia Enloe's observation that "nationalism typically has sprung from masculinized memory, masculinized humiliation and masculinized hope" (Enloe 1989, 44). As I have pointed out, in *Fengru feitun* the Chinese male's unproductive sexuality (according to patriarchal principles) creates an opportunity for the foreign Other to violate the symbolic female body. The novel's preoccupation with the sexual power of the foreign Other stems from and is ultimately an anxiety about the Chinese self. This anxiety finally finds relief in the redemption of the Chinese male and the suppression of the illegitimate son's masculinity. A sharp contrast to his father's sexual success, the bastard son's abject failure can be interpreted as a retribution for the elder's sin against the Chinese patriarch, a rejection of the potency of the alien *zhong*. If the vigor and vitality of the foreign father are reluctantly acknowledged through the birth of a son, his alien power is nonetheless contested by the author. The son's loss of sexual energy, and by corollary the reproductive power, robs the foreign Other of the chance to regenerate. Jintong's emasculation in the end both cancels out the previous victory of the foreign father and closes off any possibility of a reenactment.

Furthermore, the denial of the bastard son's sexual strength and maturity problematizes not only his foreign association but also the very mode of his production. I commented at the beginning of this chapter that the search for an effective model to balance China's needs for self-preservation and self-rejuvenation in the pursuit of modernity underlies Chinese intellectuals' reflections and speculations about China and the world. As the country's history proves, modernization involved westernization and, consequently, the bastardization of China and its culture. The slaying and bloodshed accompanying Jintong's birth points to the violent and destructive nature of this bastardization, calling to mind China's defeat in the foreign wars. The incompetence he embodies further questions the efficacy of the union, as it has only produced offspring with innate weaknesses. If social vicissitudes are to blame for the degeneration of *zhong* in *Red Sorghum*, the introspection, or extrospection, in *Fengru feitun* identifies a different source—a dubious hybridization of the native with the foreign. Yet the birth of the bastard has improved Mother's position and power in the novel, just as China has undeniably benefited from westernization.

Fengru feitun thus reveals the author's deep ambivalence toward China's inevitable bastardization. A critique of the model of merging and coproduction at one level, the novel nevertheless offers the reader no ready solution. Neither the native's solitary struggles nor its integration with the foreign Other turns out to be successful. *Fengru feitun* in the final analysis can be seen as yet another endeavor by Chinese intellectuals to look for a durable configuration to ensure the country's survival and growth in the world. An unending project, the examination of the self and the foreign Other will continue to be part of China's efforts to negotiate and create a modern identity for itself.

In my analysis in chapters 5 and 6, I have sought to place the stories not only within their immediate social realities but also within a larger historical scheme. The affinity I established between the authors' narrative designs and recurring patterns and themes in modern discourses of the self should make it clear that these post-Mao explorations are part of a shared intellectual tradition that has consistently made China and the national self the object of its reflections, critiques, and examinations. Endorsed by generations of writers since Lu Xun, the archetype of the devoted social critic, this approach points to an understanding that locks the fulfillment of the intellectual self, the representing consciousness, with the study of the narrated self, the object of representation. From an epistemological point of view, this is a vision of unity. Because it assumes no chasm between the interests of the intellectual and the people, it identifies the concerns and anxieties of the representing with the represented. By treating both as sort of general, unitary categories, this stance equates the intellectual's self-realization with the national project of rejuvenation. This convergence of the representing with the represented satisfies the intellectuals' existential needs by making their endeavors politically and ideologically meaningful; at the same time, it is a strategic deployment whereby the intellectuals legitimize their authority and importance in society. But this vision of unity was challenged by changing realities in the 1990s, when divergent self-interests, which could be absorbed into the official reform program only in the broadest terms, would force Chinese intellectuals to reexamine many of the premises underlying their perception of themselves and their relation to the community. What happens when the people's and the intellectuals' aspirations are not identical, when the unison between them falters? The circumstances that impelled the intellectuals to engage in serious soul-searching and finally fix the gaze upon themselves are the topic of the next chapter.

7 Appropriation and Representation
The Intellectual Self in the Early 1990s

The fictional characters' lack of subjective powers I have discussed so far unquestionably contradicts the humanist model of individual worth, rationality, and self-autonomy. But this should not lead to a simplistic denial of the recovery of the writers' own creative agency. As Lacan would tell us, the attempt to represent absence is the first step toward replacing the void, opening up possibilities for signification. The breadth and depth of the postrevolutionary inquiry into the Chinese soul in literature attest to the autonomy the writers have reclaimed from Mao's dictatorial cultural policy. Behind the variegated representations of the subject, there is a heightened impulse common to all the writers—the impulse to appropriate, defined by Robert Weimann in simple terms in his theory of representation as "making things (relations, books, texts, writings) one's own" (Weimann 1987, 183). Although the urge to imitate left over from the formulaic Communist past surfaced periodically in bloated, tendentious trends in the 1980s, the majority of post-Mao writers prized individuality, vying with one another to erect their own signposts in the literary landscape. On the collective level, literary appropriations, through which the writers voiced their concerns, commented on social problems, and presented their visions, facilitated their return to the forefront of social development, a position denied them by Mao's manipulation and monopoly of power. But no matter how much the intellectual-writers would like to aggrandize and perpetuate the glory of literature, it was only part of the post-Mao reconstruction, one project among other social engagements reshaping contemporary China. In an age of radical transformation beyond the realm of ideology, literature had to compete with a powerful rival on the historical stage for audience attention: the discursive revolution had to share space with the economic reforms taking place concurrently throughout the country. When Deng Xiaoping reaffirmed his support of the modernization program in early 1992, more than two years after the Tiananmen incident, economic reforms gained new momentum, giving rise to a surge of material appropriation among the population. Emphasizing the accumulation of individual wealth, thus appealing to people's desire to improve their lives, the new trend sucked millions into a frenzy of money-making and consumption, displacing the memories of the ill-fated pro-democracy movement of 1989.

The massive shift of public interest from politics to personal enrichment in the 1990s threatened the centrality Chinese intellectuals had aspired to and to a certain extent secured for themselves in the 1980s, inducing a new crisis for them as subjects in real history in the post-1989 era. This chapter examines the intellectual's changing image in the reforms and the role different appropriating activities played in the process. I take Jia Pingwa's much-debated 1993 novel *The Ruined Capital* as a case study to show how, in one instance, literary representation as an appropriating practice mediates among subject, text, and history to enable the decentered intellectual to deal with his marginalization in a world of fiction.[1] By "intellectuals" in this chapter, I refer to the *renwen gongzuozhe* (humanist workers) or cultural intellectuals, the writers in particular and the scholars who teach and conduct research in the humanities and the social sciences in general. The economic reforms in the past three decades have greatly increased the social and political diversity of contemporary China, redefining existing groups and creating new categories of wealth, power, and alliances. As a result, concerns felt by one segment of the intellectual population may not bother another. Therefore, it is necessary to distinguish the cultural intellectuals from the scientific intellectuals, technicians, professionals, and engineers, for example. Determined by the nature of their profession and the subject matter of their study, the former participated actively in the cultural debates and, rising to prominence in the idealistic 1980s, came to regard themselves as the cultural elites *(wenhua jingying)* of the society. The latter were engaged in more practical undertakings and were less conspicuous and influential ideologically, though a few of them, such as the liberal activist Fang Lizhi, were also at the center of the political storms.[2] The continual emphasis in the 1990s on technological development created a great demand for the expertise of specialists, improving their financial status and offering them options and freedom not enjoyed by the cultural intellectuals. As a result, the scientists were spared in large part the crisis confronting their colleagues in the humanities and the social sciences, who were growing more and more disconcerted by the public's indifference toward intellectual pursuits and the moral values they promoted.

The scope and fast pace of change also make it necessary for us to distinguish the early 1990s from the second half of the decade. The early 1990s witnessed a number of significant events: the acceleration of economic reforms; the advent of a pleasure-oriented popular culture modeled on that of the West, Hong Kong, and Taiwan; and an officially encouraged consumer revolution that favored spending over thrift. These interrelated developments drastically affected the cultural intellectuals' social position and the way their profession was viewed and practiced, producing in them a great deal of anxiety and anguish. Thus, the first few years of the decade marked the onset of the crisis, when the social changes and their ideological, financial, and psychological effect on the intellectuals were most acute. For this reason I situate my discussion of the intellectual self and the formation of the crisis in this period, which is also the social setting of Jia Pingwa's novel. All the factors contributing to the crisis (the aftermath of Tiananmen, political apathy, marketization of the economy, commercialization and commodification of cultural production) still existed in the second half of the decade, but when the practices that disturbed the intellectuals became more or less the norm, their initial shock and dismay gradually turned into resigned acceptance. Though they complained from time to time, aware of the futility of their grumbling and resistance, many intellectuals tried to adapt to the situation and searched for strategies to deal with and even benefit from the new reality. Some advocated retreat into their profession, and some soon found in new conservatism and new nationalism a gratifying platform to reengage culture, politics, and the nation. I offer some reflections on later developments in the Epilogue.

In choosing appropriation as the focus of my argument, I am indebted to Weimann's theory on this subject. In a 1987 article on modern narratives, Weimann reiterates the role of appropriation in representation in response to two popular conceptions, the classical theories of mimesis and the structuralist and poststructuralist dogma of the autonomy of the signifier. The referential theory assumes a closure between the text and history, granting the subject total reflecting powers over the historical real. The modern obsession with signification, in contrast, introduces a rupture between the signifier and the signified, locating meaning in the self-determining referentials in the linguistic system of language. Challenging the idealism of the signifier, poststructuralists such as Michel Foucault stress the predetermined discursive usage of language, bringing social mechanisms of power into the understanding of the dissemination of linguistic knowledge. The insistence on the discursive nature of language, Weimann contends, proscribes the subject as an active agent in the production of meaning (Weimann 1987, 177–179).

Unhappy with the monolithic approach of both traditional hegemony of the subject and its annihilation in twentieth-century theories, Weimann reintroduces the concept of representation as a calculated activity of appropriation to avoid viewing the subject as "purely a function of discourse but discourse not, simultaneously, as a function of the subject" (Weimann 1987, 177).[3] In returning the subject to the representational act and yet not treating it as a free consciousness outside history and language, Weimann addresses textual and extratextual dimensions in representation alike, linking appropriation in literary representation with that in the realm of the sociohistorical. He points out that appropriation as a fundamental mode of human existence involves both discursive practices and nondiscursive activities concerning proprietary and economic rights, and that history unfolds as such activities relate and react to each other. This being the case, changing conditions of social production and ownership as well as the transformed relationship between the represener and his community inevitably affect the modes and functions of representation. As the "social energies and conflicting interests . . . assert themselves within and without the text," representation becomes a performance, a site of interaction between the subject and history (177). An "[act] of intellectual acquisition of imaginative assimilation" (183), representation brings together the subject, the text, and political, social, and economic events. It allows the subject to project itself into the text, thereby maneuvering its position in actual history. Through this appropriation, the gap or link between what is representing and what is represented is either affirmed and magnified or contested and denied (175–191).

Weimann's theory offers two useful perspectives: to recognize representation as a radically historical activity that simultaneously participates in and is affected by other sociohistorical activities and to emphasize not only the performative nature of literary representation, treating it as the subject's self-projection, but also the correlation between the changes in representational strategy and the socioeconomic conditions that give rise and account for such changes. My analysis in this chapter is divided between these two perspectives. In the first part, I discuss the historical conditions leading to the crisis of self-representation for Chinese intellectuals in the 1990s. Specifically, I focus on two stages in the development of the crisis, relating them to various appropriating activities (discursive and nondiscursive) in the reform era: post-Mao intellectuals' efforts to return to the discursive center through ideological appropriation in the first stage and their marginalization in society due to the rise of intense material appropriations since the late 1980s in the second stage. In the second part of the chapter, I look at the representational strategies used in *The Ruined Capital* to recenter the problematized intellectual. I propose to read the novel as a deliberate, appropriating project designed to enable the male intellectual to negotiate his anxiety in the 1990s. By appropriating female subjectivity and enlisting it in the service of the male, the author creates a phallocentric fictional world to compensate for the intellectual's loss of power in real history. I contend that valorizing intellectual authority through male sexuality merely reduces its potency, limiting the intellectual's relevance to society, thus deepening the crisis.

Moving toward the Center

Appropriation as the most basic activity of mediation between the subject and the object no doubt had always been part of life in Communist China. Its existential significance did not become apparent to the Chinese people, however, until noninstitutionalized, individual appropriation was legitimized after Mao's death. The first wave of nationally significant appropriating activities after the Cultural Revolution—the debates on practice as the criterion for testing truth, humanism, and the socialist alienation—was intellectual, ideological, and political in nature. Since at the time China was still recovering from the disastrous political movement, people responded to its conclusion in kind. When the Party's reassessment of its previous policies and campaigns opened up ground for new interpretations, comprehensive reconfiguration became the order of the day. Released from their former ideological pigeonholes, various social groups must reposition themselves in post-Mao China. The intellectuals were the most vocal in redefining their relationship to the state.

What evolved as a result was a complex relationship, which nonetheless had some discernible patterns. It was fluid and changeable, by turns promising and gloomy. Even though Deng's policy toward the intellectuals in general was more tolerant and conducive to intellectual freedom, it followed a familiar Maoist model of integration and control. On the one hand, the modernization program promoted by China's new leaders needed the knowledge, advice, and cooperation of the intellectuals more than ever. On the other, it was hard for the old-timers at the top to shake off their suspicion of the intellectuals. The reinstated veterans proved themselves perfectly willing to resort to Mao-style political censorship to curb the intellectuals' power whenever they thought they had detected threatening moves from those quarters. The campaign against "bourgeois liberalization" targeting Bai Hua ended only after the artist made a public self-criticism in November 1981, admitting his mistakes in doubting the Party's ability to rectify itself. Although the "anti–spiritual pollution" drive was short-lived after its introduction in 1983, because of resistance from the reform leaders within the Party and lack of support from intellectuals without, it further testifies to the Party's continued mistrust of the intellectuals.

The volatility of the relationship often reflected not only the cleavage between the conservatives and younger liberals of the new power elite in the Party but also the division among the ranks of the intellectuals, between those who spoke for the Party's reform program and the critical-minded who pressed for institutional changes (Hamrin 1987). It took some intellectuals about a decade to transcend the traditional school of thought, which sought no political autonomy outside existing governmental structures. It was not until the eve of the bloody showdown in 1989 that the intellectuals finally relinquished their hope of reform from within the political system. Goldman, Link, and Su show that the intellectuals' relationship with the Party went through distinct stages. In the early years after the Cultural Revolution, the majority identified with the official modernization program, adopting a "restorationist" approach in helping the Party return to "genuine Marxist practices." From 1982 to the Tiananmen Square bloodbath, doubts about the sanctity of the system began to build, strengthened each time the Party initiated repressive measures to silence criticism. Deepening frustration and skepticism about the effectiveness of political action within the system led in the end to the call for reform of the system. The reality of the June Fourth crackdown eventually brought some intellectuals around to the opinion expressed by Liu Xiaobo, considered too radical a few years before, that to be truly loyal to the nation, the intellectuals should go into the opposition, thus abandoning their traditional position as moral advisers begging the regime to reform itself (Goldman, Link, and Su 1993).

One thing remains clear in the eventful relationship. Intellectual appropriation—the efforts to redefine, or add new categories to, China's ideological-political vocabulary—was the means the intellectuals adopted to assert their influence in the post-Mao era. As soon as the ideological thaw began in 1976, the intellectuals lost no time in launching polemical discussions on the subjects I dealt with in chapter 2, Marxism, humanism, subjectivity, Chinese culture, and modernization, even though these debates started under a range of historical circumstances, served divergent purposes, and invoked different responses from the Party.[4] Intellectual appropriation in turn proved itself time and again a source of provocation to the Party, and this was where it struck back, as evidenced by the aborted minicampaigns.

The post-Mao ideological debates carried out by the intellectuals served two general functions. First, they were condemnations of Mao's destruction of genuine appropriation in the realm of intellectual thought. Thanks to his forceful collectivization at every level of social life, the boundaries between public and private spheres in Mao's authoritarian China were practically nonexistent. All intellectual activities—thinking, writing, and reading—were made uniform and publicized. Take literature, for example. The writers' role in the so-called collective creation (*jiti chuangzuo*), a practice popularized in the late 1960s and 1970s, was often defined as *zhibi* (writing down). Their creative agency nullified, writers were allowed to do no more than holding the pen in recording collective decisions. Reading was likewise contaminated. Under tight control by the media and the watchful eye of local Party organizations, the unpredictability of the naturally heterogeneous activity was greatly reduced. The ritual of "collective study" (*jiti xuexi*) created a group atmosphere that turned private reception into public consumption, replacing individual assimilation with collective absorption of prescribed information. With the Party assuming the critical role as the storyteller who had every power to restrict audience choice and interpretations, China virtually became a gigantic storytelling theater, void of its traditionally relaxed atmosphere. The collective experience forestalled "misreading," ensuring unity along the Party line on both physical and psychological levels.

In this type of collective venture, "appropriation" was an empty term. When ideological conformity left the subject little to appropriate, the operative principle of "making things one's own" was suspended, and individual agency vital to the act of appropriation could not come into play. Taking appropriation out of the hands of the participants, the Party monopolized the role of appropriator, functioning as both the ultimate author and the only privileged interpreter of the Communist "master narrative." Is it any wonder that homogeneity on the whole defines Mao's China?[5] The writer's position in the monolithic Communist system was not very different from that of epic poets in a communal society described by Weimann: "The author's function is to assert known and publicly acknowledged ideals; it is not to appropriate any area of thought or experience that has not previously been appropriated in (early feudal or courtly) society itself" (Weimann 1987, 187). This explains the epic poets' acceptance of previous literary efforts as shared property and their free use of existing stories with known characters and events. Revolutionary literature presents a similar case. The creation of stereotypical characters and predictable plots is essentially a recycling of a few basic Communist patterns from collective resources. There is, however, a significant difference. Since the epic poets' identification with the communal values of their times was voluntary, complete, and congenial, they did not feel the need for individual appropriation. On the contrary, Chinese intellectuals' association with Party ideology in many instances after the late 1950s was involuntary and coerced. The periodic sprouting of "poisonous weeds" is testimony to the intellectuals' constant attempts at true appropriation.[6]

Second, the post-Mao ideological debates not only declared the intellectuals' opposition to the revolutionary practice but also simultaneously helped them move toward the center that they had lost to the Maoist brand of Communist discourse. The fight over political and ideological nomenclature was a fight over the power to name, a battle against the Party's monopoly over language. By challenging the Maoist discourse, the intellectuals sought to reestablish their own authority. Chinese intellectuals' aggressiveness in repossessing the center came from their confidence in their ability to represent the people. The ruthless repression they received at the hands of Mao's regime gave the intellectuals the credibility to speak on behalf of people who suffered the same fate, and the prestige they traditionally enjoyed in Chinese society added further weight to their opinion. The immense appeal of the "literature of the wounded" proved the validity of the intellectuals' self-assessment. Although the literary trend had the official blessing, its popularity with readers was spontaneous and overwhelming. Later, fiction and reportage exposing government corruption and social problems, such as Liu Binyan's 1979 "Ren yao zhi jian" (People or monster?) and Liu Xinwu's 1985 "Gonggong qiche yongtandiao" (The aria on a bus), continued to exert great influence over society. The willing destruction of their official image as the mouthpiece of Mao's leftist policies after the Cultural Revolution obviously did not affect the intellectuals' role as representatives. The message changed, but the messenger did not.

Moreover, the messenger-intellectuals had much to boost their image in the eyes of society. Under the aegis of Deng Xiaoping's policy, the intellectuals' social and economic status improved: they were reintegrated into the ranks of the working people, their admission into the Party was made easier, and they were given academic titles and promotions (L. T. White 1987). But more important to the intellectuals was the part they came to play in the reforms. Their professional knowledge was deemed indispensable to the modernization program, and their advice was sought at high levels, which allowed them direct input into the decisionmaking process.[7] If not exactly ready to replace the CCP, the intellectuals certainly felt that they could share with it the position as the vanguard setting the course for the nation's transformation. This posture is obvious in the title of a book series launched by the intellectuals, *Zou xiang weilai* (Marching toward the future), which had the ambitious goal of publishing 100 books to provide spiritual guidance for the people. The objective of another megaseries, managed by Gan Yang, *Wenhua: Zhongguo yu shijie* (Culture: China and the world), was to translate 470 books by foreign authors, including Lacan, Foucault, Sartre, and Camus.[8] The air was saturated with a sense of euphoria in the 1980s. In this information age when "knowledge is power," the intellectuals, it seemed, should be the leaders.[9]

Crisis in the Making

While intellectual pursuits reclaimed authority and representational power for the intellectuals in the postrevolutionary era, they also prepared conditions for their erosion. The reform age the ideological debates helped usher in would eventually frustrate the intellectuals, introducing unexpected changes in their relationship to the society. Fearing that a political reform would cause fast dilution of its power, the Party decided first to experiment with economic reforms. Its unprecedented move to relinquish the utopian goal to allow a part of the population to get rich before everyone else soon led to a second wave of appropriation that stressed material gain in no uncertain terms. The public's appropriating instinct, which had been condemned and strictly contained within the official channels in the past, was awakened, and people followed it with great vehemence. Privatization and increased social productivity suddenly presented people with colossal possibilities for making wealth. Relieved of the ideological shackles and restrictive policies, people now realized that they could set their own terms of living with their daring and innovativeness. Poverty and frugality, glorified in Mao's thinking, became a disgrace to be hidden and overcome.

Unlike the ideological appropriation in the late 1970s, whose major players were for the most part intellectuals, material appropriation after the mid-1980s developed into a new national obsession shared by hundreds of millions of people from every conceivable background. A contemporary parody of Mao's slogan *"quan min jie bing"* (turning the whole nation into soldiers) describes the rage for starting private businesses as *"quan min jie shang"* (turning the whole nation into merchants). "Making things one's own" was now a social craze, a distinctive characteristic of the current mode of life. As material appropriation mounted, Mao's artificially designed and enforced egalitarian society crumpled with surprising speed. The newly rich popped up, and the phenomenal gap between them and the poor kept widening.[10] As the reforms deepened, living expenses rapidly climbed.[11] While the poor still had problems making ends meet, the new monied elite enjoyed a lifestyle in every respect comparable to that of the upper middle class in the West. Tales of fancy housing and sumptuous feasts circulated widely. Of course only a tiny percentage of the populace could indulge in luxury. In sharp contrast to the openly displayed extravagance of the rich, a noticeable number of people sank into poverty as a result of losing the "iron rice bowl."[12] The new system of contracting out enterprises to individuals often led to job cuts. At the same time, unprofitable factories or firms were allowed to merge and lay off workers on a part- or full-time basis.[13] *Xiagang,* the Chinese term for laying off workers, was a favorite conversation topic among city inhabitants and was often staged in TV series in the early 1990s. It was up to the *xiagang* workers to find ways to supplement their meager wages (50 percent or so of their original pay) to cover skyrocketing living expenses.[14]

Those feeling the economic pinch of the times were not just employees of foundering enterprises. Intellectuals were also affected. Admittedly, as government employees, they did not have to face layoffs and downsizing.[15] A small number of them were even quite well off. Best-selling authors who were able to have their works adapted to the big screen fared extremely well financially. But the less popular were not so fortunate. This was not because writers published less. Since the Cultural Revolution, channels for publication had greatly expanded. According to *Zhongguo chuban nianjian, 1997* (China statistical yearbook of publications, 1997), the total number of publishing houses rose from 105 in 1978 to 550 in 1994; that of journals and magazines made a spectacular jump from 930 in 1978 to 7,325 in 1994, among which 567 were devoted to literature and art (8, 17). Increased publication possibilities, however, did not necessarily fatten the writers' pocketbooks. Only 3 to 4 percent of the profit was paid to the writers; the largest piece of the pie (20 to 50 percent) went to the retailers (Li Shulei 1995, 55). Unless a work was able to sell hundreds of thousands of copies, the author could not expect to make a fortune. To writers in the 1990s, hearing that in the 1950s and 1960s one could make a very decent living on money received from publishing three or four short pieces a year was like "listening to stories from the reign of Tianbao (741–755)." That Du Pengcheng, the author of the revolutionary novel *Baowei Yan'an* (Defending Yan'an), was able to spare tens of thousands of yuan to pay for his Party membership dues in the 1950s sounded like "a tale out of the *Arabian Nights*" (Xiao Haiying 1993b).

Without generous remuneration to defray galloping prices, life became difficult for some writers and scholars in the early 1990s. A number of premature deaths were reported. She Shusen, a professor known for his studies of twentieth-century prose, died in his fifties, leaving his widow to support his two school-age children with her monthly salary of a couple of hundred yuan. When Lu Yao, the author of the well-known "Rensheng" (Life), died leaving little inheritance for his orphaned daughter, the Chinese Literary Foundation stepped in to provide her with money to continue her education. When Zhu Xingyi, a prize-winning short-story writer, died in his middle age, his colleagues had to collect donations for his three unemployed children (Zhang Zhizhong 1994, 89). Meanwhile, many struggled to deal with their declining standard of living, trying hard to comprehend what they perceived to be a glaring income gap between themselves and those who were traditionally of a much lower social status, such as peasants and street vendors.[16] Scholar and writer Lin Fei commented wryly that his neighbor, an old melon peddler by trade, earned enough money to buy a van in a few summers. Knowing what was in store for a scholar financially, Lin felt extremely guilty about his Ph.D. program applicants. He was afraid that "they might repeat the poor life of [his] generation of intellectuals."[17] The famous film director Xie Jin was excited over the 2,000 yuan he received as a consultant for a film, which, he told his friend Sha Yexin, far exceeded his regular monthly pay. Sha noted sadly that one of his friends in business once spent more than 2,300 yuan on a dinner for three (Li Shulei 1995, 55).

Circumstances—economic difficulties, disappointment with the 1989 democracy movement, danger of radical political intervention, and no doubt in many cases the lure of money—compelled the intellectuals to join in the fad of material appropriation. Unable to give substantial salary raises to intellectuals, the government in the mid-1980s began to allow academics and professionals to take up second jobs to augment their state incomes. Encouraged by official policy, university departments started "create income" *(chuang shou)* programs to offer extracurricular services and classes to help with school budgets.[18] It was truly a situation of *ba xian guo hai, ge xian shentong* (the Eight Immortals crossing the sea, each one showing his or her special prowess). Science and technology departments formed partnerships with enterprises to develop new products or took on projects to generate money. Having a harder time selling their expertise, those in the humanities and the social sciences sometimes had to settle for less academic ventures.[19] Many intellectuals also individually "put out to sea" *(xiahai):* they gave up secure government jobs to work in the private sector. Entertainers and athletes, who were often categorized along with the writers as members of the arts and sports circles, led the trend and reportedly made a fortune. China's world-famous gymnast Li Ning organized his own sporting-goods company, turning his name into a successful brand name. The versatile film star Liu Xiaoqing headed several entertainment businesses and, according to popular belief, ranked among China's richest women.

But *xiahai* was not so easy for the intellectual-writers, who had to overcome more psychological hurdles. To engage in business and making money was traditionally held beneath the dignity and integrity of the literati. In 1998, a year after Zhang Xian's death, his widow still found it necessary to defend the writer's financial success from making popular TV plays (Qin Zhiyu 1998).[20] When Wei Minglun, a playwright nationally accredited for his innovative *chuanju* dramas *Bashan xiucai* (The scholar from Bashan) and *Pan Jinlian,* had to give up his creative career, he was grief-stricken and indignant.[21] He told his readers that he had always despised money and had been content living a simple life even though his monthly salary was only a couple of hundred yuan. He revealed that the remuneration from all his works was less than 2,000 yuan and that his twenty-year-old son had never even been to Chengdu, the provincial capital. Wei went on to say that, sustained by his pride in his literary creations, he had never felt inferior on account of his financial status. Why now, he asked, "are Chinese intellectuals so worthless?" He informed his readers that he had abandoned his literary career because his "standard of living and working conditions affected [his] creation, hurting [his] sense of dignity and honor."[22]

Other writers went into private business to help tide their fellow writers over economic difficulties. Zhang Qie, the secretary of the Secretariat of the Chinese Writers' Association, calls this *"yingong chuhai"* (going out to sea on official business) (Xiao Haiying 1993a). Zhang Xianliang, a writer famous for his fiction on life in labor camps, said that he decided to start a company because among the government departments at the provincial level, the Ninghai Federation of Literature and Arts was a *qingshui yamen* (nonprofitable office). As chairman of the federation, he did not even have sufficient funds to run the office. His purpose in going into business was to earn money to create more favorable working conditions for the writers affiliated with the Ninghai Federation. He was doing this at his own expense, which meant the suspension of his creative career and the misunderstanding, possibly contempt, his decision could induce from fellow writers (Zhang Zhizhong 1994, 88).

Most writers treated their colleagues' new vocation as an individual choice, but "writers going out to sea" *(zuojia xiahai)* did arouse distress. "China is not short of merchants but writers," Chen Guokui implored. He cited statistics to support his view: "Japan's population is only 20 percent of China's, but it has three times as many writers as China." Feng Jicai, vice chairman of the China Federation of Literature and Arts and a prolific writer in his own right, could hardly hold back his anguish: "If in their time Cao Xueqin opened a restaurant and Lu Xun set up a vending stall on the street, what a tremendous spiritual loss this would have been for the Chinese nation." The veteran playwright Xia Yan even tried a scare tactic, telling the writers that "your separation from the commodity economy made you neglect a commonsense fact, that is, there are high risks involved in the 'sea.' Business and literary creation are two entirely different trades. You writers who are 'going out to sea,' do you have the [business] talent?" (Xiao Haiying 1993a).

Losing the Center

The tidal wave of material appropriation did not just affect intellectuals financially, causing a few changes of heart. It precipitated a profound sense of crisis. From antiquity to the modern period, Chinese intellectuals had always been at the center of society. On the strength of their knowledge of Confucianism, the dominant philosophical and ideological basis of premodern China, the traditional intelligentsia had monopolized access to officialdom since the Tang dynasty via the civil service examination and were revered by the ruling and the ruled alike. The May Fourth intellectuals' mutiny against the Confucian tradition later in the modern period did not hurt their prestige. By redefining what China needed for survival in the international arena, the new intellectuals retained their authority as the guiding force of social progress. Privileged by their education in the West and in Japan and their ability to transmit modern ideas through their mastery of foreign languages, the May Fourth intellectuals presented themselves as the sole competent designers of a program of national rejuvenation. Identifying completely with the new epochal discourse, modern intellectuals endowed themselves with an irrefutable authority as the native source of a modernizing movement vital to their country's well-being, unlike the prestige their predecessors derived from their interpretative ability of the Confucian canon in the past.

Precisely because of their knowledge of Western thought, the intellectuals gradually lost their discursive power when the Communist ideology in Mao's interpretation became the only legitimate social discourse in the People's Republic. Establishing itself as the new authority, the Communist Party came to occupy the center. Even though the negation of their authority took the discursive power out of the hands of the intellectuals, however, it did not move them from the center of attention. On the one hand, the intellectuals' discursive capability made them potentially the most subversive force in the eyes of the Party and consequently the most censured social group in Mao's China. On the other hand, the Party had to rely on the intellectuals as "thought workers" to propagate its ideology through the activities they were engaged in. Chinese intellectuals' unique position as both the target of ideological purges and the operator of what Louis Althusser calls the state ideological apparatuses landed them in the middle of social life in revolutionary China, turning them into involuntary stars in Mao's political dramas.

But the secularization of Chinese culture and the stepped-up commercialization after the late 1980s threatened to de-center the intellectuals. After enjoying the limelight for about a decade following the Cultural Revolution, the intellectuals found themselves pushed to the periphery. Besides the financial difficulties many of them had, various factors contributed to their marginalization. First, political and economic reform (no matter how limited the former was) brought with it a plurality of social discourses, which not even the Party could easily stamp out.[23] As a result, instead of one discursive center, contemporary China has an array of divergent "small narratives." In an age of multiplicity, the intellectuals could not possibly hope to prevail. In fact, the attempt to hold the absolute center is a residue of the Maoist legacy.

Second, the appeal of literature as a crucial part of the post-Mao discourse of change rested primarily on its serving as a vehicle for public complaint and protest. However, the futility of mass protest and the Party's new authoritarian policies in the wake of the Tiananmen demonstrations discouraged political participation. The bloody crackdown of 1989 and the ensuing purges made barbed commentary and confrontational politics risky and dangerous. Radical intellectuals were arrested, persecuted, or went into exile. In addition, as the economic reforms gathered force and the prospects of getting rich by individual effort were becoming more promising, the excessive enthusiasm in politics cultivated by Mao's ideology diminished on the popular level. At the same time, the public's disinterest in politics was shared by literature itself even before the events of 1989. Tired of being an ideological tool forever trying to keep up with the fickle Party line, some writers advocated a return to "pure" literature. As the metafiction represented by Ma Yuan demonstrates, literature is chartered as the writer's exclusive territory, an insider's game with little political significance. If in the early 1980s the political thrust of literary avant-gardism was still recognized and appreciated by the reading public, in the changed situations of the reform age radical technical experimentalism could appeal only to a shrinking elite and was recycled among a few "club members."[24] Thus, literature and readers seemed to be mutually deserting each other beginning in the mid-1980s. The gradual disengagement of literature from ideology and political concerns was illustrated in the writers' retreat from social intervention. The previous fascination with the political and cultural subject that we witnessed in the previous chapters cooled into passionless observation, as shown in the trend of the "new realism," the representative feature of which is the author's "zero involvement" in the literary presentation of ordinary people's lives. The typical narrator of a "new realist" work makes no moral judgments, neither condemning nor condoning.[25]

Third, when reduced to a form of entertainment without a strong political and ideological agenda, literature must compete directly with other pastimes. As in all areas of life, people were now flooded with entertainment choices. Contemporary China has been a revolving stage, putting on show after show of new trends and fashions in quick succession. Even the film industry, which used to provide the most popular form of entertainment, felt the threat. Boasting a viewership of over 800 million, TV came out a big winner, thanks to the decentralization of the state TV network, which gave the audience access to a wider range of channels and programs.[26] Although the film industry sought external funding and catered to popular tastes, ticket sales were disappointing. Even structural changes (such as partitioning seats into small boxes to give filmgoers more privacy) and selling drinks and snacks in theaters failed to lure TV audiences away from the comfort of their living rooms.[27] Emblematic of China's rush toward modernity, pop and consumer culture also charged in from abroad and across the Taiwan Strait with a vengeance. Health clubs, beauty salons, and cosmetic clinics were booming businesses. In the evenings many young and middle-aged people went to the bars to eat and sing karaoke; others flocked to nightclubs to rock and disco away their spare time.[28] Zhang Kangkang, a female educated–youth writer who emerged after the

Cultural Revolution, wondered "if there would be a day when China's invention of paper would not be that important anymore."[29]

This is not to say that literature is completely displaced. It is still widely read; however, readers' tastes underwent essential changes. Exhausted by a faster pace of life and the business of moneymaking, readers turned away from serious literature. Profound thinking seemed too tiring. In the ambiance of material betterment, an escapist approach to literature was obvious. Bookstalls lining the streets peddled popular stories featuring murder, sex, legendary robberies, kung fu, and palace intrigues. In the writer Xiao Fuxing's words, "Nowadays the majority of readers are content with one-time-use, fast-food type of literary works" (Xiao Haiying 1993b). The marketization of the publishing industry further empowered consumers.[30] When reading was reprivatized into a matter of individual choice, the publishing houses had to respect reader preferences if they wanted to sell their products. A commodity now, literature had to descend from its lofty position, obey the rules of the market, and be a part of it.[31] Business terms even entered the vocabulary of literary criticism, adding a commercial color to the intellectual's language of disenchantment. Literary creation was said to be "in a slump," and adopting a marketing strategy to boost the sales of a book was called *chao zuo* (literally, "to stir-fry a literary work"), the same *chao* as in *chao gupiao* (speculation in stocks), which was a new national rage in its own right after China's first stock market opened in Shanghai and Shenzhen, in 1992 (Zhang Rulun et al. 1994).

The society's changing needs and its reduced dependence on literature for emotional catharsis and moral guidance forced Chinese intellectuals to readjust their perception of their relationship to the community. With their image as social prophets (only lately restored after the Cultural Revolution) radically problematized, the intellectuals suddenly felt that they were alienated and discarded by society. The psychological effect of the dissolution of their alliance with the people should not be underestimated, for it historically provided the moral basis for the intellectuals to legitimize and fight for their prestige and privileged status in society. To understand the trauma the scission brought to Chinese intellectuals, we may look to Pierre Bourdieu's theory of the field of cultural production (Bourdieu 1993). Although his theory is not fully applicable to the situation in China, the modifications we could make to some of his key concepts when dealing with the Chinese field (in the same spirit of contextualization that underlies Bourdieu's own approach) could help us highlight what is unique and has shaped Chinese cultural practice in the twentieth century.

Crucial to Bourdieu's theory is his explication of various forms of capital, whose (re)distribution among its agents, that is, members of the field of cultural production, creates the dynamics of the field: the symbolic capital, the cultural capital, and the economic capital. "Symbolic capital" refers to the celebrity, honor, accumulated prestige, and recognition the agents enjoy. "Cultural capital" is defined as a form of knowledge or an internal code, obtained through education, that provides the agent with competence to appreciate and decipher cultural products. In other words, possession of cultural capital allows the agent to participate meaningfully in the production and consumption of cultural artifacts. "Economic capital," as the name suggests, refers to material wealth in the form of property and monetary gains. While all these forms of capital are involved in the production of cultural goods, they are not of equal importance in the hierarchical order of the cultural field, which Bourdieu calls "the economic world reversed" because of its disavowal of the economic interest. Based on his analyses of the French field of cultural production in the nineteenth century, Bourdieu points out that the internal logic of the cultural field, which serves to distinguish it from other social fields, is built upon an overruling principle of artistic autonomy—the refusal to give in to demands outside the field, for example, the ideological needs of the dominant class or the taste of the popular cultural market. This emphasis on independence, Bourdieu further explains, is effected through the adoption of the mode of "restricted production," a production that aims at a small audience made up of other agents in the cultural field who share similar artistic dispositions with the works' producers themselves. What is at stake in this insistence on artistic autonomy for the agents is obviously not the economic profit but the symbolic capital, the consecration by one's fellow producers. Thus guided by its preference for autonomy, the cultural field places on the inferior end of its scale those who are successful only in making economic gains through the "large-scale production" that targets the public. As a result, those who are high in economic capital are low in symbolic capital (Bordieu 1993, pt. 1, in particular 29–73, 112–141).

It is apparent from Bourdieu's discussion of the execution of the autonomous principle that the restricted production is to a large extent an internal love affair, so to speak, in the sense that the two parties involved, the producer and the consumer, are both insiders. How is this significant to the generation of symbolic capital? It is the insider's appreciation and recognition that ultimately form and confirm the value of symbolic capital. It is precisely on this point that the cultural field in modern China differs greatly from the French model. Studies on the genesis of modern Chinese literature have made it amply clear that it was conceived in a moment of national crisis and that its development was inextricably intertwined with China's pursuit of modernity and social progress. The partnership between literature and revolution, which was not only entered into willingly but was also forcefully advocated by progressive-minded modern intellectual-writers, further strengthened the didacticism and functionalism already deeply rooted in the Confucian literary practice, a part of the tradition the intellectuals inherited despite their repudiation of other Confucian principles. As a result, the European art for art's sake, an essential component of the autonomous principle, was consciously rejected by the majority of modern writers, who were keen on instigating social transformation through the literary word. Instead of taking pride in the limited circulation of their creations among those in the know in the field, as the French autonomous artists did, modern Chinese writers tried, at least in intention and theory, to reach as wide a readership as possible in their project of revolution and change. As Michel Hockx asserts, national considerations had become "part of their practice" (Hockx 1999, 12).

The courting of an external readership thus significantly redefined the literary-ideological hierarchization in the Chinese cultural field. While commercial success was looked upon with suspicion and remained at the low end of the scale, the autonomous principle was very much suspended within the mainstream left-wing practice. Works carrying explicit, strong moral messages in the iconoclastic spirit of the times were lauded, and various modernist, formal experiments perceived to be at a distance from the immediate reality and lacking social urgency were coldly received. In the subsequent Mao era, the Communist proletarianization of literature institutionalized through various policies and censorship further reinforced the May Fourth tendency to politicize and popularize. Wooed into the Chinese configuration, the people became an indispensable element in deciding how the symbolic capital was conceived and received. Having been turned into the ideal(ized) audience, the people became a necessary legitimizing force with social, political consequences. Only in the political and social arena, at the intersection between the production of the cultural goods and their reception by the people, was the symbolic capital realized. The people's recognition and acknowledgment of the value of symbolic capital served to validate the social significance of both the cultural products and their producers. Thus, even though Chinese writers have always held an elitist attitude toward the people, they paradoxically also sought their acceptance and approval. Even if the representation of the people and their voice was often manipulated by the CCP in its scheme to achieve social, political power, the intellectual-writers had long ago internalized service to the people as a crucial standard in assessing their social position and self-worth.

As I mentioned above, because of their importance in the production of social meaning and power, the people, particularly in Communist China, have often been used as a strategy for political purposes. The Party justified its suppression of the intellectuals by naming them enemies of the people; the intellectuals, wherever possible, legitimized their dissent and demand for freedom and autonomy in the name of the people. For example, in Mao's regime, the Party's tactic of identifying the country's needs with its own made patriotism outside the Communist political order impossible. As a countermove after the Cultural Revolution, post-Mao intellectuals brought loyalty to the nation and the people into the new three-part structure of Party-country-intellectuals in their relationship to the state, thus sundering the previous Communist conflation of the state and the nation.[32] The new platform allowed the intellectuals to disagree and to advise as representatives of the people, providing them with a brand-new leverage in the post-Mao era. While some intellectuals continued the traditional practice of gaining a voice through political patronage, many sought support by forming connections with nonofficial, nongovernmental associations (Bonnin and Chevrier 1996; Goldman 1999). Indeed, it was surmised that some of them, embittered by the 1989 crackdown, "might no longer conceive of themselves as intermediaries between the government and the people and move completely over to the side of the people" (Goldman, Link, and Su 1993, 153).

The foundation on which the intellectuals hoped to build an opposition collapsed beneath them. Only a few years after the heady months in 1989, they had to admit that "the traditional 'honeymoon' relationship between writers and society is over" (Chen Fumin 1993). They realized that the age when a single literary work could create a national furor was gone forever. Some ten years before, Jiang Zilong's 1979 reformist story "Qiao changzhang shangren ji" (Manager Qiao reports to work), which portrays a new manager's efforts to reform a bankrupt factory, brought him hundreds of letters of support from readers. Similarly, Ye Wenfu was greeted by a full house at each of his public readings of the critical 1979 poem "Jiangjun, buneng neiyang zuo" (General, do not do this), which admonishes a high-ranking army officer for abusing his power. But because of the paucity of entertainment choices, literature had virtually no competition in those days. In sharp contrast to the savior image Mo Yan creates for his intellectual protagonist in "White Dog and the Swings" (discussed in my introduction), a critic in the 1990s exhorted his fellow intellectuals to give up their "public-square consciousness" *(guangchang yishi)*, referring to the role Chinese intellectuals had played in leading public protests in modern and recent history. He told them they should not expect that "at a wave of their arms, hundreds will respond" *(zheng bi yi hu, yingzhe yunji)* (Chen Sihe et al. 1993, 69). Another critic called intellectuals today "garbage collectors" gathering what society no longer treasured—humanistic concerns and social morals (Chen Fumin 1993).

Feeling the landslide, the intellectuals were at a loss how to position themselves in society and how to deal with the public's indifference. Many acknowledged that they were facing "an existential crisis" in the 1990s (Wu Xuan et al. 1994; "Zhongguo wentan"). According to the popular fiction writer Wang Shuo, "Intellectuals are the group least able to find its position in society. They, more than the people in other social strata, have the strongest sense of crisis in the face of the surge of commercialization" (Wang Shuo 1993, 65).[33] As a social group, Chinese intellectuals tend to thrive on controversy. Even the government's negative attention was an acknowledgment of their importance in society. Now all of a sudden they were ignored. Not only was the public too busy going about getting rich to be interested in intellectual polemics, but the government had finally learned to give intellectuals more leash to head off confrontations.[34] With their opponents and allies alike in retreat, there was no one for the intellectuals to pick a fight with and no one to fight for. And unlike Cervantes' hero, they could not be consoled with a chivalrous illusion. The absence of government provocation and belligerence coupled with the public's lack of zeal created a feeling of loss among the intellectuals.[35] The critic Li Shulei puts it succinctly: "Chinese intellectuals are used to being at the center. [They] may be able to adapt to [government] suppression because of too much attention; but they found it hard to swallow the neglect of being left out in the cold. Neglect poses a real threat to the intellectuals' sense of self-value and self-respect" (Li Shulei 1995, 54).

As society's need for the cultural intellectuals changed, a painful self-reevaluation was in order. Again, as Bourdieu emphasizes, the pursuit of symbolic capital rather than material gratification distinguishes the field of cultural production from other social fields. Chinese intellectuals had always placed great value on their cultural knowledge, which gave them the ability to provide spiritual guidance to society. This had been the source of their social worth, winning them respect from the people and personal satisfaction. But after the mid-1980s material possessions became the accepted standard for judging a person's success or failure. "Million-yuan households" were the envy of everyone. The issue here is not so much that material wealth was the intellectuals' chief object of desire: the majority of them still took great pride in their studies and pursuit of humanistic ideals. It had more to do with how intellectuals felt they were being judged in the eyes of society. The era when Tao Yuanming (365–427) could be tranquil and even self-celebratory about his poverty was over. The famous poet certainly did not have to daily witness his neighbors' affluence. Nor did the literati's social status depend on their bank accounts in those days. As Wei Minglun reveals, he was content with his meager pay until that of an ordinary worker surpassed it. Let us return to Wei's sorrowful question: "Zhongguo de zhishifenzi jiu zeme bu zhiqian?" (Why are Chinese intellectuals worth so little money?). *Zhiqian*, which can be a metaphor, has to be understood literally now. In popular conception, individuals' amassed economic capital equals their accomplishments and social respectability. When the intellectuals were forced to feel ashamed of their thin pocketbooks while upstarts without much cultural capital could squander ten times the amount of their monthly salary on one dinner, the idea of being a modern Tao Yuanming was rather unpalatable.

Representation Problematized

Having discussed the dramatic changes in Chinese intellectuals' position and function in society since the Cultural Revolution, anchoring the fluctuation in various appropriating activities in the post-Mao era, I turn to how representation wrestles with this historical reality. To regard the text as a juncture of representation and history is to subscribe to the position that both emphasizes literature's situatedness in history and recognizes it as a signifying activity that fulfills certain representational aims. Jia Pingwa's *The Ruined Capital* offers an intriguing case for my study on two counts.[36] First, it reveals a strong historicity in its presentation of the intellectuals' loss of authority through the figure of the artist. Second, and more fascinating, it shows us how this loss is recouped in the same text by the use of certain representational strategies. I seek to prove that reviving an outdated discourse of male superiority over women as pure sex objects in the fictional world, the text tries to counterbalance the marginalization of the intellectual in real history only to have the mirage deconstructed when its own textual basis crumbles.

Jia Pingwa is a familiar name to readers of contemporary Chinese literature. Born in 1952 to a large peasant family, Jia grew up in the Shangzhou area, Shaanxi province, which later became a permanent backdrop for his fiction. When his middle school education was cut short by the start of the Cultural Revolution, he returned to his village and lived with his family in poverty and political disgrace after his father, a local schoolteacher, was named a "historical counterrevolutionary" and lost his job. In 1972 Jia was lucky enough to be admitted into the Chinese department of Northwestern University in Xi'an. Having tried his hand at poetry writing without much success, Jia turned to fiction and excelled. After graduation he worked as editor for various publishing houses and journals. A prolific writer who in 1985 alone published ten novellas, Jia is now a member of the council of the Chinese Writers' Association. His well-received "Shangzhou chu lu" (Preliminary records of Shangzhou), and a series of stories and novellas set in the mountainous area around his hometown are fine specimens of *xungen* literature. Famous for his vivid and colorful descriptions of local customs and his insights into the people's emotional and psychological "turbulence" (as the title of one of his stories characterizes it) during the reforms, Jia has produced many powerful stories about life at the crossroads of modernization.

Besides his vigorous examination of indigenous traditions and social changes, the appeal and aesthetic beauty of Jia Pingwa's work come from his fine artistic sensibility and superb mastery of the Chinese language. The author's appreciation of traditional culture and literature is clearly reflected in the grace, elegance, brevity, and descriptive power of his language. Many of Jia's depictions of Shangzhou scenery are as exquisite as those in traditional travelogues. His fiction has won numerous literary awards and has been translated into many languages. Critics and readers alike regard him as one of the finest writers in China today. Partly because of his reputation, the appearance of *The Ruined Capital* shocked many of Jia's colleagues, critics, and readers.

In spite of its length, the novel has a rather simple story line. It centers on a famous writer, Zhuang Zhidie, who faces a libel lawsuit brought against him by a former female colleague, Jing Xueyin, for publishing an account of his alleged affair with her. Much of the novel is devoted to detailed descriptions of Zhuang's sexual escapades with his mistresses and his various attempts to win his legal battle. With his reputation and health destroyed, Zhuang ends up losing the lawsuit as well as his lovers.

The Ruined Capital was a huge sensation both before and after its publication. The marketing of the book was cited by critics as a perfect instance of the *chao zuo* phenomenon (Chen Xiaoming et al. 1994b). The public was goaded into eager anticipation long before the novel was scheduled to reach bookstores. Advertisements calling it a modern *Honglou meng* or *Jin ping mei* appeared everywhere, capitalizing on these traditional novels' misconstrued pornographic reputation. In the frenzied hype, rumors about the book and its author quickly circulated and were as quickly put to rest. It was reported that Jia had sold the book for more than a million yuan; almost immediately that figure was denied. From then on each news release about the book further fanned the public's interest. This marketing ploy produced the desired result. Hundreds of copies of the journal *Shiyue* (October), which ran the novel in full, were sold out. The 480,000 copies of the first print run in book form by Beijing Publishing House also failed to satisfy demand, and there were thousands of pirated copies in circulation. In the summer of 1993, Jia even succeeded in usurping the crown from the king of popular literature, Wang Shuo, as *The Ruined Capital* drove Wang's best-sellers into temporary obscurity. The *chao zuo* did not stop there. Subsequent reports of a pending government ban sent many hunting for a precious personal copy before it was too late. Overnight *The Ruined Capital* became ubiquitous. It was on store shelves, in readers' hands, in people's conversations, and in the media.

Indeed no other book in post-Mao China has evoked as much controversy among critics as did *The Ruined Capital*. Opinions were sharply divided and tempers were hot.[37] The chief editor of *Shiyue*, Xiao Lei, and deputy chief editor of *Xiaoshuo pinglun* (Fiction review) proclaimed it "a work worth handing down to future generations" *(chuanshi zhi zuo)* (Zhang Yan 1994, 76). Some critics applaud Jia Pingwa for his "remarkable artistic achievement" in boldly describing the destroyed moral values in contemporary life. "It continues the realistic tradition of the Ming-Qing novel and offers an unembellished reflection of modern city life. Its description of the characters' daily experience is sharp, careful, and unreserved," writes one critic (Chen Juntao et al. 1993, 37). The fin-de-siècle anxiety the author demonstrates over the ruined culture gives the book "an epochal significance," states another; this "extraordinary book" awakens readers from the numbness and oblivion of their real existence and saves the human subject (Zhong Benkang 1993b, 53; Han Luhua 1993).

But the majority of critics and writers were disgusted with the way the book was marketed and profoundly disappointed with Jia Pingwa for pandering to low taste. One critic, Chen Zhichu, wrote an article called "Jia Pingwa, kexi le" (Jia Pingwa, what a shame) (Chen Zhichu 1994). Others dubbed the book a "carnival on ruins," "a crazed dance of a spiritual decadent," and "a novel on prostitution," likening it to the American magazine *Playboy* (Chen Zhichu 1994; Chen Xiaoming 1994; Chen Xiaoming et al. 1994b; Meng Fanhua 1994; Zhaxi Duo 1994; Li Jiefei 1993; Yi Yi 1993). They charged the author with presenting a carnivalesque picture of uninhibited lust, debauchery, betrayal, and destruction of cultural values without any critical, authorial intervention; they were dismayed that Jia Pingwa had given up his position as a responsible social and cultural critic and degenerated into "a man without a soul." Li Shulei asks, "How could it be that in a matter of a few years Jia Pingwa changed from being a pure, sensitive, serious artist into a pop fiction writer with vulgar tastes?" Detractors accused Jia of betraying the intellectual tradition, saying he was emblematic of the self-abandonment of Chinese intellectuals: "What we saw [in *The Ruined Capital*] is the disappearance of the intellectuals' heroism and idealism. When our nation was facing great hope and at the same time a grave danger, the intellectuals failed to demonstrate their deep concern for and insight into the fate of the nation" (Li Shulei 1994, 125–126). Female writers and readers, for their part, were angry with Jia for portraying women as playthings to satisfy male fantasies (Zha 1995, 154–156). Some also maintained that the novel not only lacks a strong moral standard but it is artistically flawed, its form and literary techniques nothing more than a patchwork of classical literary images and expressions (Zhang Fa 1993).

Jia Pingwa's explicit description of sexual activities is clearly a major point of controversy. The author's presentation of sex is open, graphic, vulgar, and at times lewd.[38] The question here is not whether candid discussions of sex as part of human experience should be allowed. Nearly two decades into commercialization, China has already swept aside the Communist taboo on this topic.[39] The question is what representational purpose the extravagant portrayal of sex serves in the novel. Thus, what most interests me in my discussion is how the narrative focus on sexual relationships fits into the overarching framework of *The Ruined Capital* as a representation of the intellectual in the 1990s. The feminist cry of foul play can be explored further to reveal how the male self and the intellectual self conflate in an imaginary space where the marginalized intellectual transforms his social frustration into sexual victory over the female body, thus creating a fictive subject-position for himself.

In his afterword to the novel, Jia Pingwa says that he has lived in the city for twenty years but has never written a story about it (Jia 1993, 519). *The Ruined Capital* is the author's first literary creation of urban life. The city in question is Xi'an, called Xijing in the novel, the ancient capital of twelve dynasties in China's history. A modernized metropolis bustling with commerce, Xijing's streets are filled with thriving private and semiprivate businesses, noisy restaurants, shops, vending stalls, nightclubs, and of course bookstores and newsstands hawking sensational stories. In a word, Xijing is a miniature of the new China, in which all social interests seem to have converged on consumerism, the excitement of making and spending money. The inhabitants most significant in this fictional world are four famous personages in the city's cultural circles; the novel is thus foremost a book about intellectuals. The choice of a developing urban center as a setting makes the intellectuals' experience historically specific: *The Ruined Capital* depicts the problematics of the intellectual self in a modernization driven for the most part, if not exclusively, by the impulse of commercialization. Moreover, since the fictional intellectuals of consequence are all male, the novel is a representation of the intellectual self reified through the experience of the male self.

The beginning of the novel is obviously modeled after the second chapter of *Honglou meng*, "Leng Zixing yanshuo Rongguo Fu" ("Leng Zi-xing Discourses on the Jias of Rong-guo House," in David Hawkes' translation). The narrator introduces us to the intellectual characters through the words of Meng Yunfang, who, a member of the city's Research Institute of Culture and History, is an intellectual himself. What he presents is consequently an insider's view. The four famous figures Meng tells us about are Wang Ximian, a painter; Gong Jingyuan, a calligrapher; Ruan Zhifei, head of a private performing troupe; and Zhuang Zhidie, the counterpart of the author, a renowned writer. Considered by Meng "the best of the best," Zhuang is the most revered among the four, his profound influence earning him a large following in both Xijing and his hometown.

It is significant that none of the four is a scientist. The novel is therefore not about Chinese intellectuals in general but about a specific group, the "cultural workers." That the fictional intellectuals all deal with representation of one form or another makes creative agency a poignant issue. But problematic representation and lack of agency characterize the figure of the artist. Despite the aura surrounding him, the representative intellectual, the writer Zhuang Zhidie, epitomizes the self-doubt of the contemporary literati, his name betraying their confusion and uncertainty in the 1990s: "Zhuang Zhidie" originates from the famous Daoist anecdote in which Zhuang Zi, upon waking up from a dream about butterflies, questions if he is not a butterfly dreaming of being a person (Chuang Tzu 1968, 49). The writer in *The Ruined Capital* becomes the "butterfly of Zhuang Zi" (Zhuang zhi die 庄之蝶). But rather than evidence of transcendence and freedom that the Daoist parable may suggest, Zhuang Zhidie is confounded at his identity, a being without a definite existence, born of the legendary imagination of a consciousness skeptical about its own realness. The fluidity implied in the origin of the name "Zhuang Zhidie" also explodes the conclusive relationship between the artist as the representing and reality as the represented. Lost in the shift between the signifying and the signified, the dreaming and the dreamed, the fictional writer is deprived of a solid ground from which he can exercise his contestatory agency.

The deficiency in the artists' representational powers is also obvious in their self-deprecation and in the way they practice their professions. When Meng Yunfang describes them to the reader, he juxtaposes the four characters with people with whom intellectuals are seldom associated traditionally: the city's notorious hooligans, thugs, underworld ringleaders, and swindlers. This juxtaposition rudely undercuts the social value of the intellectual figures, granting them no privileged position over the morally dubious and subversive in society. Indeed, none of the intellectuals is dedicated to socially constructive creations. Wang Ximian, the painter, is not famous for his original work; he is known for his superb skill in producing forgeries. He is able to imitate to perfection the styles of both reputable painters from the past and living talents. Wang gives up the chance to create authentic art at the Institute of Traditional Painting, trading it for an opportunity to make easy money by copying other artists and selling his products to foreign tourists. As he assumes a different identity each time he passes off his fake as the real thing, Wang waives his right to individual representation, leaving the self mutating and dangling between the misrepresentations. Ruan Zhifei, the actor, has similarly deserted his creative career. He leaves the city's Qinqiang opera troupe to form his own company, building his success on performing trendy Western songs and dances.[40] Chasing after new fads in the hope of attracting more customers, Ruan betrays art and originality. A compulsive gambler, Gong Jingyuan, the calligrapher, is a total disgrace to his profession. Whenever his debtors press him, he writes a few couplets for them as payment. The careless mass production of his calligraphy reduces Gong's work to scrip.

Zhuang Zhidie, the writer, is exactly like his cohorts. Although Meng Yunfang paints him as a man above material concerns, he does not seem so aloof when a prosperous businessman, Mr. Huang, approaches him with a proposition. Huang wants Zhuang to write and publish a newspaper article about a certain pesticide, offering to pay him 5,000 yuan. The writer readily agrees, promoting a product that turns out to be a hoax. On another occasion Zhuang is told that he will be paid 4,000 yuan a month to create advertisements and work reports for the neighborhood factories. Zhuang and his intellectual friends have abandoned their free agency. They are producing a new type of "command literature/art" (zunming wenxue), which has succeeded the political model that Chinese intellectuals were compelled to follow during Mao's tenure. Material temptations have taken over the role once played by the coercive Communist ideology.

What the intellectuals do in fiction has a parallel in real history. The corruption of the genre of reportage is a case in point. Highly respected for its independent spirit in exposing social problems and official misdeeds in the 1980s, the reportage is in danger of becoming paid advertisement in the 1990s. A new standard procedure took hold in the media: a business that wants publicity pays a magazine or newspaper, which then solicits the services of a writer to produce a piece on the topic and gives the author part of the money received from the business. Deploring the absence of responsible journalists today, one critic blames the decline of the important genre on this kind of "paid reportage."[41] Nor is literary criticism immune from the practice: critics are paid to participate in orchestrated discussions of literary works, making it uncertain whether they are offering independent reviews or merely trumpeting praises to please the sponsors of the meetings ("Zhongguo wentan").

With the interests of the buyers tipping the scale, these arrangements have fundamentally destroyed the representational autonomy of the intellectuals. Intellectual productions have in consequence lost their moral force. When the exchange value of intellectual activities took top priority, the intellectuals revoked their status as spokespeople of social conscience. In *The Ruined Capital* the depreciation of intellectual writing is shown in what happens to a copy of Zhuang's *Collected Works of Zhuang Zhidie*, which the writer has autographed and presented to a friend: the book ends up on the shelf of a secondhand bookstore. The writer himself has even contributed directly to his degradation. To boost business, the manager of the bookstore Zhuang sponsors comes up with a plan to sell forgeries. He asks Zhuang to write a few comments of appreciation on the scrolls so that customers can be tricked into believing their authenticity. Agreeing to lend his name to forgeries, Zhuang betrays people's trust for the writer as well as his authority and respectability. When genuine representation is forsaken, the fake takes its place.

The reduction of the intellectuals' power to represent is also manifested in their narrowed sphere of operation. Retreating from their traditional project of representing the world and humanity, they direct their attention inward, to themselves. Their writing as a result loses social significance. The best example is the "love letters" Zhuang writes to his friend Zhong Weixian, chief editor of the *Journal of the Western Capital*. An unfortunate victim of Mao's political movements, Zhong lost touch with his college girlfriend, who was branded a rightist and, like Zhong, exiled to a remote area during the Anti-Rightist Campaign. Zhong has lately heard that his old love, now divorced, is teaching in a middle school in Anhui province. He falls in love all over again and writes her four letters. Although none of his letters is answered, he routinely visits the mailroom. His hope of reuniting with his former lover becomes the only meaningful pursuit in Zhong's unsuccessful professional career.

Hearing the story, Zhuang Zhidie decides to disguise his handwriting and reply to Zhong's letters to his sweetheart, hoping in this way to end Zhong's misery. He asks Ah Can, one of the women he is involved with, to forward to her sister, who works in a post office in a small town in Anhui, the letter he concocts. Ah Can's sister is to send the letter to the editor in a different envelope, using her own address. When Zhong writes back to the imaginary girl, Ah Can's sister will relay the letter to Zhuang in Xijing so that he can continue the correspondence. Writing these love letters becomes Zhuang's chief—and only—literary project: notwithstanding the narrator's assurances of Zhuang's fame, he produces nothing else as the novel unfolds. Writing to each other, Zhuang and Zhong are engaged in an attempt to return to a pre-Mao plenitude, to retrieve an irretrievable past. When the object represented is an unrecoverable romance spoiled by decades of political turmoil, the representation is undermined by the vacuity of the project. Although Zhong is unaware of the truth of the letters, in reality the intellectuals' desire for repletion is reciprocated only between themselves. The fictitious nature of the letters shows that this fantasized love between two intellectuals is based on self-pity and deception. It is narcissism externalized in an illusory love affair that can be sustained only by a writing whose presence signals an absence. It is a self-love bouncing back and forth between the intellectual and his mirror image. Ironically, this deception gives the editor's life purpose. Whenever he gets a letter from his so-called sweetheart, he goes over it again and again. By the time Zhong dies of cancer, he has accumulated a whole box of them. Writing these bogus letters in turn creates an ongoing engagement to which Zhuang Zhidie can devote his time and energy. He throws himself wholeheartedly into it, often weeping over the letters he manufactures. Thoroughly enjoying the imaginary love, and confusing fabrication with reality, the two writers build their lives on duplicity, wasting their creative energy on producing a pure fiction relevant only to themselves, which even as self-expression is false and delusive.

Self-representation for the intellectual is further problematized when the writer himself is turned into an involuntary object to be represented and appropriated. Zhou Min, a young man from Zhuang's hometown, makes himself famous in Xijing by trumping up a sensational story about Zhuang Zhidie's affair with his former colleague Jing Xueyin. Zhou's article leads to the publication of yet more stories about the repercussions caused by the article until the whole business becomes a profitable industry. Enraged by the story, Jing, now married, sues Zhuang for libel. When Zhuang loses the lawsuit, another book appears on the market detailing how he came to be involved in this sensational scandal. Zhuang discovers that even his own bookstore is distributing the book in large numbers for sale in the suburban counties. The bookstore manager justifies his decision by saying that if other people are making money by selling books about Zhuang, his own store might as well cash in. Zhuang realizes that there are a large number of people who live on telling stories about him, and he admits that he never expected to "make money out of his own scandal" (Jia 1993, 509).

This incident completely reverses the writer's relationship to himself and his world. He goes from being the representing to being the represented. His story manipulated by others, the writer is expelled from his traditional role of reading the world; the world is reading a misrepresentation of him. Zhuang says mournfully, "My name is mine, but it is mostly used by others" (Jia 1993, 124). The writer not only loses his voice in telling his story, but he has no power to correct the misrepresentations, which renders the very act of representing invalid and counterproductive. When Zhuang tries to explain in a letter to Jing the truth of the publication of Zhou Min's story, she uses it as evidence in court and wins her lawsuit. Zhuang is punished for attempting to give the true version of the story.

On a higher level, the dismissal of the writer's role as an effective voice of truth is evident in his deposition as a social critic. This post is taken over in *The Ruined Capital* by a trash collector, a deranged former schoolteacher who roams the city, supporting himself by selling what he can salvage from garbage. The madman is well known in Xijing for chanting ditties exposing government corruption, irrational policies, and shady business dealings. The verses tell about people's discontent with the moral degeneration of society and they satirize the writers who sell their consciences for money and fame. What we normally expect from intellectual writings now comes out of the mouth of the old man. When he says his verses, spectators gather around him, asking him for more. The lunatic has become such an outlet for the people to vent their frustration that they miss him when he is absent from the city for a while.

If Chinese writers' "obsession with China" has been transferred to a madman in *The Ruined Capital*, their anxieties about humanity have become the concern of an old cow who has a special bond with Zhuang Zhidie. When the cow's owner, Sister Liu, brings the cow into the city to sell fresh milk on the streets, she stops by to see Zhuang. The cow moos to greet the writer whenever he is in sight, and she allows Zhuang to drink milk directly from her udder (if others try to do the same, the cow kicks and jumps to drive them away). The affinity is more importantly shown in the cow's contemplation about human existence. Hearing Zhuang's comment that the cow "looks like a philosopher," magically "the cow started to think like a human being, examining the city from the perspective of a philosopher" (Jia 1993, 55). This bovine philosopher demonstrates the typical "worrying mentality" *(youhuan yishi)* of Chinese intellectuals, who have traditionally taken it upon themselves to be concerned about the well-being of the nation and the people.[42] On several of her visits to the city, the cow goes into lengthy soliloquies regarding her anxieties about humanity and urban life. To the cow, which shuttles between the city and the country, the latter is an idyllic world where human beings and animals live in harmony. The city, on the contrary, is an artificial construction that alienates humanity from its natural existence. Isolation, apathy, and tension characterize people's relationships in urban centers. They crowd into limited space and yet remain strangers to one another. Despite advanced technology and new discoveries in medicine, urban life ruins people's health. The urbanites nonetheless stick to this unhealthy world, refusing to return to the country. The cow foresees the approach of doomsday.

The cow's thoughts hark back, albeit with significant modification, to a recurrent theme in modern Chinese literature, the urban-rural dichotomy. Yingjin Zhang's study of the topic shows that the configuration of the city in modern Chinese literature and film presents a heterogeneous picture. Both the city and the country were given multiple identities in intellectual and literary imaginings. The city is at once the source of light—a place of Enlightenment ideals of knowledge, freedom, science, technology, and the new nation—and a source of darkness, harboring contamination, moral corruption, and promiscuity. It is a center of hope and a center of disillusionment for the aspiring young. Portrayed as the site of innocence and arcadian harmony, the country nevertheless also presents a bleak landscape of poverty, ignorance, and backwardness (Yingjin Zhang 1996, 3–16). In *The Ruined Capital* the May Fourth intellectuals' ambivalence toward the symbolic significations of the city and the country and their search for a possible site of modernity between the two is replaced by a rather simplistic nostalgia, a presentation of a black-and-white picture. In the cow's vision the city induces degeneration and alienation, and the country promises a natural order of peace and serenity. The moral struggle of the May Fourth writers to position themselves in the complexities of nation building delineated through the dichotomy of city and country is consequently absent. The problematic of the contemporary world in the cow's contemplation is distanced from the sociopolitical reality and "naturalized" into a matter of preference over different modes of living. The city and the country in this treatment become transcendental categories beyond the turmoil of the reforms. Thus the cow betrays not only a tendency toward displacing modernization as the true source of the contemporary intellectual's agony and anxiety but also a sort of elitist attitude toward the silly masses who, unlike the cow, fail to make an intelligent choice.

Allowing marginal figures like the madman and an animal to stand in for the intellectuals after their successful comeback in the 1980s has its obvious ironies. Although Jia Pingwa's deranged garbage collector suggests the famous madman Lu Xun created, on both textual and contextual levels Jia's creation is inferior. Lu Xun's madman offers sharp insights into the workings of traditional Chinese society, exposing the cannibalistic nature of institutionalized Confucian practices. The sense of urgency and the individual's fear are poignantly portrayed in the paranoia of the young scholar as a loner in a wolfish crowd. By nature of its form, the diary whose producer is at the same time its sole intended and legitimate reader presents a pre-enclosed world, reinforcing the incommunicability of the madman's vision, frustration, and anxiety. In this light it is significant that an unintended reader, the narrator in the frame of the story, is given a chance to read the diary only after the madman's "madness" is characterized as a "dreadful disease" in the opening section. The diagnosis provides a safe framework to preempt misreading, bringing into sharp focus the opposition between the madman's voice of truth and an orthodoxy that seeks to suppress it by circumscribing its interpretive possibilities. The ostracized madman is a fighter who insists on asking questions to prick the numbness and psychological oblivion of his compatriots. In the context of modern nation building, Lu Xun's story produced resounding echoes for decades to come. In comparison, Jia Pingwa's garbage collector is a bizarre old man who pokes fun, stirring up a few laughs in his audience. While the laughter may carry some subversive force, it nonetheless functions as a safety valve for the spectators to let off emotional steam. The old man's jests and eccentric behavior trivialize his message, canceling out much of its critical power. The sting of the laughter dulled by the audience's awareness and acknowledgment of the unconventional nature of the gatherings, the marginalized festivity is contained within the carnivalesque moment, disappearing once it expires. The transience and ineffectuality of the contemporary madman are proven by the (non)response he receives. Lu Xun's young scholar poses a social threat and must be "cured"; Jia Pingwa's disgruntled garbage collector appears quite harmless and is left undisturbed to run his business in the city. There is also a meaningful difference in the crowds. That Lu's madman is surrounded by a hostile throng adds force to the crisis of the individual. The receptive onlookers in *The Ruined Capital*, in contrast, make the absence of a significant, compelling speaker all the more noticeable. The presence of the audience, however small, seems to suggest that there are still people who are willing to listen to the intellectual. But where is the noteworthy spokesperson?

It is disconcerting to find the post-Mao intellectual transformed from a vociferous, eager social architect in the 1980s to a resigned, mute spectator in the image of a cow in the 1990s. The philosophical animal, of course, is not an original creation. Well versed in Marxist jargon, Zhang Xianliang's righteous horse in his novella "Nanren de yiban shi nüren" (Half of man is woman) is able to talk his hero into political action. The animals in both Zhang's and Jia's stories obviously represent an inner core of the besieged, fragmented intellectual self. In Zhang Xianliang's world, it stands for the repressed true Marxist who is battling a skeptical counterpart disheartened by the political reality of Mao's repressive movements. The cow's existential anxiety in *The Ruined Capital* speaks to the traditional intellectual's deep urge to be the savior and guardian of the human soul. But while the divided selves in Zhang's political world can face each other in dialogue, which eventually brings them together through the character Zhang Yongling's decision to take action, politics is no longer available as a source of redemption and synthesis in the 1990s. The cow stays a soliloquist in Jia Pingwa's fiction. Sharing no moral values with its secularized double, the writer Zhuang Zhidie in the human world, the self of sacred social responsibility remains isolated and suppressed. Voiceless, it can only murmur to itself.

Furthermore, if the garbage collector still offers feeble social commentary in the writer's stead, the cow is a silent thinker without access to the human beings she worries about. The narrator concedes, "The cow does not speak human language, therefore the humans do not know this philosopher's thoughts" (Jia 1993, 55). Unspoken and, as a result, buried entirely in its self-musings, the cow's apprehension, concern, and emotional torment for humanity lack public connection. Troubled communication besets the intellectual's alter ego. He either fails to speak forcefully when there is an audience, or he is unable to talk at all. The intellectuals' self-confidence and their complete identification with the people in the early years of the postrevolutionary era have dissipated. There is now a rift evidenced by the disappearance of a common language between the intellectual's substitute in the novel and the people. They stand outside each other's meaning system. Significantly, speechlessness is not only the cow's problem. Jia Ping-wa's intellectuals have difficulties with both of the essential subjective powers I have discussed in previous chapters, the ability to speak and perceive. Incompetent to contest the lawsuit in court on his own behalf, Zhuang Zhidie leaves his defense to his friend and is found guilty. Later in the story, Meng Yunfang unexpectedly goes blind in one eye while Ruan Zhifei, having lost one eye after being beaten up by some hooligans, replaces it with a dog's eye. These mishaps undoubtedly signify the intellectuals' problematized agency, the loss of their power to discern and intervene.

Constructing a New Center: Representation Rescued

Locating the correlatives between the historiography in the text and social reality is doing half the job. To regard *The Ruined Capital* as a simple admission of the crisis of the intellectuals' discursive power would be to reduce representation to the referential function, overlooking a central aspect: through appropriation, the subject attempts to cope with conflicting pressures in real history by creating a world of self-projection and imaginary assimilation in works of fiction. In other words, by dint of the performative function, the world in the book is appropriated in such a way that it enables the writing self to negotiate reality on its own terms.

In striking contrast to the disintegration of the intellectuals' subjective agency in the novel is a world of glory that the author builds around them. This is most obvious in the fame Zhuang Zhidie enjoys. Known to everyone in town, the writer is raised to godlike stature. A member of the Municipal People's Congress, Zhuang often has meetings with the city's top officials. He is a celebrity on TV, with fans in all walks of life, from the lawless to the lawful. One ringleader says, "If you ask me who the governor of the province is, I won't be able to tell you. But I sure know who Zhuang Zhidie is" (Jia 1993, 476). Zhuang's name works wonders. One day Sister Liu and her cow are stopped at an intersection by a policeman who is keeping traffic at a standstill to allow the car of an important official from Beijing to pass. When Sister Liu informs the officer that she has to go across the street to deliver milk to Zhuang, he immediately salutes the woman, letting her and her cow pass while the rest of the crowd waits and watches.

After shaking hands with Zhuang, Mr. Huang vows not to wash it until his wife also has a chance to shake it. Zhuang Zhidie himself puts it jokingly that his hand is now as sacred as Chairman Mao's.[43] Even thieves are awed by the writer's prestige. Once a pickpocket tries to sell Zhuang a pair of sunglasses he had stolen. When Zhuang shows him his business card, the thief clicks his heels together, giving Zhuang a big salute, telling him that he is greatly honored to meet him and that he has dreamed of becoming a writer since attending one of Zhuang's lectures.

But Zhuang's most ardent admirers are women. They include Tang Waner, a small-town beauty who elopes with Zhou Min to Xijing, deserting her husband and her three-year-old son; Liu Yue, a young maid of the Zhuangs from the countryside; painter Wang Ximian's wife; Ah Can, a factory worker Zhuang comes to know by chance; and even a prostitute. The narrator makes it perfectly clear to the reader that Zhuang's attraction for women is not physical. He is short and thin with disheveled hair and a noticeable paunch. At their first encounter, Tang Waner, who is soon to become Zhuang's number-one mistress, is surprised that the writer's appearance in no way matches his great fame. The author makes Zhuang an ordinary man in appearance in order to highlight his irresistible charisma as a literary talent. His leading role at a discussion session many years ago suffices to turn the head of Wang Ximian's wife, who has since dreamed of becoming Zhuang's wife and has only abandoned her hopes after learning of his marriage to Niu Yueqing. We are not told exactly which of Zhuang's works his admirers have read, but the simple fact that Zhuang is a writer is enough to make him desirable to women. This conjoining of the male self with the intellectual self allows the author to invest some symbolic significance in the male-female relationship, as I discuss shortly.

Without exception, women's infatuation with the writer translates into their eagerness to give themselves to him body and soul. Thus, the consecration of the intellectual is effected through the desecration and dedication of the female body. It seems that as soon as a woman comes near Zhuang, her wish is to sleep with him. The very first time Tang Waner and her lover Zhou Min invite Zhuang over for dinner, Tang feels hopelessly stirred by romantic feelings for her guest. It takes only five days for her to get into bed with him. Ah Can's affair with Zhuang Zhidie is even more ludicrous. Ah Can happens to be home when Zhuang comes looking for her sister. Hardly are they left alone in the house when Ah Can, whom Zhuang has never met before, takes off all her clothes to let Zhuang do whatever he wants with her. She begs Zhuang to believe that she is "not a bad woman" and that she cannot help herself when such a great writer as

Zhuang is there with her. Liu Yue, the Zhuangs' maid, insists on having sex with the writer the night before her wedding; she does not even resent Zhuang for arranging her marriage to the mayor's crippled son in exchange for the mayor's support in Zhuang's lawsuit. The most unbelievable of his trysts is with a middle-aged prostitute. Discovering that she has a venereal disease, Zhuang refuses her services. No disappointment: the narrator does not need a prostitute to launch another bout of sexual encounters (of which the novel has plenty already); what the narrator is looking for is one more woman's confession of love and reverence for the intellectual. The sordid business of flesh is magically sublimated once the woman finds out her customer's identity. She tells Zhuang that on her way to see him she planned to give him only an hour with an extra fee since she was summoned at such short notice. "But," she sobs her heart out at Zhuang's rejection, "once I saw you, [I realized] you're the most attractive man I've ever met. I'll entertain you for two or even three hours free of charge" (Jia 1993, 316).

The female characters are keen on sleeping with Zhuang because they regard it as a great honor to be associated with the writer. Tang Waner's wish is to replace Niu Yueqing as Zhuang's wife and become the envy of the whole city. In her own words, she is convinced that her confidence in herself comes from Zhuang, that if she is magnificent it is only because Zhuang has shed some of his shining "sunlight" on her. After sleeping with the writer, Ah Can thanks him profusely. Committing adultery with Zhuang is a "glorious experience" for her. She is not only physically gratified, but her "very soul is content." Her despair is gone; with a literary celebrity like Zhuang fond of her, she now has "confidence to go on living." Liu Yue, the maid, competes with Tang Waner for Zhuang's affection, crediting the writer with "creating a wholly new person" out of her and Tang, and "giving [them] courage and confidence to start a new life" (Jia 1993, 460). But other than the destruction of their lives, we do not find any evidence of a "glorious," or even "new" future in store for Zhuang's women. When Tang Waner is kidnapped and brought back to her hometown by her husband, Zhuang Zhidie is unable to save her from daily physical and sexual abuse by her spouse. Liu Yue is sacrificed by the Zhuangs into a loveless marriage. Ah Can purposely disfigures herself as a farewell gesture, after having sex with Zhuang for the second time, and vanishes from the novel.

As described above, the female characters in the novel fall into the familiar category of self-effacing women. Ah Can's self-mutilation is typical behavior for the "chaste woman," who proves her loyalty to the male by physical sacrifice. The consciousness behind the creation of the female characters in *The Ruined Capital* is blatantly phallocentric. Their intelligence and talent are used exclusively in trying to outwit each other to secure Zhuang's favor. As some Chinese critics have pointed out, if stripped of their modern dress and high-heeled shoes, these women could walk out of traditional fiction (Lei Da 1993; Zhang Fa 1993). To make the female characters' selfless devotion possible, the author has to redomesticate women. He does this not so much by sequestering them in the inner living quarters, as in premodern China, as by limiting the social paradigm on which they can locate themselves. The vibrant social reforms, the real source of the intellectuals' frustration, are muted and play no significant part in the lives of the women. Tang Waner does not work after eloping with Zhou Min to Xijing. She either stays at home all day dreaming and waiting for Zhuang to visit her, or she invents excuses to meet him in their love nest. Liu Yue's regular job is working as the Zhuangs' maid. These women have to be confined within the domestic sphere so that they have no careers, no ambitions, no personal goals to distract them from their passion for the writer. As a result of this redomestication, the male-female relationship, specifically, the relationship of these women to the writer, becomes the women's only reference point for self-definition. Ahistorical outside broader social changes, the female characters are cemented in the subservient, traditional mold.

The male-centered perception is also ingrained in the novel's intellectual characters. Their typical, traditional Chinese male gaze is characterized by their obsession with women's feet. Ruan Zhifei is particularly fond of women's shoes and has accumulated enough to fill an entire closet. Zhuang Zhidie insists that the essential feature of a woman's beauty is her feet, deeply resenting his wife's wide and fleshy feet. Part of Tang Waner's sexual attraction for Zhuang lies in her small, exquisite feet. At the sight of them, "Zhuang Zhidie couldn't help giving a long whistle [of amazement]" (Jia 1993, 53). Tang's feet are endowed with the same qualities that define the "beauty" of the infamous bound feet: pointed, slender, and supple, they have an astonishingly high arch. Even though almost a century has elapsed since the times of the literati lotus-lovers described by Feng Jicai in *The Three-Inch Golden Lotus*, their contemporary counterparts are still drawn to small feet. The voyeurs, of course, do not stop there; the entire female body has to be aestheticized to enable the body politics to work. Zhuang particularly enjoys staring at the naked female body, pinning the woman at the end of his "look." Under the objectifying gaze, the woman is completely externalized and reduced to a mere composite of physiological parts. Zhuang's ideal lovers are very cooperative; they meet and accept Zhuang's gaze with absolute ease and willingness.

As Weimann points out, "The process of making certain things one's own becomes inseparable from making other things (and persons) alien, so that the act of appropriation must be seen always already to involve not only self-projection and assimilation but alienation through reification and expropriation" (Weimann 1987, 184). To appropriate the female is simultaneously to expropriate her, to make her alien to herself. Declaring her love for Zhuang in an emotional outburst, Tang Waner promises to make him "forever happy": "I will adjust myself to suit you so that you'll always find something new, something fresh in me. To suit you doesn't mean there's no me anymore. On the contrary, this will make my life fresh and meaningful. ... Women's function is to contribute [their] beauty" (Jia 1993, 124). Tang perceives her identity entirely from the point of view of her usefulness to Zhuang. The very substance of her existence is paradoxically the absence of her self. There is nothing solid in her that she can call her own. Her femininity functions merely to affirm the primacy of the writer's masculinity. Tang assumes a fluidity, but one contrary to that advocated in feminist practice to frustrate patriarchal definitions.[44] Her mutability is not a means to defy but a means to comply. Thus, Tang is insubstantial and formless to herself but perfectly predictable to the defining male. Zhuang's desire and preference dictating her transformations both psychologically and physically, she allows the man the ultimate power to shape her existence. She literally twists and abuses her body to present herself in ever-changing images to catch Zhuang's attention.

But the insubstantiality of Zhuang Zhidie's experience with women is inevitably exposed in the relatively low social status and lack of education of the women he conquers. Drawn by Zhuang's reputation, they have fallen in love with his status as writer. While these women hold Zhuang in a sort of religious reverence, Zhuang's own wife, Niu Yueqing, knows him too well as a common man. She says bluntly, "I'm married to a man, not an idol. He [Zhuang] was spoiled by those around him. Little did they know that he has athlete's foot and decayed teeth. He talks in his sleep, he eats and farts and enjoys reading over a shit" (Jia 1993, 40). Recognizing his human triviality, Niu Yueqing rejects the myth of Zhuang as a great writer. Unlike the other women, she does not submit to his whims, often refusing to adopt new positions in bed to cater to his desires. In the absence of an appreciative audience, Zhuang's sexual prowess evaporates. He has great trouble performing in his own bedroom and has failed to produce a child after years of marriage, though he easily impregnates his mistress Tang Waner. Similarly, the "invincible" writer suffers defeat in his relationship with another, more educated woman. The only female in the novel Zhuang

Zhidie covets but fails to get is Jing Xueyin, his colleague many years ago in the office of the magazine *Western Capital.* Jing is a college graduate from a senior cadre's family with powerful connections. In spite of his secret love for Jing, Zhuang never even dared to shake hands with her. The presence of other social relationships (professional and political) proves to be an effective deterrent to the writer's rampant sexuality. Unable to forget Jing, Zhuang Zhidie can only dream of a wedding with her. In a self-delusive moment after losing the lawsuit to Jing Xueyin, he imagines taking his revenge by arousing her desire only to desert her at the last minute when she is begging him for sex. To the writer sex is obviously a symbolic action, a game of power and dominance. What Zhuang cannot obtain in reality, he achieves in his fantasy, transferring his own desire for recognition to the female consciousness. Zhuang's foiled sexuality with insubordinate women recalls Keith McMahon's findings in his study of the traditional "beauty-scholar" romances. McMahon concludes that when the women exceeded the men in literary talent and wit, their superior intellectuality allowed them a more forceful role in their relationships with their husbands, and they could enjoy a more or less monogamous marriage. In McMahon's words, "where there is the superior woman, there is no sex" (McMahon 1995, 124). Zhuang's story in *The Ruined Capital* is a traditional plot with a twist. Whereas the premodern, effeminate *caizi* (talent) gives up his right to polygamy, the contemporary Zhuang Zhidie, who is frustrated in his sexual relationship with more independent women at home and at work, seeks consolation from his multiple, fantastic affairs outside of wedlock.

Indeed, we have reason to question whether *The Ruined Capital* is a multilevel fantasy indulged in by the subject both in and outside the text. Not only is the portrayal of the female characters a reproduction of the contested conventional image, but the entire novel is cast in a sort of quasiclassical Chinese. Repeating many details from the traditional fiction, it reads very much like a Ming-Qing production in its diction, description, and narration. The peculiarity of Liu Yue's body (she has no pubic hair) and Tang Waner's strategy of letting Zhuang Zhidie have sex with Liu Yue so that the maid will not divulge their illicit affair are familiar devices. Even the sex scenes are similar to those in certain classic narratives.[45] And the imitation extends beyond descriptive details. McMahon's conclusion with regard to the absence of sex involving the superior woman applies to the text in terms of narrative strategies as well. He discovers that in stories containing talented women, sex is either displaced by the couple's exchange of poems or toned down by the use of euphemisms. In contrast, if the woman is inferior, the narrator is unconcerned about her chastity, indulging in lengthy, explicit, erotic descriptions (McMahon 1995, chaps. 5, 6, and 8). The vision and narrative mode of *The Ruined Capital* coincide with the latter. The author provides some sixty sex scenes and, were it not for the cuts made by the editor and the author himself out of the concern that the novel might be censored, there would have been more.[46]

Likewise, the characters in the text also consciously follow past models. In their farewell "lovemaking," Zhuang Zhidie and Ah Can abandon themselves to sexual pleasure: "They forgot all their pain and worries. They did everything described in classical books, all along uttering the language used in them." But because the couple does, after all, live in the 1990s, "They also imitated whatever they saw in foreign videotapes in addition to trying all the postures of the ancients they read about.... They copied what wild animals—pigs, dogs, cattle, and sheep—did and even threw in a few moves of their own" (Jia 1993, 303). The scene is downright chaotic and farcical. Patterning themselves after a hodgepodge of sources, the characters are shams completely devoid of authenticity. Fabrication as well as duplication takes place both internally and externally, both in the self-formation of the characters and over the creation of the novel. When converted into a borrowed, outdated discourse, the glory, enormous popularity, and tremendous prestige of the intellectual in the world of fiction are debunked, becoming a mere representational mirage.

This representational mirage is predicated on undermining an essential accomplishment of twentieth-century China, the emancipation of women. But before discussing this issue, I must first comment on the author's stylistic preferences. As I have said, the language of the novel is close to the traditional vernacular used in premodern fiction. Such a linguistic choice is never an innocent move, as experienced writers and readers all know. Without denying the influence of other social factors, we might say that the national identity of modern China was written into existence. By successfully staging a cultural revolution through a new kind of writing, the May Fourth writers forever changed the social, moral, and psychological fabric of the nation. The awareness that language implies certain social perspectives can be seen in Lu Xun's handling of the traditional and modern vernacular in his first *baihua* story, the celebrated "Kuangren riji" (Diary of a madman). The tension produced by his intentional juxtaposition of a more literary language in the frame of the story with the vernacular in the diary proper shows that Lu Xun chooses the former to represent the institutionalized voice that misinterprets the madman's vision and the latter to convey the immediacy of the individual's true experience covered up or denigrated in the ideologically charged classical mode of writing.

I am not proposing that we should uncritically inherit the May Fourth radical iconoclasm, discrediting the use of traditional language and techniques altogether in literature today. In fact, the reintegration of traditional forms and techniques has played a positive role in enlivening post-Mao literature, and quite a number of writers (Jia Pingwa among them) have used them with great success. Most of the successful stories, however, are set in the countryside or secluded areas where life is inextricably entangled with ancient beliefs and practices. Jia Pingwa's own fiction provides good examples. The use of traditional-flavored language and fictional techniques helps create a fitting environment for him to develop the theme of conflict between social progress and entrenched customs.[47] But against the backdrop of a modern metropolis in the 1990s, the pronounced classical accent in *The Ruined Capital* sounds anachronistic.

And so is the author's portrait of the intellectual and his women anachronistic. They can exist only in the kind of world found in orthodox, traditional writings, where male subjectivity is legitimized at the expense of female subjectivity without being challenged. On many occasions when the narrator expatiates on Zhuang Zhidie's sexual encounters, the writer's female partner stops being a person with a name. She is referred to as *nei furen* (that woman) after the manner of a typical traditional narrator. Meng Yue and Dai Jinhua point out that as defined in *Liji* (Book of rituals), *Yili* (Rites and rituals), and *Lunyu* (Analects), the term *fufu* (husband and wife), which emphasizes the gendered role of the couple, is different from *nannü* (man and woman) as a referent to the natural sexes. In the *fufu* relationship, *furen* (women, kinswoman) is positioned in the kinship system where *fu* (women) is equated with *fu* (obeying) (Meng and Dai 1993, 11). To the narrator of *The Ruined Capital*, a woman involved in a sexual relationship with Zhuang is recognizable and referable to only by her disadvantaged, gendered slot in the hierarchy. She is not so much a *nü* as a *fu* to the male intellectual.

To revive the traditional discourse of male supremacy is to reverse the modern revolution. The female consciousness we observe in the novel is drastically different from that in modern fiction. Since the male-female relationship in *The Ruined Capital* is embedded in the (mis)use of the female body, it is helpful to look at the modern woman's relationship to her physical form. Wendy Larson's findings of the modern woman's uneasiness about her body are particularly pertinent here. In her 1998 study on women and writing in modern China, Larson shows that May Fourth women writers found it problematic to relate to the female body when they assumed the role of writer. Under the moral weight of *de* (virtues) as a centrally feminine quality, the female body in opposition to *cai* (talent) as a dominantly masculine quality "appears as an obstacle to fulfillment" in their literary aspirations. In stories by female writers, women who write are often sick, weak, or commit suicide; the modern woman had difficulty reconciling two gendered concepts: woman and writing. As a result, the female body had to be effaced through sickness or death to allow the emergence of the male activity of writing (often in the mediated form of letters and diaries) (Larson 1998, 125, 123–130). What we see in *The Ruined Capital* is just the opposite. The new woman's alienation from her body is completely suppressed. Zhuang Zhidie's women are comfortable with their bodies precisely because they have no intention of venturing into any new meaning construction outside the traditional code of *nüzi wucai bian shi de* (to be without [male] talent constitutes virtue for a woman). Unlike the May Fourth women writers, they are not trying to represent; they are content with being represented. Consequently, they are at peace with the female body. Except for their lovesickness for Zhuang, they are healthy. Their bodies do not need to be effaced, and indeed they are indispensable: their bodies are the anchors of their identities, incarnating the self-value they have internalized. Ah Can thus dances naked for Zhuang, "trying her hardest to show every part of her body" (Jia 1993, 303). Presented as anything but a mystery, the female body is offered as a blank signified to be freely inspected and inscribed by the male gaze.

If we put the contemporary artist's appropriation of women into historical perspective, we can discover an underlying pattern. It seems that at various moments when the Chinese male intellectual's subjectivity was in question, he would turn to the representation of the female for "salvation" (Martin Huang 1995, 76–88; Shuhui Yang 1998, 115–124). As Martin Huang argues, the distress at having to compete for the favor of the emperor, the unpredictability of a political career, and a resultant sense of insecurity created an experience of marginality for the male literati in premodern China. It was as stressful as the anxiety the females (wives and concubines) underwent in their daily struggle to preserve their positions in polygamy. "Mainly because of this shared marginality, literati authors liked to adopt a feminine voice (to view and present themselves as women) in their lyrical discourse as a plea for appreciation of their value" (Martin Huang 1995, 79). Chinese literature is marked by a long tradition of "transsexualism," so to speak. The persona in the *Chu ci* (Songs of the south) switches freely from male to female; evidence of adopting the female identity and speaking in the woman's voice is legion in Tang poems, Song lyrics, and Ming-Qing fiction.[48] Whether the purpose is to alleviate the male's fear of castration by the father (Meng and Dai 1993, 19–23), to allay the literati's "anxiety of service" (Shuhui Yang 1998, 124–152) or to express "private, unmanly... emotions, and of erotic love and passion in particular" (Fong 1994, 109), the woman in these practices is no more than the male's projection that can be momentarily invoked for temporary relief. Rather than disturbing the gendered social order, the willing identification with the female in these situations serves to affirm the supremacy of the yang, the authority appealed to, be it the emperor or his surrogates.

Modern history offers further examples. Scholarship on gender studies since the late 1980s contends that the Chinese women's liberation movement has failed to achieve an independent status (Zarrow 1988; Barlow 1994). As I mentioned in chapter 6, the movement, as well as the representation of women, was subsumed under other primary sociopolitical discourses—nation building in the modern period and socialism in Communist China. At the center of these appropriations is the male consciousness, substituting its own desire and needs for the woman's in the name of the nation or the state. In my analysis of Mo Yan's novel, I situated the male and female dichotomy within a framework of an international or racial conflict; here I instead stress the domestic and internal factors. When the young intelligentsia in the beginning of the twentieth century found themselves incapacitated by Confucian ethics, they empathized with women as the fellow oppressed, using liberation of women as a weapon toward the destruction of the Confucian tradition, which reduced the young to the same subordinate position of the female yin vis-à-vis the patriarch in the yin-yang hierarchy.[49] Women's emancipation in a patriarchal society and the freedom of the young male from the dominance of the father thus became related issues in the broader social context of cultural rejuvenation. Sublating the woman as the marginalized Other into himself empowered the young male in his challenge to the Confucian system. And here lies the central difference between the identification with the female in traditional literary discourse and that in the modern period. While the former sought to augment the social hierarchy expressed through the yin-yang dichotomy, the latter aimed at toppling the symbolic authority of the patriarch, the very foundation of that hierarchy. That women's liberation obeyed imperatives other than purely its own interests in the May Fourth era does not detract from the movement's liberating effects on women's welfare in such areas as health, education, career, and participation in national affairs, nor should the positive part male intellectuals performed in bringing this to pass be denied.

If male intervention in the modern period served a good cause, the contemporary intellectual's choice of action as represented through the narrative position in *The Ruined Capital* can only be detrimental. The question then has to be asked: What accounts for the radical shift in the representational strategy in which the male intellectual deviates from the May Fourth tradition? In raising the question, I do not mean to appoint the author as the spokesman for other male intellectuals. The scathing remarks about the novel made by Chinese critics and many of Jia Pingwa's fellow writers (predominantly male) should at least show that they found his approach alarming, though they have tended to focus more on the author's graphic sexual descriptions than on the problematic portrayal of women. But as long as we believe that individual consciousness is inevitably colored by the zeitgeist, I would suggest that the changes in representational strategies in *The Ruined Capital* should be related to the changing relationship between the intellectual and his community. In her critique of contemporary experimental fiction, Lu Tonglin identifies a misogynistic trend in works by male writers, arguing that because women's rise to power through massive participation in production was enabled by the Communist discourse, women came to be associated with it. As a result, "certain attacks supposedly directed against communism, are actually directed against women, as if they were indeed identified with communism" (Lu 1995, 7). Lu convincingly reasons that their appropriation by Communist ideology deprived women of a subjective voice, forcing them to speak through the official discourse, and she also demonstrates with ample evidence the presence of misogyny in post-Mao literature. What remains less convincing is the link Lu seeks to establish between the misogynistic practice and the male writers' misplaced desire to subvert Communism through it. The alleged relation is more speculative than proven. I would attribute the misogynistic approach to a rebound of the tendency for the male intellectual to appropriate the female as a means to cope with his marginalization, as occurred repeatedly in his literary and intellectual tradition, and I would locate this reaction in the crisis that contemporary intellectuals experienced in the 1990s.

Admittedly, Chinese intellectuals had been talking about crises throughout the twentieth century. What made the 1990s crisis different was that the intellectuals lost their elitist position as commentators who tackled the crises on behalf of the nation. Unlike their May Fourth counterparts during the national emergency in the modern era, post-Mao intellectuals could no longer rally public support in the name of fighting a common enemy in dealing with their frustration after Tiananmen. The crisis they were facing this time affected no one but themselves. The anxiety they felt was unsharable; the pain was theirs and theirs alone. Fighting an exclusive battle, the contemporary literati were on their own. The post-Tiananmen crisis had a different dynamic. The ultimate male authority the premodern scholars appealed to and the tyrannical father the modern intelligentsia rebelled against were both absent.[50] The intellectuals' adversary was their preconception of self-importance unsustainable in a society that came to value real capital much more than symbolic capital. Unless they learn to rechannel their energies, the incongruity between desire and reality will continue to be a source of pain and humiliation. When intellectual authority is weakened in the reorientation of national and individual priorities, the author and his male characters readopt the discourse of subjugation of women to shore up the intellectual's problematized subjectivity; they use the age-old male-female dichotomy to neutralize the historical trauma. Fiction steps in to counteract the real: the intellectual's precarious position in the reform age is balanced by his male supremacy in the world of fiction. In his relationship with the misrepresented Other, the intellectual's respectability and centeredness are projected through the adoration and homage the female characters pay to Zhuang Zhidie. Surrounding the writer with devoted, submissive women, the text creates a new center for the marginalized intellectual, whereby the superfluousness of the intellectuals and the absence of their creative power are salvaged. Turning the writer into the locus of universal female desire, the fictional world compensates for the intellectual's loss of centrality in real history. Women's presence as sex objects and his easy invasion of the female body prove to Zhuang his status as a male subject. Zhuang "feels like a man" only when he is with his mistresses. Therapeutic, the woman's body becomes the site where his subjectivity finds expression and is valorized and reified. When his problematized agency is reaffirmed in bed, it in turn provides the writer with an imaginary space for self-representation over the female as the signified. The female, as a result, is appropriated both sexually and, on a symbolic level, textually.

But the wishful equation between discursive authority and male sexuality simply testifies to the writer's diminished representational power. When Zhuang's creative agency transfers to his penis, the world he can represent dwindles to the domain of the bedroom. And when the writer's social responsibility is displaced by tricks and techniques in bed, new sex adventures become his only venue for self-expression. In this light, *The*

Ruined Capital offers the reader a curious combination of eulogy and elegy. For when the intellectual's creative power is celebrated through male sexual superiority, the eulogy is simultaneously turned into an admission of his privation of social relevance in the era of reforms. In the final analysis, representation is a creation. The world of illusion becomes unsustainable once the understructure crumples. After the women exit from his life, bringing the projected sexual politics to an end, Zhuang Zhidie suffers a fatal stroke. Once the fantasized foundation disappears, the male subject collapses.

In the end, the finale of Zhuang Zhidie and his story deconstructs the very logic upon which the fictive male/intellectual authority is imagined. Having indulged in a cathartic excess in the text, the narrating self admits the futility and transience of the misrepresentation of women. The destruction of Zhuang's sexual/representative power offers us a glimpse into the dilemma of the intellectual self in the 1990s by problematizing various discursive options or positions by means of which it could define itself in the new age. Clearly, neither the orthodox of service and engagement nor the hedonistic self-abandonment is a solution to the intellectual's difficulties in the commercialized era of modernization. A fitting image of the dislocated self of idealism and dedication, the philosophical cow is an outsider in the urban center, the locale of feverish actions and new possibilities. Because she is extraneous to a changing reality, the cow has trouble relating to the social transformation. She is a "tragic muse" haunted by an unattainable desire that fails to reach an audience; she finally succumbs to exhaustion and perishes, crystallizing the intellectual's awkward position in the contemporary world. Zhuang Zhidie, the corrupted intellectual whose sexual wantonness reflects the uninhibited fin-de-siècle mentality, also dies, at the train station just before catching a train out of town; he leaves the world with a face twisted by a stroke. A distorted self transfixed on the edge of a thwarted desire for change, the degenerated intellectual becomes a permanent fixture on the cultural ruins of the modernizing city. Neither resorting to the traditional moralistic position nor submitting to current dubious practices provides an escape. Paralyzed in between, the intellectual self is stuck. The text inevitably ends, but the crisis of the subject outside it continues.

Epilogue

The representation of the disenchanted agent constitutes a recent chapter in a convoluted national narrative that Chinese intellectuals have been writing since the country's entry into the modern world. With its debut some eight decades ago, the humanist hero, one of the central tropes of this national narrative, embarked on a long and arduous journey only to come to a problematic stop in the last decade of the twentieth century. The sound and fury of the Enlightenment ideals having finally been drowned out in the din of modernization and commercialization in the 1990s, we can now look back on the human subject from a distance to assess and understand its failings against the desires and imperatives behind its inception and textual execution.

Since the post-Mao subject was envisioned as an antidote to the Communist hero, its inadequacy should be examined first in that light. Symbolizing the political suppression the nation suffered for decades, the problematic subject's recurrent trouble with vision and language, as Han Shaogong, Can Xue, and Yu Hua have shown us, is undeniably a pointed negation of the falsehood imposed on its subjectivity by the Party's manipulation of these basic vehicles of human agency. To the extent that self-envisioning can be formulated and articulated only through the mediation of language, language is of paramount importance and lies at the bottom of the subject's deficiencies. My reflection on the troubled subject in relation to both Maoist and post-Mao discourses of the self focuses on this point. Overwhelmed by the official interpellation, the Communist subject is a victim of language. It was not only used by the revolutionary discourse, but it was also asked to use it. Jean-François Lyotard's insight into the operation of the Marxist ideology is particularly illuminating here. Lyotard points out that the Communist master narrative inflicts injustice on its participants by fixing in advance all the narrative functions:

> As a citizen of one of these regimes, you are taken at the same time for the co-author of its narrative, for the privileged listener, and for the perfect executor of the episodes that are assigned you. Your place is thus fixed in the three instances of the master-narrative and in all the details of your life. Your imagination as a narrator, listener or actor is completely blocked. . . . A mistake in execution, an error of listening, a lapsus of narration, and you are locked up. . . . You are forbidden narration. (Lyotard 1977, 31–32)

As Lyotard lays it out, the revolutionary language game is full of paradoxes. The forceful and involuntary indoctrination is nevertheless effected through the recipient's active contribution that requires the subject to perform multiple functions in its own interpellation. Until it makes a mistake and is denied a part in the Marxist historical drama of class struggle, it must first narrate and be the coproducer of a story about itself already prescribed in both principle and practice by the ultimate author, the ruling party. The subject has to speak.

But this self-narration is a façade. The Communist hero is by no means a speaking subject: it only speaks its own spokenness. Simultaneously the narrating and the narrated, the subject is given the responsibility of narrating its own constructedness. Ann Anagnost's analysis of the Maoist practice of "speaking bitterness" *(suku)* illustrates clearly how the Party used it as a technology of control to create an all-encompassing class identity for PRC citizens. Through the act of speaking and listening at the *suku* meetings, an emotional bond was established among the narrator and the audience. The practice of identifying common targets and offering reciprocal commiseration instills in the participants an illusion of a homogeneous subjectivity. By routinely recalling and voicing bitterness against the class enemies— rich peasants, landlords, capitalists, and the reactionaries of the Guomindang—historical memories were not only frozen for those who had experienced it but were also created and perpetuated for the "revolutionary successors" who would otherwise have no knowledge of the preliberation hell (Anagnost 1997, 17–44). The *suku* strategy was a handy weapon wielded whenever there was "a new trend in class struggle" *(jieji douzheng xin dongxiang)* to remind the masses where their loyalties should lie. Affecting everyone, the *suku* ritual fixed people into class categories, cementing cross-generational ties. Memorizing and repeating over and over again an assigned script, the Communist subject is led into a restricted but coherent subject-position, reinforcing and regenerating its imposed subjectivity each time it opens its mouth.

The *suku* method is but one instance of the verbal reproduction of the official ideology in the Communist game of power. Mao's China was a country controlled by the words the state machine ratified. Each and every political movement entailed concerted efforts at learning, echoing, and reciting sets of Communist slogans pounded into public consciousness by the indefatigable media. While Mao was obviously convinced that "political power came from the barrels of guns," he was equally adamant that this power, once achieved, was consolidated by the ideologization of words.[1] The emphasis on the spoken word in particular was a shrewd move. It secured the participation of millions of illiterate peasants, engendering among the entire populace a political and emotional solidarity the more solitary experience of reading might not be able to foster as successfully.

Against the prominent oral tradition in Mao's China, the post-Mao subject's loss of voice and the attendant loss of vision repeatedly proven by the authors I have discussed no doubt amount to a vehement rejection of the inauthentic pledges the subject was forced to utter for decades. But this is as much a willful gesture of silence as an involuntary muteness registered by representation. The subject's voicelessness is a reticence pushed to the ontological extreme. The post-Mao self is a tortured soul pulled between the past and the future. The Maoist subject, as Aunt Yao's flighty stepdaughter announces, "must die." The ideological principles fed to the revolutionary self have become obsolete in the reform era; so has the subject they have nurtured and raised. Changing social conditions in post–Cultural Revolution China demanded a new being with provenance in itself to participate in the reconstruction. Having been denied access to a productive use of language in meaningful communication, however, the subject is no longer able to envisage a self and narrate it.

But narrate it must. The Maoist regime of the past was not the only social force that wanted the subject to speak. The success of the post-Mao overhaul championed by the intellectuals depended on the subject's gaining a voice to express its moral outrage and desired autonomy. It is now required to speak against its spokenness, thus beating the Communist system at its own game. Profoundly ironic, the psychological and spiritual cleansing the literature of the wounded and literature of self-reflection hoped to achieve was in a way a continuation of the *suku* tradition. It constituted another round of nationwide "speaking bitterness," this time pointing an accusing finger at the inventor of this device, Mao's regime.

Venting the post-1949 bitterness was not the ultimate purpose, however. The subject had to go beyond catharsis so that the country could "march toward the future" and "march toward the world." But the voicelessness, the nonsensical utterances, and the loss of seeing power revealed by Chinese authors have become a permanent state of being. The subject has tremendous trouble rising above its debilitation. Consumed by its ontological weaknesses, it remains a solitary being. Mired in a sticky cultural and political history and thus paralyzed, it is a rude sabotage of the humanist credo of self-creation and self-determination, the ideological and philosophical basis of the discursive revolution of the 1980s. The subject created by the writers is an antihero who neither signifies as the Communist superman nor is it able to negotiate new positions to replace it. Self-production stops, and the being becomes an existential blank continuously reenacting a story of perennial absence.

This kind of discursive subject is obviously of little use to post-Mao reconstruction. The newly designed collective project of modernization needed the initiative of a fully functional agent. Unless the subject was able to transcend the regurgitation of the past, the creation of a humanist China would land in an impasse and there would be no new story. It is in the subject's inability to advance to the crucial stage that we can uncover another dimension of the crisis. A being of nonaction, the subject presented for the post-Mao audience fails at the most fundamental level. As I have said, even the Communist discourse requires action. The total incapacity for decision and choice robs the post-Mao subject of the potential to exercise agency and resistance. The nonspeaking, nonseeing being creates a dilemma. It introduces a hiatus between past and future, dashing the hopes of rejuvenation, thus problematizing the very design that has brought it into being.

On the metanarrative level, the difficulties of the subject in the text resonate with those encountered by the writing self outside it. Proof of the fissure between the humanist utopian vision and its realization, the incongruity between the Enlightenment principle of rationality and self-determination and its execution through literary representation reveals significant moments of anxiety and doubt. Like the internal subject, post-Mao writers also did not operate in isolation. Human imagination may be boundless, but it does not exist in a social and ideological vacuum. Despite the post-Mao urge to bury it and move on, the revolutionary legacy had a tenacious hold on the nation's psyche even after being publicly discredited. Whether acknowledged or not, it circumscribed the literary imagination, restricting the fictional subject's choice of action in a realistic setting, thus making realization of the enlightenment project a theoretical mirage and conceptual fantasy. A self-conscious project aiming at nothing less than designing a national model for China's renewal, the literary search was a story in the future tense. But none of the writers treated here achieved the goal. What comes next after the death of the Maoist subject and the disillusionment with the humanist and culturalized hero? No new actor is staged for a post-Mao performance. The aborted mission makes the question unavoidable: Did post-Mao writers overestimate their creative power in their eagerness to resume the social enlightenment initiated by their May Fourth predecessors in the early twentieth century? While recognizing the social impact of the strategy of adopting Western ideas, looking back and forward, we have to also raise doubt about the feasiblility of making the transplantation of Western concepts and ideals the nucleus of China's reconstructive projects, as if they were universal categories that could transcend the sociopolitical specificities of both the original and recipient cultures. Additional problems reside in that, in many cases, Chinese scholars' understanding and interpretation of Western concepts, often contended terms among Western theorists to begin with, tended to be partial and pragmatic.

For the critics and writers, the literary search was also ultimately a strategy of self-positioning. By assuming responsibilities for their country's future and making the nation their object of creation, Chinese intellectuals planted themselves at the center of social development and gave their endeavors a national import, as had been the case in the May Fourth era. Yu Hua's stories of the traveler and Mo Yan's contemplation of the foreign Other are fine examples of the approach consistently adopted by Chinese writers. Representing, exploring, and speaking for the nation through literature and cultural criticism have enabled the intellectuals to function as a meaningful and significant social force in the nation's history. But this posture works only if their role as representatives of the people is accepted by both performers and audience. The very assumption that the intellectuals could represent national conscience became a point of contention in the new economic boom following Deng Xiaoping's trip to the south in 1992. As demonstrated by the confused and degenerated Zhuang Zhidie in Jia Pingwa's novel, the intellectual's own identity, representational power, and moral integrity became an issue. The intellectuals' trouble with retaining representational authority in the 1990s posed a fundamental threat to their social image; it directly challenged their relevance and value in the reforms. On the one hand, the government's ruthless suppression of political dissidence made it dangerous to demand political reforms. On the other, the public simply lost interest in intellectual projects that had no direct bearing on their daily existence in an increasingly competitive world. Thus, the intellectual's problematized relationship to the people and politics was the essence of their crisis in the early 1990s. When they were denied the choice of radical politics and when public zeal for political intervention was replaced by a fervor for moneymaking, the intellectuals had to face the alienating market that obeyed only the rules of supply and demand. The marketization, once set in motion, dragged all social activities into its orbit, in the process dissipating the aura intellectual and literary pursuits had enjoyed for centuries. Like everything else in China today, intellectual writings are products of labor and therefore exchangeable commodities. In the post-Tiananmen avoidance of confrontational politics, speculation in stocks has an appeal far greater than speculation in literature, no matter how much thinking has gone into the latter. When literature carries little political weight and is worth no more and no less than its exchange value, does it matter what it says? Commercialization and consumerism seem to have finally exploded the myth of the power of words cultivated by China's own cultural tradition and Mao's propaganda machine.

Literature stopped playing its orthodox role in society not only because the didacticism of *wen yi zai dao* (use words to impart moral lessons) was hard to practice in a secularized culture but also because ideological diversity had made the vision of a national subject with universal appeal naively idealistic. Unlike in Mao's China, there is no unitary Dao in today's pluralistic society. Different groups have conflicting interests and demands. The vast contingent of unemployed workers has very different views about the reforms from the newly emerging middle class that has a vested interest in current state policies. The floating population from rural areas seeking opportunities in the cities do not want the same thing as urban dwellers, who view the influx as a threat to public safety and job security. Nor do regional governments have the same agenda and priorities as the central state. With the advent of numerous small narratives, the notion of a unified national subjectivity is no longer sustainable. Chinese intellectuals now do not have a privileged voice in prescribing the national story. In what one observer calls a "trendless" *(wu ming)* age, they have to realize that their narration is only one among a multitude of versions enacting China's drama of modernization.[2] Is it finally time for the intellectuals to let go of their "obsession with China" and practice what they have always asked for in their complaint against the Party's authoritarian control: separation of literature from ideology and of academic learning from politics? But what would this position entail for the intellectuals in terms of their relation to the nation, politics, and themselves? And are there alternatives?

How did the intellectuals cope with their marginalization after absorbing the initial shock, and where did they invest their energies to ensure their presence as a meaningful group with some identifiable characteristics in a society that continued to change at a rapid pace? The Chinese cultural field since the mid-1990s was as fragmentary as the society that it endeavored to understand and interpret. This, however, is hardly the place for an in-depth analysis of the diversified opinions and their critiques, or even the labels pinned on various groups.[3] I single out the following two trends to take the question of intellectual identity beyond my focus in the preceding chapter: the discussion of the "humanist spirit" *(renwen jingshen)* and the "post-ist" theories *(hou xue)*, to adopt Yiheng Zhao's coinage. In my brief comment on their general tendencies, I treat the trends as self-positioning strategies and discuss how they moved in opposite directions on the central issue of whether to engage or disengage the nation and politics in an effort to remap the intellectual's relationship to the nation and politics.

The discussion of the "humanist spirit" started in 1994 and continued for a couple of years. Launched in recognition of their superfluity and diminishing influence in a rampant consumerist cultural market, it provided an opportunity for the humanists to hold each other's hands and assure themselves of the worth and goal of their intellectual undertakings. Among the questions often voiced at the time were: What constitutes a "humanist spirit," and what should the cultural scholars be concerned with when the humanist morals they had promoted had lost their public appeal? The catchphrase in many of the deliberations was *"zhongji guanhuai"* (the ultimate concern), the alleged final goal of all humanistic studies, whether history, cultural criticism, or literature. Though frequently used, neither the term "ultimate concern" nor "humanist spirit" has generated any clear, agreed-upon definitions. To some, the "humanist spirit" resides in the intellectuals' personal conscience *(geren liangzhi)*, a moral conviction in such values as truth and justice that enables them to resist corruptive market forces and the cynicism in their own circles. To others, the "ultimate concern" refers to finding universal meanings of human existence. Since the real value of humanistic studies lies in realizing the "ultimate concern," these studies, some remind their colleagues, would not produce any immediate social effect. The intellectuals should therefore prepare to put up with loneliness and not be disheartened by the lack of instant gratification and public recognition. The way for the intellectuals to deal with their peripheral status is to acknowledge that their previous prominence in society was an abnormal state of things resulting from radical politicization of their profession. It was proposed that the scholars should take advantage of the economic reforms to return things to normal by devoting themselves to learning without imposing on intellectual pursuits any political purpose.[4]

The disappearance of the nation from the discursive horizon of the "ultimate concern" rationale is a significant difference between the debates on humanism and subjectivity in the 1980s and the current "humanist spirit" discussion. Although the intellectuals formulated the theories of humanism and subjectivity on the basis of their own desires and experiences, the primary object of their exploration and interest in the 1980s was the nation and the country. On behalf of the Chinese people, the intellectuals took up the "emancipation of thought" as a crucial step toward modernization. In contrast, the participants, intended audience, and immediate beneficiaries of the discussion in the 1990s were more exclusively the intellectuals themselves. While humanism was envisioned as a universal principle for the soul of the nation in the previous decade, no such grand illusion was entertained in the 1990s. The discourse of "humanist spirit" and the "ultimate concern" was prescribed only for the moral health of the intellectuals, therefore a limited club affair. The purpose of the discussion was to help intellectuals battle frustration and pessimism by clarifying for them the value of their endeavors so that they would not lose sight of their profession's importance in a materialistic society. Thus, the two projects proceeded from very different understandings of the intellectual's position in society. The search for a new national subject in the 1980s was initiated on the assumption that the intellectuals were the rightful vanguard of their country's transformation; talk of the "humanist spirit" came about precisely because such an assumption had lost its validity. The admission that the intellectuals could no longer superimpose their vision on that of the nation carries certain ambiguities. By releasing their self-imposed national mission, the intellectuals seemed to have shed some of their arrogance toward the people, but the view that they were working to realize some "ultimate concern" beyond the comprehension and reach of the masses reinforced the elitism deeply ingrained in the intellectuals' self-perception.

How the "humanist spirit" discussion positioned itself in relation to politics is another characteristic that distinguishes it from the intellectual climate of the 1980s. The first round of debates on humanism and subjectivity targeted the disregard of human values in the Communist practice and was consequently a step of active engagement. The "ultimate concern" rhetoric charts a course of disengagement and retreat. This can be seen in that the former humanism was an ideologically and historically specific discourse of social change. It was given a clear set of principles (freedom, independence, rationality, and truth) in contradistinction to the Communist denial of individual autonomy. The "ultimate concern" about universal humanity, on the contrary, takes on a transcendental quality above immediate social and political conflicts. In the same way that the definition of "humanist spirit" and the "ultimate concern" is vague, the relation between their realization and daily social struggles is also fuzzy. There is a considerable distance between individual conscience as a purely private matter of self-cultivation and the overgeneralized and consequently hard-to-define concept of the "history of humanity." How is a person to move from one to the other to integrate self-perfection with effective social action? In what ways can the pursuit for the "ultimate concern" of humanity be tied up with and benefit China's continued efforts at modernization? And finally, does there exist a pure knowledge about humankind devoid of social and cultural particularities? These issues remained largely untackled, for to provide explanations, we would have to go back and question the very premise of the "ultimate concern" as moral values of universal significance. By bestowing on humanistic knowledge some metaphysical quality, the scholars introduced a distance between intellectual inquiries and the mundane world, thus carving out a space for themselves to form a new identity away from both politics and economic praxis. Relocating the "symbolic capital" within humanistic knowledge and insights, this position created a buffer between scholarly activities and commercialization. At the same time, it could also shield the intellectuals against the kind of constant manipulation by the ruling power that they had suffered under the Communist rule, making them less susceptible to suppression and persecution. The insulation of humanistic concerns from utilitarianism could finally give the intellectuals a truly independent identity, but it could also lead to their isolation and further marginalization in a vibrant society.

The "ultimate concern" proposition identified the intellectuals' superiority in their knowledge about an all-embracing humanity, developing a defense mechanism to protect them against historical contingencies. To subscribe to this vision, the intellectuals would have to give up their traditional sense of mission and their "worrying mentality" and desire to achieve immediate social effects, the very quality that had designated them as a special group in China's history, the modern era in particular. This turned out to be a difficult step for many cultural critics representing various "new conservative" positions, a label used by both the proponents at home and their critics abroad.[5] The cultural critics' refusal to detach from the sociopolitical particulars is understandable when we consider that any study of culture has to be socially and historically specific if the reflections are to have any relevance and meaning for the community involved. While the "ultimate concern" believers discovered a new site for their identity in the rupture between the academics and other nonscholarly public activities, the "new conservatives" tried to reinstate the intellectual on the national stage by engaging the very elements of social life deemphasized by the humanists: the nation and politics. This diverse group of intellectuals was dubbed "new conservatives" because their diagnosis and prescriptions for the post–New Era China *(hou xin shiqi)* were often preceded by critiques and negative reevaluations of the intellectual currents of the 1980s. The previous modernity project that privileged the enlightenment mode of thinking and the Western style of democracy was found to be too radical for China because it lacked a democratic tradition and the necessary conditions, such as an effective civil society and a stable economy, to withstand violent changes. It was feared that the youthful revolution mentality behind all the radical movements in China's history—the May Fourth iconoclasm, the Communist revolution, the Cultural Revolution, and the June Fourth protests—would only induce disorder and chaos, causing the dissolution of the country. Indeed, Li Zehou and Liu Zaifu, the two most prominent figures in the intellectual reorientation of the 1980s, publicly bid farewell to the revolution (Li and Liu 1995). Wary of extreme measures, many intellectuals were now in favor of more moderate evolutionist and realistic approaches and were willing to grant priorities to economic development over political reforms and social stability over drastic systemic changes.

When the 1980s idea of modernity came under scrutiny, its radical westernization became a common target. Arguing that post-Mao transformation should not be achieved at the expense of jeopardizing China's own tradition and values, some intellectuals promoted Chinese learning as a new model of knowledge to build a China-specific approach to modernization. Drawing strength from postmodernist and postcolonialist antihegemonic positions, others highlighted the conflict between China and the West as a chief concern on the country's agenda, rejecting the kind of blind faith in Western values and Western interpretations of modernity typical, in their opinion, of the 1980s perception of modernization. To counter Western hegemony and Western cultural imperialism, the "post-ist" theorists offered to accentuate Chineseness, determined by such anthropocentric factors as a common heritage of language, ethnicity, and culture, turning it into a foundation for an authentic national identity. The emphasis on the indigenous, the proponents believed, could ensure China's independence and cultural uniqueness in globalization. Making its own history and experience the reference point in deciding its course of modernization could empower China and help it ward off Western domination. Except for the postcolonialist stance, the traditionalist vision of the 1990s echoed the concerns about the destiny of Chinese culture and identity raised by the neo-Confucianists during the Cultural Discussion in the 1980s (Tang Yijie 2001). Going against the popular zeal for westernization, the traditionalists of the previous decade failed to gain an upper hand. By assuming an antiradical position and adopting the first world–third world dichotomy, their colleagues, however, succeeded in making China-centered approach and nationalism dominant social motifs in the 1990s.[6]

Although the efforts to redefine the intellectual self varied in their emphasis and sensibilities, the positioning pivoted on the intellectuals' relation with the people. Recognizing the heterogeneity generated by the reforms, the "ultimate concern" vision admits the futility of attempting to create and represent a unified voice for the people, resituating the intellectual in a transcendental project immune from the fluctuations of the reforms. By retreating from the public, this type of elitism locates humanistic knowledge as a stable core of the intellectual self to offset the unpredictability of social transformations. No matter how we interpret it, the various strands of the China-centered approaches, in contrast, tried to eliminate the distance between the intellectuals and the public in the marketized economy by reappropriating the scholar's traditional position as spokesperson for the society's conscience.[7] Privileging cultural generality over social diversity, the native over the foreign, and China over the West recollectivized the people, once again making them representable. By reinvigorating the idea of nation and emphasizing national interests and cultural integrity, the post-ist theorists subsumed the people under a common signification in which local differences were secondary concerns. Instead of cocooning the scholars in unpolitical professionalism and separating them from the quotidian of modernization, the nativist rhetoric reinserted the intellectuals into the center of national development and national politics. Appealing to the prevailing anti-West sentiments sanctioned by the regime, the intellectuals reworked their relation with both the people and the state. It returned them to public attention and connected them with the society, giving them another opportunity to speak for the nation, this time not through radical politics but more through realignment with popular will and the state.

The 1990s presented unprecedented challenges. The rapid transformation made the post-1989 era dynamic, promising, and confusing. The reforms could not yield any lasting and predictable patterns because there are too many contradictions. Tensions were therefore inevitable. To name a few sources: social polarization induced by the marketization; uneven development of local economies and the resultant conflict in central-local, region-region interactions; uninhibited abuse of power and increasing public resentments toward official corruption; and the uncertainties in domestic and international politics. Still, accelerating marketization, a continued openness toward the outside, and the diversification of society and economy also offered tremendous opportunities and room for maneuver. How to maintain their social integrity and critical function as intellectuals, how to establish a productive relationship with the nation and the state, and how to find a position that balanced academic passivism, radical activism, and complicitous conservatism in an age when the boundaries between global capital, state power, civil space, and intellectual autonomy have become ever harder to define continued to confront contemporary intellectuals. There can be no easy answer. As China changes, so will the paradigm in which ideas of the intellectual self can be discussed and practiced.

Notes

Chapter 1: Introduction

1. The debate was initiated by Wang Ruoshui in 1980. The crux of Wang's argument is that alienation, first discussed by Marx in relation to the capitalist mode of production, also exists in various forms in the socialist system. See Wang Ruoshui 1981, 1983.

2. *Renmin ribao*, 18 May 1979, cited in Alan P. L. Liu 1986, 332.

3. The collection showcases examples of post-Mao fiction that are subversive on many fronts: the lack of political and ideological utility, the fascination with the unspeakable sides of human nature and individual behavior as well as artistic approaches that defy established interpretive frameworks, such as politics, ethics, ideology, and aesthetics.

4. The literary and cultural studies of contemporary China in book form include Jing Wang 1996; Xudong Zhang 1997; Lu Tonglin 1995; Xiaomei Chen 1995; Gregory B. Lee 1996; Xueping Zhong 2000; Min Lin with Maria Galikowski 1999; Ben Xu 1999; Geremie R. Barmé 1999; Gang Yue 1999; Xiaobing Tang 2000; Yingjin Zhang 2002. See also the following collections: Goldblatt 1990; Widmer and Wang 1993; Liu and Tang 1993; Larson and Wedell-Wedellsborg 1993.

5. The translation of the passage is by Joseph S. M. Lau. See Lau 1993, 21.

6. This question underlines Robert Weimann's critique of the post-structuralist position that completely subordinates the subject to the power of discourse. I discuss Weimann's view in more detail in chapter 7.

7. For studies on modern Chinese literature published since the 1990s, see Anderson 1990; Rey Chow 1991; David Der-wei Wang 1992; Barlow 1993; Lydia Liu 1995; Feuerwerker 1998; Yingjin Zhang 1996; Hu Ying 2000; Leo Lee 1999; Xiaobing Tang 2000, pt. 1; Shih 2001.

8. For a fuller discussion of the topic, see Denton 1998, 27–72. Most scholars agree that the May Fourth period includes a few years prior to the movement in 1919 and a few years afterward, in the early 1920s. The May Fourth movement is a widely discussed topic. See, for example, Chow Tse-tsung 1960; Vera Schwarcz 1986.

9. Lin explains in a note on the same page that his use of the word *totalistic* "has nothing to do with its totalitarian connotation."

10. For example, Feng Youlan has noted the conflict between loyalty and filial piety; C. K. Yang maintains that there is tension in the idea of universalistic virtue *(gong)* and familistic morality; Yu-sheng Lin points out that the basics of Confucian *ren* and *li* (ritual) assume contradictory moral principles. See Feng 1967, 78–79; C. K. Yang 1959, 134–164; Y. Lin 1974–1975, 172–204.

11. Traditional Chinese literature is a rich source for discovering the self living and resolving moral ambiguities in different social relationships. For discussions of a gallery of the self in Chinese literature, see Hegel and Hessney 1985.

12. Foreign literature so captivated the imagination of the May Fourth generation that it became fashionable to adopt Western names and mannerisms after one's fictional idols. See Leo Lee 1973, 275–296.

13. Hu Shi held a different position in his earlier essay "Ibsenism," where he situated the more enlightened individual outside the society as its spiritual guardian. See Denton 1996, 44–45.

14. Hu Shi, "Bu xiu: wo de zongjiao" (Immortality: my religion), in *Hu Shi wencun* (Collected works of Hu Shi) (Taibei: n.p., 1953), 1:693–702. Quoted in Denton 1996, 45.

15. The emphasis on the self's subordination to the country in my view provides one of the central links between the premodern, modern, Communist, and post-Communist conceptions of the self. The need to survive as a nation-state, which gave birth to nationalism and the modern self, superseded all other desires and considerations in the twentieth century and was appropriated by various political powers to rally public support for their causes. In recent years nationalism has also proven to be an effective new ideology to channel the otherwise heterogeneous social energies into the discourse of the state in post–June Fourth China. On the rise of a new nationalism in China in the 1990s, see, for example, Zheng 1999.

16. For discussions on the nuances of the concept of the individual and the whole in traditional schools of thought, see Munro 1985a.

17. That Confucianism believes strongly in the malleability of human moral character goes without saying. Scholars have also pointed out that in their own ways, both Buddhism and Daoism emphasize the transformation of human nature. The Buddhist purification of the mind by self-effort and the Daoist return to nature are predicated on the recognition that human nature can be influenced and changed. See, for example, Berling 1985; Fozdar 1973.

18. Because of the state's control over job assignments and the *hukou* (residence registration) system, social mobility, especially between rural areas and cities, was strictly limited by the government. People had no choice over their place of residence before the mid-1980s.

19. For a comprehensive discussion of how literature functioned in Communist China, see Link 2000.

20. For example, Leo Lee points out that in both the May Fourth and the post-Mao eras, the usage of Western terms often differed from their original semantic and sociopolitical context (2001, 34).

21. An English version of the story can be found in an anthology edited by Duke 1991.

22. In her book, Feuerwerker discusses the diverse ways in which the relation between the intellectual and the peasant is used as a trope of self-construction by four generations of Chinese writers.

Chapter 2: In Search of a New Subject

1. Because of the events of 1989 and the upsurge of commercialism in the early 1990s, the cultural landscape changed dramatically. See my discussion in chapter 7. Richard Trappl invented the term "textivity" to describe the post-Tiananmen situation, when there were fewer literary texts of commendable quality, although the presses continued to publish a large quantity of literary works. Trappl uses the term "to stress the fact that what has become important is not so much *what* is expressed in the published texts but *that* texts are published." See Trappl 1993; Barmé 1991.

2. The swirling new trends induced dizziness not only among readers but also in critics. Faced with this literary merry-go-round, critics experienced a kind of excited frustration and fascination. At a literary conference held in Beijing in September 1986, critics commented jokingly that now any literary trend could claim to be new only for three or five days, parodying the Qing poet Zhao Yi's observation that "the country has produced talents in each dynasty. One could lead a trend only for a couple of hundred years." About the conference, see Wang Meng's speech "Xiaoshuojia yan" (Comments from a writer), *Renmin ribao*, 22 September 1986. Huang Ziping, a prominent young critic, once said self-mockingly that "critics are chased around by the dog of innovation so that they don't even have time to stop and pee." Quoted in Li Tuo 1988, 10.

Huang Ziping's choice of image shows that the role of critics in the 1980s was no longer that of intermediary between the Party and the writer. The tables had been turned. Literary criticism no longer guided literary practices; now it was trying to catch up. The critics' compulsion and rush to "name" were also a defensive gesture to mitigate their anxiety over their loss of leadership in literary creation. For a preliminary discussion of literary criticism in the 1980s, see Wedell-Wedellsborg 1993.

3. For discussions on post-Mao reportage, see Yingjin Zhang 1993; Duke 1985, 98–122.

4. For the purpose of my study, by "intellectuals" *(zhishifenzi)*, I mean those who received a higher education, in particular, the "cultural workers," writers, artists, literary critics, and those in the social sciences and humanities. Scientists and technologists, along with the cultural workers, were targets of attacks during various movements, but they were not as directly responsible for spreading the official ideology as those working with their pens. On the relationship between Chinese intellectuals and the state in Communist China in general, see Goldman 1981; Goldman et al. 1987; see also James C. F. Wang 1985, chap. 9; Ma 1993.

5. There are complicated cultural, historical, political, and practical reasons behind the intellectuals' identification with their official function. The Confucian tradition required the literati to serve as upholders of social, ethical principles and as loyal assistants to and moral critics of the ruler when circumstances demanded. The May Fourth legacy, furthermore, placed the responsibility for national salvation and the rejuvenation of Chinese culture onto the shoulders of

the modern intellectuals, strapping them with the fate of the nation. Not only did the Communist Party later co-opt the intellectuals' patriotism and sense of mission in its struggle for power, but the Maoist ideological manipulation of language also made unity with the Party and the state politically correct and safe and practically profitable. Perry Link points out that the CCP is good at playing the language game to ensure submission from its people. For example, by holding itself up as the representative of the people (renmin) and pronouncing those with different opinions "a tiny minority" (yixiaocuo), it automatically puts the regime in the mainstream and its opposition in the minority. In Link's words, "'the tiny minority' message is a dual one. It not only carries a threat against deviation but offers comfort as a reward for docility." See Link 1992, 178.

6. For example, at a literary discussion held in January 1980, Li Zhun, a well-known veteran writer, said with deep remorse that he felt "ashamed before the people" for having produced much worthless political propaganda in his works. See Duke 1985, 32.

7. This is a well-documented subject. See the special issue on Chinese Communist literature, China Quarterly 13 (1963); Fokkema 1966, 1969; C. T. Hsia 1961, 1970; Birch 1960; Borowitz 1954; McDougall 1984; R. Wagner 1990; Anagnost 1997, chap. 1.

8. For a discussion of the use of traditional characters in revolutionary literature, see Hegel 1984.

9. These were real individuals, but their life stories were fictionalized and elevated according to the Party's standard of ideological correctness. For a discussion of the use of models in Communist China, see Munro 1977, 135–157.

10. Lei Feng was a soldier who performed numerous good deeds. He died in an accident. In 1964 Mao and the Party started the nationwide "Learn from Comrade Lei Feng" campaign.

11. Except for Hao Ran's Jinguang dadao (The golden road) (1972), no full-length novels of any weight were published during the Cultural Revolution. For seven years, from 1966 to 1972, China did not produce a single feature film. See Dangdai zhongguo dianying (Film in contemporary China), 319–329. With Jiang Qing as the standard-bearer of revolutionary literature and art, it is no wonder that there is a leading superwoman in almost every one of these model plays.

12. On the history of the PRC, see Meisner 1986.

13. During the Cultural Revolution, there were a number of hand-copied stories in circulation among young readers, most of them "sent-down" youths. Perry Link (1989) points out that rather than being dissident voices, they reflect the popular taste for detective stories, triangular love stories, romances, and pornography.

14. See Jing Wang's critique that the alienation school failed to pursue the cause of economic alienation in depth and that it overlooked the subject's own internalization of oppression, thus assuming that alienation will disappear once the external factors are eliminated (1996, 9–31).

15. On the debate, see Schram 1984, 42–56; Brugger and Kelly 1990, 139–170; Kelly 1987. See also Jing Wang 1996, 9–36.

16. Li Zehou, Pipan zhexue de pipan (A critique of critical philosophy), enl. ed. (Beijing: Renmin chubanshe, 1984). The work later appears in Li's Li Zehou shinian ji (1994).

17. An adequate presentation of Li's theory is impossible without going into the details of his Marxist appropriations of the Kantian formation of subjectivity in the three essential constituents of knowledge, will, and feeling. Interested readers should read Li's own works. Li's *Mei de licheng* [The path of beauty] now has an English version; see Li Zehou 1994b. For critical views of Li Zehou's theory, see Liu Kang 1993; Gu Xin 1995; Jing Wang 1996, 93–114; Lin and Galikowski 1999, chap. 2; Liu Xiaobo 1989.

18. The most important essays are collected in Liu Zaifu 1986a, *Liu Zaifu lunwen xuan* [Selected essays by Liu Zaifu].

19. Liu Zaifu did not make clear what he meant by "traditional intellectuals" nor which dynastic era he was referring to. Different periods had different notions of individuality and tolerated it to varying degrees. See Munro 1985a.

20. Liang Qichao built his argument in "Lun xiaoshuo yu qunzhi zhi guanxi" (On the relationship between fiction and the government of the people) on the assumption that fiction has irresistible power over the reader's mind. The essay is reprinted in *Zhongguo jindai lunwen xuan* (Selected writings on literature in modern China), 2 vols. (Beijing: Renmin wenxue, 1962), 1:157–161. Even for Hu Feng, whose theory of the "subjective fighting spirit" brought him endless political trouble under Mao's regime (as I discuss briefly later in this chapter), the "subjective spirit" applies only to the writer. Despite the difference between the slogans of Hu Feng's *hua dazhong* (to enlighten the masses) and Mao's *dazhonghua* (popularization of literature), the underlying belief is the same, that is, the reader is the one to be educated.

21. Hu Feng's clashes with Communist literary authorities dated back to the 1930s in Shanghai in the factional conflict within the League of Left-Wing Writers. Later, in the early 1940s and early 1950s, Hu Feng was again at the forefront of the controversies between independent, nondoctrinaire writers and the Party's literary representatives. For collections of Hu's essays, see Hu 1984, 1985.

22. Hu Feng shared with most of the May Fourth writers a strong sense of mission and a firm conviction that the Western realism represented by such nineteenth-century writers as Honoré de Balzac, Émile Zola, Stendhal, Romain Rolland, and Henrik Ibsen was the literary mode that would enable writers to get to the truth of Chinese society and rejuvenate Chinese culture. Understandably, in his unflinching commitment to the program of nation building, Hu Feng considered literary trends other than realism as "corrupt forces in society itself" (1967, 64).

23. Hu Feng's plea for the autonomy of writers and truthfulness to real life finally brought about his downfall in 1955, when he was condemned as the head of an "anti-Party" clique and arrested on charges of organizing counterrevolution. Hu was released from prison in 1979, but his final exoneration did not come until 1987. On the Hu Feng event, see Goldman 1962 and 1967, chap. 7; Fokkema 1965, 19–26; Liu Kang 1993, 26–30; Denton 1998. For a source in Chinese, see Li Hui 1989.

24. Even though Li Zehou stresses social, economic practice over language in his theory, his having fought his battle in the discursive field shows that he is very conscious of the power of language.

25. For discussions on the "literature of the wounded," see Duke 1985, 63–68; Louie 1989, 1–13; H. Martin 1982.

26. On these two works, see also Goodman 1986; Cheng Yingxiang 1986.

27. Though the experimentation has not always been successful, it is nonetheless a sign of the awakening and assertion of the writer's subjectivity. See Duke's criticism of Dai Houying in Duke 1985, 149–181.

28. Li Zehou, "Letters to L.J.," *Wenyibao* 2 (1981): 44, quoted in Li and Schwarcz 1983/1984, 52.

29. The sense of loss, frustration, betrayal, awakening, and hope is well documented in the collection of interviews of writers from this generation conducted by Laifong Leung (1994). The middle-aged generation constitutes the fifth generation, according to Li and Schwarcz. They were shaped by the Soviet model of education, and Li and Schwarcz characterize them as sincere, eager believers in the revolution; timid; and narrow in their views. See Li and Schwarcz 1983/1984, 51–52. Li Zehou himself belongs to this generation, but he holds a pessimistic view about his own peers. The voluminous "educated youth literature" is another excellent source for studying the frustration, aspiration, and in some cases romanticization of the Cultural Revolution generation.

30. Some of the middle-aged writers, notably Wang Meng and Dai Houying, should be commended for their pioneering role in adopting new literary techniques. Their political beliefs are less radical than those of the younger generation, however, and sometimes get in the way of their technical innovation. See Leo Lee 1985a, 1990; Tay 1984.

31. Chinese critics named this tendency *danhua* (despecification). See Cao Wenxuan 1986. Aspects of despecification listed by Cao include plot, theme, setting, and emotions.

32. The Four Principles were keeping the socialist road and upholding the dictatorship of the proletariat, the Party leadership, and the Marxism-Leninism–Mao Zedong thought.

33. For an excellent in-depth study that spells out the nuances and contradictions of the representative views, see Jing Wang 1996, 37–136; see also Xudong Zhang 1997, pt. 1. For a concise discussion in Chinese, see Chen Kuide 1991.

34. In this book, Jin spells out his theory about the superstable structure of traditional society.

35. Neo-Confucianism started at the end of the 1950s and peaked in the 1970s. Tu Wei-ming considers these scholars Confucianists in the third period. The first period is from Qin, Han to Tang (202 B.C.–A.D. 907), the second from Song, Ming to Qing (A.D. 960–A.D. 1911). See Tu 1989, 26–28. See also Feng Zusheng 1989.

36. The Asian tigers, Taiwan, Hong Kong, South Korea, Singapore, and Japan, or the "five little dragons" as they were called in mainland China, were cited as supporting evidence by the advocates of the view that Confucianism and modernity may overlap. See, for example, Tu 1989, 347–352. The flourishing of neo-Confucianism in the 1970s was also due to the economic boom of these countries and regions.

37. Pang Pu admits that Confucianism's neglect of the study of science is a drawback. But he argues that industrialization also created "machinelike, emotionless humans." The "humanism" of Confucianism, in his view, can help compensate for the loss of humanity induced by modernization. See Pang Pu 1988, 76.

38. For example, Tu Wei-ming holds that modernity takes specific forms

even within the Western world. Therefore it is erroneous to assume that there is only one modern culture and one type of modernity. See Tu 1989, 289–295.

39. Other art forms such as film and painting were also involved in the "culture fever." For a discussion of post-Mao art, see Gao Minglu 1989. On post-Mao films, see Xudong Zhang 1997, pt. 2; Yingjin Zhang 2002.

40. "Roots" writings started as early as 1982, with Jia Pingwa's "Shang-zhou chu lu" (Stories of Shangzhou), Li Hangyu's series of stories of the Gechuan River, Duore'ertu's hunting stories, and Zhong Acheng's "Qiwang" (Chess king). After Han Shaogong's article "The 'Roots' of Literature" was published, the trend not only got its name but also surged through the literary world.

41. For example, Feuerwerker's analyses of three *xungen* writers, Han Shao-gong, Mo Yan, and Wang Anyi, demonstrate that the writers' imaginings of rural China and the writing self have little in common. See Feuerwerker 1998, chap. 6.

42. In her essay "The Anxiety of Out-fluence: Creativity, History and Postmodernity," Bonnie S. McDougall chides modern as well as contemporary Chinese writers for copying Western literary fashions, thus forsaking creativity. McDougall's criticism is not without validity. But in the age when the information superhighway was quickly becoming an accustomed channel of communication, influence, or "out-fluence," to use the critic's own word, is inevitable. In my opinion, as long as there is the attendant "anxiety," influence can be a blessing. See McDougall 1993.

43. Some of the prominent writers associated with the traditional forms are Wang Zengqi, Lin Jinlan, and Jia Pingwa. For a collection of works written in the literary sketch form, see Zhong Benkang 1993a.

44. On the rise of modernism and the nativist school in Taiwan literature and their oppositional relationship, see Sung-sheng Chang 1993.

45. For example, Han Shaogong's two representative works "Pa Pa Pa" and "Woman Woman Woman" blend traditional *baimiao* (simple and direct descrip-tion) with García Márquezian magical realism.

46. In his engaging and vigorously argued essay on contemporary visual art, Yuejin Wang analyzes a group of portraits of parental figures and comes to the conclusion that "the question 'who are you, father?' finally boomerangs to become 'who am I?'" (1993, 268).

47. Fokkema's study of Communist literary doctrine proves that these literary principles were kept vague so that the Party could always adapt them to the needs at hand. Those who attempted an explanation based on their own under-standing were invariably criticized or denounced for advocating a separatist, erro-neous policy in opposition to the Party's (Fokkema 1965, 256).

48. For a summary discussion of the debates in Chinese, see Xu Zidong 1989. For English sources, see Wendy Larson 1989, 1993; Wedell-Wedellsborg 1986. More recent views on the subject can be found in Jing Wang 1996, 137–194, and Xudong Zhang 1997, 122–142.

49. In the following presentation of Chinese critics' arguments, the word *modernism* does not refer strictly to the Western use of the term for the trend that was started at the turn of the century and gradually subsided in the 1930s with such representative figures as T. S. Eliot, Franz Kafka, William Faulkner, Joseph Conrad, James Joyce, and Virginia Woolf.

50. The earliest attempts at producing modernist writings were made by a group of young poets later known as the "obscurists" or "misty poets." In fiction Bei Dao, Bai Hua, Dai Houying, and Wang Meng were already experimenting with such techniques as stream of consciousness, dream sequence, and nonlinear narration.

51. The essay later appears in the collection *Xifang xiandaipai wenxue wenti lunzhengji*, 568–613. For discussions on *menglong shi* (obscure or misty poetry), see Tay 1985; Golder and Minford 1990.

52. See, for example, Chen Daixi 1984.

53. Chinese writers in the 1980s had a definite advantage over their May Fourth predecessors in that they did not have the country's sovereignty to worry about. As a result, they were much more responsive to other literary trends besides realism. Not only could contemporary writers experiment in a much more leisurely manner (unlike the May Fourth writers, they were financially secure, supported by the state under the *danwei* [work unit] system), but the social milieu in the 1980s was also more conducive to literary adventures.

54. Yu Hua, for example, seems to take particular pleasure in dissecting the human body and casually scattering the fragments around in his fiction. On a symbolic level, under the new-wave writers' assault on the categories of human consciousness, memory, and history, the humanist hero as the arbiter of all knowledge has died many an inglorious death. For discussions of the new-wave writers, see Jing Wang 1996, 224–259; Xudong Zhang 1997, 143–200.

Chapter 3: The Spoken Subject

1. See Wang's comment quoted in chapter 1.

2. Li Jie 1988, 118; Wang Xiaoming 1988, 27; Chen Dazhuan 1986, 136; Li Qingxi 1986, 51.

3. Four of the stories in English translation are collected in Han Shaogong, *Homecoming? and Other Stories*, trans. Martha Cheung (Hong Kong: Research Center for Translation, Chinese University of Hong Kong, 1992).

4. See Duke 1989a, 42 n. 11. In his interview with Shi Shuqing, Han admits that he found *The Sound and the Fury* quite a challenge because of its constant shifting from one scene to another. He listed Faulkner several times, along with James Joyce, Gabriel García Márquez, Franz Kafka, and the French "new novelists," as the most popular among China's young readers. See Shi 1989, 138–139.

5. I used Martha Cheung's translation except that I retained the character Bing Zai's name, which the translator rendered as "Young Bing."

6. Lacan talks about the mirror relationship in the following passage:

> We have only to understand the mirror stage as *an identification,* in the full sense that analysis gives to the term: namely, the transformation that takes place in the subject when he assumes an image.... This jubilant assumption of his specular image by the child at the *infans* stage, still sunk in his motor incapacity and nursing dependence, would seem to exhibit in an exemplary situation the symbolic matrix in which the *I* is precipitated in a primordial form, before it is objectified in the dialectic of identification with the other, and before language restores to it, in the universal, its function as subject. (Lacan 1977, 2)

7. As can be seen here, for Lacan the ego from the very beginning is an alienated image mistaken for the being's real self. Lacan calls this "the self's radical eccentricity to itself." Ibid., 171.

8. In his discussion entitled "Lacan and the Discourse of the Other," Wilden offers a brilliant introduction to and analyses of many Lacanian concepts.

9. Jacques Lacan 1961, "La Direction de la cure," 198, quoted in Wilden 1968, 176.

10. In spite of his playfulness, Lacan's play with words nonetheless points to the importance he places on language: *"lettre"* for Lacan becomes *"l'être"* (being). Also compare the statement from the linguist Emile Benveniste: "It is a speaking man whom we find in the world, a man speaking to another man, and language provides the very definition of man" (Benveniste 1971, 224).

11. Wilden explains the "zero" thus: "for mathematics the function of zero is to be the concept under which no object falls (all objects being defined as identical with themselves), because in order to 'save the truth,' zero is assigned to the concept 'not identical with itself' (Frege). Zero makes a lack (but not a 'nothing') visible, and thus it provides for the linear movement of integers in the same way as absence constitutes the subject of the *Fort! Da!*, who has previously known only the asubjectivity of total presence. In other words, the lack of object is what enables the child to progress to the subjectivity of 'I,' or, in the mathematical metaphor, from the not-nothing-not-something of zero to the status of 'One,' who can therefore know two. The subject *is* the binary opposition of presence and absence, and the discovery of One—the discovery of difference—is to be condemned to an eternal desire for the nonrelationship of zero, where identity is meaningless" (Wilden 1968, 191).

12. Liu Zaifu sees Bing Zai's two expressions as a reflection of the either-or mentality of the Chinese people. To the idiot, people belong to either the friendly "Papa" category or the "F—— Mama" enemy camp (Liu Zaifu 1988c).

13. I have modified the translation here. The Chinese original is *xue zhe zenyang zuoren* (learning to be a man). Martha Cheung translates this as "teaching him this or that."

14. One would have no trouble detecting García Márquez's *One Hundred Years of Solitude* behind this scene. On the influence of magic realism on Han Shaogong, see Chen Dazhuan 1986.

15. In Duke's opinion Old Black represents the "thoroughly modern young woman." See Duke 1989a, 44–45.

16. Duke interprets Aunt Zhen as a rural version of the traditional self-denying Chinese woman, while Aunt Yao stands for the urban type. See Duke 1989a, 43–44.

17. In the Chinese original, "a certain person" *(yige shenme ren)* is highlighted. The author obviously wants to emphasize the expectation.

18. This is the note provided by the translator: "According to the author, there are two schools of explanation for the word *'xu'*. One is that it was used in ancient times as a term of address by the people of Hunan and Hubei for their elder sisters. Another is that it was used in ancient times as a term of address by the people in Hunan and Hubei for all their female relatives." In the novella Han Shaogong clearly is using the term in the second sense.

19. That very few if any *zhiqing* actually returned to the countryside only proves the split between the generation's psychological need to salvage their *zhiqing* experience and their realization of the physical reality.

20. Qu Yuan was an honest minister in the court of King Huai (reigned 328–299 B.C.) in the state of Chu. It is generally believed that because of slander, Qu Yuan was banished and deprived of public service. Later he wrote the famous "Li sao" as a protest (his authorship of other *Chu ci* poems remains controversial) and drowned himself in the Miluo River.

21. See, for example, Leo Lee 1985c, 10; Yu-sheng Lin 1985, 111–112.

Chapter 4: In the Madding Crowd

1. *The Birthday Party* by Harold Pinter came out in Chinese as early as 1978. Samuel Beckett's *Waiting for Godot* even spawned a Chinese counterpart on the theme of waiting, in a Chinese situation, in Gao Xingjian's *Chezhan* (Bus stop). On this play and its affinities to and differences from the theater of the absurd, see Tay 1990. The full text of *Chezhan* in English can be found in *Theater and Society: An Anthology of Contemporary Chinese Drama*, ed. Haiping Yan (Armonk, N.Y.: M.E.Sharpe, 1998), 3–59. An anthology of Gao's plays in English is also available. See Gao 1999.

2. *Xifang xiandaipai wenxue wenti lunzhengji* has an index of all essays on Western literature published in China between 1978 and 1982.

3. See also Cheng Depei 1988, 1–19. Other critics obviously share this opinion. Psychoanalysis underlines part of Lu Tonglin's essay on Can Xue and is the framework of Jon Soloman's reading of the author's story "Skylight." See Soloman 1988; Lu 1993a; the essay later appears in Lu 1995, chap. 3.

4. In her feminist reading of Can Xue, Lu Tonglin offers another explanation for Chinese male critics' reactions to the author. She holds that Can Xue's experiment with language is doubly subversive, undermining not only the official ideology but also the newly institutionalized male-centered fictional discourse in post-Mao China. Lu charges that their mysogynistic attitude leads Chinese male writers and critics to celebrate male writers' experiments with language and discredit Can Xue's efforts as symptomatic of a woman's paranoia and hysteria. See Lu 1995, chap. 3.

5. Personal correspondence between the author and her translator, quoted in Janssen 1989, 164. See also Shi Shuqing 1989, 234–247.

6. In Mao's call to the students to rebel against established authorities, officials, and administrative cadres at different levels were accused of being "capitalist roaders" and were dispatched in large numbers to the so-called cadre schools in the country to reform their thinking. For a memoir of life in a cadre school, see Yang Jiang 1983.

7. Unless otherwise noted, all quotations from the author's short stories are from Janssen and Zhang's translation.

8. The most notable exception is Can Xue's first creation (1989a), "Yellow Mud Street," in which the characters are the inhabitants of the title street. In her later works, the community shrinks to the core and extended family.

9. See Sigmund Freud (1996), *The Interpretation of Dreams*, 218–276. See also Freud 1955–1974; lecture 10 has a complete discussion of dream symbolism.

10. Because mention of the speaker's sex is unavoidable in the English translation, the translators decided to treat the narrator as a female. Given the author's predilection for female protagonists, this is not a totally arbitrary choice, but it nonetheless has an unfortunate delimiting effect, as the individual's experience is not specifically gender related. Since the use of a possessive pronoun is a grammatical necessity, I follow the translators in treating the protagonist as a female in my discussion of the story.

11. I used the translation in Duke's 1991 anthology. Further references to the story are from this translation.

12. See the index in *Xifang xiandaipai wenxue wenti lunzhengji*.

13. The collection entitled *Sate yanjiu* (On Sartre) (1981) has some of Sartre's essays on literature and excerpts from his novel *Nausea* and the plays *The Flies* and *No Exit*. The volume also devotes a section to reference materials, including a chronological table of Sartre's major publication dates, activities, and synopses of all his literary works. The book concludes with a group of essays on Sartre by Western critics.

14. See articles indexed in *Xifang xiandaipai wenxue wenti lunzhengji*, 851–854.

15. I modified the translation here. Janssen and Zhang's version—"he would utter the curse that made the son-in-law so angry"—gives the impression that the old man in the quoted passage is Geng Shanwu's father-in-law. In fact, the old man is Ma Laowu.

16. In his discussion Sartre does not objectify "I" as a third person but uses it as a first person. For the most part I am following his practice in my presentation of his ideas in this section.

17. To Sartre, two looks cannot meet, for just as I cannot be an object for an object, I cannot be a subject for another subject. The significance of the look and its ontological power is aptly illustrated by the angry look feminists gave Freudian and Lacanian theories. They contend that the psychiatrists' explanations of female sexuality and identity reduced women to the inferior and underprivileged. Refusing to be objectified and fixed by the male look, they gazed back at Freud and Lacan and started feminist theories so as to establish the female as the subject in her own right.

18. García Márquez is an indisputable influence in this scene, which recalls the last days of the world of Macondo in *One Hundred Years of Solitude*.

19. On housing problems facing young couples in the 1980s, see Honig and Hershatter 1988, 137–166.

20. Lu Tonglin 1995 comments that "Can Xue's special resentment against motherhood may be perceived as a rebellion against the significant role of mother assigned to Chinese women by the traditional culture," 97.

21. For a Freudian reading of Can Xue's description of the mother-daughter relationship, see Soloman 1988, 238–241.

Chapter 5: The Post-Mao Traveler on the New Long March

1. Yu Hua 1990, 1992. English translations of the stories are available in Yu Hua, *The Past and Punishments*, trans. Andrew Jones (Honolulu: University of Hawai'i Press, 1996). Unless otherwise noted, I used these translations. There are

two English versions of "A Soul in Bondage" by Zhaxi Dawa, one in *Best Chinese Stories: 1949–1989* (Beijing: Chinese Literature Press, 1989); the other appears in Jeanne Tai, comp. and trans., *Spring Bamboo: A Collection of Contemporary Chinese Short Stories* (New York: Random House, 1989). I used the translation in *Best Chinese Stories* and modified it where necessary.

2. See, for example, Wedell-Wedellsborg 1996; Jianguo Chen 1998.

3. Tang has presented a forceful discussion, with stimulating analyses, of the narratives of the self as (post)modernist representations. See also Larson 1993, 185–187.

4. Jing Wang regards the aggressive attitude toward the future in the post-Mao era as a new promotion of the Great Leap Forward mentality and a "recycling" of the Sinocentric vision. See Jing Wang 1996, 233–242.

5. The reference to the Red Army's celebrated strategic retreat (1934–1935) was deliberate and well calculated. From the late 1970s through the early 1980s, before the image of the People's Liberation Army was tarnished by its role in the infamous June Fourth crackdown on prodemocracy demonstrators in 1989, the Red Army and its heroic endeavor were still a revered myth. The implications invoked by the historic journey are manifold. First, just as the first Long March led to the survival of the Communists and the founding of a new China, the post-Mao journey similarly promised an eventual victory. Second, the reference invites confidence in the resumed "correct" leadership of Deng Xiaoping as a guarantee to success. Third, even though the present regime did not necessarily want to emphasize the heavy casualties suffered during the costly Communist march, the subtle reminder of those enormous sacrifices required people to be prepared. The modernization program demanded loyalty and assiduity.

6. After 1976, millions of middle school students and college graduates moved back to the cities from the countryside; hundreds of thousands of ex-rightists, "capitalist roaders," and people accused of one crime or another were reassigned jobs and traveled to take up new posts. Many of the *xiafang ganbu* (government cadres sent down to the countryside to engage in physical labor as part of Mao's strategy against bureaucratism) and urban dwellers who had been persuaded to give up their city residences as a countermeasure to the resistance to socialist transformation were also allowed to return.

7. Before the reform in the 1980s, population mobility, especially between rural and urban areas, was strictly controlled by the government. In 1983 the State Council made a decision to grant peasants temporary city-residence certificates to encourage them to start businesses there. For discussions of the *hukou* (household registration system), see Cheng Tiejun 1992. For a revised version in English, see Cheng and Selden 1994. See also Solinger 1999; Mallee 2000.

8. Owing to the success of the four special economic zones set up in the Guangdong and Fujian provinces in 1979 and the opening up of fourteen additional coastal cities to foreign participation in 1984, these places rapidly became the preferred destinations. As a result, these cities swelled. Before 1978, for instance, Shenzhen was a small fishing town with a population of about 20,000; by the mid-1980s the figure had grown to around two million. See Ng Yen-tak 1983.

9. In the winter of 1988 and 1989, hundreds of thousands of peasants from China's poverty-stricken northwestern regions swarmed into Guangdong province.

The migration became such a grave issue that Premier Li Peng publicly urged them to go back to their villages to engage in agricultural production. See "Li Peng Urges Poor Peasants to Go Home," *Far Eastern Economic Review,* 13 April 1989, 14.

10. *Renmin ribao,* 24 February 1995.

11. This view is, of course, in line with the dominant May Fourth realistic approach of using language and literature to expose and correct social ills.

12. The translation is mine.

13. Many scholars have discussed the dilemma of China's reforms. See, for example, Joseph Cheng 1989; Goldman and MacFarquhar 1999.

14. See the discussions on various forms of resistance in contemporary China in Perry and Selden 2000.

15. Younger writers such as Ge Fei, Su Tong, Sun Ganlu, and Yu Hua himself, in my opinion, eventually turned this "lack" to their advantage. Less haunted by memories of the Cultural Revolution, they ventured into a broader scope of thematic concerns and literary experiments. As a result, their subversions of both cultural and literary conventions prove even more radical than those by older writers.

16. For a systematic discussion of the device, see Dällenbach 1989.

17. I have modified the translation. "The Lord of the Lotus" refers to Padma-sambhava.

18. See also Nisbet 1970. Nisbet contends that the genealogical assumption about time may have resulted from man's confusing genetic descent with simple temporal sequence.

Chapter 6: Mirror of the Self

1. As many scholars have noted, this ambivalence rises out of the paradox of nationalism and iconoclasm embedded in the modern revolution. To thwart foreign ambitions concerning China, China must model itself after the same alien powers that threatened its sovereignty; to oppose imperialism, China must adopt the very values that fostered the aggressive spirit; to establish a modern identity for itself as an independent entity, China must break down its existing political order and what little unity it had; and finally, to build a strong nation on an equal footing with the rest of the world, China must turn its back on its own traditions and uproot its past. See, for example, Yu-sheng Lin 1979; Hunt 1993; Denton 1996, 10.

2. The word used in Mo Yan's novel is *zazhong.* When the referent is a person (as opposed to an animal or plant), it denotes either a descendant of an interracial marriage or an illegitimate child. Both meanings obviously apply in *Fengru feitun.* While it is not an exact equivalent of the English word "bastard," which does not carry any racial overtones, *zazhong* similarly can be used as a term of abuse for an offensive person. Here I am using it only to refer to an illicit child. No moral judgment is intended.

3. For a review of various positions, see Betts 1993/1994.

4. Huntington's essay and responses from Asian scholars can be found in Rashid (1997).

5. See, for example, Shen Hong 1995, 1996; Chen Lai 1994.

6. *Zhongguo zuojia zishu* (Self-portrayals by Chinese writers) (Shanghai: Shanghai jiaoyu chubanshe, 1998), 132.

7. Xu Huaizhong thinks that "the title errs on the side of not being serious," Su Tong is afraid that "the title may stir up controversy among readers," and Wang Zengqi's argument that "the title is not everything the novel is" nonetheless betrays his uneasiness about the author's choice of words. See Zhang Jun 1996, 213.

8. See Feuerwerker's discussion of the narrative complexities in *Red Sorghum* in her 1998 book, 214–225.

9. I failed to locate any significant discussions by historians or anthropologists. Literature also seems to be reticent on this issue. For example, while erotic fiction is often spiced with adultery, illegitimacy seldom finds representation in descriptions of debauchery. Nonetheless, fiction offers some typical solutions to sidestep illegitimacy. First, it is prevented by the death of the adulteress. Take the Ming novel *Shui hu zhuan* (The water margin) by Shi Nai'an and Luo Guanzhong, for example. Wu Dalang's wife, Pan Jinlian, and Song Jiang's wife, Yan Poxi, are both killed because of their infidelity, eliminating the possibility of illicit births. Second, polygamy, which allowed a man to have multiple wives, makes the admission of paternity less a problem. For instance, in the banned Qing novel *Wu meng yuan* (A dream romance) the illicit child fathered by the protagonist Wang Song is legitimized when Wang makes his mistress his concubine.

10. Judging by the copious literary representations, bastardy is more prevalent in the West. Alison Findlay's study documents in Renaissance drama over seventy plays with bastard characters between 1588 and 1652. See Findlay 1994, appendix.

11. Margaret Bozenna Goscilo argues that the novel's marginality as a genre that developed outside the mainstream of classic conventions and its emphasis on the individual make it particularly sympathetic toward the bastard character who shares with it a dubious origin and a spirit of nonconformity. See Goscilo 1990, chap. 1.

12. In fact, bastardy is also an issue carrying historical and religious weight. One of the most controversial figures is Jesus Christ. Some scholars argue that his mother's virgin birth endows Christ with a bastard identity. See, for example, Schaberg 1987.

13. As Findlay reasons, bastardy merely reinforces women's marginal status, as they were already excluded from family inheritance and social power in a patriarchal society, whereas for men it had a more radical effect. As a result, bastard characters are more often than not male (Findlay 1994, 5). Findlay's argument is supported by other studies. The bastards Goscilo discusses are also males.

14. This "internal mirror" is one type of *mise en abyme* discussed by Dällenbach (1989).

Chapter 7: Appropriation and Representation

1. I use the masculine pronoun on purpose, for the intellectual in Jia's novel is a male image presented by a male-centered imagination.

2. For discussions of the scientific intellectuals in the post-Mao era, see Simon 1987.

3. Weimann holds that René Girard's theory of appropriation limits it to the level of individual instinctive action, ignoring the social reproductive dimen-

sion of appropriation. For his critique of poststructuralist uses of appropriation, see Weimann 1982.

4. For example, the direct target of the discussion of "practice as the sole criterion for testing truth" was CCP chairman Hua Guofeng and his cohorts, who insisted that Mao's instructions be taken as the absolute truth. The campaign was in fact a political movement backed by Deng, which eventually led to Hua's replacement. See Schoenhals 1991.

5. This was manifested in literature in what Cyril Birch (1977) calls a "great return," the abandonment of individual style and the creation of exemplary characters emphasizing communal interests in the revolutionary literature.

6. In Maoist discourse any literary work slightly deviating from the Party's current policy was condemned as a "poisonous weed."

7. Successful examples include the intellectuals' involvement in Tigaisuo (The research institute for system reform), which masterminded China's famous rural reform in the late 1970s and early 1980s, and Wang Meng's appointment as minister of culture in 1986.

8. For a discussion of the intellectual roots of the series, see Chen Fong-ching 2001.

9. For a critique of the elitist and utopian tendencies of the post-Mao intellectuals during this period, see Jing Wang 1996, 37–117.

10. For a discussion of the increase of social inequality in the 1990s, see Davis 1996.

11. In April 1992 the cost of living in China's thirty-five largest cities jumped by 14 percent over what it had been in April 1991. See Jefferson 1993, 51.

12. In mid-1995 about 14 million town and city inhabitants (about 4.5 percent of the urban population) lived below the urban poverty line (on an annual family income of 5,000 yuan, or 1,540 yuan [about $185] per person) (Riskin 1997, 93). The "iron rice bowl" is a term used in China to refer to a permanent job.

13. It was reported that during the first five months of 1992 about 1.4 million workers lost their jobs through the reorganization of the state sector (*Vokskrant* [Amsterdam], 15 June 1992, quoted in Saich 1993, 27). Bankruptcy was experimented with beginning in 1985. Experimental closures and layoffs occurred in 1986, and in September of that year, the Shenyang Explosion-Proof Equipment Factory was the first Chinese firm to actually declare bankruptcy since 1949. But bankruptcy was practiced with great caution. Up until 1992, only a few dozen bankruptcies were recorded per year. After a more vigorous implementation of the bankruptcy law in 1993, when 900 cases were processed in court, it again slowed down in 1995. On this topic see Brugger and Reglar 1994, 169; Chi-Wen Javons Lee 1996.

14. Poverty among the *xiagang* workers became such a widespread phenomenon that local governments found it necessary to declare their own poverty lines to offer government aid to families falling below these lines. In 1999 the figure set for the city of Shenzhen was the highest (319 yuan [about $38] a person per month), and that for Huhehaote, Yinchuan, and Nanchang the lowest (143 yuan, equivalent to about $17). See "Zhongguo de shehui baozhang tixi" (China's social security system), *Lianhuabao*, 5 October 2000. According to official statistics, in Beijing 10.5 percent of the unemployed received relief payments in 1996 (*Zhongguo tongji nianjian*, 1997, 142).

15. In the late 1990s government offices and universities also began to trim their personnel, encouraging many employees to seek positions elsewhere.

16. The intellectuals' resentment was not wholly warranted but was primarily a psychological reaction. As a result of rural reforms, peasants' standards of living improved more dramatically than the city dwellers' in the early 1980s. But on the whole there are still considerable income differentials between the cities and the countryside. In 1995 the per capita net income of peasants stood at 1,550 yuan while the urban incomes were 3,855 yuan. See *Renmin ribao*, 6 January 1996.

17. *Xuezhe zixuan sanwen jinghua: qiu shi juan* (The best prose written and selected by the scholars: autumn fruit) (Taibai wenyi chubanshe, 1995), 48, quoted in Li Shulei 1995, 55.

18. The extra money earned was divided among the administration, the department, faculty, and staff.

19. The history department of Yunnan University ran a fruit stall on the streets (Chan 1991, 110). The Research Institute of Philosophy of Shanghai Academy of Social Sciences rented out its office space on the Huaihai Road in the busy shopping district, using the rent collected as a secondary source of income for its members (personal conversation with Wang Miaoyang, former director of the institute).

20. Zhang Xian was the author of many stories, films, and TV plays, including *Tang Ming Huang* (Emperor Ming of Tang), "Bei aiqing yiwang de jiaoluo" (The corner forsaken by love), and "Jing" (The well).

21. *Chuanju* is a variation of the traditional drama popular in the Sichuan area.

22. "'Gui cai' yu xiahai: mai diao ming he cai—Wei Minglun beifen hua 'touhai'" (The talented going into business: selling off fame and talent—Wei Minglun talks about "going out to sea" in sorrow and indignation), *Zhongguo wenhuabao*, 4 June 1993.

23. Cogent examples are the revival of popular rituals and the changing concepts of marriage and family values. Studies show that in rural areas lavish ritual observations (condemned as feudal superstition under Mao) with public displays of family wealth were increasingly widespread. The super-stable family encouraged by both Chinese tradition and the Communist government after the 1950s was fast dissolving. Divorce in present-day China threatened to become epidemic. For a collection of essays on various aspects of social life in post-Mao China, see, Link, Madsen, and Pickowicz 1989.

24. The Ma Yuan "narrative trap" style can be found in a number of writers' works, such as those by Sun Ganlu and Ge Fei.

25. According to some critics, new realism appeared around 1990. Among the writers often cited as representatives of the new realism are Chi Li, Liu Heng, Liu Zhengyun, and Fang Fang. For a discussion of this style, see Song Suiliang 1993. For a sample of the new-realist fiction, see Liu Zhengyun, "Danwei" (Work unit), in Liu Zhengyun 1995, 103–174.

26. "Dalu dianshimi chaoguo bayi ren" (Over eight hundred million TV fans in the mainland), *Shijie ribao*, 3 January 1997, A10.

27. On contemporary Chinese cinema, see Clark 1993. For a discussion of television in post-Mao China, see Zha 1997.

28. For a discussion of contemporary Chinese culture, see Barmé 1999, chap. 5.

29. "Zhongguo wentan: shouzhu liangxin zhunze, yinling biange shidai" (Literary world in China: maintaining the principles of conscience and leading the reform era), *Gongren ribao*, 3 February 1996.

30. After Deng Xiaoping's 1992 speech calling for bolder reforms, publishing houses were given more autonomy in deciding what to print. In general, whatever sells goes, as long as it is not overtly pornographic or politically sensitive. See Zha 1997, 125–131.

31. In the mid-1990s there was a heated debate among Chinese writers on how they should respond to the spread of popular literature; see Barmé 1999, chap. 11.

32. Goldman and his colleagues point out that in the early and mid-1980s, before the confrontation that led to the Tiananmen demonstrations, the Party and the intellectuals compromised to make the country the center in their new relationship. See Goldman, Link, and Su 1993, 147.

33. Perhaps Wang is perfectly qualified in passing this judgment; after all, he successfully gauged and played into the mood of the 1990s and became a phenomenon of popular culture himself. For discussions on Wang Shuo, see Jing Wang 1996, 261–286; Barmé 1999, chap. 4.

34. After a short relapse, more relaxed cultural policies were continued. At his meeting with some forty leading cultural figures on March 1, 1991, Party general secretary Jiang Zemin promised his audience that criticism and counter-criticism would be carried out in a "friendly and comradely fashion." See *Wenyi-bao*, 9 March 1991.

35. This was a familiar situation. In the late 1980s, before the storm of June Fourth, Perry Link noted the *meijin* (listless) mentality of Chinese intellectuals and concluded that there is an underlying interest in political engagement among the intellectuals (1992, 122–123, 275).

36. All my quotations from the novel are to the 1993 edition. The translations are mine.

37. In general, critics in the coastal cities in the south were indifferent; those in Beijing, Nanjing, and Shanghai had scathing words for the author; and critics and writers from Jia's home province stood by their *laoxiang* (fellow townsman). See Zha 1995, 161.

38. As some critics put it, you can find wetness and hair everywhere in the novel. See Chen Juntao et al. 1993, 42.

39. For a discussion of China's belated obsession with sex, see Zha 1995, 129–164.

40. A local variant of the traditional drama popular in Shaanxi.

41. Yang Pin 1995, quoted in Li Shulei 1995, 57.

42. Liu Zaifu holds that *youhuan yishi* is a crucial part of the intellectual's subjectivity. See Liu Zaifu 1986b, 291. Perry Link 1992 finds it a persistent characteristic of the mental makeup of China's intellectuals, 249–255.

43. During the Cultural Revolution, those who had the good fortune to shake hands with Mao considered it such an honor that they refused to wash their

hands for days so that they could prolong the glory and let other people share it with them by shaking their hands.

44. For example, Hélène Cixous advocates a feminine writing that refuses unitary meaning or a single identity by tuning language to the female's bodily emotion and by conveying in syntax the rhythm of the woman's libidinal drive. See Cixous 1980.

45. The late Ming literati novel *Jin ping mei* comes to mind. Jia admitted that he was influenced by traditional fiction but insisted that the inspirations for his sexual descriptions came from the porn videos in rampant circulation in China then. See Zha 1995, 150.

46. Zha 1995, 149. The self-censored parts are represented in the text by blank squares and sometimes by the narrator's parenthetical statements that a certain number of words were deleted.

47. See, for example, Jia's stories "Shangzhou chu lu" (Preliminary records of Shangzhou) and "Gubao" (Ancient castle) in Jia Pingwa 1992.

48. See, for example, the discussion in Fong 1994, 107–118; Martin Huang 1995, chap. 3; Shuhui Yang 1998, 115–152.

49. In his study on the development and application of the yin-yang concept to social relationships in premodern China, Bao Jialin points out that in the Han scholar Dong Zhongshu's theory, yin-yang cosmology is not only complimentary but also relational. A son is in a position of yin to his father's yang. Bao further argues that women do not have the same mobility enjoyed by men in their positioning. Women were always at the base position of yin. See Bao Jialin, "Yin yang xueshuo yu funü diwei" (The concept of yin-yang and women's social status), in Bao 1988, 39.

50. Chinese government successfully diverted social attention to economic development and consumerism in the early 1990s. As I discussed earlier in the chapter, after an initial purge, the government relaxed its control over cultural production. Contrary to what was predicted, after the crackdown of the prodemocracy movement in 1989, intellectuals in mainland China did not go into radical opposition against the state. In fact, the revolution mentality of the movement was critiqued and some intellectuals advocated various approaches in support of the official position on patriotism and nationalism. I comment on this in my Epilogue.

Epilogue

1. For a discussion of the Communist formalization of language, see Schoenhals 1992.

2. Chen Sihe 1997 holds that the primary characteristic of literature in the 1990s was its diffuseness. Whereas in the previous two decades literature could be described by a few major tendencies *(gong ming)*, it now became "trendless and nameless" *(wu ming)*.

3. For book-length studies in English on the dynamic cultural studies since the mid-1990s, see Xudong Zhang 2001; Ben Xu 1999; Min Lin 1999; G. Davis 2001. See also Yingjin Zhang 2002, in particular, the "Conclusion."

4. More influential articles published during the discussion can be found in five consecutive issues of *Dushu* (March–July 1994).

5. See for example Xiao Gongqin 1997; Yiheng Zhao 1995, 1997; Ben Xu 1999.

6. For additional discussions on the various "post-ist" and nationalist positions, see, for example, Song Qiang et al. 1996a, 1996b; Li Xiguang et al. 1996; Ji Xianlin et al. 1995; Chen Xiaoming et al. 1994b; Zhang Kuan 1996.

7. Scholars such as Ben Xu and Yiheng Zhao have been very critical of the "new conservatism" for abandoning the 1980s intellectual activism with its pursuit of democracy and retreating from the intellectual's social responsibility (Xu 1999; Zhao 1995, 1997). But one could argue that the post-ist privileging of the native engages the nation on different terms. Yingjin Zhang contends that while Xu's polemic targets the undemocratic state, defining intellectual trends only in binary terms of either opposing or colluding with the state, supporting or deserting democracy reveals the critic's "own intolerance for intellectual freedom and democracy" (Zhang 2002, 337–338).

Bibliography

Althusser, Louis. 1971. *Lenin and Philosophy and Other Essays.* Trans. Ben Brewster. New York: Monthly Review Press.

Anagnost, Ann. 1997. *National Past-times: Narrative, Representation, and Power in Modern China.* Durham, N.C.: Duke University Press.

Anderson, Marston. 1990. *The Limits of Realism: Chinese Fiction in the Revolutionary Period.* Berkeley: University of California Press.

Ba Jin. 1979. *Suixiang lu* (Random thoughts). Hong Kong: Sanlian shudian.

Bao Jialin, ed. 1988. *Zhongguo funüshi lunji xuji* (Sequel to the collection of materials on the history of Chinese women). Taibei: Daoxiang chubanshe.

Barlow, Tani E., ed. 1993. *Gender Politics in Modern China: Writing and Feminism.* Durham, N.C.: Duke University Press.

———. 1994. "Theorizing Woman: *Funü, Guojia, Jiating.*" In *Body, Subject and Power in China*, ed. Angela Zito and Tani E. Barlow. Chicago: Chicago University Press.

Barmé, Geremie R. 1991. "An Iron Fist in a Velvet Prison: Literature in Post–June 1989 China." *China News Analysis* 1443 (September): 1–9.

———. 1999. *In the Red: On Contemporary Chinese Culture.* New York: Columbia University Press.

Benveniste, Emile. 1971. *Problems in General Linguistics.* Trans. Mary Elizabeth Meek. Miami Linguistics Series no. 8. Coral Gables, Fla.: University of Miami Press.

Berling, Judith. 1985. "Self and Whole in Chuang Tzu." In *Individualism and Holism: Studies in Confucian and Taoist Values*, ed. Donald J. Munro. Ann Arbor: Center for Chinese Studies, University of Michigan.

Best Chinese Stories: 1949–1989. 1989. Beijing: Chinese Literature Press.

Betts, Richard K. 1993/1994. "Wealth, Power and Instability: East Asia and the United States after the Cold War." *International Security* 18, 3 (winter): 34–77.

Birch, Cyril. 1960. "Fiction of the Yenan Period." *China Quarterly* 4:1–12.

———. 1977. "Change and Continuity in Chinese Fiction." In *Modern Chinese Literature in the May Fourth Era*, ed. Merle Goldman. Cambridge, Mass.: Harvard University Press.

257

Bonnin, Michel, and Yves Chevrier. 1996. "The Intellectuals and the State: Social Dynamics of Intellectual Autonomy during the Post-Mao Era." In *The Individual and the State in China*, ed. Brian Hook. New York: Clarendon.

Borowitz, Albert. 1954. *Fiction in Communist China*. Cambridge, Mass.: MIT Press.

Bourdieu, Pierre. 1993. *The Field of Cultural Production: Essays on Art and Literature*. Ed. Randal Johnson. New York: Columbia University Press.

Brugger, Bill, and David Kelly. 1990. *Chinese Marxism in the Post-Mao Era*. Stanford: Stanford University Press.

Brugger, Bill, and Stephen Reglar. 1994. *Politics, Economy and Society in Contemporary China*. Stanford: Stanford University Press.

Cai, Rong. 2002. "The Mirror in the Text: Borges and Metafiction in Post-Mao China." *Tamkang Review* 32, no. 2:35–67.

Calinescu, Matei. 1987. *Five Faces of Modernity: Modernism, Avant-garde, Decadence, Kitsch, Postmodernism*. Durham, N.C.: Duke University Press.

Can Xue. 1988. *Tiantanglide duihua* (Dialogues in paradise). Beijing: Zuojia chubanshe.

———. 1989a. *Huangnijie* (The yellow mud street). Taibei: Yuanshen chubanshe.

———. 1989b. *Dialogues in Paradise*. Trans. Ronald R. Janssen and Jian Zhang. Evanston, Ill.: Northwestern University Press.

———. 1991a. *Old Floating Cloud: Two Novellas*. Trans. Ronald R. Janssen and Jian Zhang. Evanston, Ill.: Northwestern University Press.

———. 1991b. "The Hut on the Hill." In *Worlds of Chinese Fiction: Short Stories and Novellas from the People's Republic, Taiwan and Hong Kong*, ed. Michael S. Duke. Armonk, N.Y.: M. E. Sharpe.

Cao Tiancheng. 1986. "Dangdai xiaoshuo de xin leibie" (New categories in contemporary fiction). *Yuwen daobao* 6:18–23.

Cao Wenxuan. 1986. "Danhua qushi: shi xi yizhong xin de wenxue xianxiang" (The tendency of despecification: a tentative discussion of a new literary phenomenon). *Baijia* (Hefei) 1:17–25.

Chan, Anita. 1991. "The Social Origin and Consequences of the Tiananmen Crisis." In *China in the Nineties*, ed. David S. G. Goodman and Gerald Segal. New York: Clarendon.

Chang, Sung-sheng Yvonne. 1993. *Modernism and the Nativist Resistance: Contemporary Chinese Fiction from Taiwan*. Durham, N.C.: Duke University Press.

Chen Daixi. 1984. "Ping 'Xin de meixue yuanze zai jueqi': yu Sun Shaozhen tongzhi shangque" (On 'The rising of a new aesthetic principle': discussions with Comrade Sun Shaozhen). In *Xifang xiandaipai wenxue wenti lunzhengji*.

Chen Dazhuan. 1986. "Han Shaogong jinzuo he lamei mohuan jiqiao" (Han Shaogong's recent creations and the techniques of magical realism in Latin American literature). *Wenxue pinglun* 4:135–136.

Chen Fong-ching. 2001. "The Popular Cultural Movement of the 1980s." In *Voicing Concerns: Contemporary Chinese Critical Inquiry*, ed. Gloria Davies. New York: Rowman and Littlefield.

Chen Fumin. 1993. "Shei shi jinri zhi 'shilajizhe': guanyu wenxue weiji yu xiandai wenren mingyun de duanxiang" (Who are the garbage collectors of today? Thoughts on the crisis of literature and the fate of contemporary men of letters). *Shanghai wenxue* 12:70–72.

Chen Jianguo. 1998. "Violence: The Politics and the Aesthetic—Toward a Reading of Yu Hua." *American Journal of Chinese Studies* 5, 8:8–48.

Chen Juntao, Bai Ye, and Wang Fei. 1993. "Shuobujing de *Feidu*" (The inexhaustible *Ruined Capital*). *Dangdai zuojia pinglun* (Shenyang) 6:36–45.

Chen Kuide. 1991. "Wenhuare: beijing, sichao ji liangzhong qingxiang" (The culture fever: background, trends of thought, and two tendencies). In *Zhongguo dalu dangdai wenhua bianqian, 1978–1989* (The cultural transformation in contemporary mainland China, 1978–1989), ed. Chen Kuide. Taibei: Guiguan tushu.

Chen Lai. 1994. "Rujia sixiang yu xiandai dongya shijie" (Confucian ideas and the modern East Asian world). *Dongfang* 3:10–13.

Chen Sihe. 1992. "Yu Hua xiaoshuo yu shijimo yishi" (Yu Hua's fiction and the fin-de-siècle consciousness). *Zuojia* (Changchun) 5:77–80.

———. 1997. " 'Wuming' zhuangtai xia de jiushi niandai xiaoshuojie" (Fiction in the trendless age of the 1990s). *Xiaoshuojie* 1:182–186.

Chen Sihe, Gao Yuanbao, Yan Feng, Wang Hongtu, and Zhang Xinying. 1993. "Dangdai zhishifenzi de jiazhi guifan" (The values of contemporary intellectuals). *Shanghai wenxue* 7:64–71.

Chen, Xiaomei. 1995. *Occidentalism: A Theory of Counter-Discourse in Post-Mao China*. New York: Oxford University Press.

Chen Xiaoming. 1994. "Feixu shang de kuanghuanjie: ping *Feidu* ji qita" (The carnival on the ruins: on *Ruined Capital* and other things). *Tianjin shehui kexue* 2:61–74.

——— et al. 1994a. "Dongfangzhuyi yu houzhimin wenhua" (Orientalism and postcolonial culture). *Zhongshan* 1:126–148.

——— et al. 1994b. "Jingshen tuibaizhe de kuangwu" (Crazed dance of a spiritual decadent). *Zhongshan* 6:142–162.

Chen Zhichu. 1994. "Jia Pingwa, kexi le" (Jia Pingwa, what a shame). *Xinhua wenzhai* 2:127–128.

Cheng Depei. 1988. Preface to Can Xue, *Tiantang li de duihua* (Dialogues in paradise). Beijing: Zuojia chubanshe.

Cheng, Joseph Y. S. 1989. "Epilogue: Whither China's Modernization?" In *China: Modernization in the 1980s*, ed. Joseph Y. Cheng. Hong Kong: Chinese University Press.

Cheng Tiejun. 1992. "Zhongguo hukou zhidu de xianzhuang yu weilai" (The household registration system in China). In *Zhongguo dalu de shehui, zhengzhi, jingji* (The political economy of contemporary China), ed. Li Shaomin. Taibei: Guiguan.

Cheng Tiejun, and Mark Selden. 1994. "The Origin and Social Consequences of China's Hukou System." *China Quarterly* 139:644–668.

Cheng, Yingxiang. 1986. "Writers as Heralds and Spokesmen of Intellectuals in the PRC." In *Cologne-Workshop 1984 on Contemporary Chinese Literature*, ed. Helmut Martin. Cologne: Deutsche Welle.

Chow, Rey. 1991. *Women and Chinese Modernity: The Politics of Reading between West and East*. Minneapolis: University of Minnesota Press.

Chow Tse-tsung. 1960. *The May Fourth Movement: Intellectual Revolution in Modern China*. Cambridge, Mass.: Harvard University Press.

Chuang Tzu. 1968. *The Complete Works of Chuang Tzu*. Trans. Burton Watson. New York: Columbia University Press.

Cixous, Hélène. 1980. "The Laugh of the Medusa." In *New French Feminisms: An Anthology*, ed. Elaine Marks and Isabelle de Courtivron. New York: Schocken Books.

Clark, Paul. 1993. "Chinese Cinema Enters the 1990s." In *China Briefing, 1992*, ed. William A. Joseph. Boulder, Colo.: Westview Press.

Cumings, Bruce. 2000. "The More Things Change, the More They Remain the Same: The World, the United States, and the People's Republic of China, 1949–1999." In *China Briefing: The Continuing Transformation*, ed. Tyrene White. Armonk, N.Y.: M. E. Sharpe.

Dai Houying. 1980. *Ren ah ren* (Oh, humankind). Guangzhou: Huacheng chubanshe.

———. 1992. "On Behalf of Humanism: The Confession of a Former Leftist." In *Modern Chinese Writers: Self-Portrayals*, ed. Helmut Martin and Jeffrey Kinkley. Armonk, N.Y.: M. E. Sharpe.

Dällenbach, Lucien. 1989. *The Mirror in the Text*. Trans. Jeremy Whiteley with Emma Hughes. Chicago: University of Chicago Press.

"Dalu dianshimi chaoguo bayi ren" (Over eight hundred million TV fans in the mainland). 1997. *Shijie ribao*, 3 January, A10.

Dangdai zhongguo dianying (Film in contemporary China). 1989. Beijing: Zhongguo shehui kexue chubanshe.

Dauenhauer, Bernard P. 1980. *Silence: The Phenomenon and Its Ontological Significance*. Bloomington: Indiana University Press.

Davies, Gloria, ed. 2001. *Voicing Concerns: Contemporary Chinese Critical Inquiry*. New York: Rowman and Littlefield.

Davis, Deborah S. 1996. "Inequality and Stratification in the Nineties." In *China Review 1995*, ed. Lo Chin Kin, Suzanne Pepper, and Tsue Kai Yuen. Hong Kong: Chinese University Press.

Denton, Kirk A. 1996. Introduction to *Modern Chinese Literary Thought: Writings on Literature, 1893–1945*, ed. Kirk A. Denton. Stanford: Stanford University Press.

———. 1998. *The Problematic of Self in Modern Chinese Literature: Hu Feng and Lu Ling*. Stanford: Stanford University Press.

Ding Maoyuan. 1986. "Xu tan 'Dangdai xiaoshuo de xin leibie'" (Follow-up commentaries on "New categories in contemporary fiction"). *Yuwen daobao* 8:54–56.

Dittmer, Lowell, and Samuel S. Kim, eds. 1993. *China's Quest for National Identity*. Ithaca, N.Y.: Cornell University Press.

Doleželová-Velingerová, Milena, and Oldřich Král, eds., with Graham Sanders. 2001. *The Appropriation of Cultural Capital: China's May Fourth Project*. Cambridge, Mass.: Harvard University Asia Center.

Duara, Prasenjit. 1995. *Rescuing History from the Nation: Questioning Narratives of Modern China*. Chicago: University of Chicago Press.

Duke, Michael S. 1985. *Blooming and Contending: Chinese Literature in the Post-Mao Era*. Bloomington: Indiana University Press.

———. 1989a. "Reinventing China: Cultural Exploration in Contemporary Chinese Fiction." *Issues and Studies* (August): 29–53.

———. 1989b. Introduction to *Modern Chinese Women Writers: Critical Appraisals*, ed. Michael S. Duke. Armonk, N.Y.: M. E. Sharpe.

———, ed. 1991. *Worlds of Chinese Fiction: Short Stories and Novellas from the People's Republic, Taiwan and Hong Kong*. Armonk, N.Y.: M. E. Sharpe.

Enloe, Cynthia. 1989. *Bananas, Beaches and Bases: Making Feminist Sense of International Politics*. Berkeley: University of California Press.

Esslin, Martin. 1973. *The Theater of the Absurd*. Rev. ed. Woodstock, N.Y.: Overlook Press.

Feng Youlan. 1967. *Xin shi lun* (New commentaries of history). Taibei: Commercial Press.

Feng Zusheng, ed. 1989. *Dangdai xin rujia* (The contemporary neo-Confucianists). Beijing: Sanlian.

Ferruccio, Rossi-Landi. 1990. *Marxism and Ideology*. Trans. Roger Griffin. Oxford: Clarendon.

Feuerwerker, Yi-tsi Mei. 1998. *Ideology, Power, Text: Self-Representation and the Peasant "Other" in Modern Chinese Literature*. Stanford: Stanford University Press.

Findlay, Alison. 1994. *Illegitimate Power: Bastard in Renaissance Drama*. Manchester, UK: Manchester University Press.

Fokkema, D. W. 1965. *Literary Doctrine in China and Soviet Influence, 1956–1960*. London: Mouton.

———. 1966. "Chinese Criticism of Humanism: Campaign against the Intellectuals, 1964-65." *China Quarterly* (April/June): 68–81.

———. 1969. "Chinese Literature under the Cultural Revolution." *Literature East and West* 13, nos. 3–4:335-358.

Fong, Grace S. 1994. "Engendering the Lyric: Her Image and Voice in Song." In *Voices of the Song Lyric in China*, ed. Pauline Yu. Berkeley: University of California Press.

Foucault, Michel. 1977. *Power/Knowledge: Selected Interviews and Other Writings 1972–1977*. Ed. Colin Gordon. Trans. Colin Gordon, Leo Marshall, John Mepham, and Kate Soper. New York: Pantheon Books.

———. 1979. *Discipline and Punish: The Birth of the Prison*. Trans. Alan Sheridan New York: Vintage Books.

Fozdar, Jamshed. 1973. *The God of Buddha*. New York: Asia Publishing House.

Freud, Sigmund. 1955-1974. *Introductory Lectures on Psycho-Analysis (1915–16)*. Vol. 15 of *The Standard Edition of the Complete Psychological Works of Sigmund Freud*, ed. and trans. James Strachey. London: Hogarth.

———. 1964. *Beyond the Pleasure Principle*. Vol. 18 of *The Standard Edition of the Complete Psychological Works of Sigmund Freud*, ed. and trans. James Strachey. London: Hogarth.

———. 1996. *The Interpretation of Dreams*. Trans. A. A. Brill. New York: Gramercy Books.

Gan Yang. 1989. "Bashi niandai wenhua taolun de jige wenti" (Some issues in the cultural discussion in the 1980s in China). In *Zhongguo dangdai wenhua yishi* (The cultural consciousness in contemporary China), ed. Gan Yang. Hong Kong: Sanlian shudian.

Gao Minglu. 1989. "Dangdai zhongguo meishu yundong" (Fine arts in contemporary

China). In *Zhongguo dangdai wenhua yishi* (The cultural consciousness in contemporary China), ed. Gan Yang. Hong Kong: Sanlian shudian.

Gao Xingjian. 1981. *Xiandai xiaoshuo jiqiao chu tan* (Preliminary discussions on the techniques of modern fiction). Guangzhou: Huacheng.

———. 1998. *Bus-stop*. In *Theater and Society: An Anthology of Contemporary Chinese Drama*, ed. Haiping Yan. Armonk, N.Y.: M. E. Sharpe.

———. 1999. *The Other Shore: Plays by Gao Xingjian*. Trans. Gilbert Fong. Hong Kong: Chinese University Press.

Gilmartin, Christina K. et al., eds. 1994. *Engendering China: Women, Culture, and the State*. Cambridge, Mass.: Harvard University Press.

Goldblatt, Howard, ed. 1990. *Worlds Apart: Recent Chinese Writing and Its Audiences*. Armonk, N.Y.: M. E. Sharpe.

———, ed. 1995. *Chairman Mao Would Not Be Amused: Fiction from Today's China*. New York: Grove Press.

Golder, Séan, and John Minford. 1990. "Yang Lian and the Chinese Tradition." In *Worlds Apart: Recent Chinese Writing and Its Audiences*, ed. Howard Goldblatt. Armonk, N.Y.: M. E. Sharpe.

Goldman, Merle. 1962. "Hu Feng's Conflict with the Communist Authorities." *China Quarterly* 12:102–138.

———. 1967. *Literary Dissent in Communist China*. Cambridge, Mass.: Harvard University Press.

———. 1977. *Modern Chinese Literature in the May Fourth Era*. Cambridge, Mass.: Harvard University Press.

———. 1981. *China's Intellectuals: Advise and Dissent*. Cambridge, Mass.: Harvard University Press.

———. 1993. "The Intellectuals in the Deng Era." In *China in the Era of Deng Xiaoping: A Decade of Reform*, ed. Michael Ying-Mao Kau and Susan H. Marsh. Armonk, N.Y.: M. E. Sharpe.

———. 1999. "The Emergence of Politically Independent Intellectuals." In *The Paradox of China's Post-Mao Reforms*, ed. Merle Goldman and Roderick MacFarquhar. Cambridge, Mass.: Harvard University Press.

Goldman, Merle, Timothy Cheek, and Carol Lee Hamrin, eds. 1987. *China's Intellectuals and the State: In Search of a New Relationship*. Cambridge, Mass: Council on East Asian Studies, Harvard University, distributed by Harvard University Press.

Goldman, Merle, Perry Link, and Su Wei. 1993. "China's Intellectuals in the Deng Era: Loss of Identity with the State." In *China's Quest for National Identity*, ed. Lowell Dittmer and Samuel S. Kim. Ithaca, N.Y.: Cornell University Press.

Goldman, Merle, and Roderick MacFarquhar, eds. 1999. *The Paradox of China's Post-Mao Reforms*. Cambridge, Mass.: Harvard University Press.

Goodman, David S. G. 1986. "PRC Fiction and Its Political Context, 1978–82: To Write the Word of 'Man' across the Sky'." In *Cologne-Workshop 1984 on Contemporary Chinese Literature*, ed. Helmut Martin. Cologne: Deutsche Welle.

Goscilo, Margaret Bozenna. 1990. *The Bastard Hero in the Novel*. New York: Garland.

Grice, Paul. 1989. *Studies in the Way of Words*. Cambridge, Mass.: Harvard University Press.

Gu Xin. 1995. "Hegelianism and Chinese Intellectual Discourse: A Study of Li Zehou." *Journal of Contemporary China* 8:1–27.

Guan Yimin. 1994. "Lun Yu Hua" (On Yu Hua). *Hebei xuekan* 3:73–78.

"'Gui cai' yu xiahai: mai diao ming he cai—Wei Minglun beifen hua 'touhai'" (The talented going into business: selling off fame and talent—Wei Minglun talks about "going out to sea" in sorrow and indignation). 1993. *Zhongguo wenhuabao*, 4 June.

Hamrin, Carol Lee. 1987. "Conclusion: New Trends under Deng Xiaoping and His Successors." In *China's Intellectuals and the State: In Search of a New Relationship*, ed. Merle Goldman, Timothy Cheek, and Carol Lee Hamrin. Cambridge, Mass.: Council on East Asian Studies, Harvard University, distributed by Harvard University Press.

Han Luhua. 1993. "Shijimo jingshen yu dongfang yishu jingshen: *Feidu* tiyi jiedu" (The fin-de-siècle spirit and oriental art: understanding the theme of *Ruined Capital*). *Dangdai zuojia pinglun* 6:53, 54–59.

Han Shaogong. 1985. "Wenxue de 'gen'" (The "roots" of literature). *Zuojia* 4:2–5.

———. 1992a. *Homecoming? and Other Stories.* Trans. Martha Cheung. Hong Kong: Research Center for Translation, Chinese University of Hong Kong.

———. 1992b. "After the 'Literature of the Wounded': Local Cultures, Roots, Maturity, and Fatigue." In *Modern Chinese Writers: Self-Portrayals*, ed. Helmut Martin and Jeffrey Kinkley. Armonk, N.Y.: M. E. Sharpe.

He Xin. 1991. *Fansi yu tiaozhan* (Reflections and challenges). Taibei: Fengyun shidai chubangongsi.

Hegel, Robert E. 1984. "Making the Past Serve the Present in Fiction and Drama: From the Yan'an Forum to the Cultural Revolution." In *Popular Chinese Literature and Performing Arts in the People's Republic of China, 1949–1979*, ed. Bonnie S. McDougall. Berkeley: University of California Press.

Hegel, Robert E., and Richard C. Hessney, eds. 1985. *Expressions of Self in Chinese Literature.* New York: Columbia University Press.

Hirst, P., and P. Wooley. 1982. *Social Relations and Human Attributes.* London: Tavistock.

Hockx, Michel. 1999. Introduction to *The Literary Field of Twentieth-Century China*, ed. Michel Hockx. Honolulu: University of Hawai'i Press.

Honig, Emily, and Gail Hershatter. 1988. *Personal Voices: Chinese Women in the 1980's.* Stanford: Stanford University Press.

Hsia, C. T. 1961. *A History of Modern Chinese Fiction, 1917–1957.* New Haven, Conn.: Yale University Press.

———. 1970. "Literature and Art under Mao Tse-tung." In *Communist China, 1949–69: A Twenty-Year Appraisal*, ed. Frank N. Trager and William Henderson. New York: New York University Press.

Hsia, Helen. 1987. "Zhi mian beilun de Han Shaogong" (The frank and unconventional Han Shaogong). *Meizhou Huaqiao ribao*, 28 February.

Hu Feng. 1967. "Realism Today." In *Literature of the People's Republic of China*, ed. Kai-yu Hsu. Bloomington: Indiana University Press.

———. 1984, 1985. *Hu Feng pinglunji.* 2 vols. Beijing: Renmin wenxue chubanshe.

Hu Shi. 1953. "Bu xiu: wode zongjiao" (Immortality: my religion). In *Hu Shi wencun* (Collected works of Hu Shi), vol. 1. Taibei: n.p.

Hu Ying. 2000. *Tales of Translation: Composing the New Women in China, 1899–1918.* Stanford: Stanford University Press.

Huang, Joe C. 1973. *Heroes and Villains in Communist China: The Contemporary Chinese Novel as a Reflection of Life.* New York: Pica Press.

Huang, Martin. 1995. *Literati and Self-Re/Presentation: Autobiographical Sensibility in the Eighteenth-Century Chinese Novel.* Stanford: Stanford University Press.

Hunt, Michael H. 1993. "Chinese National Identity and the Strong State: The Late Qing Republican Crisis." In *China's Quest for National Identity,* ed. Lowell Dittmer and Samuel S. Kim. Ithaca, N.Y.: Cornell University Press.

Innes, Charlotte. 1991. Foreword to Can Xue, *Old Floating Cloud: Two Novellas.* Trans. Ronald R. Janssen and Jian Zhang. Evanston, Ill.: Northwestern University Press.

Janssen, Ronald. 1989. "Can Xue's Attack of Madness." Afterword to Can Xue, *Dialogues in Paradise.* Trans. Ronald R. Janssen and Jian Zhang. Evanston, Ill.: Northwestern University Press.

Jefferson, Gary H. 1993. "The Chinese Economy: Moving Forward." In *China Briefing, 1992,* ed. William A. Joseph. Boulder, Colo.: Westview Press.

Ji Xianlin et al. 1995. "'Wenhua zhiminzhuyi' xianxiang hai xu shen toushi" (Exploring the phenomenon of "cultural colonialism"). *Jingji ribao,* 3 November.

Jia Pingwa. 1992. *Jia Pingwa huojiang zhongpian xiaoshuo ji* (Prize-winning fiction by Jia Pingwa). Xi'an: Xi'an daxue chubanshe.

———. 1993. *Feidu.* Beijing: Beijing chubanshe.

Jie Min, ed. 1989. *Dangdai zuojia bairen zhuan* (A hundred autobiographies of contemporary writers). Beijing: Qiushi chubanshe.

Jin Guantao, and Liu Qingfeng. 1989. *Xingsheng yu weiji: lun zhongguo fengjian shehui de chao wending jiegou* (Prosperity and crisis: on the ultrastable cultural structure of China's feudal society). Taibei: Fengyun shidai chuban gongsi.

Jones, Andrew. 1994. "The Violence of the Text: Reading Yu Hua and Shi Zhicun." *Positions* 2, 3:570–602.

Kau, Michael Ying-Mao, and Susan H. Marsh, eds. 1993. *China in the Era of Deng Xiaoping: A Decade of Reform.* Armonk, N.Y.: M. E. Sharpe.

Kelly, David A. 1987. "The Emergence of Humanism: Wang Ruoshui and the Critique of Socialist Alienation." In *China's Intellectuals and the State: In Search of a New Relationship,* ed. Merle Goldman with Timothy Cheek and Carol Lee Hamrin. Cambridge, Mass.: Harvard University Press.

King, Ambrose Y. C. 1985. "The Individual and Group in Confucianism: A Relational Perspective." In *Individualism and Holism: Studies in Confucian and Taoist Values,* ed. Donald Munro. Ann Arbor: Center for Chinese Studies, University of Michigan.

Krieger, Murray, ed. 1987. *The Aims of Representation: Subject/Text/History.* New York: Columbia University Press.

Lacan, Jacques. 1968. *The Language of the Self: The Function of Language in Psychoanalysis.* Trans. Anthony Wilden. Baltimore: Johns Hopkins University Press.

———. 1977. *Ecrits: A Selection.* Trans. Alan Sheridan. New York: Norton.

Larson, Wendy. 1989. "Realism, Modernism, and the Anti-'Spiritual Pollution' Campaign in China." *Modern China* (January): 37–71.

———. 1993. "Literary Modernism and Nationalism in Post-Mao China." In *Inside Out: Modernism and Postmodernism in Chinese Literary Culture*, ed. Wendy Larson and Anne Wedell-Wedellsborg. Aarhus, Denmark: Aarhus University Press.

———. 1998. *Women and Writing in Modern China*. Stanford: Stanford University Press.

Larson, Wendy, and Anne Wedell-Wedellsborg, eds. 1993. *Inside Out: Modernism and Post-Modernism in Chinese Literary Culture*. Aarhus, Denmark: Aarhus University Press.

Lau, Joseph S. M. 1993. "Han Shaogong's Post-1985 Fiction." In *From May Fourth to June Fourth: Fiction and Film in Twentieth-Century China*, ed. Ellen Widmer and David Der-wei Wang. Cambridge, Mass.: Harvard University Press.

Lee, Chi-Wen Javons. 1996. "The Reform of the State-Owned Enterprises." In *China Review 1996*, ed. Maurice Brosseau, Suzanne Pepper, and Tsang Shu-ki. Hong Kong: Chinese University Press.

Lee, Gregory B. 1996. *Troubadours, Trumpeters, Troubled Markers: Lyricism, Nationalism, and Hybridity in China and Its Others*. Durham, N.C.: Duke University Press.

Lee, Leo Ou-fan. 1973. *The Romantic Generation of Modern Chinese Writers*. Cambridge, Mass.: Harvard University Press.

———. 1985a. "The Politics of Technique: Perspectives of Literary Dissidence in Contemporary Chinese Fiction." In *After Mao: Chinese Literature and Society, 1978–1981*, ed. Jeffrey C. Kinkley. Cambridge, Mass.: Harvard University Press.

———. 1985b. "The Solitary Traveler: Images of the Self in Modern Chinese Literature." In *Expressions of Self in Chinese Literature*, ed. Robert E. Hegel and Richard C. Hessney. New York: Columbia University Press.

———, ed. 1985c. *Lu Xun and His Legacy*. Berkeley: University of California Press.

———. 1990. "Beyond Realism: Thoughts on Modernist Experiments in Contemporary Chinese Writing." In *Worlds Apart: Recent Chinese Writing and Its Audiences*, ed. Howard Goldblatt. Armonk, N.Y.: M. E. Sharpe.

———. 1999. *Shanghai Modern: The Flowering of A New Urban Culture in China 1930–1945*. Cambridge, Mass.: Harvard University Press.

———. 2001. "Incomplete Modernity: Rethinking the May Fourth Intellectual Project." In *The Appropriation of Cultural Capital: China's May Fourth Project*, ed. Milena Doleželová-Velingerová, and Oldřich Král with Graham Sanders. Cambridge, Mass.: Harvard University Asia Center.

Lei Da. 1993. "Xinling de zhengzha: *Feidu* bianxi" (Struggles of the soul: exploring *The Ruined Capital*). *Dangdai zuojia pinglun* (Shenyang) 6:20–28.

Leung, Laifong. 1994. *Morning Sun: Interviews with Chinese Writers of the Lost Generation*. Armonk, N.Y.: M. E. Sharpe.

Li Hui. 1989. *Lishi beige: Hu Feng jituan yuanan shimo* (A tragic song in history: the truth of the unjust verdict on the Hu Feng clique). Hong Kong: Xiangjiang chuban youxiangongsi.

Li Jie. 1988. "Lun zhongguo dangdai xinchao xiaoshuo" (On contemporary Chinese new-wave fiction). *Zhongshan* 5:116–138.

Li Jiefei. 1993. "*Feidu* de shibai" (The failure of *The Ruined Capital*). *Dangdai zuojia pinglun* (Shenyang) 6:29–35.

Li Jiefei, and Zhang Ling. 1986. "Yijiubawunian zhongguo xiaoshuo sichao" (Fictional trends in China in 1985). *Dangdai wenyi sichao* (Lanzhou) 3:35, 57–64.

Li Qingxi. 1986. "Shuo 'Ba ba ba'" (On *Pa pa pa*). *Dushu* 3:49–58.

Li Shulei. 1994. "Xiandai renge de lunsang" (The loss of modern human dignity). *Xinhua wenzhai* 2:125–126.

——. 1995. "Lun shichanghua jingji dui wenhuaren de yingxiang" (On the impact of marketization on the intellectuals). *Touzi yu hezuo* 12:52–58.

Li Tuo. 1988. "Ye tan 'wei xiandaipai' ji qi piping" (Additional comment on "fake modernist school" and its criticism). *Beijing wenxue* 4:4–10.

——. 1990. "Xue beng he chu" (Where did the avalanche start?). Preface to Yu Hua, *Shiba sui chumen yuanxing*. Taibei: Yuanliu.

——. 1993. "The New Vitality of Modern Chinese." In *Inside Out: Modernism and Post-Modernism in Chinese Literary Culture*, ed. Wendy Larson and Anne Wedell-Wedellsborg. Aarhus, Denmark: Aarhus University Press.

Li Xiguang et al. 1996. *Zai yaomohua zhongguo de beihou* (Behind the demonization of China). Beijing: Zhongguo shehui kexue chubanshe.

Li Zehou. 1981. *Mei de licheng* (The path of beauty). Beijing: Wenwu chubanshe.

——. 1988. *Li Zehou ji* (A collecton of the works of Li Zehou). Harbin: Heilongjiang jiaoyu chubanshe.

——. 1994a. *Li Zehou shinian ji* (Collection of works of Li Zehou in the past ten years). 4 vols. Heifei: Anhui wenyi chubanshe.

——. 1994b. *The Path of Beauty: The Study of Chinese Aesthetics*. Trans. Gong Lizeng. New York: Oxford University Press.

Li Zehou, and Liu Zaifu. 1995. *Gaobie geming* (Farewell to revolution). Hong Kong: Cosmos Books.

Li Zehou, and Vera Schwarcz. 1983/1984. "Six Generations of Modern Chinese Intellectuals." *Chinese Studies in History* (winter): 42–56.

Liang Qichao. 1962. "Lun xiaoshuo yu qunzhi zhi guanxi" (On the relationship between fiction and the government of the people). Reprinted in *Zhongguo jindai lunwen xuan* (Selected writings on literature in modern China). 2 vols. Beijing: Renmin wenxue, 1962.

Lin, Min, with Maria Galikowski. 1999. *The Search for Modernity: Chinese Intellectuals and Cultural Discourse in the Post-Mao Era*. New York: St. Martin's Press.

Lin, Yu-sheng. 1972. "Radical Iconoclasm, Nationalism, and Internationalism in the May Fourth Movement." In *Reflections on the May Fourth Movement: A Symposium*, ed. Benjamin I. Schwartz. Cambridge, Mass.: East Asian Research Center, Harvard University Press.

——. 1974–1975. "The Evolution of the Pre-Confucian Meaning of *Ren* and the Confucian Concept of Moral Autonomy." *Monumenta Serica* 31:172–204.

——. 1979. *The Crisis of Chinese Consciousness: Radical Antitraditionalism in the May Fourth Era*. Madison: University of Wisconsin Press.

——. 1985. "The Morality of Mind and Immorality of Politics: Reflections on Lu Xun, the Intellectual." In *Lu Xun and His Legacy*, ed. Leo Ou-fan Lee. Berkeley: University of California Press.

Link, Perry. 1989. "Hand-Copied Entertainment Fiction from the Cultural Revolution." In *Unofficial China: Popular Culture and Thought in the People's*

Republic, ed. Perry Link, Richard Madsen, and Paul G. Pickowicz. Boulder, Colo.: Westview Press.

——. 1992. *Evening Chats in Beijing: Probing China's Predicament.* New York: Norton.

——. 2000. *The Uses of Literature: Life in the Socialist Literary System.* Princeton, N.J.: Princeton University Press.

Link, Perry, Richard Madsen, and Paul G. Pickowicz, eds. 1989. *Unofficial China: Popular Culture and Thought in the People's Republic.* Boulder, Colo.: Westview Press.

Liu, Alan P. L. 1986. *How China Is Ruled.* Englewood, N.J.: Prentice-Hall.

Liu Fangtong. 1984. "Cunzaizhuyi yu wenxue" (Existentialism and literature). In *Xifang xiandaipai wenxue wenti lunzhengji* (Collection of essays on Western modernist literature). Beijing: Renmin wenxue chubanshe.

Liu Kang. 1993. "Subjectivity, Marxism, and Cultural Theory in China." In *Politics, Ideology, and Literary Discourse in Modern China: Theoretical Interventions and Cultural Critique,* ed. Liu Kang and Xiaobing Tang. Durham, N.C.: Duke University Press.

Liu Kang, and Xiaobing Tang, eds. 1993. *Politics, Ideology, and Literary Discourse in Modern China: Theoretical Interventions and Cultural Critique.* Durham, N.C.: Duke University Press.

Liu, Lydia H. 1994. "The Female Body and Nationalist Discourse: Manchuria in Xiao Hong's *Field of Life and Death.*" In *Body, Subject and Power in China,* ed. Angela Zito and Tani Barlow. Chicago: University of Chicago Press.

——. 1995. *Translingual Practice: Literature, National Culture, and Translated Modernity—China, 1900–1937.* Stanford: Stanford University Press.

Liu Mingjiu. 1984. "Xuanbianzhe xu" (Foreword to *Studies of Sartre*). In *Xifang xiandaipai wenxue wenti lunzhengji* (Collection of essays on Western modernist literature). Beijing: Renmin wenxue chubanshe.

Liu Xiaobo. 1989. *Xuanze de pipan: yu sixiang lingxiu Li Zehou duihua* (Critique of choice: dialogues with the intellectual leader Li Zehou). Taibei: Fengyun shidai chubangongsi.

Liu Zaifu. 1986a. *Liu Zaifu lunwen xuan* (Selected essays by Liu Zaifu). Hong Kong: Dadi tushu gongsi.

——. 1986b. "Lun wenxue de zhutixing" (On subjectivity in literature). In *Liu Zaifu lunwen xuan* (Selected essays by Liu Zaifu). Hong Kong: Dadi tushu gongsi.

——. 1988a. *Lun zhongguo wenxue* (On Chinese literature). Beijing: Zuojia chubanshe.

——. 1988b. "Ba Jin 'Suixiang lu' de biaozhixing yiyi: zuojia de liangzhi zeren he wenxue zhong de chanhui yishi" (The symbolic significance of Ba Jin's "Random thoughts": on the conscience of writers and the consciousness of penitence in literature). In *Lun zhongguo wenxue* (On Chinese literature). Beijing: Zuojia chubanshe.

——. 1988c. "Lun Bing Zai" (On Bing Zai). *Guangming ribao,* 4 November.

——. 1993. "The Subjectivity of Literature Revisited." In *Politics, Ideology, and Literary Discourse in Modern China: Theoretical Interventions and Cultural Critique,* ed. Liu Kang and Xiaobing Tang. Durham, N.C.: Duke University Press.

Liu Zhengyun. 1995. *Liu Zhengyun wenji: Yi di jimao* (Collection of stories by Liu Zhengyun: *Strewn with Chicken Feathers*). Nanjing: Jiangsu wenyi chubanshe.

Louie, Kam. 1989. *Between Fact and Fiction: Essays on Post-Mao Literature and Society.* Sidney: Wild Peony.

Lu Tonglin. 1993a. "Can Xue: What Is So Paranoid in Her Writings." In *Gender and Sexuality: Twentieth-Century Chinese Literature and Society,* ed. Lu Tonglin. Albany: University of New York Press.

———, ed. 1993b. *Gender and Sexuality: Twentieth-Century Chinese Literature and Society.* Albany: University of New York Press.

———. 1995. *Misogyny, Cultural Nihilism, and Oppositional Politics: Contemporary Chinese Experimental Fiction.* Stanford: Stanford University Press.

Lukács, Georg. 1971. *History and Class Consciousness.* Cambridge, Mass.: MIT Press.

Lyotard, Jean-François. 1987. *Instructions païennes* (Paris: Falilée, 1977), quoted in David Carroll, "Narrative, Heterogeneity, and the Question of the Political: Bakhtin and Lyotard." In *The Aims of Representation: Subject/Text/ History,* ed. Murray Krieger. New York: Columbia University Press.

Ma, Stephen K. 1993. "Dangerous Game: Deng and the Intellectuals." *Journal of Contemporary China* 2:53–68.

Mallee, Hein. 2000. "Migration, Hukou and Residence in Reform China." In *Chinese Society: Change, Conflict and Resistance,* ed. Elizabeth J. Perry and Mark Selden. New York: Routledge.

Martin, Helmut. 1982. "Some Remarks on 'Literature of the Scar' in the People's Republic of China (1977–1979)." *Asian and African Studies* 18:53–74.

———, ed. 1986. *Cologne-Workshop 1984 on Contemporary Chinese Literature.* Cologne: Deutsche Welle.

Martin, Helmut, and Jeffrey Kinkley, eds. 1992. *Modern Chinese Writers: Self-Portrayals.* Armonk, N.Y.: M. E. Sharpe.

Martin, Wallace. 1986. *Recent Theories of Narrative.* Ithaca, N.Y.: Cornell University Press.

Marx, Karl. 1967. *Capital.* Vol. 1. New York: International Publishers.

McDougall, Bonnie S., ed. 1984. *Popular Chinese Literature and Performing Arts in the People's Republic of China, 1949–1979.* Berkeley: University of California Press.

———, ed. 1993. "The Anxiety of Out-fluence: Creativity, History and Postmodernity." In *Inside Out: Modernism and Post-Modernism in Chinese Literary Culture,* ed. Wendy Larson and Anne Wedell-Wedellsborg. Aarhus, Denmark: Aarhus University Press.

McMahon, Keith. 1995. *Misers, Shrews, and Polygamists: Sexuality and Male-Female Relations in Eighteenth-Century Chinese Fiction.* Durham, N.C.: Duke University Press.

Meisner, Maurice. 1986. *Mao's China and After: A History of the People's Republic.* New York: Free Press.

Mellard, James M. 1991. *Using Lacan, Reading Fiction.* Urbana: University of Illinois Press.

Meng Fanhua. 1994. "Yibu 'piaoji xiaoshuo'" (A novel of prostitution). *Xinhua wenzhai* 2:126–127.

———. 1997. *Zhongshen kuanghuan: dangdai zhongguo de wenhua chongtu wenti* (The

Dionysian dance: cultural conflicts in contemporary China). Beijing: Jinri zhongguo chubanshe.

Meng Yue, and Dai Jinhua. 1993. *Fuchu lishi dibiao: zhongguo xiandai nüxingwenxue yanjiu* (Voices emerging into the foreground of history: a study of contemporary Chinese women's literature). Taibei: Shibao wenhua chubangongsi.

Mo Yan. 1993. *Red Sorghum: A Novel of China*. Trans. Howard Goldblatt. New York: Penguin Books.

———. 1995a. *Fengru feitun* (Large breasts and full hips). Beijing: Zuojia chubanshe.

———. 1995b. "*Fengru feitun* jie" (On *Large breasts and full hips*). *Guangming ribao*, 22 November.

Munro, Donald J. 1977. *The Concept of Man in Contemporary China*. Ann Arbor: University of Michigan Press.

———, ed. 1985a. *Individualism and Holism: Studies in Confucian and Taoist Values*. Ann Arbor: Center for Chinese Studies, University of Michigan.

———. 1985b. "The Family Network, the Stream of Water, and the Plant: Picturing Persons in Sung Confucianism." In *Individualism and Holism: Studies in Confucian and Taoist Values*, ed. Donald Munro. Ann Arbor: Center for Chinese Studies, University of Michigan.

Ng Yen-tak. 1983. "Shenzhen jihua renkou ji laodongli zhi yinjin" (Planned population and labor introduction in Shenzhen). In *Zhongguo zuida de jingji tequ—Shenzhen* (Shenzhen: the largest special economic zone in China), ed. D. K. Y. Chu. Hong Kong: Guangjiao.

Nisbet, Robert. 1970. "Genealogy, Growth, and Other Metaphors." *New Literary History* 3:351–364.

Nivison, D. S., and A. F. Wright, eds. 1959. *Confucianism in Action*. Stanford: Stanford University Press.

Ou Litong. 1984. "Ping Sate wenxue de zhexue qingxiang" (On the philosophic tendencies in Sartre's literary works). In *Xifang xiandaipai wenxue wenti lunzhengji* (Collection of essays on Western modernist literature). Beijing: Renmin wenxue chubanshe.

Pan Xiao. 1980. "Rensheng de lu ah, zenme yue zou yue zhai…" (Why is the path of life getting narrower and narrower…). *Zhongguo qingnian* 5:3–5.

Pang Pu. 1988. *Wenhua de minzuxing yu shidaixing* (The national quality and epochal characteristics of culture). Beijing: Zhongguo heping chubanshe.

Perry, Elizabeth J., and Mark Selden, eds. 2000. *Chinese Society: Change, Conflict and Resistance*. New York: Routledge.

Qin Zhiyu. 1998. "Xie gei Zhang Xian" (To Zhang Xian). *Shouhuo* 5:124–131.

Rank, Otto. 1952. *The Myth of the Birth of the Hero: A Psychological Interpretation of Mythology*. Trans. F. Robbins and Smith Ely Jelliffe. New York: Robert Branner.

Rashid, Salim, ed. 1997. *"The Clash of Civilizations?": Asian Responses*. Oxford: Oxford University Press.

Renxing, Rendaozhuyi wenti taolunji (Discussions on issues of human nature and humanism). Beijing: Renmin chubanshe, 1983.

Riskin, Carl. 1997. "Local Development, Quality of Life and the Environment." In *Crisis and Reform in China*, ed. E. Bliney. Commack, N.Y.: Nova Science Publishers.

Saich, Tony. 1993. "Peaceful Evolution with Chinese Characteristics." In *China Briefing, 1992*, ed. William A. Joseph. Boulder, Colo.: Westview Press.

Sartre, Jean-Paul. 1956. *Being and Nothingness: An Essay on Phenomenological Ontology.* Trans. Hazel E. Barnes. New York: Philosophical Library.

Sate yanjiu (On Sartre). 1981. Beijing: Zhongguo shehui kexue chubanshe.

Schaberg, Jane. 1987. *The Illegitimacy of Jesus: A Feminist Theological Interpretation of the Infancy Narrative.* San Francisco: Harper and Row.

Schoenhals, Michael. 1991. "The 1978 Truth Criterion Controversy." *China Quarterly* 126 (June): 243–268.

———. 1992. *Doing Things with Words in Chinese Politics: Five Studies.* Berkeley: Institute of East Asian Studies, University of California.

Schram, Stuart. 1984. *Ideology and Policy in China Since the Third Plenum, 1978–1984.* London: Contemporary China Institute SOAS, University of London.

Schwarcz, Vera. 1986. *The Chinese Enlightenment: Intellectuals and the Legacy of the May Fourth Movement of 1919.* Berkeley: University of California Press.

Schwartz, Benjamin I., ed. 1972. *Reflections on the May Fourth Movement: A Symposium.* Cambridge, Mass.: East Asian Research Center, Harvard University Press.

Sha Yexin. 1995. *Jingshen jiayuan* (Spiritual home). Shanghai: Shanghai renmin chubanshe.

Shen Hong. 1995. "Shenme shi wenming?" (What are civilizations?). *Zhanlue yu guanli* 5:88–98.

———. 1996. "Jingjixue zenyang tiaozhan lishi" (How does economics challenge history?). *Dongfang* 1:49–55.

Shi Shuqing. 1989. *Wentan fansi yu qianzhan: Shi Shuqing yu dalu zuojia duihua* (Looking back and into the future: dialogues between Shi Shuqing and mainland writers). Hong Kong: Mingbao chubanshe.

Shih Shu-mei. 2001. *The Lure of the Modern: Writing Modernism in Semicolonial China, 1917–1937.* Berkeley: University of California Press.

Simon, Denis Fred. 1987. "China's Scientists and Technologists in the Post-Mao Era: A Retrospective and Prospective Glimpse." In *China's Intellectuals and the State: In Search of a New Relationship,* ed. Merle Goldman with Timothy Cheek and Carol Lee Hamrin. Cambridge, Mass.: Council on East Asian Studies, Harvard University, distributed by Harvard University Press.

Smith, Paul. 1988. *Discerning the Subject.* Minneapolis: University of Minnesota Press.

Solinger, Dorothy J. 1999. "China's Floating Population." In *The Paradox of China's Post-Mao Reforms,* ed. Merle Goldman and Roderick MacFarquhar. Cambridge, Mass.: Harvard University Press.

Soloman, Jon. 1988. "Taking Tiger Mountain: Can Xue's Resistance and Cultural Critique." *Modern Chinese Literature* 4:235–262.

Song Qiang, Zhang Zangzang, and Qiao Bian. 1996a. *Zhongguo keyi shuo bu* (China can say no). Beijing: Zhongguo gongshanglian chubanshe.

———. 1996b. *Zhongguo haishi neng shuo bu* (China can still say no). Hong Kong: Mingbao chubanyouxiangongsi.

Song Suiliang. 1993. "Ping jibu 'xin xieshi' changpian xiaoshuo" (Commentaries on several new realist novels). *Wenxue pinglun* 5:68–75.

Sun Shaozhen. 1984. "Xin de meixue yuanze zai jueqi" (The rising of a new aesthetic principle). In *Xifang xiandaipai wenxue wenti lunzhengji* (Collection of essays on Western modernist literature). Beijing: Renmin wenxue chubanshe.

Tai, Jeanne, comp. and trans. 1989. *Spring Bamboo: A Collection of Contemporary Chinese Short Stories*. New York: Random House.

Tang Yijie. 2001. "Some Reflections on New Confucianism in Mainland Chinese Culture of the 1990s." In *Voicing Concerns: Contemporary Chinese Critical Inquiry*, ed. Gloria Davis. New York: Rowman and Littlefield.

Tang, Xiaobing. 1993. "Residual Modernism: Narratives of the Self in Contemporary Chinese Fiction." *Modern Chinese Literature* 7:7–31.

——. 2000. *Chinese Modern: The Heroic and the Quotidian*. Durham, N.C.: Duke University Press.

Tao Wan. 1996. "Waiqu lishi, chouhua xianshi" (Distortion of history and reality). *Zhongguo xiandai, dangdai wenxue yanjiu* 9:200–206.

Tay, William. 1984. "Wang Meng, Stream-of-Consciousness, and the Controversy over Modernism." *Modern Chinese Literature* 1 (September): 7–24.

——. 1985. "'Obscure Poetry': A Controversy in Post-Mao China." In *After Mao: Chinese Literature and Society, 1978–1981*, ed. Jeffrey C. Kinkley. Cambridge, Mass.: Harvard University Press.

——. 1990. "Avant-garde Theater in Post-Mao China: *The Bus-Stop* by Gao Xingjian." In *Worlds Apart: Recent Chinese Writing and Its Audiences*, ed. Howard Goldblatt. Armonk, N.Y.: M. E. Sharpe.

Tobin, Patricia Drechsel. 1978. *Time and the Novel: The Genealogical Imperative*. Princeton, N.J.: Princeton University Press.

Todorov, Tzvetan. 1971. "The Two Principles of Narrative." *Diacritics* (fall): 37–44.

Trappl, Richard. 1993. "'Textivity,' or the Dissolution of Literary Discourse: Beyond a Postmodern Horizon in Contemporary Chinese Literature." In *Inside Out: Modernism and Post-Modernism in Chinese Literary Culture*, ed. Wendy Larson and Anne Wedell-Wedellsborg. Aarhus, Denmark: Aarhus University Press.

Tu Wei-ming. 1985. *Confucian Thought: Selfhood as Creative Transformation*. Albany: State University of New York Press.

——. 1989. *Ruxue disanqi fazhan de qianjing wenti: dalu jiangxue, wennan he taolun* (Prospects of Confucianism in the third period: lecturing, critiquing, and discussing in mainland China). Taibei: Lianjing.

Tucker, Nancy Bernkoft. 2000. "Dangerous Liaisons: China, Taiwan, Hong Kong, and the United States at the Turn of the Century." In Tyrene White, ed., *China Briefing: The Continuing Transformation*. Armonk, N.Y.: M. E. Sharpe.

Wagner, Marsha L. 1997–1999. "The Subversive Fiction of Yu Hua." CHINOPERL Papers 20–22:219–244.

Wagner, Rudolf G. 1990. *The Contemporary Chinese Historical Drama: Four Studies*. Berkeley: University of California Press.

Wang Chuanbin. 1989. "Shilun yishiliu xiaoshuo zai zhongguo de yanbian" (On the development of stream-of-consciousness fiction in China). *Zhongzhou xuekan* 5:65–69.

Wang, David Der-wei. 1988. "Jirenxing: dangdai dalu xiaoshuo de zhongsheng 'guai' xiang" (Pantheon of the deformed: the "bizarre" visage of life as seen in contemporary PRC fiction). In *Zhongsheng xuanhua* (Heteroglossia). Taibei: Yuanliu.

———. 1992. *Fictional Realism in Twentieth-Century China: Mao Dun, Lao She, Shen Congwen*. New York: Columbia University Press.

———. 1993a. Introduction to *From May Fourth to June Fourth: Fiction and Film in Twentieth-Century China*, ed. Ellen Widmer and David Der-wei Wang. Camridge, Mass.: Harvard University Press.

———. 1993b. "Lu Xun, Shen Congwen, and Decapitation." In *Politics, Ideology, and Cultural Literary Discourse in Modern China: Theoretical Interventions and Cultural Critique*, ed. Liu Kang and Xiaobing Tang. Durham, N.C., and London: Duke University Press.

———. 1997. *Fin-de-Siecle Splendor*. Stanford: Stanford University Press.

Wang Derong. 1996. "Qian tan *Fengru feitun*: guanyu lishi de cuowu miaoxie" (Preliminary discussion of *Fengru feitun*: erroneous description of history). *Zhongguo xiandai, dangdai wenxue yanjiu* 9:206–208.

Wang, Gungwu. 1996. *The Revival of Chinese Nationalism*. Leiden: International Institute for Asian Studies.

Wang, James C. F. 1985. *Contemporary Chinese Politics: An Introduction*. 2d ed. Englewood Cliffs, N.J.: Prentice-Hall.

Wang, Jing. 1996. *High Culture Fever: Politics, Aesthetics, and Ideology in Deng's China*. Berkeley: University of California Press.

Wang Meng. 1986. "Xiaoshuojia yan" (Comments from a writer). *Renmin ribao*, 22 September.

Wang Ruoshui. 1981. *Ren shi Makesizhuyi de chufadian* (Humans are the starting point of Marxism). Beijing: Renmin chubanshe.

———. 1983. "Tantan yihua wenti" (On the issue of alienation). In *Renxing, rendaozhuyi wenti taolunji* (Discussions on issues of human nature and humanism). Beijing: Renmin chubanshe.

Wang Shuo. 1993. "Wang Shuo zibai" (Wang Shuo in his own words). *Wenyi zhengming* 1:65–66.

Wang Xiaoming. 1988. "Buxiangxinde he buyuanyi xiangxinde: guanyu sanwei 'xungen' pai zuojia de chuangzuo" (Things one doesn't believe and things one doesn't want to believe: on the creations of three *xungen* writers). *Wenxue pinglun* 4:24–35.

Wang, Yuejin. 1993. "Anxiety of Portraiture: Quest for/Questioning Ancestral Icons in Post-Mao China." In *Politics, Ideology, and Literary Discourse in Modern China: Theoretical Interventions and Cultural Critique*, ed. Liu Kang and Xiaobing Tang. Durham, N.C.: Duke University Press.

Wang Zheng, and Xiao Hua. 1989. "Hubu de qingnian yishi: yu Su Tong youguande huo wuguande" (The complementary youth consciousness: things relevant or irrelevant in relation to Su Tong). *Dushu* (July/August): 102–107.

Wedell-Wedellsborg, Anne. 1986. "Chinese Modernism?" In *Cologne-Workshop 1984 on Contemporary Chinese Literature*, ed. Helmut Martin. Cologne: Deutsche Welle.

———. 1993. "The Ambivalent Role of the Chinese Literary Criticism in the 1980s." In *Inside Out: Modernism and Post-Modernism in Chinese Literary Culture*, ed.

Wendy Larson and Anne Wedell-Wedellsborg. Aarhus, Denmark: Aarhus University Press.

———. 1996. "One Kind of Chinese Reality: Reading Yu Hua." *Chinese Literature: Essays, Articles, Reviews* 18:129–143.

Weimann, Robert. 1982. "Appropriation and Modern History in Renaissance Prose Narrative." *New Literary Theory* 14, 3:459–495.

———. 1987. "History, Appropriation, and the Uses of Representation in Modern Narrative." In *The Aims of Representation: Subject/Text/History*, ed. Murray Krieger. New York: Columbia University Press.

White, Gordon. 1994. "Democratization and Economic Reform in China." *Australian Journal of Chinese Affairs* 31 (January): 73–92.

White, Lynn T. 1987. "Thought Workers in Deng's China." In *China's Intellectuals and the State: In Search of a New Relationship*, ed. Merle Goldman with Timothy Cheek and Carol Lee Hamrin. Cambridge, Mass.: Council on East Asian Studies, Harvard University, distributed by Harvard University Press.

Widmer, Ellen, and David Der-wei Wang, eds. 1993. *From May Fourth to June Fourth: Fiction and Film in Twentieth-Century China*. Cambridge, Mass: Harvard University Press.

Wilden, Anthony. 1968. "Lacan and the Discourse of the Other." In Jacques Lacan, *The Language of the Self: The Function of Language in Psychoanalysis*. Trans. Anthony Wilden. Baltimore: Johns Hopkins University Press.

Wu meng yuan (A dream romance). 1994. In *Si wu xie hui bao* (Collections of erotic fiction), ed. Chen Qinghao and Wang Qiugui. Vol. 16. Taibei: Taiwan daying baike.

Wu Xuan, Wang Gan, Fei Zhengzhong, and Wang Binbin. 1994. "Women xuyao zenyang de renwen jingshen" (What kind of humanist spirit do we need?). *Dushu* 6:66–74.

Xiao Gongqin. 1997. "Dangdai zhongguo xinbaoshouzhyuyi de sixiang yuanyuan" (The ideological roots of new conservatism in contemporary China). *Eeshiyi shiji* 40:126–135.

Xiao Haiying. 1993a. "Shangchao jiao luan wenren meng" (The commercial tide disturbs the intellectuals' dreams). *Guangming ribao*, 17 June.

———. 1993b. "Chulu: zhi neng shi wenxe" (Literature is the only way out). *Guangming ribao*, 19 June.

Xifang xiandaipai wenxue wenti lunzhengji (Collection of essays on Western modernist literature). 2 vols. Beijing: Renmin wenxue chubanshe, 1984.

Xu, Ben. 1999. *Disenchanted Democracy: Chinese Cultural Criticism after 1987*. Ann Arbor: University of Michigan Press.

Xu Daoming, and Zhu Wenhua. 2000. *Xinbian zhongguo dangdai wenxue zuopinxuan* (A new collection of contemporary fiction). Shanghai: Fudan daxue chubanshe.

Xu Jingya. 1983. "Jueqi de shi qun" (A flourishing group of poets). *Dangdai wenxue sichao* 1 (January): 14–27.

Xu Zidong. 1989. "Xiandaizhuyi yu zhongguo xinshiqi wenxue" (Modernism and Chinese literature in the New Era). *Wenxue pinglun* 4:21–34, 60.

Xu Zhaohuai. 1989. "Shilun Han Shaogong de tuibian yishi" (On Han Shaogong's consciousness of change). *Baijia* 1:60–63.

Yan, Haiping, ed. 1998. *Theater and Society: An Anthology of Contemporary Chinese Drama*. Armonk, N.Y.: M. E. Sharpe.

Yan Wenjing. 1985. "Wo shibushi ge shangle nianji de Bing Zai?" (Am I an old Bing Zai?). *Wenyibao*, 24 August.

Yang, C. K. 1959. "Some Characteristics of Chinese Bureaucratic Behavior." In *Confucianism in Action*, ed. D. S. Nivison and A. F. Wright. Stanford: Stanford University Press.

Yang Jiang. 1983. *Six Chapters from My Life "Downunder."* Trans. Howard Goldblatt. Hong Kong: Chinese University Press.

Yang Pin. 1995. "Shiluo de baogao wenxue" (The decline of reportage). *Shanxi fazhan daobao*, 18 March.

Yang, Shuhui. 1998. *Appropriation and Representation: Feng Menglong and the Chinese Vernacular Story*. Ann Arbor: Center for Chinese Studies, University of Michigan.

Yi Yi. 1993. "*Feidu*: huangdi de xinyi" (*The Ruined Capital*: the emperor's new clothes). *Wenyi zhengming* 5:47–52.

Yu Hua. 1990. "Shiba sui chumen yuanxing" (On the road at eighteen). In *Shiba sui chumen yuanxing* (On the road at eighteen). Taibei: Yuanliu.

———. 1992. "Xianxue meihua" (Blood and Plum Blossoms). In *Mianhua duo* (Cotton piles), ed. Department of Research on Creative Writing, Chinese Writers Association. Changchun: Shidai wenyi chubanshe.

———. 1996. *The Past and Punishments*. Trans. Andrew Jones. Honolulu: University of Hawai'i Press.

Yu, Ying-shih. 2001. "Neither Renaissance nor Enlightenment: A Historian's Reflection on the May Fourth Movement." In Doleželová-Velingerová and Král, *The Appropriation of Cultural Capital*.

Yue, Gang. 1999. *The Mouth That Begs: Hunger, Cannibalism, and the Politics of Eating in Modern China*. Durham, N.C.: Duke University Press.

Zarrow, Peter. 1988. "He Zhen and Anarcho-Feminism in China." *Journal of Asian Studies* 4 (November): 796–813.

Zha Jianying. 1995. *China Pop: How Soap Operas, Tabloids, and Bestsellers Are Transforming a Culture*. New York: New Press.

———. 1997. "China's Popular Culture in the 1990s." In *China Briefing, 1995–96: The Contradictions of Change*, ed. William A. Joseph. Armonk, N.Y.: M. E. Sharpe.

Zhang Fa. 1993. "*Feidu*: duo ziwei de chengbai" (*The Ruined Capital*: multilevels of success and failure). *Wenyi zhengming* 5:50–52.

Zhang Jun. 1996. "Mo Yan: Fanfeng yishujia—Du *Fengru feitun*" (Mo Yan: an artist of irony—reading *Fengru feitun*). *Zhongguo xiandai, dangdai wenxue yanjiu* 9:212–217.

Zhang Kuan. 1996. "Guanyu houzhimin piping de zai sikao" (Rethinking postcolonial criticism). *Yuandao* 3:406–424.

Zhang Rulun, Wang Xiaoming, Zhu Xueqin, and Chen Sihe. 1994. "Renwen jingshen shifou keneng" (Humanistic spirit: possibilities and probabilities). *Dushu* 3:3–13.

Zhang, Xudong. 1997. *Chinese Modernism in the Era of Reforms: Culture, Avant-Garde Fiction, and the New Chinese Cinema*. Durham, N.C.: Duke University Press.

———, ed. 2001. *Whither China: Politics in Contemporary China.* Durham, N.C.: Duke University Press.

Zhang Yan. 1994. "Zenyang pingjia *Feidu*" (How to evaluate *The Ruined Capital*). *Zuopin yu zhengming* 4:76–79.

Zhang, Yingjin. 1993. "Narrative, Ideology, Subjectivity: Defining a Subversive Discourse in Chinese Reportage." In *Politics, Ideology, and Literary Discourse in Modern China*, ed. Liu Kang and Xiaobing Tang. Durham, N.C.: Duke University Press.

———. 1996. *The City in Modern Chinese Literature and Film: Configurations of Space, Time, and Gender.* Stanford: Stanford University Press.

———. 2002. *Screening China: Critical Interventions, Cinematic Reconfigurations, and the Transnational Imaginary in Contemporary Chinese Cinema.* Ann Arbor: Center for Chinese Studies, University of Michigan.

Zhang Zhizhong. 1994. "Weiji, xuanze yu ziyou: wentan yu wenhua jinkuang shuping" (Crisis, choice, and freedom: an overview of recent situations in cultural and literary circles). *Dangdai zuojia pinglun* 4:88–97.

Zhao Yibing. 1995. "Zhongguo liudong renkou wenti zhi wo jian" (My view on the floating population in China). *Renmin ribao* (the overseas edition), 13 October.

Zhao, (Henry) Yiheng. 1991. "Yu Hua: Fiction as Subversion." *World Literature Today* (summer): 415–420.

———. 1995. "'Houxue' yu zhongguo xinbaoshouzhuyi" ("Post-studies" and China's neoconservatism), *Ershiyi shiji* 27:4–15.

———. 1997. (Henry Y. H. Zhao). "Post-Isms and Chinese New Conservatism." *New Literary History* 28:31–44.

Zhaxi Dawa. 1989a. Zhaxi Dawa, "Xiaozhuan" (An autographical sketch). In *Dangdai zuojia bairen zhuan* (A hundred autobiographies of contemporary writers), ed. Jie Min. Beijing: Qiushi chubanshe.

——— (Tashi Dawa). 1989b. "A Soul in Bondage." In *Best Chinese Stories: 1949–1989.* Beijing: Chinese Literature Press.

———. 2000. "Ji zai pishengkou shang de hun." In *Xinbian zhongguo dangdai wenxue zuopinxuan* (A new collection of contemporary Chinese fiction). Vol. 2, ed. Xu Daoming and Zhu Wenhua. Shanghai: Fudan daxue chubanshe.

Zhaxi Duo. 1994. "Zhengjin weizuo shuo *Feidu*" (Talking seriously about *The Ruined Capital*). *Xinhua wenzhai* 2:128–129.

Zheng, Yongnian. 1999. *Discovering Chinese Nationalism in China: Modernization, Identity, and International Relations.* Cambridge: Cambridge University Press.

Zhong Benkang, ed. 1993a. *Xin biji xiaoshuo xuan* (Selected works of the new literary sketches). Hangzhou: Zhejiang wenyi chubanshe.

———. 1993b. "Shijimo: shengcun de jiaolü—*Feidu* de zhuti yishi" (Existential anxiety in the fin de siècle: subjectivity in *Ruined Capital*). *Dangdai zuojia pinglun* 6:46–53.

Zhong, Xueping. 2000. *Masculinity Besieged? Issues of Modernity and Male Subjectivity in Chinese Literature of the Late Twentieth Century.* Durham, N.C.: Duke University Press.

Zhongguo chuban nianjian, 1997 (China statistical yearbook of publications, 1997). Beijing: Zhongguo chuban nianjianshe.

Zhongguo jindai lunwen xuan (Selected writings on literature in modern China). 1962. 2 vols. Beijing: Renmin wenxue.

Zhongguo tongji nianjian, 1997 (China statistical yearbook, 1997). Beijing: Zhongguo tongji chubanshe.

"Zhongguo wentan: shouzhu liangxin zhunze, yinling biange shidai" (Literary world in China: maintaining the principles of conscience and leading the reform era). 1996. *Gongren ribao*, 3 February.

Zhongguo zuojia zishu (Self-portrayals by Chinese writers). 1998. Shanghai: Shanghai jiaoyu chubanshe.

Zhu Hong. 1978. "Lun huangdanpai xiju" (On the theater of the absurd). *Shijie wenxue* 2. Reprinted in *Xifang xiandaipai wenxue wenti lunzhengji* (Collection of essays on Western modernist literature). 2 vols. Beijing: Renmin wenxue chubanshe, 1984.

Zhu Wei. 1990. "Guanyu Yu Hua" (About Yu Hua). In Yu Hua, *Shiba sui chumen yuanxing*. Taibei: Yuanliu.

Zito, Angela, and Tani E. Barlow, eds. 1994. *Body, Subject and Power in China*. Chicago: University of Chicago Press.

Zong Pu. 1987. *Zong Pu daibiaozuo* (Representative works by Zong Pu). Zhengzhou: Huanghe wenyi chubanshe.

Index

absurdist literature, 11, 21, 92–96, 108
A Cheng, 89
adultery. *See* Mo Yan: female sexuality and promiscuity; sexual transgression
agency, intellectual, x, 10, 22, 24
Ai Wu, 130, 135
alienation, 24, 94, 109; critiques of alienation school, 35n. 14; discussion of, 35, 40; and Marxism, 35; socialist, 8, 10, 20, 23, 41
Althusser, Louis, 33
Anagnost, Ann, 225–226
appropriation: ideological and intellectual, 183, 184–185, 187; literary, of women, 219–221; in Maoist China, 185–186; material, 180, 187–188, 189, 191; in the theory of Robert Weimann, 179, 181–182
"A Soul in Bondage." *See* Zhaxi Dawa
autonomy, x, 10, 14, 18, 30, 41, 61, 179, 226; artistic, 28, 55, 57–59
avant-garde, ix, 2, 11

Bai Hua, 34, 43–44, 184
Ba Jin, 51
bastard, 26. *See also* Mo Yan
Beckett, Samuel, 94
Bitter Love. See Bai Hua
"Blood and Plum Blossom." *See* Yu Hua

body, female, 26. *See also* Jia Pingwa: feminity and female subjectivity; Zhuang Zhidie and women; Mo Yan: female body
Bourdieu, Pierre, 194–195, 198

Calinescu, Matei, 5
Camus, Albert, 94
Can Xue, xi, 21, 25, 92, 127; antagonism between self and Other, 25–26, 93, 99, 126; biography, 98; decay and death, 104, 121; dehistoricization, 122, 124; dehumanization, 105–106, 124; dream and nightmare, 26, 92, 98, 100, 106, 120; eyes, 108, 109–110, 112; failure of communication, 93, 101–103; family relationships, 97, 99, 100; fear of persecution, 93, 104–106, 120–121; inner reality, 92, 98–99, 106; insects and worms, 119, 121; and literature of the wounded, 97; lonely self, 99; madness, 121, 123; mirror, 103, 104, 112, 116, 121; nonrealist mode, 92–93, 96–97; obsession, 93, 101–104; parental figures, 104–108, 112–113, 121, 124–126; scopophilia and scopophobia, 93, 111, 117, 119–120, 123; and searching for roots literature, 92; sexual symbolism, 102. Works: "The Date," 99, 106;

About the Author

Rong Cai received her Ph.D. in comparative literature and Chinese at Washington University in St. Louis. She is presently assistant professor of Chinese at Emory University. Her articles on post-Mao literature have appeared in *Modern Chinese Literature, Modern China,* and other journals.

Production Notes for
Rong Cai / *Subject in Crisis in Contemporary Chinese Literature*

Cover and Interior designed by UH Press Production Department
in Giovanni, with display type in Korinna

Composition by UH Press Production Department

Printing and binding by The Maple-Vail Book Manufacturing Group

Printed on 60# Sebago Eggshell, 420 ppi